I0105192

terra australis 40

Terra Australis reports the results of archaeological and related research within the south and east of Asia, though mainly Australia, New Guinea and island Melanesia — lands that remained terra australis incognita to generations of prehistorians. Its subject is the settlement of the diverse environments in this isolated quarter of the globe by peoples who have maintained their discrete and traditional ways of life into the recent recorded or remembered past and at times into the observable present.

List of volumes in Terra Australis

terra australis 40

4000 Years of Migration and Cultural Exchange

The Archaeology of the Batanes Islands, Northern Philippines

Peter Bellwood and Eusebio Dizon (eds)

Australian
National
University

E PRESS

ANU
E PRESS

© 2013 ANU E Press

Published by ANU E Press
The Australian National University
Canberra ACT 0200 Australia
Email: anuepress@anu.edu.au
Web: http://epress.anu.edu.au

National Library of Australia Cataloguing-in-Publication entry

Title:	4000 years of migration and cultural exchange : the archaeology of the Batanes Islands, Northern Philippines / edited by Peter Bellwood and Eusebio Dizon.
ISBN:	9781925021271 (paperback) 9781925021288 (ebook)
Series:	Terra Australis ; 40.
Subjects:	Prehistoric peoples--Philippines--Batan Islands. Batan Islands (Philippines)--Antiquities.
Other Authors/Contributors:	Bellwood, Peter, 1943- editor. Dizon, Eusebio Z., editor.
Dewey Number:	930.1

Copyright of the text remains with the authors, 2013. This book is copyright in all countries subscribing to the Berne convention. Apart from any fair dealing for the purpose of private study, research, criticism or review, as permitted under the Copyright Act, no part may be reproduced by any process without written permission. Inquiries should be made to the publisher.

Series Editor: Sue O'Connor

Cover image: Fengtian nephrite artifacts from Savidug Dune Site, Sabtang, late first millennium BC. Source: Hsiao-chun Hung.

Back cover map: Hollandia Nova. Thevenot 1663 by courtesy of the National Library of Australia.
Reprinted with permission of the National Library of Australia.

Terra Australis Editorial Board: Sue O'Connor, Jack Golson, Simon Haberle, Sally Brockwell, Geoffrey Clark

Contents

Preface

This monograph contains a series of archaeological reports on investigations undertaken between 2002 and 2007 in the Batanes Islands, located in the northern Philippines, half-way between Taiwan and Luzon. Because of this location, the Batanes Islands occupied a strategic position for all prehistoric human migration from southern China, through Taiwan, into Luzon and the Philippines, and sometimes possibly in the other direction as well (e.g. from the Batanes to Lanyu Island). The prehistory of these islands reflects very greatly on the early migrations of the Austronesian-speaking peoples, a phenomenon dating between 4500 and 3000 years ago for its earliest Malayo-Polynesian manifestations beyond Taiwan, as inferred from current investigations in comparative linguistics, archaeology, and biological anthropology (Blust 2013; Bellwood 2013; Cox 2013).

The bulk of this monograph presents archaeological data as its primary purpose. It is not intended to serve as a commentary on the Austronesian origins debate, or even to provide a firm statement on this issue, although the issue of links between Taiwan and the northern Philippines is necessarily an ever-present topic of discussion in the text. The first chapter introduces the project and the islands themselves. Three chapters then cover excavations and other investigations on the islands of Itbayat, Batan and Sabtang. The remainder of the volume deals with various categories of material culture and subsistence through time, particularly pottery, lithic and nephrite items, animal (including fish) bones, and marine shells.

The Batanes research project was designed originally in 2001 by Atholl Anderson, Peter Bellwood and Eusebio Dizon to throw light on the migrations of Neolithic populations from Taiwan to Luzon, or perhaps vice versa (depending on one's point of view on Austronesian prehistory), between about 4500 and 3000 years ago. The results, however, date not only from this time period, but cover all of Batanes prehistory right down to the arrival of Japanese and European seafarers in the late 17th century. During this 4000 year time span, the people of the Batanes Islands forged a unique island-based culture, while remaining in fairly continuous contact with their contemporaries in Taiwan to the north (a major source of nephrite, as well as other aspects of Neolithic material culture), and Luzon to the south.

The field teams comprised the following individuals, in alphabetical order of surname:

Australian National University: Atholl Anderson, Peter Bellwood, Deirdre Cook, Daniel Davenport, Hsiao-chun Hung, Damien Kelleher, Marc Oxenham, Janelle Stevenson, Mary Clare Swete Kelly, Katherine Szabó, Michelle Wright, Shawna Hsiu-Ying Yang.

National Museum of the Philippines: Giovanni Bautista, Rey Bautista, Alexandra De Leon, Eusebio (Bong) Dizon, Jonathan Jacar, Clyde Jago-on, Ligaya (Gay) Lacsina, Antonio (Tony) Peñalosa, Erwin Sebastian, Adan Soriano.

Archaeological Studies Program, University of the Philippines: Jane Carlos, Darryl De Leon, Pamela Faylona, Andrea Jalandoni, Armand Mijares, Aileen Paguntalan, Alfred Pawlik, Victor Paz, Jessica Peña, Andrea Ragrario, Emil Robles, Eliza Romualdez-Valtos, Sharon Teodosio, Archie Tiauzon, Edwin Valientes.

Other Institutions: Hallie Buckley (University of Otago); Julien Corny (Erasmus Mundus International Masters Program in Quaternary Studies and Prehistory, Museum of Natural

History, Paris); Yoshiyuki Iizuka (Institute of Earth Sciences, Academia Sinica, Taipei); Daud Tanudirjo (Jurusan Arkeologi, Gadjah Mada University, Yogyakarta); Sophie Tynan (University of Liverpool).

Some further acknowledgements are necessary here, since this research involved input from many funding agencies and Filipino supporters. Funding for the project was received from the following agencies:

Australian Research Council Discovery Project Grant - *Understanding the Early Phases of Neolithic Dispersal in the Western Pacific* (2002-2004).

Australian Research Council Discovery Project Grant - *The Creation of Southeast Asian Peoples and Cultures, 3500 BC to AD 500* (2007-2010).

Chiang Ching–Kuo Foundation, Taiwan - *The Role of Taiwan in the Creation of Southeast Asian Peoples and Cultures, 3500 BC to AD 500* (2007-2010).

National Geographic Committee for Research and Exploration - *The Genesis of Austronesian Dispersal in Taiwan and the Philippines* (2002).

National Geographic Committee for Research and Exploration - *The Taiwan-Philippine Interaction Sphere, 2000 BC to AD 500* (2005).

Australian Institute of Nuclear Sciences and Engineering (AINSE) - *C14 dating of Neolithic Colonization and Nephrite Trade in the Batanes Islands, Northern Philippines* (2005).

Australian Institute of Nuclear Sciences and Engineering (AINSE) - *C14 Dating of a 2000 Year Old Jade Workshop in the Northern Philippines* (2007).

Australian National University, Centre for Archaeological Research - funding for the ANU and some of the Waikato C14 dates.

Australian National University, Faculties Research Grants Scheme - *Origins and Dispersals of Early Agricultural Populations in Island SE Asia* (2001).

The Australian National University - for infrastructure support in the School of Archaeology and Anthropology and the Department of Archaeology and Natural History.

The team wishes to thank the following people in the Philippines who provided permissions and assistance for the fieldwork:

In Manila: Corazon S. Alvina, former Director of the National Museum; Willie Ronquillo, former Chief of the Archaeology Division, National Museum.

In Batanes: Florencio B. Abad, former Congressman for Batanes; Vicente S. Gato, former Governor of Batanes; George Reyes, Department of Environment and Natural Resources; Rodobaldo Ponce, Julius S. Velayo, Magdalena Siazon, Ed Delfin and Tomas Ibardo, National Commission for Indigenous Peoples; William A. Agsunod, former Mayor of Mahatao; Leonor Hornedo-Belgado, Rural Health Unit, Mahatao; Ireneo Canela, Barangay Savidug, Sabtang; Romeo L. Gonzalez, former Mayor of Itbayat; Magdelena C. Ruiz, Barangay Santa Lucia, Itbayat; Gershom P. Gato, Barangay Santa Rosa, Itbayat; Faustina Cano, Mayan, Itbayat.

The following graduate student theses have been completed within the bounds of this project:

Shawna Hsiu-Ying Yang, School of Archaeology and Anthropology, ANU: Fishing Sinkers in the Batanes Islands (Philippines) and Taiwan, and Further Relationships with East Asia. MA 2006.

Armand Mijares, Department of Archaeology and Natural History, ANU: Unravelling Prehistory: The Archaeology of North-eastern Luzon. PhD 2006.

Alexandra De Leon, Archaeological Studies Program, University of the Philippines: Pottery and Cultural Interaction from 3000 to 600 BP, Batanes, Northern Philippines. MSc 2008.

Hsiao-chun Hung, Department of Archaeology and Natural History, ANU: Migration and Cultural Interaction in Southern Coastal China, Taiwan and the Northern Philippines, 3000 BC to AD 1: the Early History of the Austronesian-speaking Populations. PhD 2008.

Mary Clare Swete Kelly, Department of Archaeology and Natural History, ANU: Prehistoric Social Interaction and the Evidence of Pottery in the Northern Philippines. PhD 2008.

Fredeliza Campos, Archaeological Studies Program, University of the Philippines: The Ichthyoarchaeology of Batanes Islands, Northern Philippines. MSc. 2009.

Finally, thanks to Jenny Sheehan and Kay Dancey of CartoGIS (formerly Education and Multimedia Services) in ANU College of Asia and the Pacific for many of the maps. Most illustrations, especially those of artefacts, were prepared by the chapter authors using Adobe Illustrator or Photoshop software, except where otherwise stated. All tables were assembled by the chapter author(s) from primary data. For *Terra Australis* editorial and submission advice we thank Sue O'Connor, Sally Brockwell and Katie Hayne.

Figures

NB: Sources are included in the text, but not in this list, except for the cover picture.

Cover picture. Fengtian nephrite artifacts from Savidug Dune Site, Sabtang, late first millennium BC. Source: Hsiao-chun Hung.

Tables

NB: All tables were assembled by the chapter author(s) from primary data.

1

The Batanes Islands, Their First Observers, and Previous Archaeology

Peter Bellwood and Eusebio Dizon

The project reported on in this monograph has been concerned with the archaeology of the Batanes Islands, an archipelago that must have been settled quite early in the process of Austronesian dispersal from Taiwan southwards into the Philippines. A multi-phase archaeological sequence covering the past 4000 years for the islands of Itbayat, Batan, Sabtang and Siayan is presented in the following chapters, extending from the Neolithic to the final phase of Batanes prehistory, just prior to the late 17th century arrivals of Jirobei, William Dampier, and the first Spanish missionaries. So far, no traces of preceramic settlement have been found in Batanes, but the archaeological sequence there from the Neolithic onwards, like that in the Cagayan Valley in northern Luzon, is now one of the best established in the Philippines. This chapter opens the volume with a review of pertinent aspects of Batanes natural history and ethnohistory.

The archaeological research reported upon in this publication grew out of the Asian Fore-Arc Programme, established by Atholl Anderson in 2001 as a research initiative of the Centre for Archaeological Research at The Australian National University in Canberra. The programme was funded from 2002 to 2004 by The Australian Research Council, the National Geographic Society, and by the former Faculties Research Fund and the Department of Archaeology and Natural History at ANU. The initial research team on the first Australian Research Council grant comprised Atholl Anderson, Peter Bellwood, Janelle Stevenson and Glenn Summerhayes from ANU, working in collaboration with Eusebio (Bong) Dizon from the National Museum in Manila and Victor Paz from the University of the Philippines, together with graduate students from both Australia and the Philippines. The Asian Fore-Arc Programme was concerned with the prehistoric archaeology and palaeoenvironments of the arc of large islands, including the Ryukyus and the Philippines, that forms the boundary of the subtropical to tropical western Pacific. Between 2002 and 2004, Asian Fore-Arc Programme archaeological projects were undertaken on Batan, Sabtang and Itbayat Islands. Some of the results of this first phase of research, including the first excavation at Sunget on Batan and the palynological research of Janelle Stevenson at Paoay Lake in Ilocos Norte (Luzon), have already been published (Bellwood et al. 2003; Szabó et al. 2003; Anderson 2005; Bellwood and Dizon 2005, 2008; Stevenson et al. 2010).

After 2004, when the Asian Fore-Arc Programme terminated, the research in the Batanes Islands continued under the direction of Peter Bellwood, Bong Dizon, Marc Oxenham and Janelle Stevenson, using further grants from the National Geographic Society, the Australian Research

Council, the Chiang Ching-Kuo Foundation (Taipei), and the Australian Institute of Nuclear Sciences and Engineering (the latter for AMS C14 dates). Important results from this more recent phase of research have been the identification of initial settlement in Batanes by 4000 years ago in Torongan and Reranum caves on Itbayat; investigation of 2500-2000 year old jar burials at Savidug on Sabtang; and some remarkable information about the exploitation of Taiwan nephrite in the Batanes Islands, especially ear pendant manufacture at Anaro on Itbayat (Hung 2005, 2008; Hung et al. 2006; Iizuka and Hung 2005; Iizuka et al. 2005, 2007; Hung et al. 2007; Hung and Bellwood 2010, Bellwood, Hung and Iizuka 2011). Several overview articles have also been published on Batanes archaeology in comparative perspective (Bellwood 2005, 2006, 2007a, 2011a; Bellwood and Dizon 2005, 2008; Bellwood et al. 2011). In addition, Shawna Hsiu-Ying Yang (2006), Hsiao-chun Hung (2008), Alexandra De Leon (2008), Mary Clare Swete Kelly (2008) and Fredeliza Campos (2009) have all completed postgraduate theses on aspects of the Batanes research (as listed in the Preface).

The purpose of this monograph is to detail the research results from all the Batanes sites investigated, with a discussion of the artefacts and economic indicators found and the implications for the overall course of Batanes and Island Southeast Asian prehistory.

The Batanes Islands

The Batanes Islands lie on the northern edge of the tropics, 150 km from the southern tip of Taiwan and 200 km from the north coast of Luzon (Fig. 1.1). They are separated from Luzon by the Balintang Channel and the Babuyan Islands, and from Taiwan by the open sea of the Bashi Channel. The group consists of three inhabited islands; dumb-bell shaped *Batan*, 18 km long and the most densely populated island of the group; 10 km long *Sabtang*; and 18 km long *Itbayat*, wider than Batan and the largest island in land area. There are also a number of small and now-uninhabited islands, of which *Ivuhos*, at 4 km long, is the largest. A chain of uninhabited islands also extends north of Itbayat, and research was undertaken on the southernmost of these, *Siayan*, in 2006.

The Babuyan and Batanes Islands belong to a double volcanic arc, the two arms of which run 50 km apart in the Babuyan Islands, but converge in the Batanes (Yang et al. 1996). The western arc formed before 3 million years ago as a submarine line of subduction volcanoes, since which time its four islands – Itbayat, Sabtang, Ivuhos and Dequey – have been uplifted above the sea, eroded, mantled with reef coral, and then uplifted again during the Pleistocene. The geologically younger eastern arc contains Batan, Diogo and the islands north of Itbayat, all created as emergent volcanoes during the Pleistocene (<2.58 mya), with Mt Iraya on Batan remaining violently active until as recently as 1500 years ago (Richard et al. 1986, and see Chapter 3). Consequently, the islands of the eastern arc, especially Batan, have fertile volcanic soils with some coastal areas of raised coral. Those in the more ancient western arc have weathered volcanic rocks with more widespread uplifted coral limestone.

In terms of the human environment, Batan is by far the most fertile island in the group, particularly its central "neck" between the Iraya and Matarem volcanos. Here, a remarkable patchwork of small hedged arable and pasture fields stretches right across the island from coast to coast (see Fig. 3.2). Most of the Batan archaeological sites occur in this area, or around the coastline like the modern settlements. Iraya itself is entirely under forest and uninhabited, as is Matarem. Much of central Batan was mantled by fresh volcanic ash from an eruption of Iraya around 1500 years ago, discussed further in chapter 3.

Sabtang has a similar volcanic landscape to much of Batan but the terrain is more ancient and weathered, thus the soils are less regenerated by the fertile ash showers that underlie the rich landscape of central Batan (see Figs 4.2, 4.3). Itbayat and Ivuhos, by comparison, are less fertile again, with undulating uplifted coral limestone or eroded volcanic interiors. However, much of the surface of Itbayat is still quite suitable for swidden farming and pasture, whereas the small uninhabited Dequey is completely barren limestone and only supports a few goats today, as it did when William Dampier visited in 1687. Itbayat has only two small settlements, both in interior depressions away from the harbourless coastline with its sheer limestone cliffs.

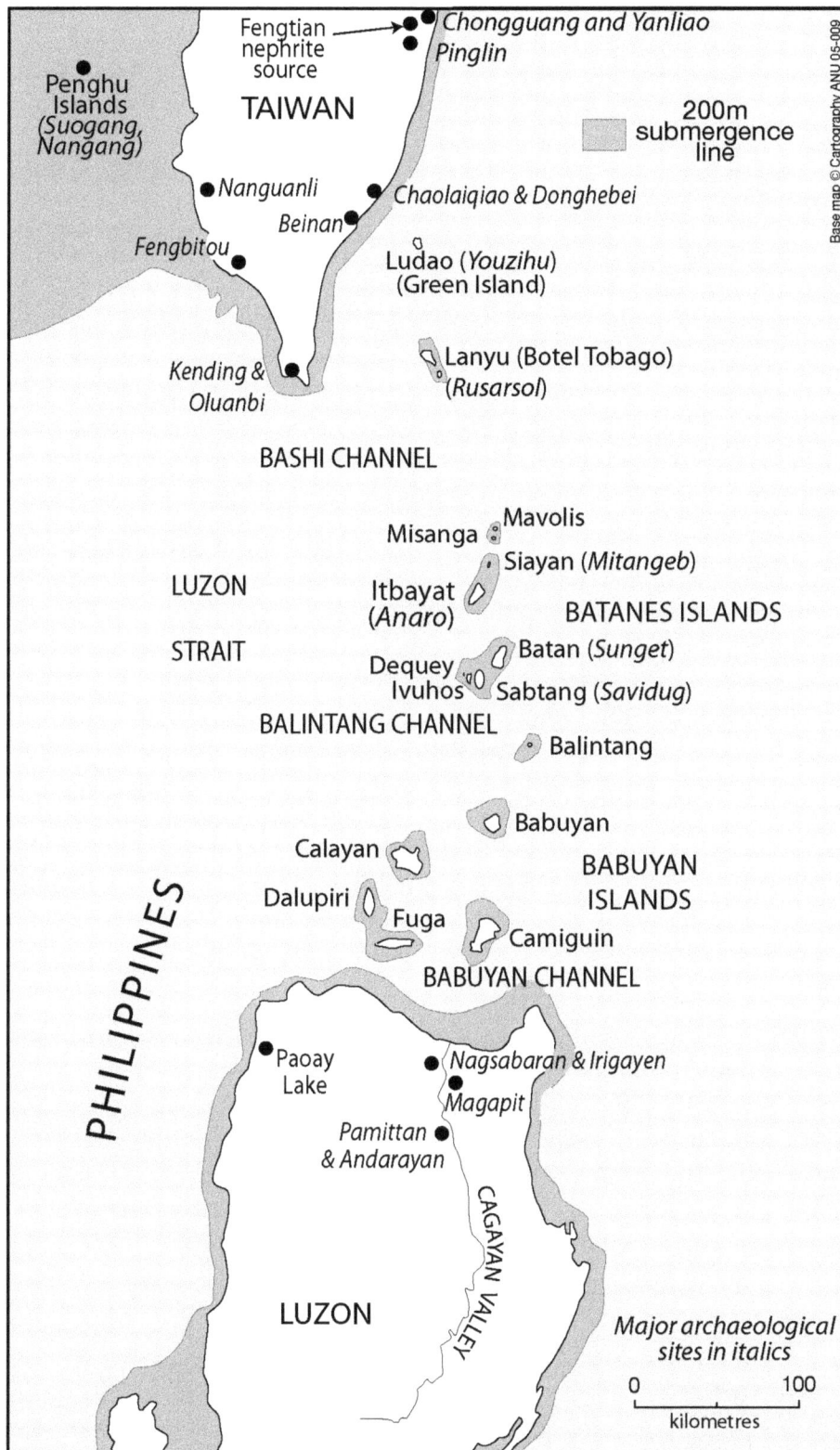

Figure 1.1. The Batanes Islands, showing their strategic location between southern Taiwan and northern Luzon.

Source: Map preparation by ANU College of Asia and the Pacific, CartoGIS.

terra australis 40

On a clear day, the islands all the way from the northern Batanes (Mavolis) south to Luzon form an intervisible chain. From Sabtang, for instance, Babuyan Island (843 m high) is very clear across 80 km of ocean (personal observations, June 2007). Lanyu, off southeastern Taiwan, and Mavolis, the most northerly of the Batanes, are 100 km apart. Lanyu rises to 548 m and Mavolis 211 m, so it is possible that they could also be intervisible in clear conditions. Indeed, Hsü (1982: 14) quotes an 1801 missionary to the effect that Lanyu was visible on clear days from somewhere unspecified in Batanes (perhaps Mavolis Island, or somewhere on the northern flank of Iraya on Batan, which rises to 1009 m above sea level). If this is correct, then there would have been a chain of inter-island intervisibility in clear weather all the way from Taiwan to Luzon, since Lanyu is visible from Taiwan and Ludao Island.

Because the Batanes are situated in the ocean strait between Taiwan and Luzon they tend to have rough seas and windy weather for much of the year, with prevailing winds from the north in the northern hemisphere winter (January) and from the south in the summer (July). Typhoons occur in late summer. William Dampier's ship (see below) was forced from its Ivuhos anchorage in early October 1687 (late summer) by a violent storm and blown out to sea. He was not able to return to the island for 6 days. Since the Batanes Islands lie at almost 21°N the winters are relatively cool, with average daytime temperatures just above 20°C, rising to an average in the upper 20s in the summer. Rainfall is very low from February to May, and peaks from August to October.

The warm Kuroshio current flows northwards up the eastern coastlines of the Philippines and Taiwan. This would have made paddling or sailing from Taiwan into the Batanes perhaps difficult at times. Indeed, Solheim (1984-5:81) believed that it would have ruled out completely any significant attempts to travel by boat from Taiwan to Luzon. However, this current produces surface counter-currents offshore from eastern Luzon (Isorena 2004), and presumably its rate of flow and longitudinal position undergo some variation throughout the year. Furthermore, there are documented drift voyages from Japan to Batanes, discussed further below, that make it clear that the Kuroshio current did not prohibit southwards movement by sea all the time. The Batanes Islands are also protected from the full force of the current by the north-eastern coastline of Luzon, and the Batanes archaeological record to be discussed makes it perfectly obvious that voyages to and from Taiwan and Lanyu must have occurred frequently in Batanes prehistory. Sailing south from Taiwan and approaching Itbayat or Batan from a north-westerly direction would presumably have taken sailors/paddlers away from the full head-on flow of the Kuroshio current.

The Batanes would have been forested before human arrival (Valerio 1995-7), but we are unable to locate any systematic reconstructions of either Batanes flora or fauna in prehuman times. Despite a great deal of "received wisdom" in the older literature that the Batanes and Babuyan Islands were part of a Pleistocene land bridge from Taiwan to Luzon, there is absolutely no geological or faunal evidence to demonstrate that this was ever the case (Heaney 1985; Bellwood 2007b). Sea bed depths in the Bashi channel attain at least 1000 metres – clearly far too deep to have been affected in terms of a land bridge by Pleistocene sea level fluctuations.

As in many of the similarly-isolated small islands of eastern Indonesia, we would expect the Batanes terrestrial mammal fauna to have been restricted to rodents and bats before human occupation – the distances from Taiwan and Luzon would have been too great even for wild pigs to swim across (Meijaard 2001). Pigs were certainly present in Batanes during human prehistory, presumably of an East Asian mtDNA lineage also found in Taiwan and elsewhere in the Philippines (Larson et al. 2007; Piper et al. 2009, and see chapter 10), although it has not yet been possible to extract and amplify ancient DNA samples from the organically degraded matrices of suid bones. Ethnographic accounts refer to a presence of deer in Batanes (Hidalgo

1996:64-5), but since neither Jirobei nor Dampier (below) referred to deer in their 17th century accounts it is unlikely that these animals were part of the native Batanes fauna. Perhaps they were humanly translocated from Taiwan or Luzon, and a few deer bones are reported from Batanes archaeological contexts (chapter 10), although none exist in Batanes today. A Japanese account of 1830 (Yamada 2007:333) also refers to monitor lizards up to 1.7 m long, but none are present in the archaeological record so it is possible that people also transported them from Luzon.

Ethnography and early historical records

Unlike Lanyu (Botel Tobago) Island off southeastern Taiwan, and Mountain Province in Northern Luzon, we have few detailed records of traditional native life in Batanes that can aid archaeological understanding. Most information is anecdotal or derived from vague missionary observations. A rather glaring example of this can be found in the huge compilation of historical documents on the Philippines by Blair and Robertson, in which it is stated (1903-9, Vol. 39, page 97, footnote) that "the present population of the Batanes is composed very largely of Ibanag from the Cagayan Valley (Luzon), introduced there as colonists by the Dominican Friars." In actuality, the Ivatan (Batan and Sabtang) and Itbayaten populations, like the Yami of Lanyu, have their own languages and customs and would perhaps be disappointed to read such an offhand dismissal of their cultural background.

As Malcolm Ross (2005; and in Bellwood et al. 2011) points out, the Batanic languages are Malayo-Polynesian, and thus belong to the single extra-Taiwan subgroup that contains all Austronesian languages, apart from those in Taiwan. But they do not subgroup uniquely with any other Malayo-Polynesian languages, nor even with the languages of northern Luzon. This makes it likely, but without absolute demonstration, that the Batanic subgroup represents a very early, perhaps even initial, split at the base of the Malayo-Polynesian genealogy. However, the three internal member languages of the Batanic subgroup - Ivatan, Itbayaten, and Yami of Lanyu – are between themselves quite closely related, suggesting the reality of mutual contacts over a long period subsequent to initial settlement. Yami, indeed, appears to be an outlier of Batanic speech adjacent to the Taiwan mainland, and as such it has probably replaced an earlier (Formosan and non-Malayo-Polynesian?) language on the island.

There exist two absolutely invaluable 17th century eye-witness ethnographic documents about Batanes, one British and one Japanese. The first was penned by the English navigator and "privateer" William Dampier, who visited the Batanes in August-September 1687 (Blair and Robertson 1903-9, Vol. 39, pp. 95-112). Dampier arrived first off Batan, which he called Duke of Grafton's Isle, and recorded the presence of "abundance of inhabitants" in at least four "large Towns". At that time, both Batan and Sabtang were thick with terraced and defended settlements on hill tops and ridges, some apparently inland and some coastal, protected wherever possible by "precipices". These defended sites are today termed *ijang*, and several have been investigated archaeologically (e.g. Savidug *ijang* on Sabtang, described in chapter 4). Unfortunately, Dampier did not record the precise locations of any of these towns, although some doubtless survive as archaeological sites today. The only one that is identifiable from Dampier's account is Chuhangin *ijang* on Ivuhos Island (called Bashee Island in 1687), described as lying "with its back next the Sea" and discussed further below in this chapter. Dampier commented that he saw no signs of artificial defences in any of these "towns" and suggested that all the precipices were natural, as indeed they clearly are when observed today. However, he did not comment on the many still-visible house terraces, often reinforced by dry stonework. These terraces were accessed by ladder from below. Dampier noted that houses, built in lines on the terraces, were quite low (for wind resistance?), built of posts and boughs with plank floors, and so rather different from the stone-walled house style, introduced by the Spanish, that is traditional in Batanes today.

Dampier also stated that Itbayat (Prince of Orange's Island) was not inhabited. But since he did not land there he was not to know that all the inhabitants then, as now, probably lived in the interior, invisible from the sea. Presumably, his informants on Batan and Ivuhos were reluctant to lose the benefits of a visiting European ship and so kept quiet about the matter. Dequey was uninhabited and used already for goat pasture, since Dampier named it Goat Island. The islands north of Itbayat were not mentioned by Dampier, but were presumably only visited by fishing parties and without permanent populations, as now.

Dampier was clearly a very keen observer of native life, like the Pacific navigator James Cook a century later. Like the Pacific peoples observed by Cook, the Batanes people were "greedy" for iron, a metal in great demand for "Hatchets" and "Utensils". Iron tools were apparently often given as a community dowry to a young groom to enable him to establish a house and farm for his family upon marriage. The inhabitants also had access to low-grade gold for making earrings. They grew bananas, pineapples, pumpkins, sugar cane, yams, cotton, and "Potatoes", a term which surely referred to the sweet potato, or *camote*, already introduced like the pineapples and pumpkins from South America to the Philippines by the Spanish during the sixteenth and seventeenth centuries. Rice was not seen growing, and no cattle or water buffalo were mentioned, even though they are universal as livestock today. Indeed, Dampier commented that buffalo hides for body armour had to be obtained from strangers, possibly from Luzon, whence he thought their iron might also have been obtained. Goats and pigs abounded, but poultry were rare. Culinary delights included fish cooked "with a very savory Stink" in the stomach contents of goats, and roasted locusts that fed on the sweet potato leaves in the fields. Sugar cane wine (*basi*) was widely consumed, as now.

Interestingly, Dampier observed no signs of religious activity or social ranking, save perhaps for the burial alive of a thief that he claimed to have witnessed. Batanes sea craft in 1687 appear to have been similar to those in use today, without outriggers and built using planks, dowels and nails, the latter presumably of iron. Dampier did not mention sails, but he did comment that the men of the islands were primarily employed in fishing. The largest boats were capable of carrying 50 people and rowed with 12-14 oars on each side. All in all, Dampier's description is a unique record of an Austronesian-speaking Iron Age society that had not yet entered the exploitative orbit of the European colonial powers.

In 2005 and 2007, we were very kindly sent translations of two further important eye-witness accounts of Batanes, dating from 1668 and 1830, by Yukihiro Yamada, a Japanese linguist who has carried out research on the Itbayaten language (Yamada 2007, Appendixes 1 and 2; see also Gaza and Yamada 1999). The most significant is an account by two crew members of a drift voyage in 1668, under the command of a certain Captain Jirobei. This commenced when they were sailing from Edo (Tokyo) for a destination in the vicinity of Nagoya, nineteen years before the visit of Dampier. While passing through the Izu Islands they were blown eastwards by a storm, then southwards and westwards until they finally landed in Batanes after 30 days of drifting. This direction is, of course, contrary to the flow of the Kuroshio Current and drives home the point that access by sea to Batanes from the north by drift or sail (and perhaps even by paddle) was not always impossible.

The Japanese probably landed in Mahatao on Batan, and the crew of 15 men was captured and made to work by the local Ivatans. After spending 16 months on Batan, from December 1668 to April 1670, they were able to escape to another village and return to Japan. Their account has points of both similarity and difference with that of Dampier. The Batanes people observed by the Japanese grew mainly root crops (unspecified) and apparently no cereals (although another part of the document states that they "plant corn"). They had pigs and cattle (Dampier did not refer to the latter), and also dogs, horses (or so the Japanese claimed), and "sheep" (goats?). Cowhide was used for body armour. No reference was made to chickens. Iron was scarce, and old people were killed when they were no longer able to work, including the unfortunate Captain Jirobei himself. Houses were of wood with cogon grass thatch. The Ivatan also visited another island, that Yamada thinks could be Taiwan, for access to bows, guns, gold and silver, although Taiwan is not certain and another possibility would of course be Luzon to the south.

Finally, the Japanese described one remarkable and rather sobering occurrence about life in a warlike society in which each village was presumably independent of, and hostile towards, its neighbours. While they were on Batan, a war occurred from April 2 to May 10 1669 between Great Makata (Mahatao) and Sekina (Ivana). During this war, a rather incredible toll was recorded in which Mahatao lost 309 killed and 900 wounded, and Ivana lost 91 killed and 407 wounded. If we can trust these figures (could they be exaggerated? If so, why?), they are without doubt surprising for such a small island, and indicate just how crowded and stressed was the population during the late prehistoric phase of intensive *ijang* occupation, as also described by Dampier. Unfortunately, however, the Japanese account does not refer to any details of settlement areas or total population size.

Spanish missionaries had also begun to pay occasional visits to Batanes commencing in 1686, and many of them recorded observations that reflect on pre-Spanish social structure and religion (summaries can be found in Gonzalez 1966; Llorente 1983; Hidalgo 1996). Few of these accounts hold information relevant for understanding deeper prehistory, although Llorente (1983:15) comments that rice cultivation was always very marginal in Batanes owing to depredation by birds and rats, and to what she terms "the dry season". Unreliability of annual and seasonal rainfall has been highlighted by Dewar (2003) as a major reason for the prehistoric disappearance of cereal cultivation in eastern Island Southeast Asia and the Pacific, and its replacement by more reliable tubers and tree crops. The Batanes Islands have almost no permanent water or flat alluvial land suitable for wet rice growing, but some swidden rice can be seen growing today in small plots on Itbayat and Batan in the summer (from May onwards).

Previous archaeological research in the Batanes Islands

Archaeology in the Batanes Islands was commenced by Tadao Kano, Otto Scheerer and Pio Montenegro in the 1930s and 1940s (see Beyer 1947:210-212). Most research at that time was focused on the so-called Jar-burial Culture, and Wilhelm G. Solheim II (1960) also described some late prehistoric jar burials from Batanes and Babuyan. A number of jar burial sites on Batan and Savidug Islands, investigated in our research, are described in the following chapters.

After these early visitors, Daniel Scheans and Joanne Laetsch reported surface finds of pottery from three locations near Uyugan in southern Batan (Scheans and Laetsch 1981). One assemblage, from their site 1, reveals possible parallels with the red-slipped pottery from Sunget, to be described in chapters 3 and 6. Following this, the first major archaeological research project in Batanes was carried out in 1982 by researchers from the University of Kumamoto (Koomoto 1983). This Japanese team surveyed and excavated sites across the central neck of Batan Island, between the Iraya and Matarem volcanic complexes, finding many assemblages of burial jars, sherds and other artefacts exposed on the present ground surface and in the walls of road cuttings. They apparently did not realise that many of the assemblages, especially those with red-slipped pottery, were buried under one or more layers of volcanic ash from a past eruption of Mt Iraya; their reports refer only to layers of unspecified "silt". Several of these buried sites have been investigated in our recent research and are discussed in the Batan chapter 3 below. One site reported by the Kumamoto team, the Sunget Neolithic site near Mahatao, was the main attraction in bringing the Asian Fore-Arc Programme team to Batanes in 2002 (Koomoto 1983:55-61; Bellwood 2007b:221).

Since 1982, there have been a number of other archaeological projects in Batanes organised by the National Museum of the Philippines and the Archaeological Studies Program at the University of the Philippines, particularly on Ivuhos, Itbayat and Batan Islands. Most have involved survey and test excavation of late prehistoric *ijang* settlements, of burials covered by boat-shaped enclosures or cairns of stones, and of further jar burials (Faylona 2003). Dizon and Santiago (1994) describe preliminary surveys in 1994 of *ijang* on Batan, Sabtang and Ivuhos, several almost certainly amongst those seen or visited by Dampier (presumably, for instance, Basco *ijang* on Batan, Savidug *ijang* on Sabtang, and Chuhangin *ijang* on Ivuhos). In 1996 and 1997, further examination took place of jar burials and boat-shaped cairns on Batan and Ivuhos (Dizon 1998-2003, 2000). Two boat-shaped cairns close to Chuhangin *ijang* on Ivuhos (the *ijang* visited by Dampier) were excavated, one covering a burial jar and the other a flexed adult male radiocarbon dated to 355±70 uncal. years before present (Dizon et al. 1995-97:38; Dizon 2000). Recent stable isotope analyses of these Chuhangin burials indicates a diet based more on marine than on terrestrial protein (Garong et al. 2010).

In 1997 and 1998, excavation was undertaken at the late prehistoric stone-terraced settlement at Racuaydi (Rakwaydi) on Batan, and further survey and excavation was undertaken on Batan and Itbayat (Dizon and Cayron 1998-2003; Mijares et al. 1998-2003; Barretto et al. 1998-2003; Mijares and Jago-on 2001). A deep excavation through alluvial/colluvial deposits was also undertaken by Victor Paz at the Holiday Camp Site, near San Vicente in southwestern Batan. This latter excavation was the first time, since the Japanese visit in 1982, that archaeological materials were recovered directly from beneath layers of redeposited colluvium and volcanic ash – in this case at a depth of 220 to 300 cm below surface, in association with red-slipped sherds, charcoal, and waterlogged wood. An AMS C14 sample from this layer gave a date of AD 70-330 (Paz et al. 1998: 26; Paz 2002: 279). Apart from further National Museum surveys and test excavations undertaken in habitation sites on Itbayat during 2001 (Mijares et al. 2003), the next phase of archaeological research in Batanes has been that described in this monograph.

2

Archaeological Excavations on Itbayat and Siayan Islands

Peter Bellwood, Eusebio Dizon and Armand Mijares

This chapter describes the layout of excavations and the stratigraphy revealed in Torongan and Reranum caves on Itbayat Island, occupied between 4000 and 3000 years ago, together with the major hill-top habitation site of Anaro, with its circle-stamped pottery and prolific evidence for working of Taiwan nephrite and slate between 3000 and 2000 years ago. Also discussed are the excavations at Mitangeb on Siayan Island, which appears to have served as a satellite settlement from Itbayat about 2000 years ago.

Itbayat Island has a land area of 92.80 square km and is the largest island in Batanes. It is basically a raised coral formation that encloses a number of highly weathered volcanic outcrops, especially Santa Rosa in the north (Karovooban in Itbayaten) and Riposed in the east, rising to 277 and 229 m above sea level respectively (Fig. 2.1). Itbayat has mainly undulating terrain, with gorges where stream beds have cut into the raised coral. The fringes of the island are almost everywhere steep coral cliffs that sometimes rise sheer to 100 metres above sea level (Fig. 2.2), but in a few places there are gorges that allow access down to rocky shelves close to sea level from which boats can be launched. There are no beaches, no sloping coastal terrain that enters the sea, and access to and from the sea can most generously be described as difficult for much of the year, involving leaping on and off heaving boats from and on to slippery quays cut into coral. Needless to say, all boats must be pulled ashore after use, and cannot be moored in the sea. Nevertheless, modern Itbayatens still go fishing and spear-diving just like their forefathers, and many archaeological sites contain large amounts of marine shell, but with the problem that some has been weathered out of the raised coral reef geology and is thus of fossil origin. There are grave dangers here if one wishes to date shell artefacts by direct dates on the shell. No such shell artefact samples have been dated in this research project, although C14 dates have been measured on marine shells in situations where they can be assumed to be food discard, where they are fresh and not rolled or weathered, and without adhering limestone matrix from the uplifted coral reefs.

Itbayat today is mainly under swidden agriculture and pasture, with secondary forest in non-farmed areas and some evergreen native forest in protected gorges. The longest river is the Torongan, that flows underground to the sea below Torongan Cave. Most stream beds on the island are dry nowadays for much of the year under natural circumstances, but they might have held more water under naturally-forested conditions in the past. Some contain pockets of permanent water, but damming to pond back water for humans and buffaloes has occurred very frequently in recent years and the presence of a dam is not always obvious without careful enquiry (see the final Appendix in this volume). Most soils are acidic clays and clay loams that support tuber crops, vegetables and fruit trees, but only very small hillside plots of dry rice are grown, and only during the monsoon season. There is no irrigated rice, neither on Itbayat nor throughout the Batanes Islands, perhaps because there are no alluvial valley bottoms that would favour irrigation and no reliable supplies of irrigation water. Terracing to grow rice has never been adopted, despite its importance in Mountain Province in nearby Luzon.

Siayan Island lies 8 km NNE of Itbayat, across a rough and exposed sea passage, and is just over one l km long. It is dominated by a volcanic pinnacle called Domnayjang (Fig. 2.3), the name apparently referring to the presence of an *ijang* fortification (Gaza and Yamada 1999:28), although no member of our team was willing to scale this relatively sheer and intimidating rock to look for it. The Mitangeb site that lies below was quite sufficient to keep us busy.

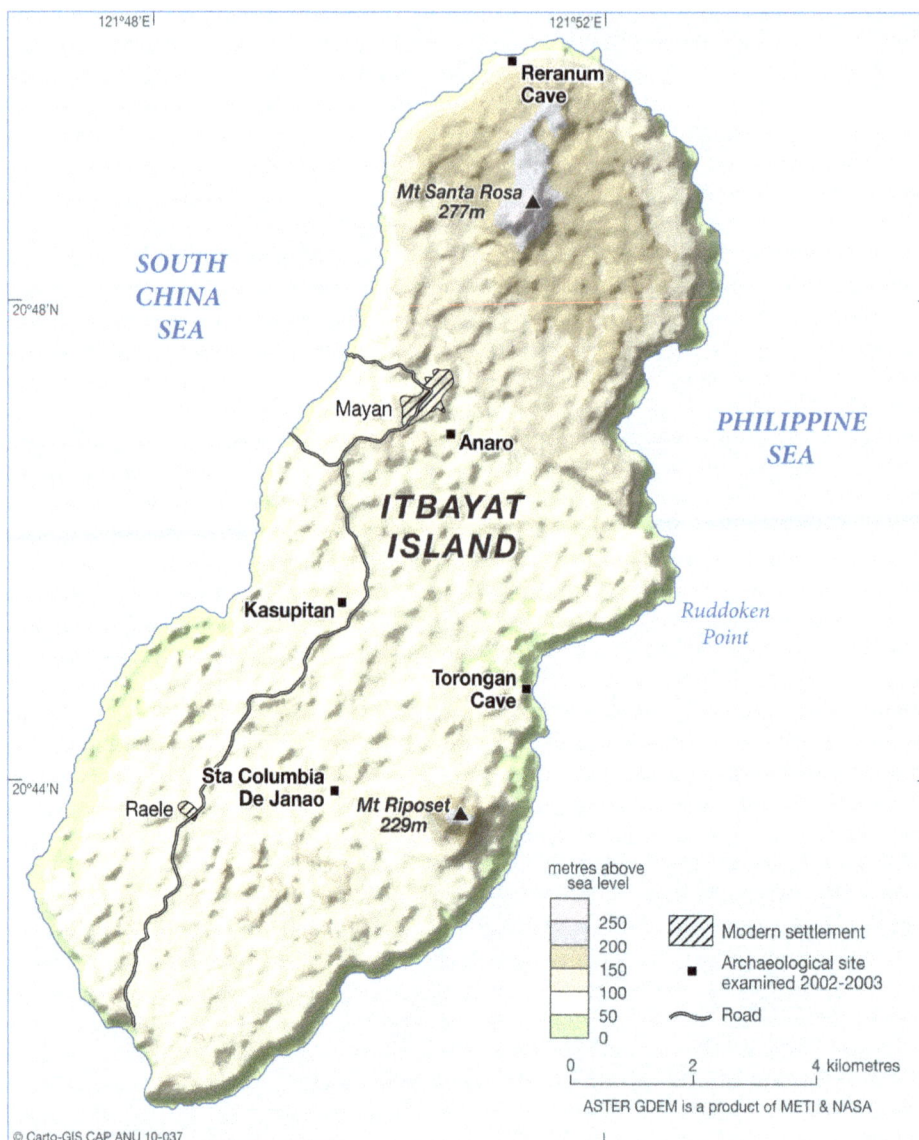

Figure 2.1. The island of Itbayat.

Source: Map preparation by ANU College of Asia and the Pacific, CartoGIS.

Figure 2.2. The eastern coastline of Itbayat, with the inland mouth of Torongan Cave in the centre (at base of cliff, hidden behind the trees).

Source: Peter Bellwood.

Figure 2.3. Siayan Island from the south, with the volcanic pinnacle of Domnayjang. Mitangeb is located just below the place marked "site".

Source: Peter Bellwood.

Torongan Cave

The oldest archaeological assemblage known so far in Batanes comes from Torongan Cave on the east coast of Itbayat. Given the verticality and height of the Itbayat cliffs and the difficulties of landing boats, it is quite possible that Torongan, which opens at sea level, would have provided a landing place for early settlers, who could have beached their canoes in the lower cave (Fig. 2.4) and then climbed up through the interior to emerge eventually on the top of the island. The lowest portion of Torongan is so close to sea level that shallow water might have penetrated into it during any putative period of mid-Holocene higher sea level (not actually attested for Itbayat, but likely until about 4000 years ago from a regional perspective – see Sathiamurthy and Voris 2006: Fig. 26). The recent geological history of Itbayat has also been one of tectonic uplift, and indeed the lower part of the cave wall next to the sea entrance has a marked overhang, perhaps due to wave action. If relative sea level has dropped since 2000 BC, then the early inhabitants of Torongan Cave could have brought in their boats during summer periods of quiet sea. The sea does not penetrate the cave today.

The cave system is a 30 m high tunnel about 150 m long, with both seaward and inland entrances (Fig. 2.5). At one time it must have been occupied by the Torongan River, which now flows underground just before it reaches the cave. The inland entrance lies behind a steep pile of roof fall that rises high above the lowest part of the cave and hides the actual entrance from external view. This has to be climbed from outside and then descended in order to get into the relatively small archaeological region of the cave, which can be seen shaded in Fig. 2.5. This archaeological deposit is located about 13 m above the base of the cave, near the top of a high cone of fallen rock and soil piled against the southwestern wall of the inland mouth (Figs 2.6, 2.7).

Figure 2.4. The Torongan Cave landing, photographed from inside the cave.

Source: Peter Bellwood.

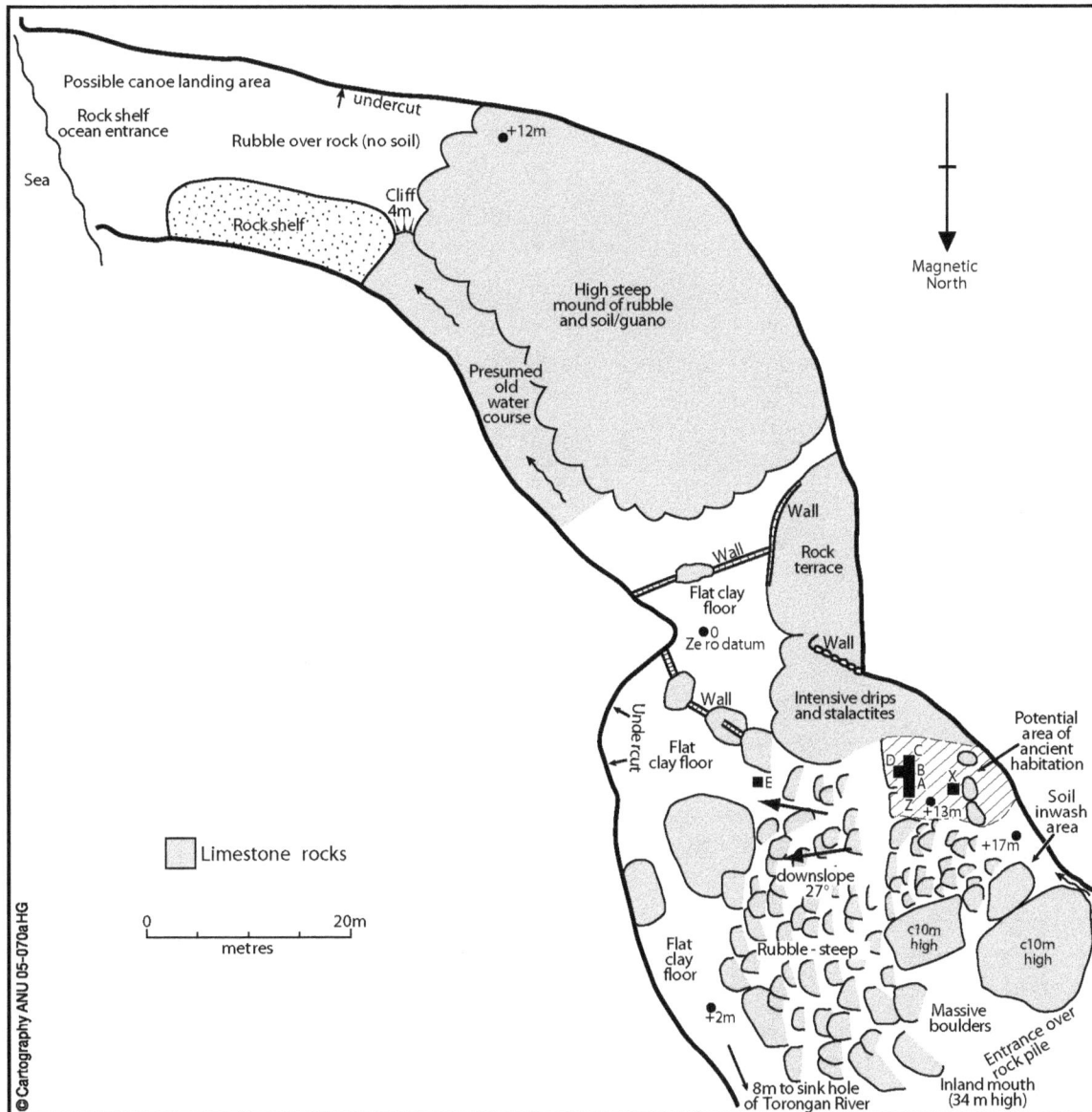

Figure 2.5. Plan of Torongan Cave, with the ocean exit at top left and the excavated area and inland mouth at bottom right. Heights in metres are above an arbitrary zero datum located in the middle of the cave.

Source: Map preparation by ANU College of Asia and the Pacific, CartoGIS.

Excavations were undertaken in 1X1 metre squares near the top of this cone in 2004 (squares A and B) and 2005 (squares C, D, X and Z). All materials in Torongan were dry-sieved through 3 and 5 mm meshes – no water was available to allow wet sieving. In squares A to D, an in-washed layer of topsoil was found at about 40-65 cm depth, presumably released into the cave down the side of the inland mouth by forest clearance and occupational activity on the land surface above. Surface traces of a former open site were noted on top of the cave in 2005, alas eroded away down to the culturally sterile clay subsoil leaving just a few remnant potsherds. Above the topsoil in squares A to D the deposit became lighter, indicating continuing inflow of subsoil after the original topsoil had been washed down, but sherds became increasingly fewer towards the surface (Table 2.1). Because squares X and Z had been disturbed by downwards movement of sediment into deep voids in the scree slope, numbers of sherds by depth are not presented for these squares. Square E, dug in 2005 in the flat clay floor at the base of the cave, was archaeologically sterile and scoured by occasional flooding through the cave.

Figure 2.6. The 2004 excavation in the rock-filled interior of Torongan Cave, photographed from the high inland mouth of the cave. The lower cave floor is down at the left, with the remains of a dry stone wall visible at the rear.

Source: Peter Bellwood.

Figure 2.7. Excavation and sieving in Torongan Cave in 2005, squares C and D.

Source: Peter Bellwood.

When we first visited Torongan we thought that all of the cultural material might have been washed in from above. However, the cave itself would also have been habitable as long as fresh water was available in the Torongan river bed outside or in the sink holes below the entrance. People could have slept on bamboo flooring laid over the rough and rocky floor of the cave, particularly over the excavated area, which was positioned away from overhanging and threatening stalactites. The cave has good light, and the *ijang*-like dry stone walls that occur further into the cave from the archaeological site (visible in Fig. 2.5) suggest that groups did live there occasionally in the recent past, perhaps hiding from enemies. For instance, a stone wall quite near the excavated area and marked on Fig. 2.5 (also visible behind and slightly to the left of the excavators in Fig. 2.6) seems to have been constructed to hide the surface of a rock terrace from prying eyes looking in from the northern mouth. However, very little midden material was found in the Torongan Cave excavations, despite good conditions for shell and bone preservation.

Table 2.1. The distribution of pottery (body sherds only) in Torongan Cave, 2004-5 excavations, squares A to D. Note the very high density in the in-washed topsoil layer (shaded). Counts for red-slipped sherds are minima, since red slip can be removed by weathering or masked by surface concretions on the sherds.

Torongan A-D	Body sherd weight gm.	Body sherd number	Red slipped sherds (positively identified)	Circle stamped
0-5	444	129	6	1
5-10	802	184	15	
10-15	553	130	13	
15-20	890	151	11	
20-25	524	178	13	1
25-30	616	193	21	
30-35	626	204	21	
35-40	934	281	19	
40-45	1723	361	50	1
45-50	1759	413	50	
50-55	1342	362	33	
55-60	744	173	11	
60-65	442	165	7	
65-70	142	58	4	
70-75	148	37	5	
75-80	5	3		
Totals	**11694**	**3022**	**279**	**3**

The calibrated C14 dates from Torongan Cave point to a chronology for the in-washed topsoil layer between 2500/2000 and 1350 BC (Table 5.1 and chapter 5), although there are younger dates from higher in the profile suggesting that the site was visited over a long period, indeed into the Ming dynasty according to a coin of the emperor Wan Li (AD 1583-1620) found just below the surface. Torongan also has three circle-stamped sherds with white lime or clay infilling occurring relatively late in the sequence (Table 2.1), similar to the sherds with stamped circles dating between 1200 and 500 BC from Sunget, Anaro and Savidug (chapter 6).

Soil Micromorphology of Torongan Cave Sections (by Armand Mijares)

Two oriented sediment samples collected in Kubiena tin boxes driven into the Torongan Cave section were impregnated, thin-sectioned, and studied under the microscope in the Archaeological Studies Program, University of the Philippines. The upper stratum (0-40 cm depth) is a fine crumbly light to dark brown sediment. The lower stratum (40-65 cm depth) of apparently in-washed topsoil is a fine dark brown to black sediment. Descriptions are based on Bullock et al. (1985) and Stoops (1998).

The upper stratum has two sub-sections differentiated by microstructure. The upper has a moderately developed angular blocky structure with channels and intra-pedal cracks. The lower has a moderately developed crumb microstructure with packing voids and poroids. The difference between the two sub-sections is probably due to the lower sub-section being subjected to more bioturbation due to faunal activity (French 2003). This sub-section has an estimated 5-10 per cent porosity.

The ground mass of the upper stratum is poorly to moderately sorted with a coarse to fine ratio of 20/80 and a texture of silty clay. The ground mass has a stipple-speckle fabric with high birefringence. The colour in plane-polarized light (PPL) is brownish yellow, and yellowish brown in cross-polarized light (XPL).

Rounded andesite fragments 120-1500 μm in size were observed. There were large fragments of limestone (750 μm-4 mm) and calcite nodules (300-700 μm). A few bone (500 μm) and shell (500-1700 μm) fragments were also observed. Other minerals observed were plagioclase (100-600 μm), amphibole (120-500 μm), pyroxene (250-250 μm), biotite (250 μm) and quartz (170-500 μm). A fragment of earthenware pottery (12 mm) was also recorded. Charcoal was the only organic material found, of rounded fragments 85-750 μm in size.

The lower stratum has a weakly developed sub-angular blocky structure. Porosity is estimated at 10% with compound packing and intra-pedal cracks. The ground mass is yellowish brown in PPL and reddish yellow in XPL. It is poorly sorted, with a silty clay loam texture. The coarse to fine ratio is 15:85. The fabric has high birefringence with stipple-speckles. It also contains shell fragments 700 μm-8 mm in size and bone fragments 7 mm in size. There are many limestone/calcite fragments (85 μm-5 mm) that are angular in shape. Other minerals observed were plagioclase (85-700 μm), quartz (50-200 μm), amphibole (50-400 μm), biotite (100-250 μm) and pyroxene (250 μm). There were rounded to sub-rounded charcoal fragments (100-850 μm), estimated at 2% by volume of the section.

Some grains or fragments have silty clay coatings. There were a lot of orange to red dirty clay peds 50-850 μm in size. Large yellowish to red coloured peds with plagioclase and amphibole inclusions were also identified. These peds are from 1500 μm to 3 mm in size and are rounded to sub-rounded.

In conclusion, the thin sections from Torongan Cave show some bioturbation, especially in the upper stratum. This can be seen in the crumbly structure and the poroids made by faunal activity. Both strata showed some degree of movement in their rounded rock fragments and charcoal inclusions. Red-orange peds and dirty clay were also observed, probably derived from outside the cave. These features are characteristic of developed soils that could have been washed into the cave from above.

Reranum rockshelter

Reranum rockshelter (Fig. 2.8) is located about half-way down the terraced raised coral northern perimeter of Itbayat Island, looking out towards Siayan Island (Fig. 2.9). This is an area where landing would have been very difficult, except in very calm seas. However, the presence of a reliable fresh water spring in the cliff below the site means that the cave would have been habitable. Boats heading for Siayan Island from the two modern landings of Mayan township, located at Chinapoliran and Paganaman, sometimes stop and take on fresh water here, since getting ashore on to the narrow limestone shelf is possible in very calm seas. Normally, however, we might expect Reranum shelter to have been accessed from the landward side, since the climb down from the island top is quite easy. The land above the cave where we camped in 2006 is gently sloping, and lightly strewn with recent potsherds.

Figure 2.8. Reranum shelter before excavation. The right hand area had most of its soil removed before our visit.

Source: Peter Bellwood.

Figure 2.9. Looking north from below Reranum shelter towards Siayan Island, with Ditarem (Mabudis) Island behind it.

Source: Peter Bellwood.

The shelter itself is very small, enclosing about 5 by 6 meters, and lies perhaps 50 m above the sea, which is accessible by a steep climb down over razor-sharp karst, past the freshwater spring. Reranum was reported by Gershom P. Gato, Captain of Barangay Santa Rosa, Itbayat, to the research team in April 2006. That same month, three 1x1 square meters (Pits A, B and C) were excavated in the shelter, as indicated in Fig. 2.10. Unfortunately, the deposit in Reranum is only a maximum of 50 cm deep (Fig. 2.11) and shows many signs of disturbance, especially in square B, where a large ash-filled pit was dug to bedrock quite late in the occupational history of the site and later sealed by fallen limestone rubble. The western end of the rockshelter has been badly disturbed by the removal of most of the deposit, perhaps by treasure hunter activity. The soil from this end had been thrown out of the cave, together with many earthenware sherds that had been collected by Mr Gato before our arrival and put in a pile inside the shelter. Many of these sherds were quite large, indicating that preservation in this part of the shelter was originally very good.

The distribution of cultural material by depth within the excavated Reranum squares is shown in Table 2.2. The single archaeological layer (layer 3 in Fig. 2.10) comprised homogenous dark soil, presumably derived from material slowly falling from upslope and behind into the shelter, entering around the sides. Sherd densities by soil volume were similar from surface to bedrock, and the latter was presumably exposed in the shelter floor when humans first utilised the site. The chronology of Reranum is discussed further in chapter 5, but the four C14 dates from it can best be described as chaotic, totally unrelated to the stratigraphy. There are probably two reasons for this, the first being simple disturbance, the second being the presence of a much younger archaeological site on the land surface immediately above the cave. Rim sherds from this ground surface are uniformly of the short everted types typical of the late, or Garayao Phase, of Itbayat prehistory (chapter 6), and sherds must have fallen down into the shelter deposits from above. Two of the C14 dates were on food residues on the inside surfaces of potsherds, and since such sherds inevitably came from the basal undecorated and unrimmed portions of pots it is impossible to guess their typological age simply by looking at them. It seems likely at Reranum that these food residues, unlike the situation in the more protected Torongan Cave, have only survived on chronologically recent sherds.

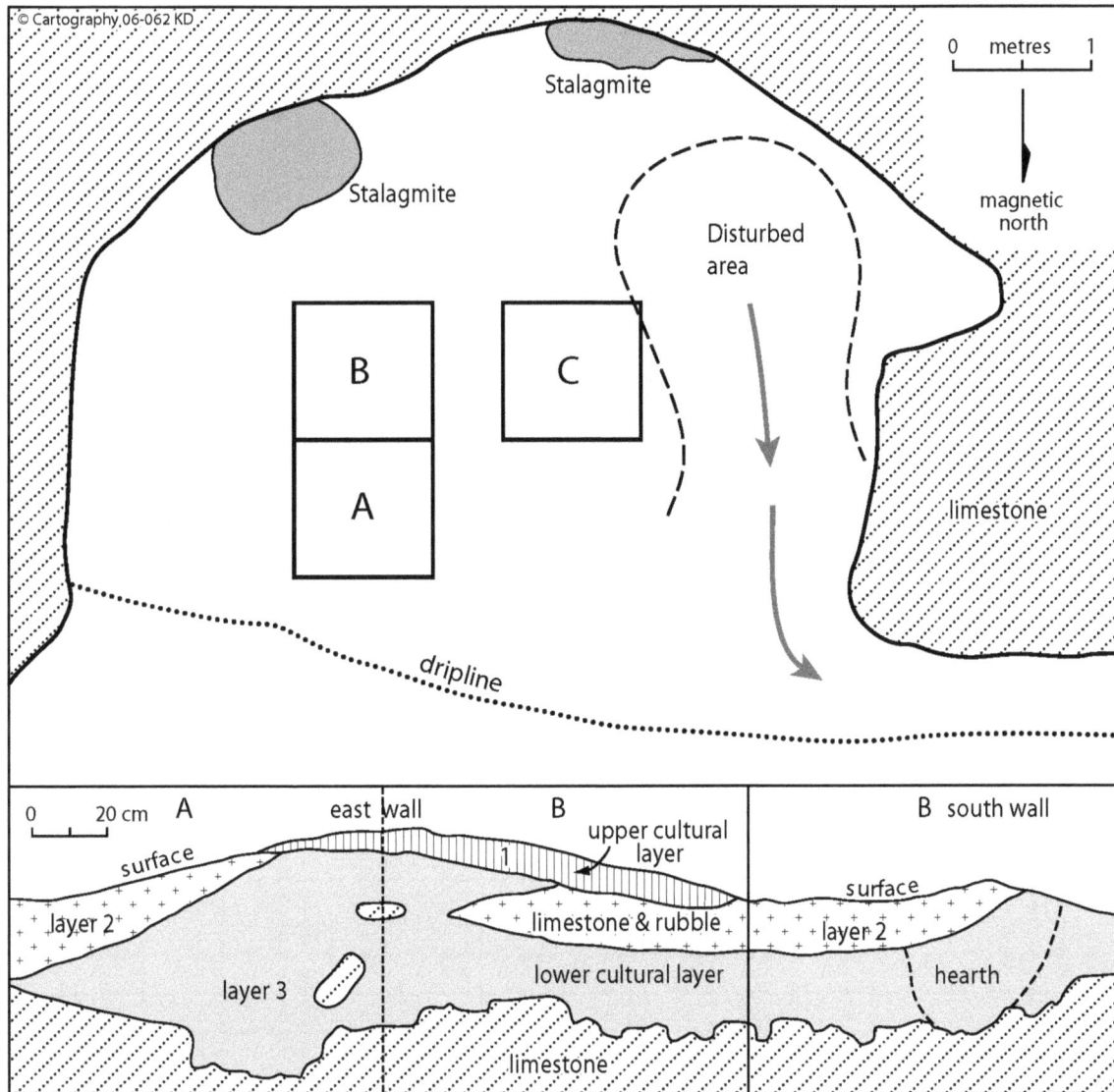

Figure 2.10. Plan and section of Reranum shelter.

Source: Map preparation by ANU College of Asia and the Pacific, CartoGIS.

Figure 2.11. The excavated eastern section of squares A and B, Reranum shelter.

Source: Peter Bellwood.

Table 2.2. The distribution of sherds by number and weight per 5 cm spit in Reranum, squares A to C. Because the floor of the shelter is very uneven, sherd counts drop off below 25 cm because smaller surface areas are represented. Given this, sherd densities by soil volume seem fairly even from surface to bedrock. Presumably the shelter had a bare and uneven rock floor when humans first occupied it.

Reranum A-C	Plain body sherds (no.)	Plain rim sherds	Fine cord-marked	Circle-stamped	Total sherd weight (gm)	C¹⁴ dates (see Table 5.1)
0-5 cm	490	9	2	0	4480	
5-10 cm	464	5	5	0	1920	768±34 BP
10-15 cm	252	6	2	0	1840	
15-20 cm	383	12	2	1	3540	479±30 BP
20-25 cm	589	21	7	0	4900	
25-30 cm	132	6	0	0	1560	3253±47 BP
30-35 cm	205	2	0	0	1790	1798±37 BP
35-40 cm	93	0	1	0	1000	
40-45 cm	15	0	0	0	40	
Total	**2623**	**61**	**19**	**1**	**21070**	

It can be seen from Table 2.2 that sherds of fine-corded marked pottery were found throughout the deposit in small numbers. Only one circle-stamped sherd was found. One significant observation about Reranum from the viewpoint of chronology is that the cord-marked sherds are all very small, suggestive perhaps of redeposition or disturbance from now-lost older layers. Cord marking had disappeared completely from southeastern Taiwan by 2000-1500 BC (Hung 2008), and its absence in Torongan Cave and in all archaeological sites in the northern Philippines, apart from Reranum, is hardly likely to be coincidental. It suggests a considerable age for the assemblage. Indeed, the rim forms of the sherds collected from Reranum by Mr Gato, to be discussed in chapter 6, also belong from a Taiwan perspective to this early period.

Anaro

The *ijang*-like hilltop site of Anaro is placed centrally within northern Itbayat, 3.5 km south of the highest hilltop on the island, Mt Santa Rosa (or Karovooban), which rises to 277 m above sea level. It lies about 500 m inland from the southeastern edge of Mayan township, from which it is separated by a valley that is normally dry. The site covers the flat limestone top and upper terrace of a long narrow promontory of raised coral that runs northwest to southeast for about 150 m, at about 100 m above sea level. At its southeastern end, Anaro is joined to another area of raised coral across a saddle, but is otherwise flanked by steep slopes strewn with fallen artefacts. The top of the promontory is a maximum of 40 m wide and the terrace that lies just below is about 3-5 metres wide (Figs 2.12, 2.13).

Figure 2.12. Anaro from the north. The cleared area in the centre of the photo contains the lower slope collection areas of Anaro 1 and 5. The low limestone cliff of the upper terrace is visible at the top of the clearing, just below the summit, with two small rockshelters (Anaro 1). The left hand end (east) is towards Anaro 2, behind the forest. Anaro 3 is over the back of the hill from the cleared area.

Source: Peter Bellwood.

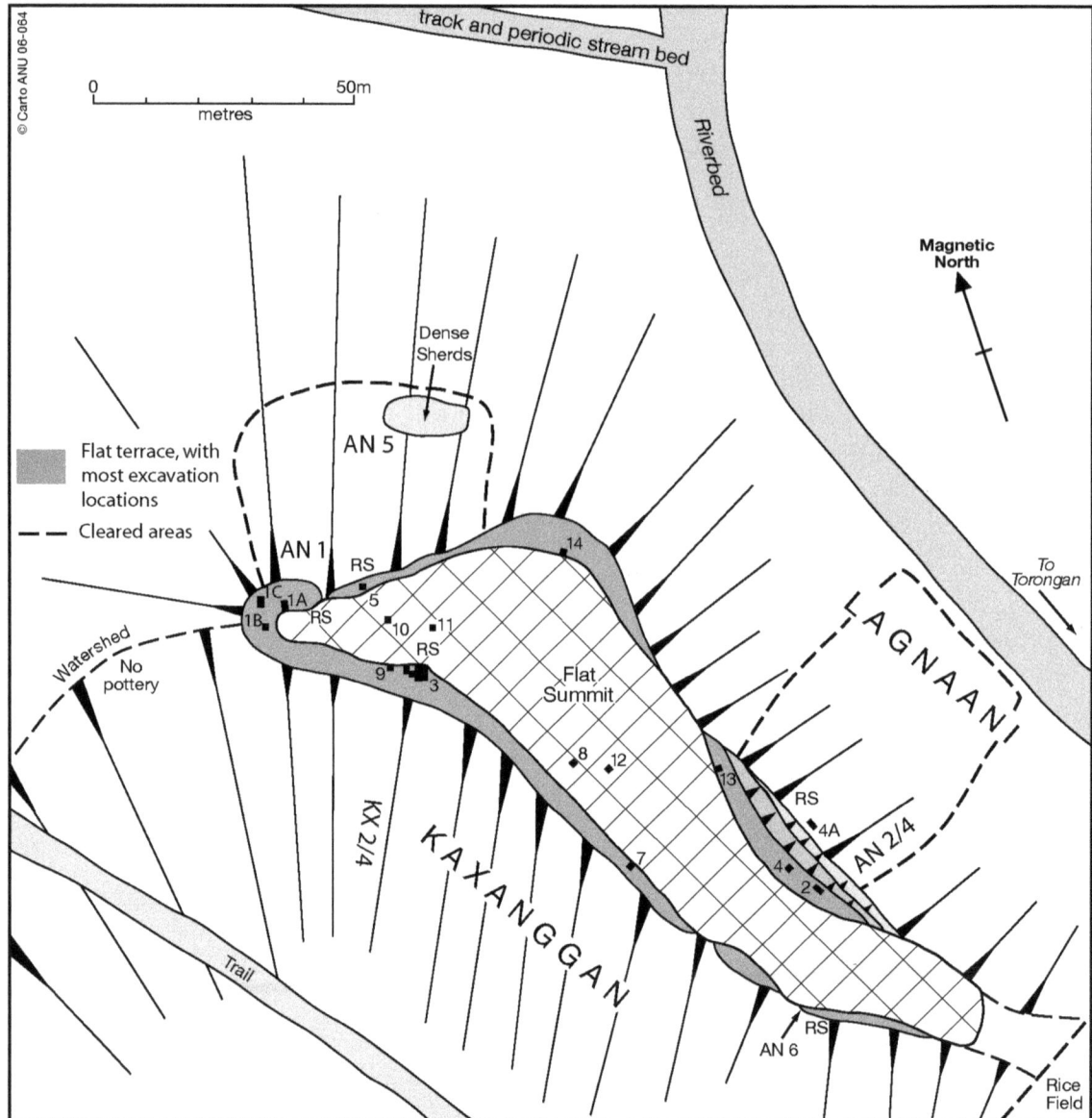

Figure 2.13. Plan of Anaro, with numbered excavation areas. The flat summit of the site is partly bare limestone and partly very thin soil with deeper pockets. No coherent archaeological stratigraphy remains here.

Source: Map preparation by ANU College of Asia and the Pacific, CartoGIS.

Anaro was originally a flat topped and steep sided coral reef, with its surface at sea level. Uplift took place, probably during the Pleistocene, in at least three episodes, indicated by the profile of the hill (Fig. 2.14). The first uplift was only about 2-3 metres, allowing the 3 to 5 m wide upper terrace that runs around most of the summit to be wave-cut, together with the rockshelters at Anaro 1 and 3. Two more uplift phases followed, cutting the two eastern cliffs below Anaro 2 and 4 that are shown in Fig. 2.13. There is also a lower level rockshelter at Anaro 6 on the western side of the hill, but this could perhaps be phreatic in origin.

The creation of Anaro

Upper terrace

Former sea levels

1. Massif still beneath sea level

2. Cutting of upper terrace and rock shelters

3. Cutting of middle terrace

4. Cutting of lowest and youngest terrace

Anaro 6 →

limestone

Anaro before human settlement

limestone

soil

soil

Situation with human settlement

houses

Anaro 3

Anaro 2

Anaro 6

Anaro 4

artifacts

artifacts

cultivation?

limestone

cultivation?

soil

soil

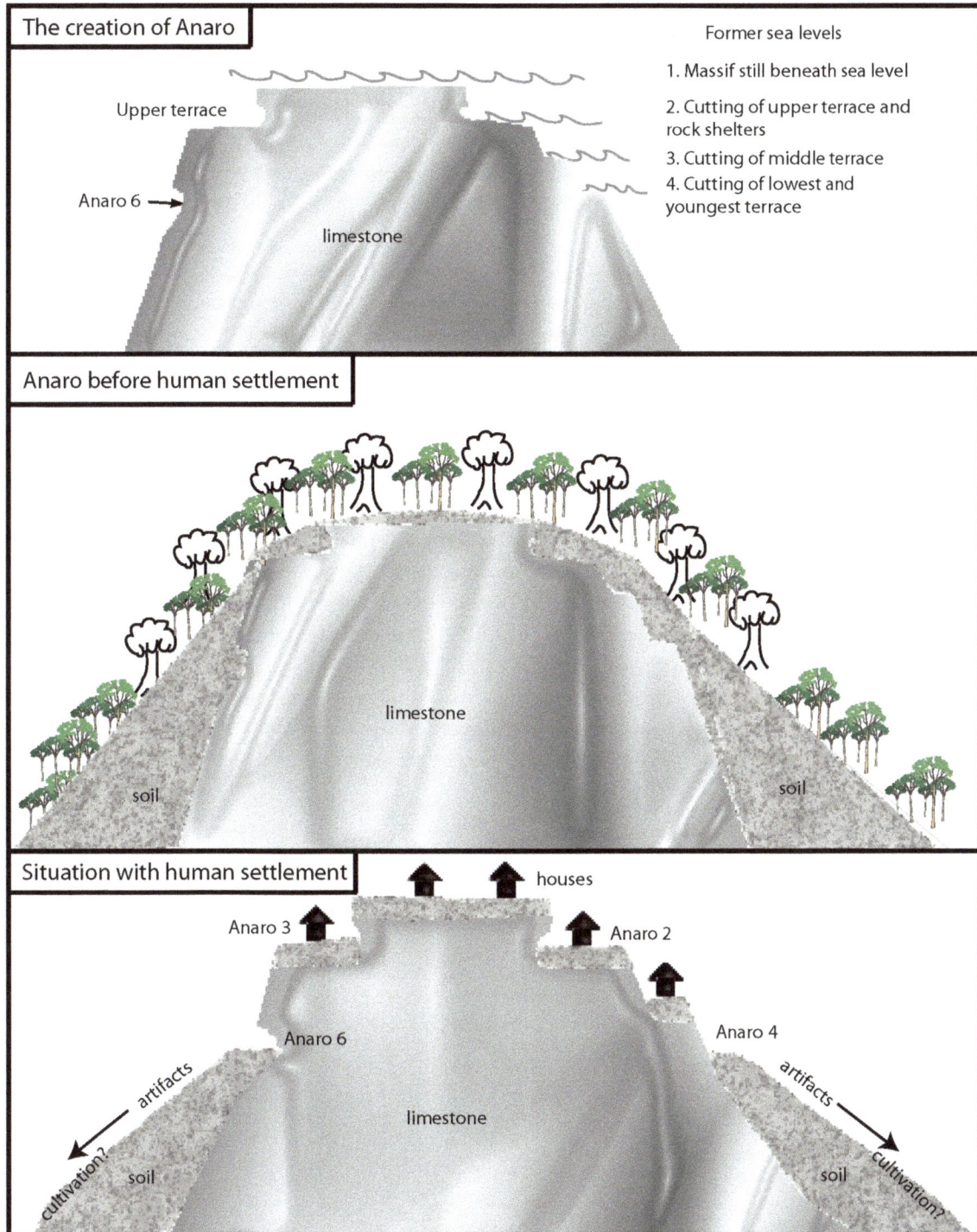

Figure 2.14. Anaro geological and occupational history. Three geological phases of wave-cut erosion are visible, not including the levelling of the flat top of the hill, presumably when it was an active reef surface.

Source: Tony Peñalosa and Peter Bellwood.

Prior to the first human arrival on Itbayat about 4000 years ago, the upper terrace would presumably have been mantled by soil (pH 8.0, alkaline) sloping down from the hill top above. Human activities have made the surface of this terrace virtually flat, especially at the northern end and down the western side, through digging stick cultivation, purposeful levelling for house floors, and so forth. During our excavations, some sections of the upper terrace were cleared for planting, as were the very steep slopes below. In recent times the flat limestone top of the site has held too little soil to support agriculture (pers. comm. from land owner Rodobaldo Ponce), being mostly now bare rock, but trees have been cut from this area in the recent past as firewood for burning lime.

Artefacts occur down to the flat bedrock base of the upper terrace in all excavated squares, especially in Anaro 2 and 3, although this need not imply that the base was bare rock when first settlement occurred. There was probably already a layer of soil. Digging stick activity would continuously have rotated artefacts through a vertical height of around 30 cm as the upper terrace deposit deepened, except during actual house-dwelling episodes. For instance, three matching rim sherds of one Anaro circle-stamped type 1 vessel (described in chapter 6) were found in square 3 at 70-80 cm, at 90-100 cm, and in neighbouring square 3G at 80-90 cm, suggesting considerable disturbance by cultivation and tree roots.

Anaro was subjected to excavation by a series of one metre squares in 2004, 2005 and 2006 (Fig. 2.13), eventually totalling 28 square metres in 16 different locations. Nine of these one metre squares were clustered at the location termed Anaro 3, where a rockshelter 1.2 m deep and 2.5 m long has been etched into the back wall of the upper terrace. Prior to excavation this shelter was filled with 75-100 cm of archaeological deposit, with only about 50 cm of vertical space remaining below its roof. The original height of the shelter when empty was thus about 1.5 m from bedrock to ceiling (Figs 2.15, 2.16). It is unlikely that it was ever formally inhabited, being too small, but it is important because it has retained a deposit approximately one metre deep, relatively undisturbed by tree roots or by the cultivation activities that have taken place outside on the terrace itself. We return to this situation later when the chronology of the site is discussed.

Figure 2.15. Anaro 3A (at rear, against exposed rockshelter wall) to 3C, excavated in 2005.

Source: Peter Bellwood.

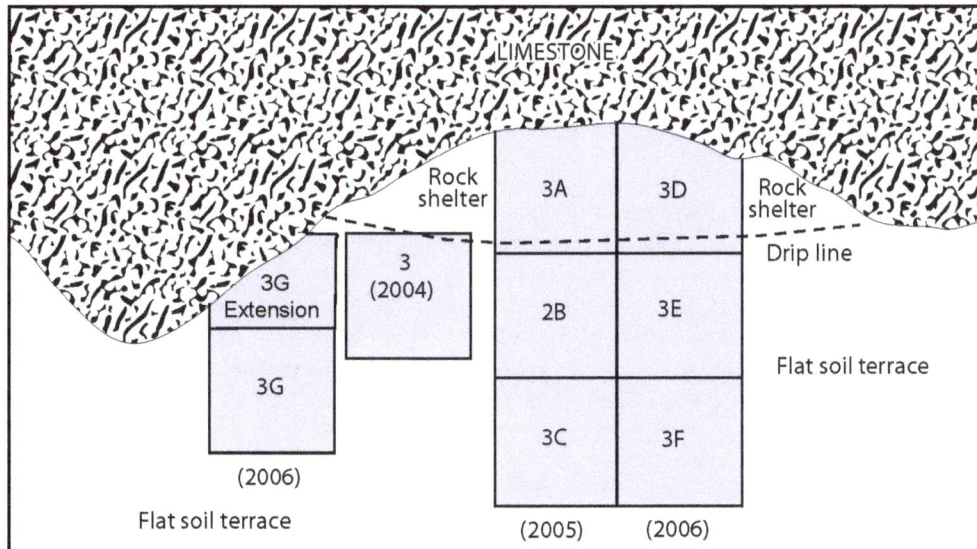

Figure 2.16. Plan of excavated squares at Anaro 3. Squares 3A and 3D lie within a small rockshelter.

Source: Peter Bellwood.

Apart from Anaro 3 and 6, the latter also a rockshelter, the other Anaro excavations mostly had very shallow deposits over bedrock in areas which had been subjected to cultivation in the past. In fact, in no trench was there any significant stratigraphic differentiation of separate soil layers. The soil deposits in all squares, outside rock shelters, were identical from surface to bedrock, consisting of a garden soil with tree roots, artefacts, shells, animal bones and so forth, in fairly similar concentrations throughout. Lower layers were usually more compact than upper, but this is to be expected due to the passage of time.

Most excavation took place in 5 cm spits, but for analytical purposes the data are discussed below by 10 cm spits. Nowhere was it evident that 5 cm spits were essential for interpretative purposes. All deposits were passed through 5 mm sieves, the soil being too hard and lumpy to pass through anything smaller. The absence of water near the site ruled out wet sieving. No charcoal concentrations were found, no hearths, and all C14 dates have come from food residues in sherds.

The excavated areas at Anaro

In this section the excavated squares are each described briefly with respect to depth and cultural content. We begin with Anaro 1, which comprised three trenches excavated at the northern end of the terrace in 2004. One 2 by 1 m trench (1A) was dug in front of a small shelter in the rock face, and another of the same size (1C) out on the terrace. A 1 by 1 m square, 1B, was dug nearby to the south. The deposits in 1A and 1C were only about 30 cm deep, had been cultivated to bedrock (this area is still planted today), and produced only very recent pottery. Evidently, any older deposits here will have cascaded downhill over the edge of the terrace in the past. Square 1B went down to 60 cm, but was mostly rock filled. It produced a sequence similar to Anaro 3 (below).

Anaro 2, a 3 by 1 m trench excavated in 2004, was located at the opposite end of the site from Anaro 1. Most of the deposit here lay between the surface and 30 cm depth, but pockets of material in the uneven limestone contained artefacts to 50 cm, including a bark cloth beater at the base of a hole in the bedrock (Fig. 8.7 D). All of the deposit seems to have been very thoroughly cultivated in the past, being garden soil throughout. A food residue AMS date of c.AD 100 (Wk 14643) came from a depth of 15-20 cm (chapter 5).

Anaro 3 is a complex area of excavation, within and in front of the rockshelter described above, with a total of 9 excavated 1 by 1 metre squares (Fig. 2.16). The single square termed Anaro 3 was dug in 2004 and is distinguished as Anaro 3 (2004) below, to avoid confusion with the use of the term Anaro 3 to refer to the whole area. Anaro squares 3A to 3C were dug in 2005, and 3D to 3G in 2006. Anaro 9 nearby was mostly loose rock. Squares 3A and 3D were actually within the rockshelter, the others in front. Depths of these deposits varied slightly; Anaro 3 (2004) and 3A reached bedrock at 110 cm, 3B and 3C at 100 cm, but 3D and 3E reached only 80 cm, 3F and 3G 90 cm. All squares had homogeneous garden soil profiles, with lots of tree roots outside the shelter.

The remaining squares, Anaro 4 and 4A, through to Anaro 14, were mostly one metre squares dug in various parts of the site. Apart from Anaro 4A, which was dug between large rocks at the top of the soil scree slope and thus "bottomless" (we dug to 100 cm but then gave up since the area was becoming too constricted), most of these squares were very shallow. Anaro 5 reached a maximum of 40 cm, Anaro 11 only 20 cm. Anaro 14 reached 50 cm. In all of these squares the bedrock is always uneven, so the deepest deposits are normally in little more than a small hole in the rock. Rock-free deposits rarely go below 20 cm from the surface, and this is true also of Anaro 2.

Anaro 6 was the only significant rockshelter excavation, apart from that at Anaro 3. However, Anaro 6 lies well below the main terrace, in the side of the hill, and gives the impression of being a phreatic "hole in the wall" rather than a wave-cut shelter. Excavation of a one metre square within the cave produced pottery down to 130 cm, with culturally sterile soil below. We never reached bedrock, since the cave probably never had a flat floor and the soil deposits doubtless continue as the scree slope for tens of metres below. Strangely, the pottery from this excavation was very homogeneous and relatively recent, with strong Mitangeb parallels. Perhaps it washed into the shelter as a result of some disturbance above, possibly during clearance and cultivation, since there were few signs that this small and dark shelter was ever actually inhabited.

Mitangeb, Siayan Island

Since Mitangeb produced a short-lived but well defined assemblage of Anaro-style plain pottery dated to about AD 1-500, the site is described here with Anaro. Getting to the uninhabited island of Siayan can best be described as an adventure, involving a 15 km small open boat trip from the Paganaman Landing near Mayan township on Itbayat. Siayan has no reliable fresh water supply so all supplies must be carried in, and visitors have to camp. The island is entirely volcanic and quite rugged (Fig. 2.3), peaking at 164 m above sea level. The site of Mitangeb, shown to us in 2004 by the Captain of Barangay Santa Rosa, Gershom P. Gato, lies on a terrace above a protected beach on the southwestern side of the island (Fig. 2.17). A small test pit dug hurriedly during our one-day visit in 2004 produced sherds at 50 to 85 cm below ground level, with the greatest density at 70-75 cm.

The general layout of the site is shown in Figs 2.17 and 2.18. The excavated area sits on a low terrace above a coral sand beach, inland from a shallow marine lagoon that is almost dry at low tide, with a reef beyond. Fig. 2.17 shows the site at high tide. Between the beach sand and the site is an area of very dense spiny pandanus, but all indications are that the site only exists above the break of slope shown on the plan, covering an area on the terrace about 25 m long by 15 m wide, according to auger holes that yielded potsherds. In 2006 we laid out three excavations, trench A at 2x1 metres, and squares B and C at 1x1 metre each. Each yielded identical stratigraphy, except that the main cultural layer 4 in C was more deeply buried, at about one metre as opposed to 60 cm in A and B. Although the surface of the site is level now, at the time of occupation the surface sloped downwards from A to C, perhaps reflecting the former presence of a gully. Trench A yielded the most interesting material, especially a layer of quite dense stones that might have belonged to a house floor or pavement of some kind, with dense sherdage in association (Fig. 2.19). This suggests the presence of a feature that could have been about 3.5 m long, given that the stone layer also appeared in the SW corner of square B.

Figure 2.17. A view of Mitangeb from the southern slope of Domnayjang. The three excavation squares can be seen behind the burnt posts in the left middle ground.

Source: Peter Bellwood.

In each square there were 5 main layers, with pH values of 6, neutral to acid. Hence the site yielded no animal bone, and little shell, mostly Turbinidae and *Thais* sp. and probably of industrial rather than food origin. Layer 1, at the surface, was simply a blown beach sand, quite deep on top of square C, where it seems to have been filling the depression or gully, but virtually absent in squares A and B. Layer 2 is a culturally-sterile topsoil, indicating that the site has not been inhabited in recent centuries. Layer 3 consists of another yellowish beach sand, also culturally-sterile. Layer 4, the main cultural layer, is a buried topsoil 20-30 cm thick that clearly formed the occupation layer for the site (Fig. 2.19). Layer 5 beneath is a culturally-sterile clay, except for a few sherds and the sinker/anvil shown in Fig. 8.10 D pressed into its top. Coring through layer 5 revealed that it is about 35 cm deep and seals in another old topsoil (layer 6), in turn about 50 cm deep, over light brown subsoil. Rocks below this terminated augering. One suggestion from this sequence could be that layer 6 is the early human phase topsoil, buried by clay soil wash released by deforestation before the Mitangeb site was inhabited. The pinnacle of Domnayjang behind Mitangeb, visible in Fig. 2.3, would certainly have produced considerable hill wash material if its lower slopes were cleared of vegetation. However, deeper investigation is required to demonstrate this possibility.

NORTH

Ditarem

Ali'i

Siayan

Mitangeb

Land over 100 m

1 km

Path

upslope

Possible extent of site

Dense pandanus

C

SEA 50 M

1 B

Slope

A

Possible extent of house floor

Dense pandanus

Erosion gully

● Auger holes

□ Excavations (A, B and C)

Slope

Path

5 m

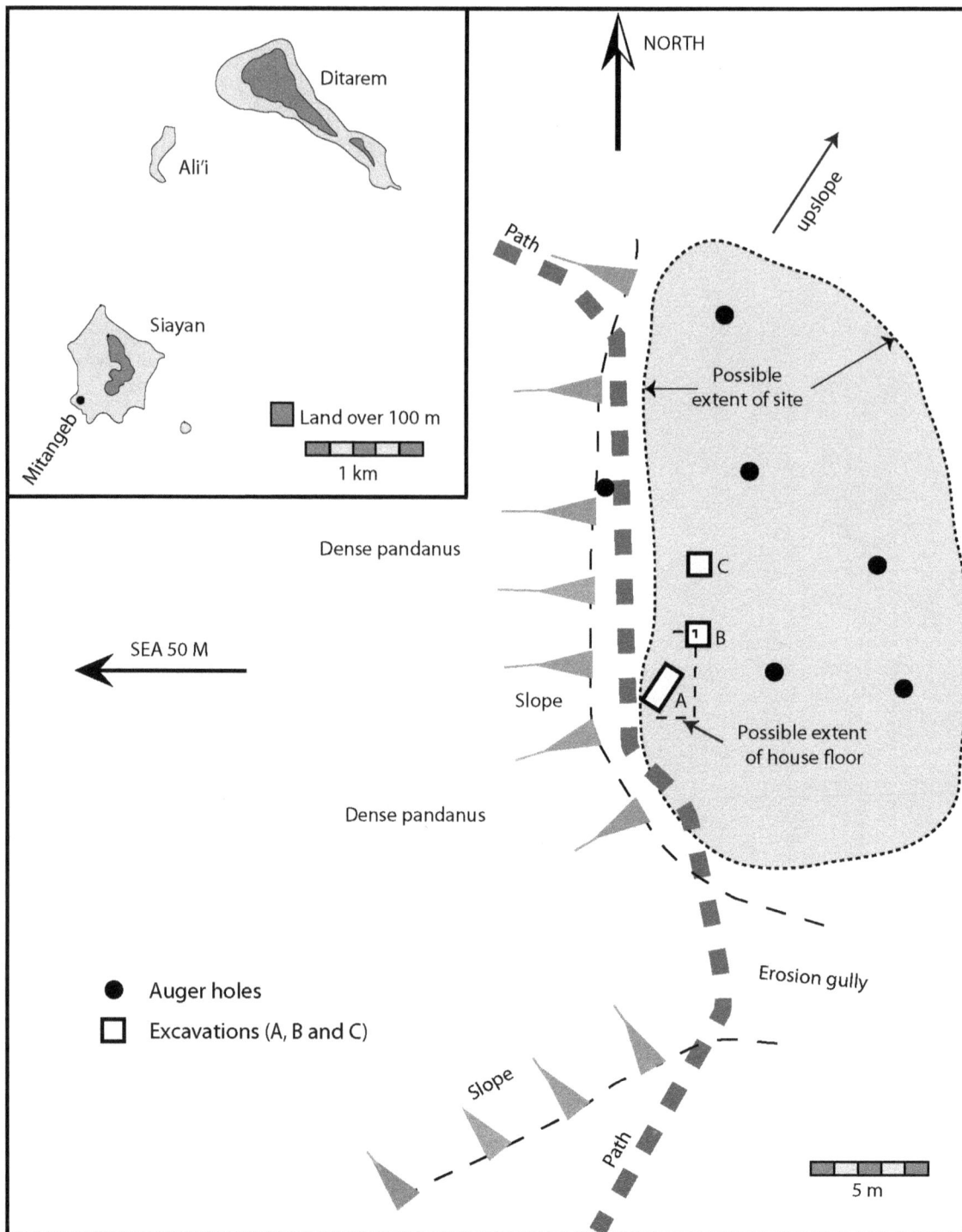

Figure 2.18. Plan of the Mitangeb site.

Source: Peter Bellwood.

Figure 2.19. Mitangeb square A, looking towards the north. The stones and dark topsoil of cultural layer 4 are clearly visible.

Source: Peter Bellwood.

3

Archaeological Excavations on Batan Island

Peter Bellwood, Atholl Anderson and Eusebio Dizon

This chapter identifies a major eruption of the Iraya volcano about 1500 years ago that buried many regions of central and northern Batan Island. It continues onwards to describe the layout of excavations and the stratigraphy revealed in the open sites of Sunget, Mahatao, Naidi, Payaman and Tayid, all buried beneath the Iraya ash. Excavations of post-eruption occupation layers in a number of caves and rockshelters are also described, and it is interesting to note that none of these caves or shelters produced any evidence for very ancient (pre-Neolithic) occupation. They seem to have been used mainly for occupation in the late prehistoric period of *ijang* warfare.

Although slightly smaller than Itbayat Island in land area, Batan is the most fertile island in Batanes. It supports most of the population and has the most settlements, including the modern administrative centre of Basco with its airport and harbour. Dumb-bell shaped, the northern part of Batan is formed by the active Iraya volcano (1009 m), the southern by the extinct Matarem (459 m), with the narrow neck between formed by volcanic soils and occasional coastal outcrops of coral limestone (Fig. 3.1). Most of the agricultural activity on the island is focused today across this central neck, roughly from Basco to Mahatao (Fig. 3.2), and around the coastal flanks of Matarem. The northeastern and northern coastlines of the island are essentially uninhabited. Not surprisingly, the distribution of known archaeological sites follows the modern distribution of settlements and agriculture very closely indeed.

Batan Island: Vulcanicity and archaeology

Before describing the archaeology of Batan, it is necessary to examine the recent volcanic history of the island. The southern volcanic complex, Matarem, is no longer active, but many sites are buried under volcanic ash from a geologically very recent eruption of the northern volcano, Iraya. This ash blanket, dated to c.AD 500 (see below), provides a very useful minimum age in central Batan for the sealed archaeological assemblages from hill and ridge top sites, such as Sunget, Naidi, Payaman and Tayid, all discussed below.

A geological report on the island by Richard et al. (1986) was the first to indicate that archaeological sites were buried beneath deep layers of volcanic ash and lapilli derived from Iraya. This team collected charcoal of archaeological origin, radiocarbon dated to 2310±80 BP (uncalibrated), from beneath ash and pumice layers at Naidi, near Basco. Wood beneath similar ash beds exposed on west Songsong Beach was also dated to 1700±210 BP. Wood from beneath another flow of coarse-grained basaltic andesite further east on Songsong Beach, closer to the volcano but *above* stratified ash beds stated to be equivalent to those at west Songsong Beach, was dated to 1480±50 BP. These dates suggested, therefore, that a major ash and pumice-producing eruption of Iraya, affecting at least the western part of Songsong Bay, occurred at some time between 1700 and 1480 BP (uncalibrated).

So far, no major program of tephrochronological research has been carried out on Batan, but our archaeological results allow us to add more to the chronology obtained by Richard et al. 1986. The five locations excavated by us that have archaeological deposits buried under volcanic ash are shown in Fig. 3.1; these are Sunget, Naidi, Mahatao Town, Payaman and Tayid. Except for Mahatao, the ash beds appear to be in primary context, not secondarily redeposited. It appears that a major ash shower fell right across the central part of the island, being thickest in the west at Sunget and thinning towards the east at Tayid and Payaman, suggesting deposition during a season with a wind from the northeast. Only one catastrophic ash-yielding eruption occurred in each of the sites examined, but Naidi and Tayid both have evidence for a minor initial eruption that preceded the major one (Table 3.1).

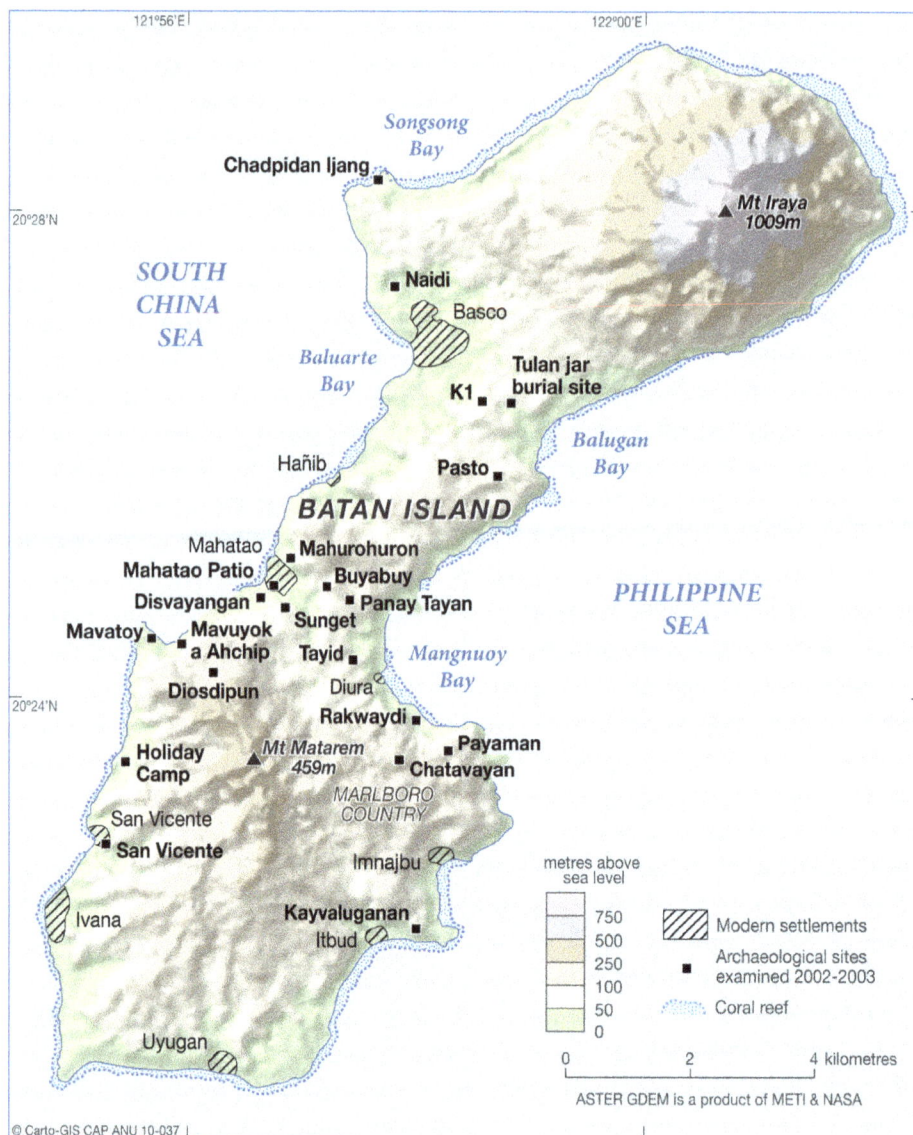

Figure 3.1. Sites investigated on Batan Island. K1, K6 and K41 are additional sites listed in Koomoto 1983 that have pre-eruption assemblages.

Source: Map preparation by ANU College of Asia and the Pacific, CartoGIS.

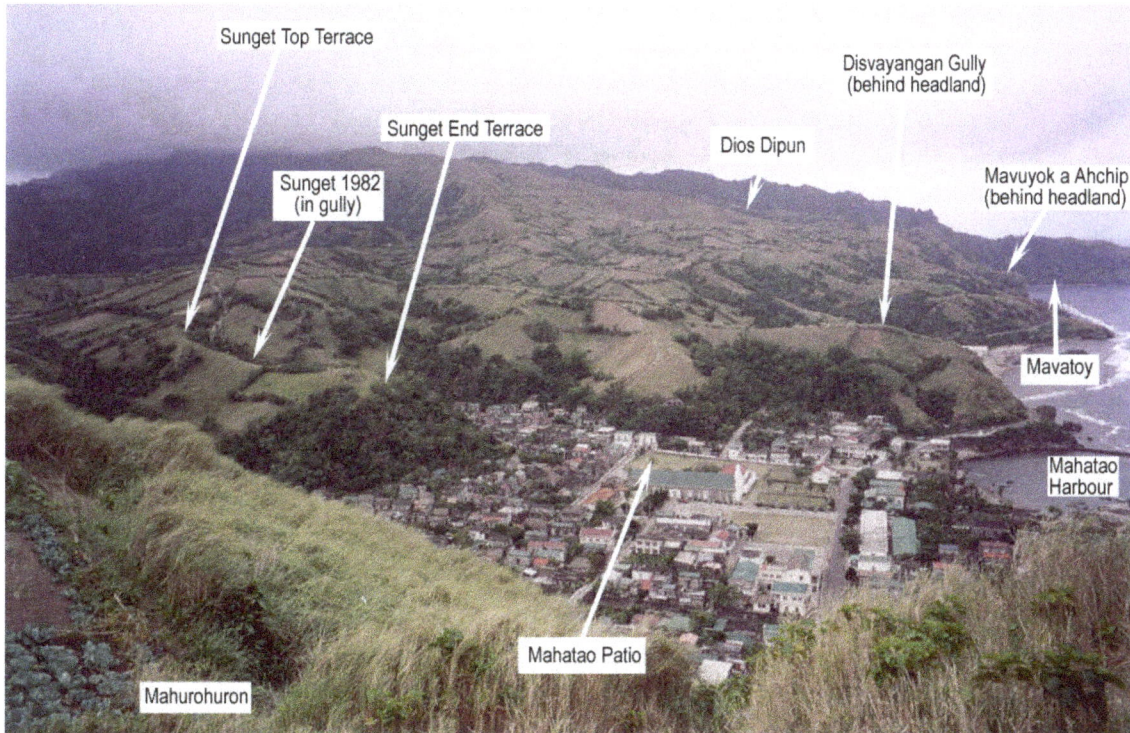

Figure 3.2. Mahatao and surroundings taken from Mahurohuron, showing the locations of the Sunget sites, Mahatao Patio, Disvayangan, Mavuyok a Ahchip (hidden behind headlands), Mavatoy, and Dios Dipun (approximate location only). The summit of Mt Matarem is under the cloud in the left background.

Source: Peter Bellwood.

Table 3.1. Ash deposits and uncalibrated C14 dates from locations in central Batan relevant for the date of the Iraya eruption (see Fig. 3.1 for locations). The dates in bold suggest that the major eruption occurred about 1500-1480 uncalibrated C14 years ago (c.AD 500).

	Basco region		Mahatao region			
	NAIDI (this project)	SONGSONG BAY (Richard et al. 1986)	SUNGET (this project)	PAYAMAN (this project)	TAYID (this project)	MAHATAO (this project)
Deposit above main ash deposit	topsoil	"nuée ardente" deposit 10-30 m. thick	topsoil	topsoil	topsoil	topsoil
Dates above main ash deposit (uncal. BP)	none	1480±50	none	none	none	Rakwaydi Phase pottery
Thickness of main ash deposit	2 metres	none given	0.7-1.2 m	30 cm	60 cm	5-6 m (in-washed into former bay)
Culturally sterile, intermediate topsoil	present	?	not present	not present	present	?
Lower ash deposit	20 cm	?	not present	not present	7 cm	?
Pre-ash C14 dates, uncal. BP	2620±30 2310±80 2240±140 1590±210	1700±210 BP (but not stated to be of archaeological origin)	2910±90 2915±49 2630±30 2383±35 2000±140	1988±47 1486±185	1842±215	2090±60 1829±80

Preliminary conclusions on Batan volcanic history can be summarised as follows, with respect to Table 3.1 (see Table 5.1 for further details of individual C14 dates):

1. Archaeological layers sealed beneath volcanic ash are widespread in central Batan. All radiocarbon indications are that these archaeological layers are older than 1486 radiocarbon years BP, this being the youngest *terminus ante quem* for the Iraya eruption.

2. The major ash fall apparently occurred between the two C14 dates of 1480 (Naidi – see above) and 1486 (Payaman) radiocarbon years BP, listed in Table 5.1. The correlation here seems almost too good to be true, since these two sites are 7 km apart. So perhaps we should be cautious and simply state that the major eruption of Iraya occurred *c.*1500 years ago. At Naidi and Tayid there was a minor pre-eruption, dating at Naidi after 1590 radiocarbon years BP, although the Naidi radiocarbon sample concerned was deficient in carbon and carbon dioxide and the date may be unreliable. In both cases, these thin preliminary ash falls were followed by short-lived topsoil formations.

This information on the recent volcanic history of Batan is important because it allows us to apportion the archaeology of the island into two separate chronological periods – *before* and *after* the volcanic eruption of *c.*1500 years ago. As we will see, the archaeological assemblages from these two chronological periods have some obvious differences, although no site actually spans the period of eruption itself, with continuous occupation below and above the ash (not surprisingly perhaps, given the extent and depth of landscape burial). Whether or not the eruption led to abandonment of the whole of Batan Island we do not know, but we did not see any deep Iraya ash deposits close to the southern coastline of Batan, or anywhere on neighbouring Sabtang Island. People presumably suffered less disruption in these locations.

The Batan Island archaeological open sites

Sunget, Mahatao

The importance of the Sunget site (Site 56 in Koomoto 1983: 55), on the limestone ridge that rises immediately behind the central part of Mahatao township in central Batan, was first indicated by a Japanese survey in 1982. They reported prolific quantities of red-slipped pottery, stone adzes and even a few items now known to be of Taiwan slate and nephrite (chapter 9) from the road cutting shown in Fig. 3.3. Our excavations at Sunget between 2002 and 2004 identified two areas of occupation located above this road cutting, about 55 m apart and separated by a steep slope. These were termed Sunget Top Terrace (Bellwood et al. 2003) and Sunget Main Terrace, the latter being located very close to and immediately above the road cutting. This is extremely important, since the materials found in the Main Terrace excavation are identical to those found by the Japanese team, and now we have a radiocarbon dated chronology. Minor excavation also took place on the Sunget End Terrace marked in Fig. 3.2, but only a very thin deposit of recent material, not discussed further, was found there. The Top Terrace excavations (2002-2004) totalled about 11 square metres, whereas the Main Terrace excavation was 2 by 2 metres, dug in 2004 (Fig. 3.3).

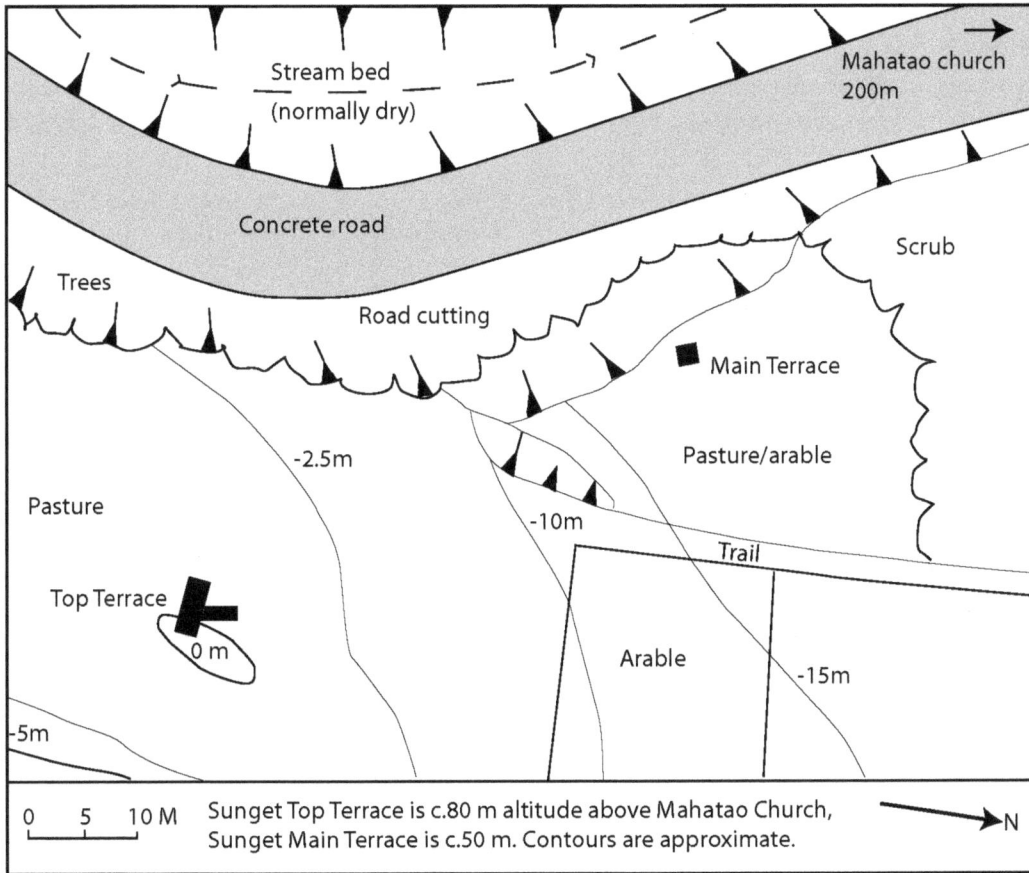

Figure 3.3. Plan of the Sunget Top and Main Terrace excavations, 2002–2004.

Source: Map preparation by ANU College of Asia and the Pacific, CartoGIS.

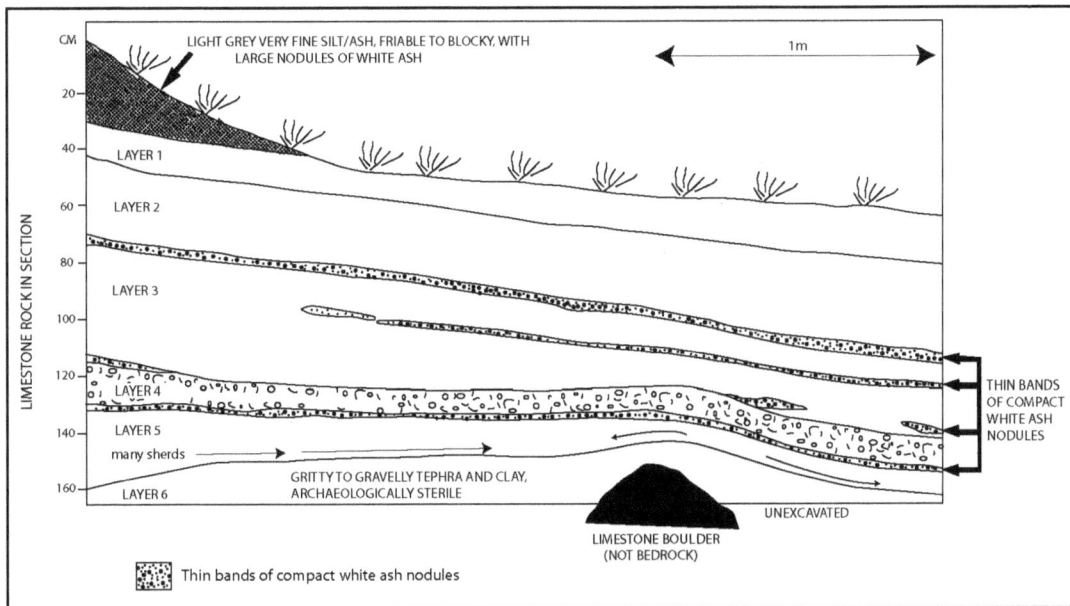

Figure 3.4. Section through the Sunget Top Terrace excavation, based on the southeastern wall of the 2002 trench. The archaeological deposit is layer 2.

Source: Lyn Schmidt.

The cultural deposit in both locations occurred within a highly weathered topsoil buried around 1500 years ago by the Iraya eruption. The Top Terrace stratigraphy (Fig. 3.4) has been discussed and illustrated previously (Bellwood *et al.* 2003: 146-7), and that of the Main Terrace is essentially the same (Fig. 3.5). Here, the overlying ash is between 70 cm and 1 m thick since the ground surface slopes markedly, and there is the same layer of gravel-sized tephra at the base of the volcanic ash as in the Top Terrace, demonstrating deposition by the same volcanic event. The weathered dark brown clay loam topsoil that contains the archaeological assemblage, beneath the Main Terrace ash deposit, is about 30 cm thick. It grades downwards into an orange brown clay, as in the Top Terrace sequence. The Main Terrace archaeological layer is about 30-35 cm thick (Table 3.2).

Figure 3.5. The Sunget Main Terrace excavation in 2004. The archaeological layer lies within the old topsoil buried beneath the yellowish mantle of volcanic ash and above the basal layer of orange clay.

Source: Peter Bellwood.

Table 3.2 shows the distribution of sherds for each area excavated at Sunget between 2002 and 2004, standardised in terms of density as the average number of sherds per square metre, within a 5 cm spit. These data reveal two interesting conclusions:

1. In the three linked Top Terrace excavations, sherds are densest against the limestone outcrop and fall off as one moves away from it. This suggests dumping of sherds against or from on top of the rock (Bellwood et al. 2003:147).

2. The Main Terrace has a single peak for the densest distribution, at 5-15 cm within the cultural layer. The occupation might, therefore, have been intensive and short-lived, with sherds subsequently dispersed by cultivation. In the Top Terrace excavation this peak was not so coherent, although there is a tendency for sherds to be most common towards the base of the old topsoil layer.

Overall, the Main Terrace archaeological sequence is very similar to the Top Terrace sequence. The high degree of standardisation of the pottery confirms that we are dealing with one relatively short and contemporary period of intensive deposition in both locations. The main difference between the Top and Main Terrace depositional sequences is that the former lies over and against outcropping limestone, whereas the latter overlies continuous volcanic deposits to an augered depth of at least 5 metres. Indeed, there is another old topsoil beneath the Main Terrace, about 3.7 metres below the upper one that holds the archaeology, but this contained no visible traces of any human presence.

Table 3.2. Sherd counts per square metre of excavated area, by 5 cm spit, for the 2002, 2003 and 2004 excavations at Sunget.

Top Terrace Layer 5, 2002 (away from limestone)	No. sherds per square metre	Top Terrace Layer 5, 2003 (against limestone)	No. sherds per square metre	Top Terrace Layer 5, 2004 (against limestone)	No. sherds per square metre	Main Terrace, cultural deposit	No. sherds per square metre
0-5	67	0-5	177	0-5	46	0-5	50
5-10	62	5-10	60	5-10	45	5-10	174
10-15	74	10-15	108	10-15	66	10-15	187
15-20	66	15-20	141	15-20	48	15-20	84
20-30 (10 cm spit)	156	20-25	109	20-25	134	20-25	42
		25-30	132	25-30	90	25-30	36
		30-35	188*			30-35	32
		35-40	178*				

* Sherds between 30 and 40 cm depth in the 2003 excavation were found concentrated in a shallow basal channel against the limestone.

As far as the date of the Sunget assemblage is concerned, we now have two almost identical calibrated AMS dates, on food residues inside potsherds, that lie between 3200 and 2950 radiocarbon years BP (Table 5.1 - note that ANU 11817 and Wk 14640 are from two different laboratories, a circumstance that supports their combined validity). OZH 776, on an external resin glaze on a sherd, is far older than expected and can perhaps be explained by the use of fossil resin as a surface glazing material. Sample ANU 11693 (c.2800 cal. BP) perhaps refers to slightly later activity on the site since it is from a concentration of charcoal, possibly derived from a former hearth. But the much younger dates Wk 15649 and ANU 11707, both late first millennium BC, are on scattered small fragments of charcoal that presumably derive from some form of agricultural activity – perhaps clearance followed by burning and later digging stick disturbance – long after the archaeological site had gone out of regular use.

The significance of the Sunget assemblage is that it represents a short-lived phase of occupation on the ridge above the current site of Mahatao town, early in the sequence of human occupation of Batan (c.1000 BC) and at a time when Mahatao Bay was still occupied by the sea. The eruption of c.AD 500 filled in the bay and buried the Sunget sites, which by that time had long been abandoned and were under cultivation. Since the eruption took place there has been absolutely no occupation of this ridge, except for agricultural activities, so the rich materials collected by the Japanese team in 1982 can only date from the period of Top and Main Terrace occupation, between 1200 and 800 BC. This is most significant because of the occurrence of items of Taiwan slate and nephrite in the assemblage – Sunget has yielded the oldest item of Taiwan nephrite found so far in Batanes (chapter 9; Fig. 9.2).

Investigations in Mahatao

When Mahatao was visited by Dizon and Bellwood in 2001, the Patio, an open grassy area next to the church, was found to be covered in pottery, much of it red-slipped like that reported from Sunget by the Kumamoto team. Unfortunately, two small excavations in 2002, near the locations of auger holes M1 and M2 in Fig. 3.6, showed that the whole area had been disturbed by grading and well-digging. The results of these excavations are not detailed here, and it is likely that much of the pottery had washed down from Sunget through a narrow valley that opens near the rear of the Patio.

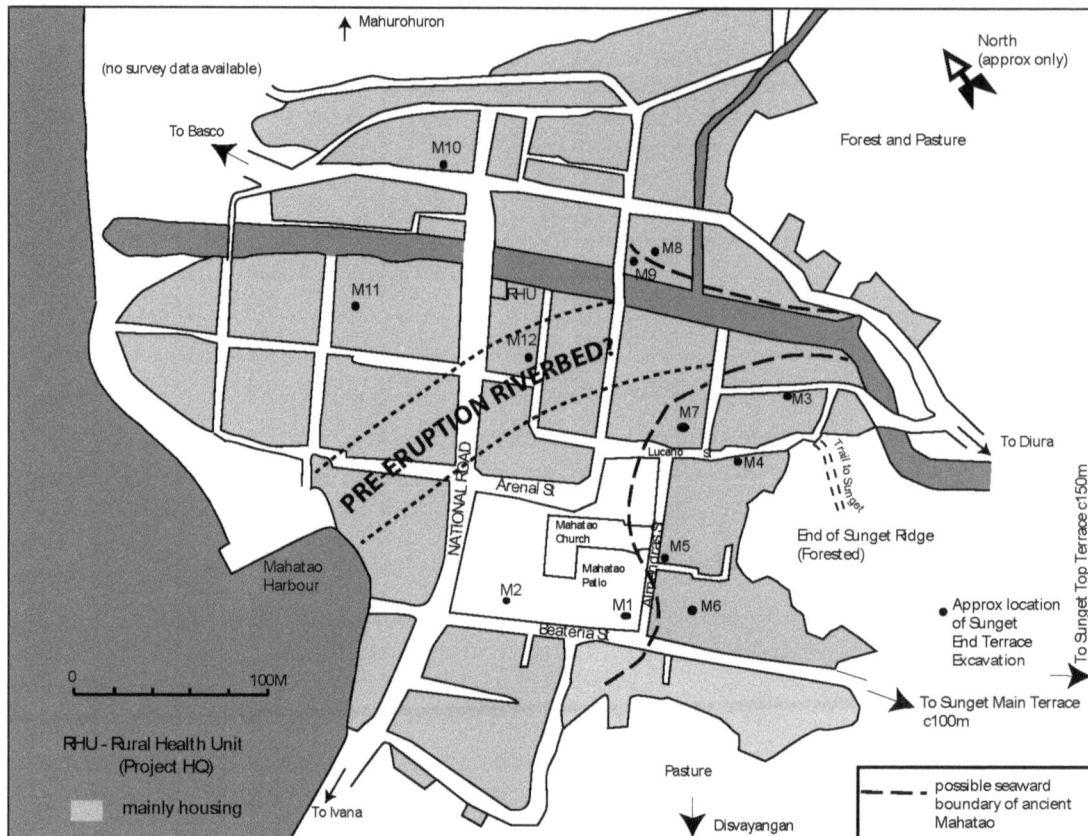

Figure 3.6. Plan of Mahatao showing auger hole locations (M1, M2, M5, M6, M7), Mahatao Septic Tank site (M3), another find-place of pottery beneath volcanic ash (M4), and the find place (M8) of the untanged and polished basalt adze 19 cm long with a reversed triangular cross-section, shown in Fig. 8.5B.

Source: Map preparation by ANU College of Asia and the Pacific, CartoGIS.

In 2003, several more auger holes were drilled in gardens below the end of Sunget Ridge in a hunt for the source of a quantity of circle-stamped pottery of Sunget type, with lots of large marine shells, that team member Shawna Yang found one day dumped alongside one of the Mahatao basketball courts near the church. We knew this material had to come from a limestone soil that preserved shell in good condition. The Sunget Ridge is limestone, and since all households in Mahatao have septic tank pits dug to a depth of about 2 metres in which artefacts are commonly found, we decided to drill a few auger holes in gardens below the end of the ridge since the most likely source must lie somewhere there. None of these auger holes, however, produced such a source, and no one could recall where the basketball court sherds came from.

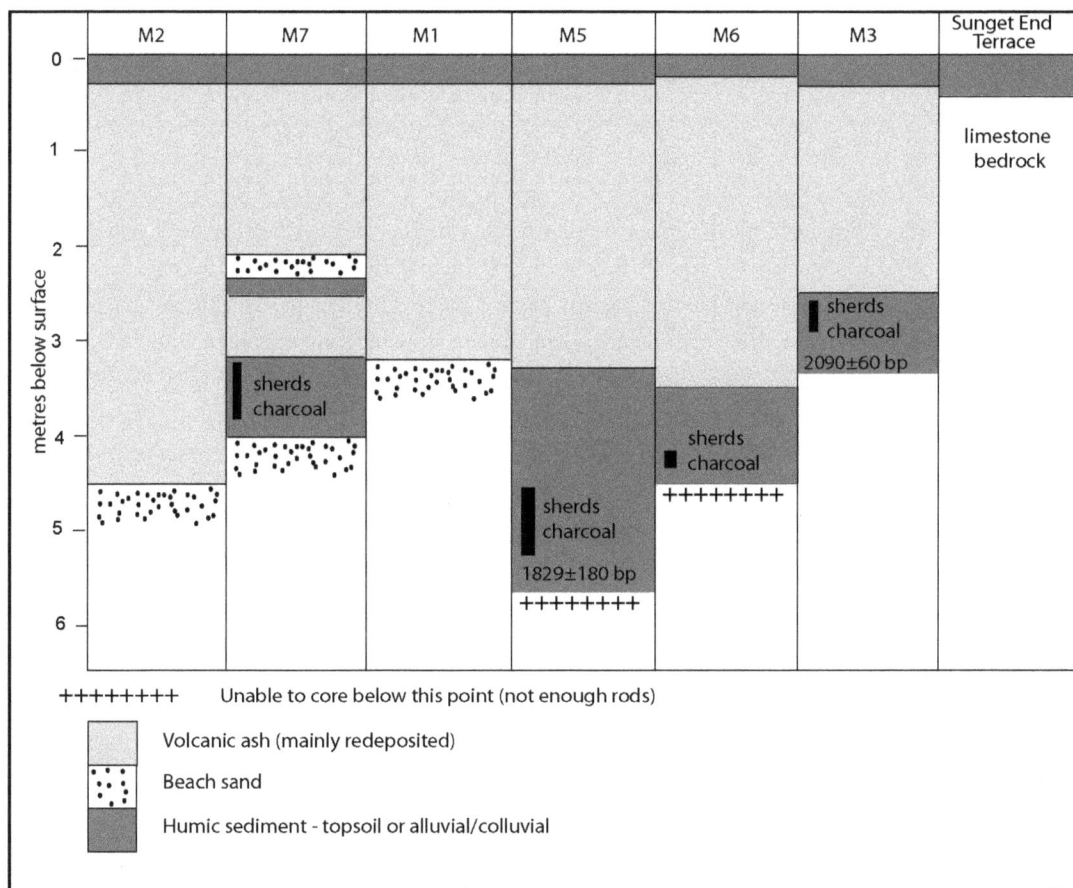

Figure 3.7. Layers revealed in the Mahatao auger holes indicated in Fig. 3.6.

Source: ANU College of Asia and the Pacic, CartoGIS.

Despite this, the auger holes do give interesting information about the disposition of the pre-eruption coastline beneath Mahatao, summarised in Figs 3.6 and 3.7. Locations M3, M5, M6 and M7 have sherds and charcoal stratified in humic dark soil layers (old topsoils) beneath redeposited Iraya volcanic ash, that was presumably washed down from Sunget Ridge after the eruption around 1500 years ago. The M3 (Mahatao Septic Tank) pottery was recovered in 2002 and is dated to 2090±60 radiocarbon years BP (ANU 11710). Locations M5, M6 and M7 also have old topsoils with sherds and charcoal beneath the ash. Unfortunately, augering in M5 and M6 had to stop before we could get below the artefact-bearing layer since we only had 4 one-metre auger rods with us in 2003 (M5 was augered to 6 metres since we were able to climb down two metres into an abandoned septic tank pit). However, we were able to establish that locations M1 and M2 (both augered in 2002) and M7 (augered in 2003) finished in clean beach sand.

These data indicate that, before the Iraya eruption, the flat embayment upon which modern Mahatao township stands did not exist, except for a narrow strip of coastal soil around the head of the bay, just above the shoreline delineated by a partly guesswork dotted line in Fig. 3.6. The eruption itself presumably helped to fill in the bay, not just by direct ash deposition but also by the subsequent in-washing of huge amounts of ash from hinterland valleys and slopes. Before the eruption, the main river of Mahatao must have debouched into the harbour between locations M3 and M8. It still flowed through the centre of the village, apparently running just north of the church, into the modern harbour until the 1940s, when it was canalised within its still-existing concrete retaining walls (William Agsunod, pers. comm.).

Given this reconstruction of ancient Mahatao it is no surprise that so many archaeological materials should have been found on Sunget Ridge, where no houses exist today. In the pre-eruption period, the population would have been restricted to a narrow coastline and people must have moved up to satellite hamlets on Sunget Ridge itself, into areas used today only for pasture and cropping. This is an important observation for the landscapes entered by Neolithic settlers in the Philippines generally, since it implies they would have been much steeper with much less low-lying flat land than one sees today. A similar presence of steep coastlines and a corresponding absence of coastal flats has also been postulated for Ilocos Norte on Luzon by Bellwood et al. (2008), as a result of research near Laoag and Paoay. Neolithic farmers in the Philippines would have had difficulty finding good flat agricultural land close to the sea at this time, just after postglacial sea level reached its mid-Holocene maximum, as they would in all of the Wallacean regions of Island Southeast Asia not flanked by shallow offshore continental shelves (Bellwood 2011b). This doubtless offered a situation remarkably different from the vast coastal and alluvial plains that support the densest modern populations of China and Southeast Asia, all mainly a result of Neolithic to modern sedimentation.

Naidi

The Naidi site is exposed beneath tephra as a single continuous archaeological layer about 20 cm thick, in a road cutting 63 metres above sea level between Basco and Songsong Beach (Bellwood et al. 2003: Fig. 7). The main exposure is on the west (upper) side, where the cutting is about 150 m long. The stratigraphy is very consistent along the section and there is no sign of any cultural material in layers beneath or above the cultural layer itself, with the exception of some unslipped sherds in the modern topsoil. The volcanic ash deposits above the archaeology here extend to a depth of 2.4 m, with intervening thin topsoil formation at about 2.1 m (see Table 3.1). Two small excavations into the side of the road cutting in 2002 yielded quite abundant pottery beneath the ash. As detailed in Table 3.1, three C14 dates from different locations (and thus not in a stratified series) are now available for this deposit, together with that of 2310±80 radiocarbon years BP from Richard et al. (1986). The calibrated range of these dates is from 835 BC to AD 900 – in actuality a much wider range that can be accommodated by such a shallow archaeological deposit. The main concentration of dates points to the late first millennium BC for the Naidi assemblage.

Payaman

The Payaman site was discovered by chance when we were searching for the source of the Mahatao basketball court pottery referred to above, which some of the Mahatao municipal labourers believed to be from near this locality. The archaeological layer had been disturbed by the grading of the Mahatao municipal dump, located high inland on the edge of Marlboro Country, and red-slipped sherds were strewn thickly around. Augering quickly located an undisturbed area near the perimeter fence of the dump, and a 2 by 1 m square was dug in 2003. The stratigraphy is very simple (Fig. 3.8, and see Bellwood et al. 2003, Fig. 8), with culturally sterile topsoil and subsoil (layer 1) over primary volcanic ash (layer 2), here much thinner than at Sunget, in turn over cultural layer 3, an old volcanic topsoil. Within layer 3, sherds were remarkably numerous, but extremely small and eroded, and concentrated heavily between 10 and 25 cm below the surface of the layer. This layer has two C14 dates of 1988±47 (Wk 13092) and 1486±185 radiocarbon years BP (ANU 12068). Like Sunget, Payaman was deserted and probably under cultivation when the Iraya ash fall occurred.

Figure 3.8. The stratigraphy of the Payaman site, Batan Island.

Source: Peter Bellwood.

Tayid

The Tayid site was originally reported by Koomoto (1983, Site 49), who noted the presence of two archaeological layers separated by "silt" layers, now known to be volcanic ash. The site is exposed in a road cutting, and two small "windows" were dug into the cutting in 2003 to check the stratigraphy. This consisted of 6 layers, as follows:

Layer 1: topsoil and redeposited volcanic ash, 50 cm thick;

Layer 2: Primary volcanic ash, 60 cm thick;

Layer 3: Old topsoil, 10 cm thick, with a small number of featureless plain body sherds;

Layer 4: Primary volcanic ash, 7 cm thick;

Layer 5: Old topsoil, 20 cm thick, containing the bulk of the archaeological sherds and with a posthole visible in section, dated 1842±215 radiocarbon years BP (Table 5.1);

Layer 6: Culturally sterile red brown clay.

About 50 metres away from the two test pits, also visible in the road cutting in 2003, lies part of a volcanic stone pavement about 2.5 metres long that underlies the ash layer 4. This suggests that the site may contain domestic architecture. Koomoto (1983: 49-52) also noted the finding somewhere on the site of a broken baked clay casting mould for a cupreous spearhead (Fig. 8.11

G). A similar baked clay mould found at Savidug on Sabtang Island in 2006 (Fig. 8.11 F) would appear to date between 2500 and 2000 BP. Without further information we cannot know if the Tayid mould came from layer 3 or layer 5, or if it was just a surface find.

Batan Island cave and rockshelter excavations

Mavuyok a Ahchip

The geomorphological location of Mavuyok a Ahchip, excavated in 2002, is in the seaward wall of a dormant and highly weathered andesitic crater that lies on the northwestern flank of the Matarem volcanic complex, on the western coast of Batan Island. The western (seaward) wall of the crater has been eroded down to about 50 m in height above sea level, and the modern road runs along the top of it. Four sea caves have been cut into this crater wall, presumably where pre-existing lava tubes or faults offered lines of weakness. Two of these caves run side-by-side right through the crater wall from the sea into the inner crater valley (Fig. 3.9). The smaller, called Mavuyok a Ahchip by local people, is high and dry at its inland mouth, where it contained an archaeological deposit that covered an area of about 4 by 2 metres in total, flanked by a deep erosion gully. The wall of this erosion gully revealed dense sherdage down to a depth of about 95 cm below the surface.

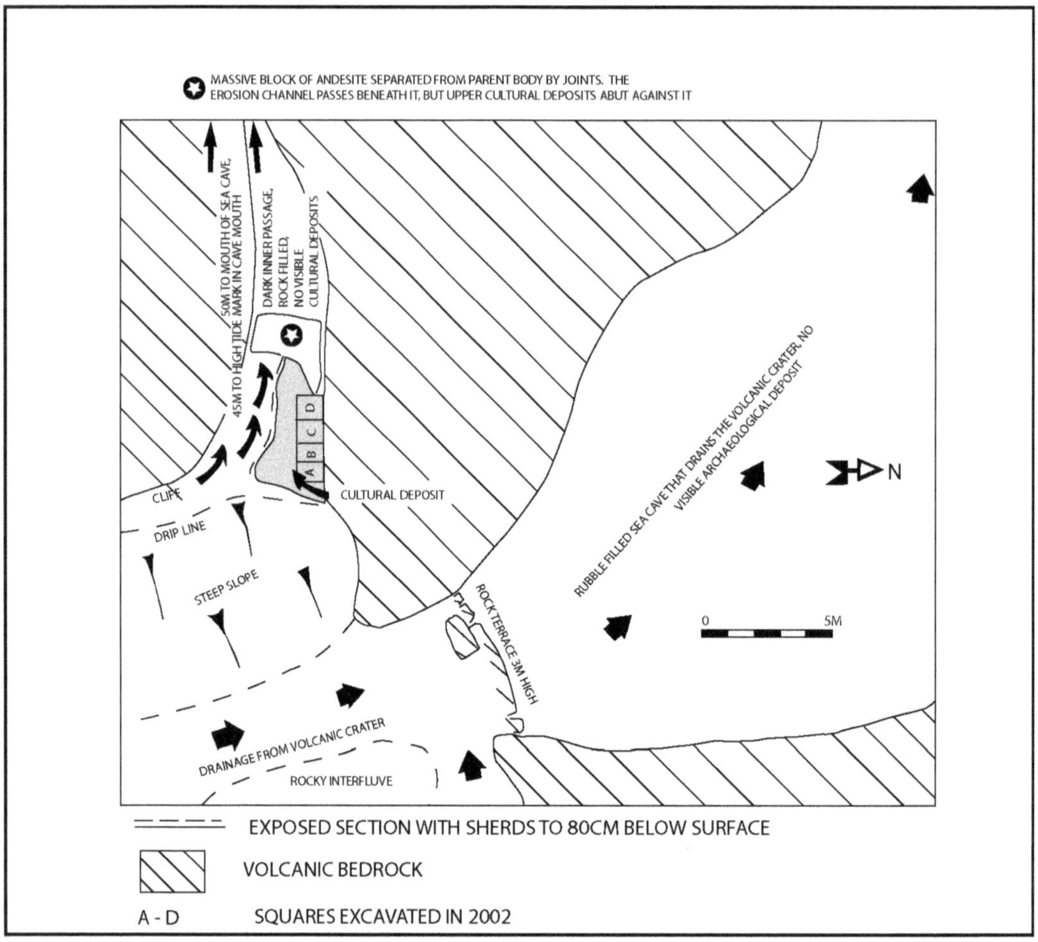

Figure 3.9. Plan of the cave of Mavuyok a Ahchip, with the archaeological deposit in its inland mouth, and the adjacent large open cave which drains the volcanic crater that lies inland.

Source: Map preparation by ANU College of Asia and the Pacific, CartoGIS.

Excavation was concentrated in an area of 2.5 by 1 m against the cave wall. The deposits were neutral (pH 6.5-7) and bone and shell preservation was good, even if economic materials turned out to be surprisingly scarce. Five layers were recognised during and after excavation, the top three being ill-defined cultural layers with very diffuse boundaries:

Layer 1: upper cultural layer, 20 cm thick: dry cave soil with a tripod hearth of three stones and plentiful ash towards the front of the cave.

Layer 2: a relatively clay-rich layer about 20 cm thick with a similar density of material culture to layer 1.

Layer 3: a cultural layer with an extremely high density of large sherds, with two side-by-side stone tripod hearths and a dense concentration of volcanic oven stones in the inner part of the cave. At times in this layer, the volume of sherdage seemed to be much greater than the volume of matrix. Much of the deposit was ash and charcoal, and the quantity of residue inside many body sherds left no doubt that this was an area of very intensive cooking.

Layer 4: soft, loose matrix similar to layer 3, but culturally sterile.

Layer 5: culturally-sterile cemented silt with many water-rolled stones, deposited by a former water course. The cave clearly drained the volcanic crater prior to the start of human usage; at present the drainage goes to the sea through the larger cave immediately to the north.

The distribution of sherds shows almost continuous deposition through about 95 cm of stratigraphy, with slight reductions in quantity between 30 and 50 cm depth. There are four charcoal C14 dates for the site, all in stratigraphic order and running from "modern" at 5-10 cm depth down to 900±60 BP near the base of layer 3 (Table 5.1). In other words, the cave sequence spans the final 600 years or so of Batanes prehistory, prior to the arrival of Dampier and the Spanish missions. It contains no Preceramic or Neolithic assemblages. Indeed, following our excavations in 2002, some treasure hunters found the cave and dug a large pit right down to bedrock, in the process destroying the site for any future research. Examination of the walls of this pit, which was left open (treasure hunters rarely backfill), indicated that no archaeological evidence existed below the excavated layers with pottery.

Dios Dipun Rockshelter

About 3 km south of Mahatao, a long ridge extends from the sea into the interior of the island. On the north side, at various points along it, are limestone rockshelters, especially just below the crest of the ridge. A series of these was inspected and the most extensive shelter, Dios Dipun, was selected for excavation in 2002. Dios Dipun encloses about 13 by 4 metres, but unfortunately the floor slopes down longitudinally, a circumstance that has promoted water flow and a tendency for cultural materials to move down to the northern end of the site, where large numbers of recent prehistoric sherds lie on the modern surface.

Only one trench in Dios Dipun produced significant finds. This was TP 2, which had a main excavated area of 2 by 1 m. Pottery, all of an unslipped late prehistoric type similar to that from Mavuyok a Ahchip, occurred sparsely down to 80 cm and then virtually ceased. On digging deeper, however, a tightly flexed burial with no associated grave goods, other than a few small pieces of red ochre, was encountered at 1.65 m depth. It was lying in a shallow, seemingly natural depression in the limestone bedrock, and was partly covered, over the cranium, by two large basalt boulders. The edges of the immediate burial pit were quite sharply defined in compact clay. Immediately above, the fill was fairly loose and dry, and included some reddish, weathered pieces of limestone. Above 1.5 m depth, compact mixed clay and abundant limestone rubble obscured any sign of the grave, so it is not clear from which level it was cut. The burial was sent to the

National Museum in Manila in 2002, where it was misplaced for a while before being recently found again (2013). We will try to obtain a C14 date on bone from it, but the result will probably arrive too late for publication in this monograph.

Existing radiocarbon dates for Dios Dipun suggest that the bulk of the deposit, except possibly for the burial and its immediate vicinity close to bedrock, is quite recent and badly disturbed. It is possible that the site has suffered from treasure hunting. One C14 date on charcoal from a depth of 175 cm is only 500±260 radiocarbon years BP (ANU 11696). Another from 120 cm is 590±110 (ANU 11736). Dios Dipun thus appears to have been occupied during a single and recent phase, and not very intensively. Both Dios Dipun and Mavuyok a Ahchip were originally excavated in the hope that they would yield early pottery and even preceramic assemblages. Neither fulfilled expectations in this regard.

Mavatoy Rockshelter

We were first shown Mavatoy rockshelter in 2002. At about 8 m long by 4 m deep, and 2 metres high in its forward portion, with a few sherds on its flat surface, it seemed to offer the promise of early deposits that we had failed to find in Mavuyok a Ahchip and Dios Dipun. The shelter underlies a large block of limestone that is encased within a massive flow of volcanic agglomerate. In 2003, a 3 by 1 m trench was excavated in its central portion (Fig. 3.10). This revealed that volcanic agglomerate forms the bedrock of the shelter and slopes down very steeply into a fairly precipitous external slope that drops to the sea. On the bedrock lies a culturally sterile brown soil (layer 5), thin and fairly patchy. On top of this lies culturally sterile and perhaps primary volcanic ash, layer 4, very similar in colour and texture to the 1500 BP Iraya volcanic ash that covers Sunget and Naidi. Archaeology begins only in layer 3, a redeposited volcanic ash with many small pieces of limestone. In square A, sherds extend down to the base of this layer, but in squares B and C they only extend down to about 30 cm below its top, and the lower portion is culturally sterile. Sherds continue upwards through layers 2 and 1, layer 2 having much charcoal and red burnt soil. The greatest density of sherds occurs between 10 and 25 cm below the surface in all squares, and all the pottery is of the recent type found at Mavuyok a Ahchip and Dios Dipun, with the exception of one red-slipped sherd of Sunget type and fabric found at the base of the pottery bearing layer. A C14 date on *Turbo* shell from close to the base of the pottery layer in square A is only 682±49 radiocarbon years BP (WK 13090).

Mavatoy, unfortunately, failed like the other Batan rockshelters to produce any pre-eruption cultural materials, in this case because its floor was simply too steep for occupation until a layer of primary or in-washed ash (layer 4) provided a sufficiently level surface. The Batan preceramic, if it exists, still eludes us. Indeed, the whole Batanes Islands preceramic, if it once existed, eludes us as well!

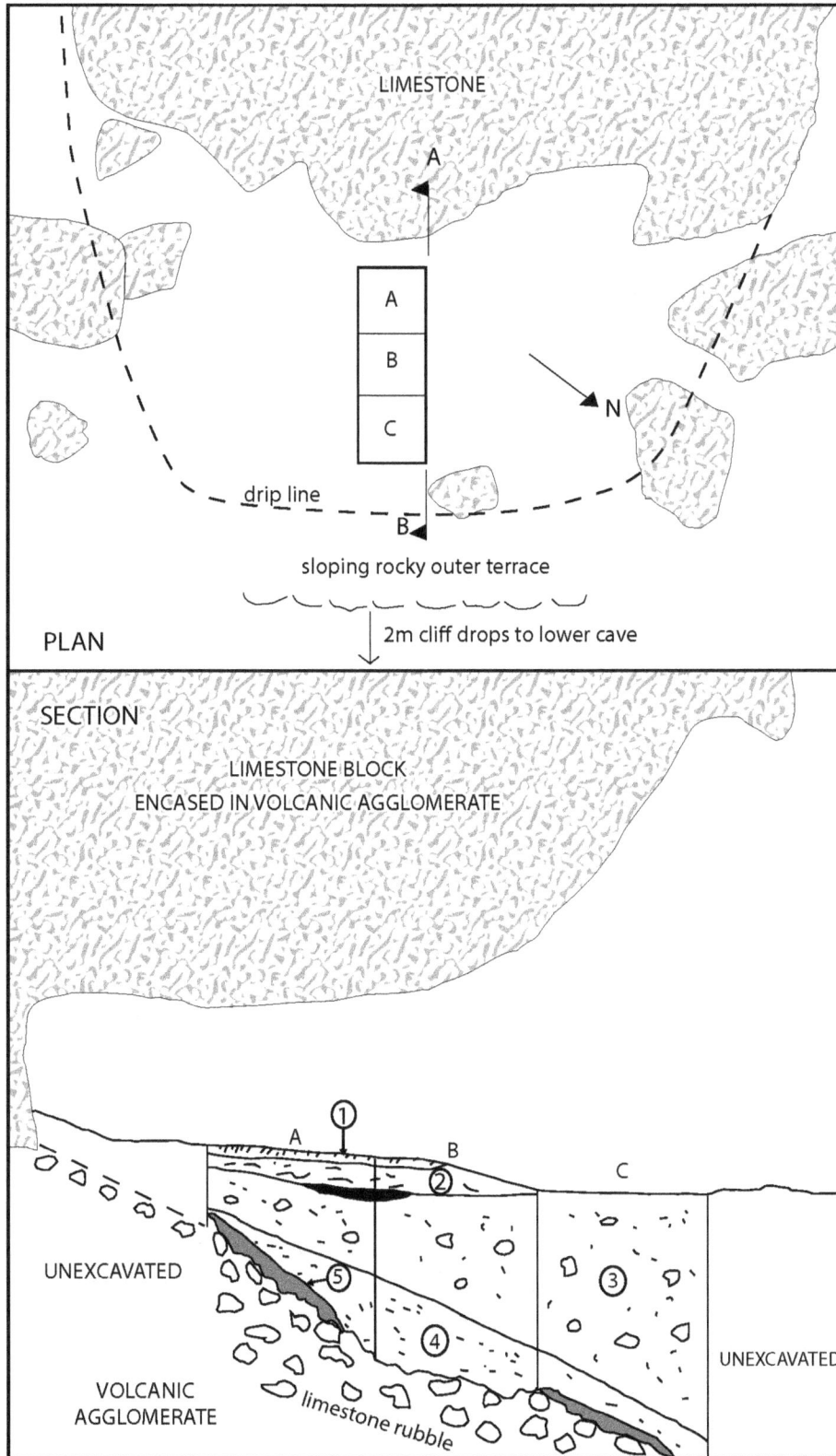

Figure 3.10. Upper: Plan of the Mavatoy rockshelter, showing the excavation trench A-C. Lower: Section of the northern wall of the Mavatoy excavation.

Source: Map preparation by ANU College of Asia and the Pacific, CartoGIS.

4

Archaeological Investigations at Savidug, Sabtang Island

Peter Bellwood and Eusebio Dizon

This chapter is focused on the site complex near Savidug village, roughly half way down the eastern coast of Sabtang Island, facing across a sea passage to the southwestern coastline of Batan. The Sabtang site complex includes an impressive *ijang* of sheer volcanic rock, which we surveyed. A sand dune to the north, close to Savidug village itself, contained two distinct archaeological phases separated by about a millennium of non-settlement in the site. We also excavated another small late prehistoric shell midden at Pamayan, inland from Savidug village.

In 2002, brief visits for reconnaissance purposes by the Asian Fore-Arc Project were made to Sabtang and Ivuhos Islands (Bellwood et al. 2003). As a result, one week was spent on Sabtang in 2003, during which time a plane-table survey and test excavations were carried out at Savidug *ijang,* and the Pamayan shell midden at the back of Savidug village was test-excavated. The location of Savidug village is indicated on Fig. 4.1, half way down the eastern coast of Sabtang and facing the southern end of Batan, 5 km across the ocean passage to the northeast.

In 2006, test-excavation was undertaken at the Savidug Dune Site (Nadapis), which yielded a sequence extending back 3000 years incorporating two separate phases of human activity commencing with circle stamped pottery dated to *c.*1000 BC and very similar to that at Anaro on Itbayat and Sunget on Batan. In 2007, Savidug Dune Site was subjected to further excavation for 3 weeks, resulting in the recovery of several large burial jars, Taiwan nephrite, and a more thorough understanding of the nature of the whole site.

Sabtang Island is mainly volcanic, geologically older than Batan and no longer active. The interior rises up to a number of volcanic ridges and pinnacles reaching a maximum of 347 m above sea level (Fig. 4.2). The central portion of the east coast consists of a dissected high terrace, possibly a former uplifted coastline (although no geomorphological survey has been undertaken), broken by a number of narrow west-to-east stream beds that are dry for most of the year. Savidug village lies just to the north of a stream bed called Padudugan. On its southern side lies the Savidug Dune Site, with Savidug *ijang* occupying a volcanic agglomerate plug in the lower part of the next valley system to the south (Fig. 4.3). The *ijang* lies about 500 m inland and about 800 m southwest of the Dune Site, as indicated on Fig. 4.1.

The central eastern coastline of Savidug, from south of the town of San Vicente to about 2 km south of Savidug, is flanked by sand dunes (Fig. 4.3) that rise behind the modern lagoon shoreline. This shallow lagoon is a valuable resource for marine products, 2-3 metres deep in places at high tide but mainly exposed sea grass, sand and rock at low tide. Both Pamayan and the Savidug Dune Site contained large quantities of exploited shellfish, particularly in late prehistoric layers when population pressure on resources was clearly very high.

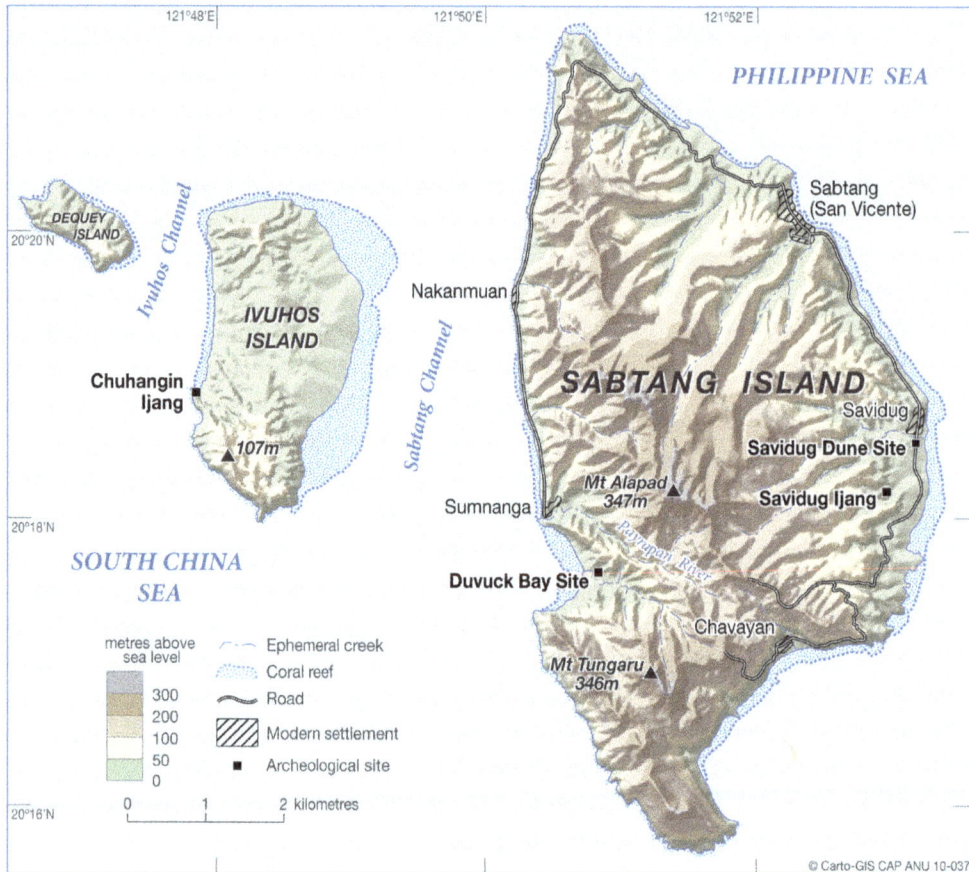

Figure 4.1. Sabtang, Ivuhos and Dequey Islands.

Source: Map preparation by ANU College of Asia and the Pacific, CartoGIS.

Figure 4.2. Sabtang Island, on approach from the south.

Source: Peter Bellwood.

Figure 4.3. Savidug *ijang*, the drum-shaped feature in the middle foreground behind the beach and sand dune.

Source: Peter Bellwood.

The Savidug sites

Savidug Ijang

Savidug *ijang* lies about 1.2 km southwest of Savidug village and is the most impressive of all the Batanes *ijang*. Dampier probably saw it in 1687, although he gives no indication of visiting the site. A very useful survey of the central part of the *ijang* was made by a National Museum team in 1994 (Dizon and Santiago 1994: Fig. 14), to which the 2003 survey added the surrounding living and agricultural terraces shown in Fig. 4.4.

The central part of Savidug *ijang* consists of a volcanic plug of agglomerate that rises like a drum, almost sheer from the surrounding terrain, up to 40 metres high on its northern side (Fig. 4.5). The plug has a small triangular summit platform of natural origin, surrounded by a large and relatively flat area that runs out to the top of the surrounding cliff. This area is now overgrown by very tall grass and shrubs since goats and cattle are unable to scale the only access point, a steep climb up a 4 metre cliff on the inland side. A few stone walls, stone piles (for defensive throwing?), and four perforated columns of prismatic andesite are still visible on the summit. In 1994 this area was apparently clear of vegetation, and a number of rectilinear stone walled enclosures were sketched on the plan made at that time (Dizon and Santiago 1994: Fig. 14). Two of the four perforated columns stand today about 4.5 m apart as though at either end of a house (the other two are recumbent), but we suspect that re-erection of these columns could have occurred in recent times (Fig. 4.6). The summit also has a surface scatter of sherds, all of recent and unslipped types. When occupied, this whole summit area would have been accessible either by ladder, as described for other *ijang* by Dampier, or by climbing up the rear access route marked in Fig. 4.4.

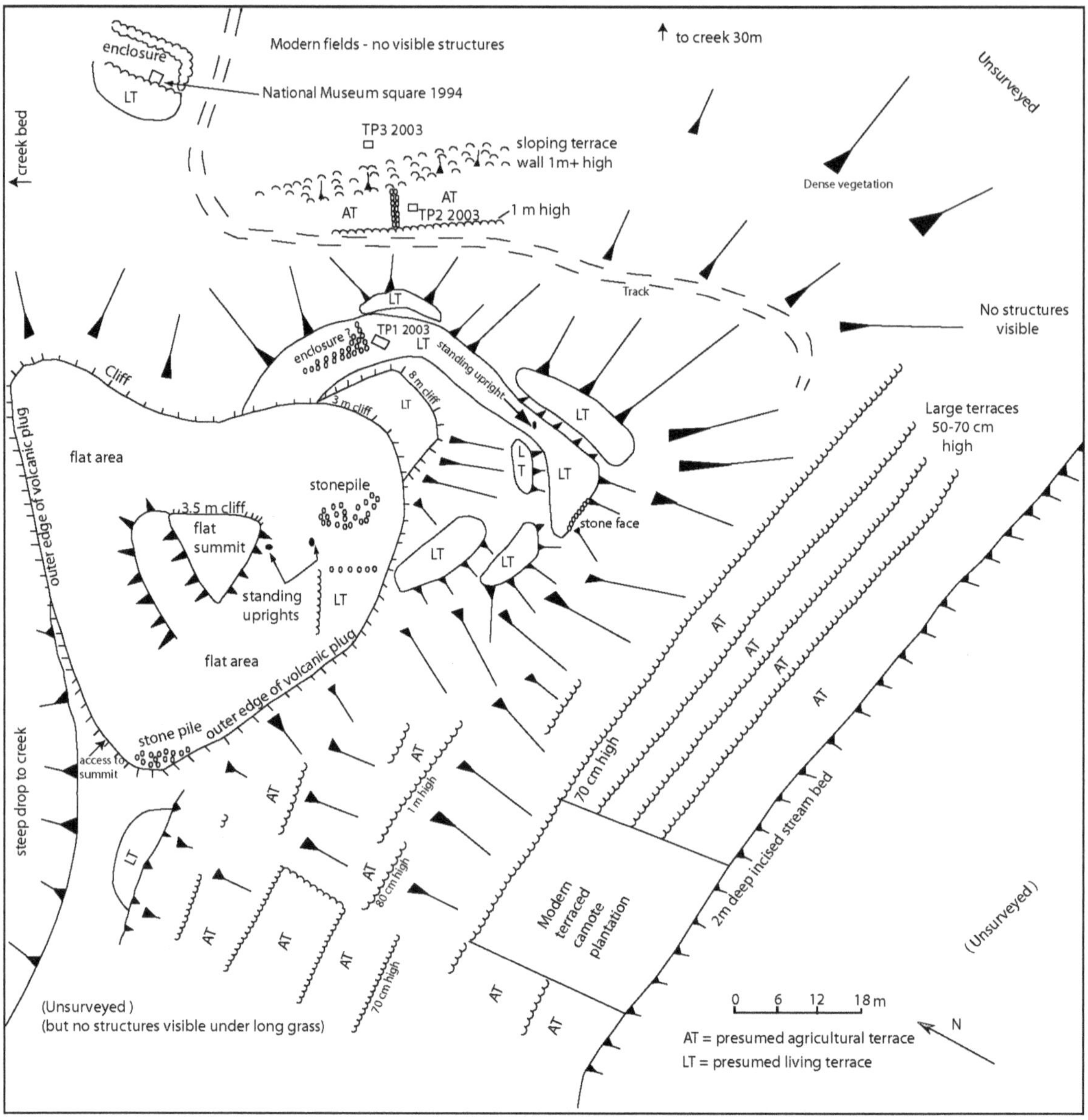

Figure 4.4. Plan of Savidug *ijang*, surveyed in 2003, showing the extent of visible terracing round the main volcanic tower.

Source: Map preparation by ANU College of Asia and the Pacific, CartoGIS.

Below the summit area, on the eastern (seaward) side of the tower, lie seven terraces. On the largest there is still one standing upright (marked on Figs 4.4, 4.5). Our excavation of a 2 by 1 m test trench in 2003 (TP1), at the other end of this terrace, produced about 20 cm of archaeological deposit over decomposed volcanic material. Three postholes about 20 cm across by 30 cm deep had been dug into the soft substrate, and they were clearly large enough to have supported prismatic stone or perhaps timber house columns (Fig. 4.7). One of these holes contained a glass bead, and all pottery found was of relatively recent date. These terraces appear to be mainly of natural origin, although some artificial levelling might have occurred; they are labelled "living terraces" (LT) on Fig. 4.4. None are stone faced, except in one small area, and all can be easily approached by walking up from the track below.

Figure 4.5. Savidug *ijang* from the ocean side. The arrows point to the location of the excavated postholes and to a surviving stone pillar that still stands on a terrace.

Source: Peter Bellwood.

Figure 4.6. Two perforated stone uprights still standing on the top of Savidug *ijang* (Daud Tanudirjo at rear, Hsiao-chun Hung at left).

Source: Peter Bellwood.

Figure 4.7. Savidug *ijang*: terrace postholes excavated in TP1, 2003. Scale is in 10 cm units.

Source: Peter Bellwood.

To the west and south of the *ijang* there are many terraces of a different type, built of soil rather than levelled into rock and all faced with dry stone walls up to one metre (up to 6 stone courses) high. Most are under pasture today, and the terrace faces have been damaged by cattle except where protected by dense vegetation. Their surfaces now slope slightly away from the *ijang*, towards the stream bed below the site, and one area is still in use with modern terrace walls for cultivation of *camote* (sweet potato). They are interpreted as agricultural rather than living terraces, and if Savidug was still in use in 1687 they could by then have been growing *camote*, as well as traditional crops such as yams, bananas and sugarcane.

Two small excavations (TP 2 and 3) were made in lower terraces on the seaward side of the *ijang* in 2003, complementary to that dug by Dizon in 1994 in an enclosure to the northeast (Dizon and Santiago 1994). All contained redeposited materials fallen down from the *ijang* above, in all cases of recent date and including Song and Yuan Chinese ceramics. TP3 was dug to a depth of 110 cm, from which level a charcoal date of 760±190 uncal. BP (ANU 12070) was processed. Neither the 2003 nor the 1994 squares reached bedrock owing to time constraints, but surface finds of red-slipped pottery identical to those dated between 3000 and 2000 BP from the lower cultural layer in Savidug Dune Site (below) were found on the seaward slope of the *ijang* in 2003, above the track close to TP 2, so occupation of this phase on or around the *ijang* is confirmed.

Pamayan, Savidug village

The Pamayan shell midden lies at the back of Savidug village, exposed by a road cutting along the base of a limestone hill that is today under forest. Our discovery of the site was accidental, when walking through the village one day in 2003. Red-slipped pottery, a broken chert pebble and a circumferentially worked operculum of a large *Turbo* indicated the existence of an interesting site that we thought then could be quite early in chronological terms. This turned out to be a little optimistic.

Two small excavation sections of 60 by 80 cm were excavated 16 m apart back into the section exposed in the road cutting, exposing shell midden to a maximum depth of 105 cm beneath the topsoil (Fig. 4.8). Sherds occurred fairly evenly and densely through this depth, together with a single shell disc bead and prolific food shells consisting almost entirely of broken small cowries. The recency of the Pamayan midden was rendered obvious by the occurrence of imported Chinese sherds down to 95 cm depth, and by the fact that bone preservation is very good, whereas at 3000-year-old Sunget on Batan, with an identical neutral pH in soil formed over limestone, it is very poor. A C14 date from the base of the cultural layer, on charcoal, is only 418±41 uncal. BP (WK 13091).

Figure 4.8. Pamayan cutting B, showing about 1 m of midden in the section. Tony Peñalosa in foreground.

Source: Peter Bellwood.

In 2007, we excavated a long cultural sequence from the Savidug Dune Site, as described below, with the uppermost phase, associated with Chinese imported ceramics, being similar in material culture to Pamayan. Both of these occupation deposits can be placed at the end of the Sabtang sequence, albeit with well-made red-slipped but otherwise undecorated pottery in the case of Pamayan. Both deposits also revealed intensive breakage of small cowrie shells, a presumed sign of late prehistoric population stress on diminishing resources (Table 4.1).

Savidug Dune Site (Nadapis)

South of Savidug village, just across Padudugan Creek, begins a large sand dune about 120-150 m wide that runs south for about 800 m to the next valley, the one that contains Savidug *ijang* (Fig. 4.9). The area has the local name of Nadapis. The archaeological site lies at the northern end of the dune, close to where it meets an 8 m bluff formed of volcanic deposits and raised coral, immediately west of the road (Fig. 4.10). Two large concrete water tanks stand on top of this bluff. The road to Chavayan runs longitudinally along the top of the dune, and where it rises up from Padudugan Creek there is a cutting up to 2 m deep, formed as a hollow way (visible in Fig. 4.10) by the long-term passage of foot, sledge, cart and sometimes vehicle traffic. In both sides of this road cutting, within the area of the grid shown on the site plan in Fig. 4.11, we first noted in 2003 a total of nine projecting burial jars exposed by erosion. On this first visit little understanding was acquired of the stratigraphy of the site, but the nine visible jars were located about 4 to 6 m apart within the area of the subsequent 2007 survey grid, with five on the inland side of the road and four on the seaward side. The latter were located close to a large number of modern lime pits dug into the sand dune to fire lime mortar for Savidug village (visible in Fig. 4.9).

Figure 4.9. Savidug Dune Site from the top of the 8 m bluff, looking southwards. To the left is excavation E1-G1/9-11, to the right QR/7-9, with spoil from K-N/27-29 just behind.

Source: Peter Bellwood.

Figure 4.10. Looking north from the Savidug Dune Site in 2006. The 2006 test pit is to the left, the bluff with the water tanks behind, the road cutting that first yielded the burial jars straight ahead, and Savidug village lies at the rear amongst the young coconut palms, across Padudugan stream bed.

Source: Peter Bellwood.

Bellwood's field notes for 2003, together with a short manuscript report by Pamela Faylona, indicate that two of the jar burials then exposed were cleaned and examined. One contained the bones of a child, of which a sample of tooth enamel was subsequently dated to 1728-1569 BP (Table 5.1, sample ANU 33938). The other, a large red-slipped jar with a girth of 62 cm, had its broken-off rim placed upside down inside, and contained only a few adult phalanges. Both jars were partly on their sides rather than vertical. No artefacts were discovered and all the jars appeared to have been disturbed, perhaps not surprisingly owing to their easy visibility from the road. The jars found in 2003 were not surveyed accurately and can no longer be related exactly to the positions of those excavated in 2006 and 2007 (Fig. 4.12).

Excavations in the Savidug Dune Site

In April 2006, we decided to undertake a test excavation in the site, and laid out a 2x1 trench in a field on top of the dune, about 8 m west of the road. This is labelled as excavation no. 5 in Fig. 4.11, and located in more detail in Fig. 4.12. It produced a sequence of five layers, beginning with 40 to 70 cm of loose ploughed soil derived nowadays from peanut cultivation (layer 1) over a dark grey sandy loam (layer 2), about 20-30 cm thick, with late prehistoric material culture similar to that from Pamayan (above). Beneath layer 2 was sterile dune sand (layer 3), then a second humic sandy cultural deposit (layer 4) with its top at about 1.4 metres below the ground surface. Layer 4, about 40 cm thick, was quite rich in material culture, with red-slipped pottery and a date of 2828±37 uncal. BP (Wk 19711) from its base at 180 cm. This pottery included a sherd of circle stamped pottery in Sunget (Batan) style, also dated at Sunget to c.1000 BC (chapter 3). A slightly more complex version of this stratigraphic sequence, recovered from Q/R7-9 in 2007, can be seen in Fig. 4.13.

Savidug 50m

stream bed
(normally dry)

N

sea

concrete
water tank

seaward edge of vegetated dune

road

hilltop 8m
above road

pasture and
arable land

ridge top

A–Z, A1–G1

1–29

3   2   1

EXCAVATION
GRID

beach
sand

seaward dune slope

inland dune slope

ephemeral
swamp

5
4

top of
dune

1 Trench E$_1$–G$_1$ / 9–11 (2007)   3x2 m
2 Trench QR 7–9 (2007)   3x1.75 m
3 Trench A–C / 9–11 (2007)   3x3 m
4 Trench K–N / 27–9 (2007)   3x3 m
5 2 x 1 test (2006)   2x1 m

0   10   20   30 metres

to Chavayan

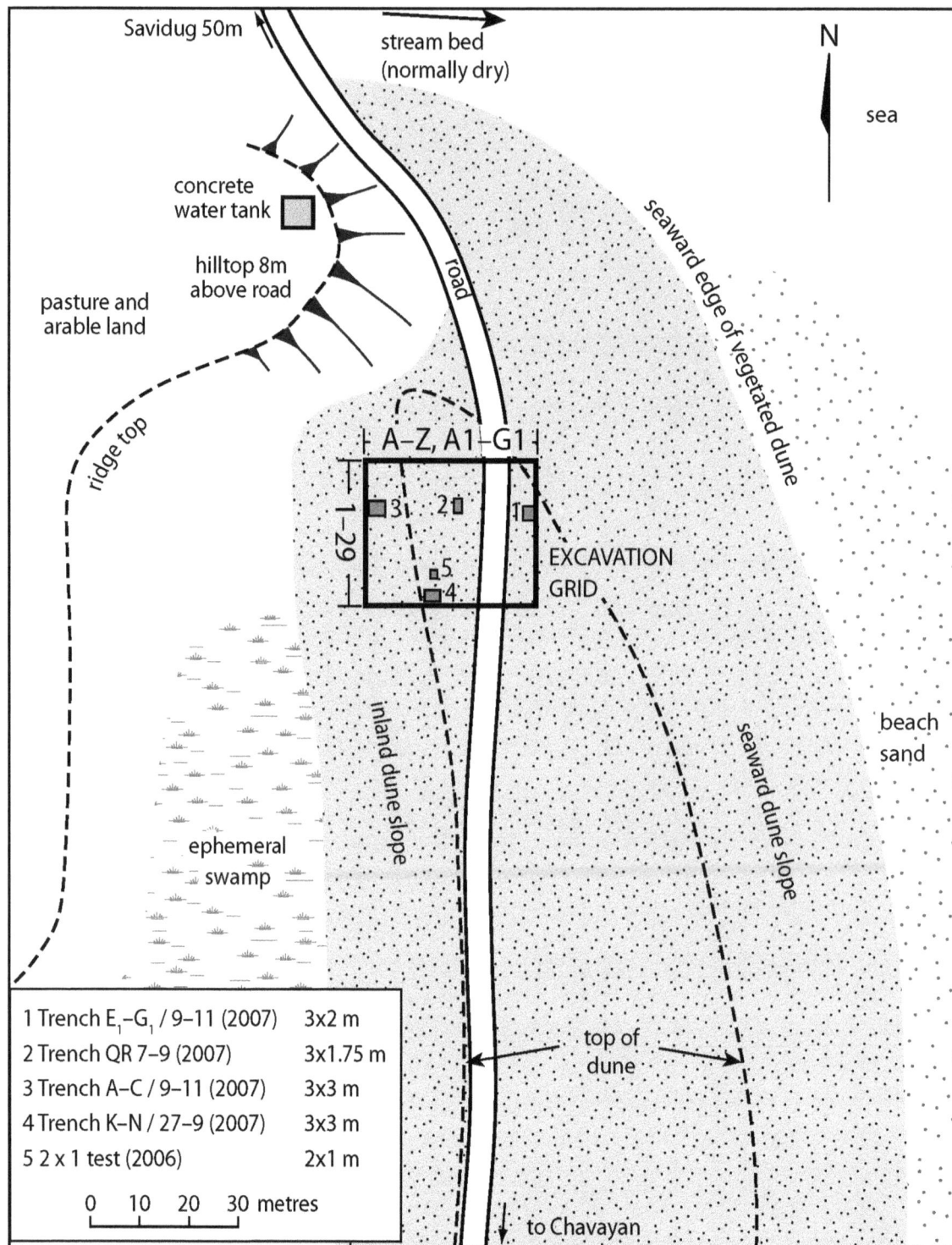

Figure 4.11. Savidug Dune Site: area plan with excavations in 2006 and 2007.

Source: Map preparation by ANU College of Asia and the Pacific, CartoGIS.

terra australis 40

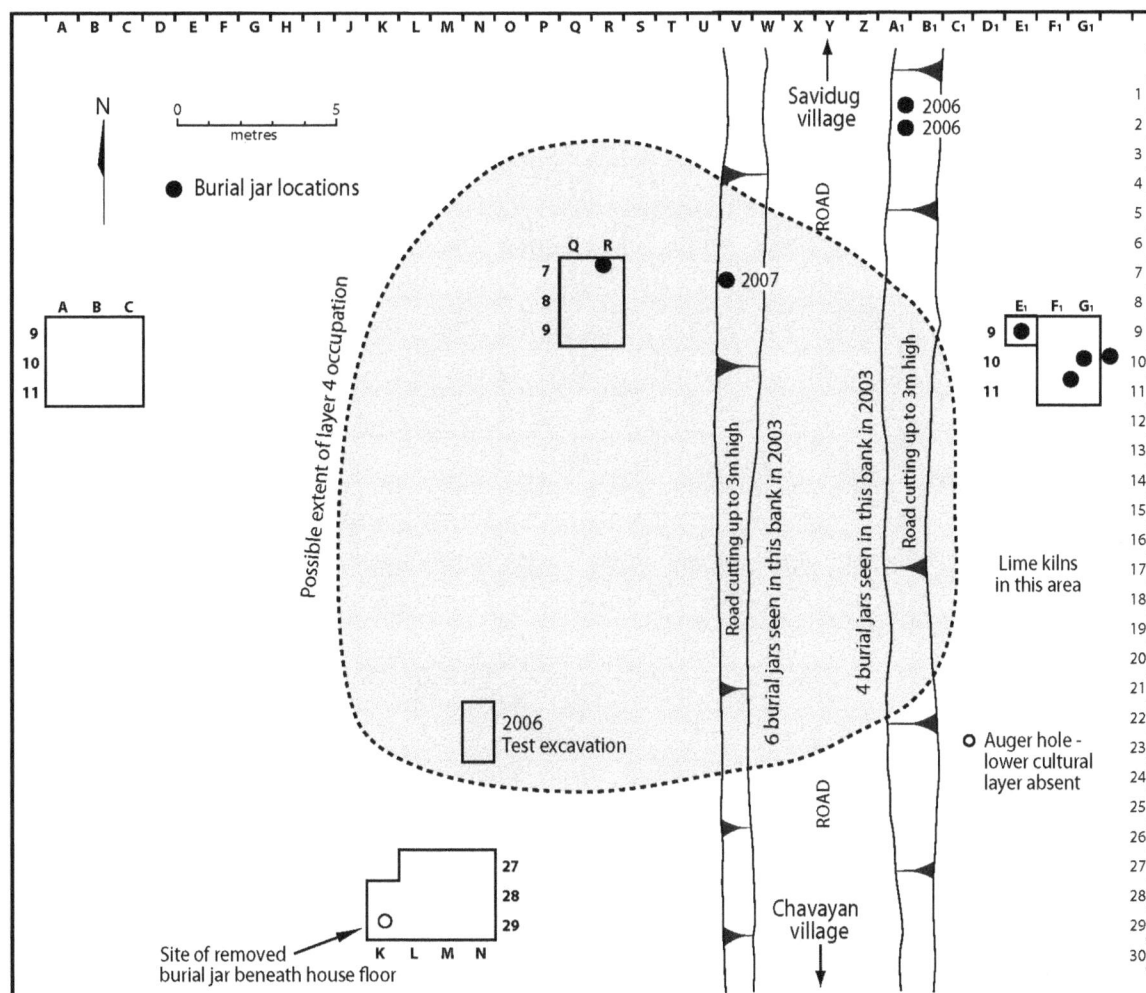

Figure 4.12. Savidug Dune Site: detailed locations of excavated areas and burial jars (circles), 2006-2007.

Source: Map preparation by ANU College of Asia and the Pacific, CartoGIS.

Beneath layer 4 lay more sterile dune sand, which we decided to auger rather than excavate since the trench walls, partly in loose dune sand, were already showing signs of collapse. Augering reached another humic sand (old topsoil) at 3.1 metres below ground level and 40 cm thick, but with no sign of any cultural presence. This overlay another culturally-sterile dune sand that continued to 4.3 metres below the surface, when augering had to stop owing to lack of rods. It is apparent that the site was not occupied beneath layer 4, at least not in this area.

Two more jar burials were observed in the seaward side of the road cutting in 2006, and one was excavated (Fig. 4.14). It consisted of a lower jar 58 cm in girth and 60 cm in surviving height, with a slightly pointed base, red slipped, and rimless. As we learnt in 2007, these burial jars had mostly had their rims removed to take primary and presumably flexed burials, like contemporary (Iron Age) burial jars in regions as far apart as Sarawak and southern Vietnam (observations by Peter Bellwood). The lid of this vessel was the lower part of another large rimless globular vessel, simply placed upside down over the mouth of the lower vessel. A virtually identical combination was also excavated in Q/R7-9 in 2007 (Fig. 4.15). As can be seen from Fig. 4.12, if we add the six jars investigated in 2007, the total from the gridded area of the site, incorporating a stretch of roadway and adjacent land about 30 m long by 29 m wide, is now 14.

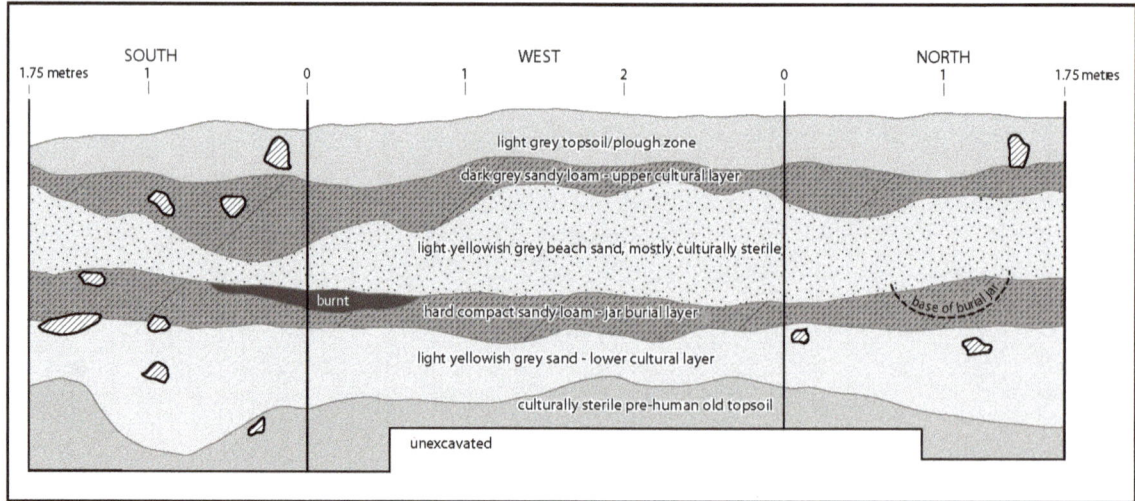

Figure 4.13. South, west and north sections of Savidug Dune Site trench QR/7-9, excavated in 2007.

Source: Map preparation by ANU College of Asia and the Pacific, CartoGIS.

Figure 4.14. Savidug Dune Site: a burial jar excavated in 2006, with a rimless lower jar, and a similar rimless jar placed upside down over the top as a lid. This contained human bone, but no artefacts.

Source: Peter Bellwood.

Figure 4.15. Savidug Dune Site: the lidded burial jar excavated in QR/7-9.

Source: Peter Bellwood.

Observation of the road section in 2006 suggested that these burial jars perhaps had their bases embedded in the top of the lower cultural layer (layer 4), but this was not really very clear and the mystery led us to return in 2007 to investigate the matter properly. One very remarkable surface find in 2006 was a baked clay casting mould found in three matching pieces in the road, broken by passing traffic, and hence an extremely lucky find (Fig. 8.11 F). We believe, but cannot be certain, that it came from layer 4, and if so it could be about 2000 years old. A small piece of copper was also found nearby in the road, subsequently analysed by Oli Pryce (pers. comm.) and shown to be actual metal rather than slag. The mould, 8.2 cm long, appears to have been one of a bivalve pair for casting a socketed tool with a slightly splayed blade, probably an adze or chisel. A similar baked clay mould was found by the 1982 Japanese team at Tayid on Batan Island (Koomoto 1983: plate 32; and see Fig. 8.11 G below), probably pre-dating 1500 BP since this site is buried under the Iraya ash layer. However, as noted in the report on Tayid in chapter 3, the Japanese team did not indicate where the mould was found – it could have been a surface find.

Nevertheless, both of these moulds are important discoveries since they indicate casting of cupreous metal in Batanes, presumably using imported scrap or ingots, at around or possibly before 2000 years ago. As with the nephrite found in the Batanes Islands (chapter 9, and see Hung et al. 2007), one wonders if itinerant metalworkers were involved, since the Batanes Islands themselves have no native copper resources, although other regions of the Philippines do.

The 2007 excavation in the Savidug Dune Site

In 2007, we decided to undertake fairly extensive excavation at Savidug Dune Site in order to find out more about lower cultural layer 4 and its relationship with the jar burials. An area of 30 by 30 metres was chosen for a surface grid of 1 m squares, running across the road where the burial jars had been found previously and over the sand dune on either side of the road. The four trenches indicated in Figs 4.11 (numbers 1,2,3 and 4) and 4.12 were excavated, and the basic results in terms of C14 dates and artefact distributions are given later in this monograph in Tables 6.6 and 8.1. These tables make clear the distinction between cultural layers 2 (upper) and 4 (lower), and the sterile sand layer 3 that lies in-between.

Excavation trench K-N/27-29

We began with a 3 by 3 m trench of 9 conjoined squares, LMN/27-29, extended later into K28 and 29 to expose an aligned 1.5 m long segment of a boulder house foundation in the upper cultural layer (layer 2). This probably held in place the base of a bamboo or cogon grass house wall in late prehistory (Fig. 4.16). A circular pit below this, about the size of a burial jar, went down into the upper part of layer 4, and we presume this represents the removal of a former burial jar protruding above the surface of layer 3, still visible at the time the house wall was constructed (see Fig. 4.12 for location). This trench produced a much higher density of upper cultural layer sherds than did the nearby 2006 test trench, perhaps because of the presence of the house. The layer sequence here was identical to that observed in 2006, but here the lower cultural layer, layer 4, contained only limited material. This area was clearly on the southern edge of the early occupation.

Excavation trench A-C/9-11

The upper cultural layer in this 3 by 3 m excavation trench was very dense in artefacts and midden material, especially at 50-60 cm. It lies at the base of a slope that descends from the rocky hillock that today supports the water tanks (Figs 4.10, 4.11). A great deal of the clay and silt matrix of layer 2 in this trench, as opposed to the sand matrix that dominates in all the other trenches, was clearly washed down in the past from this hill. Indeed, this trench also contained occasional cultural materials that appeared to be of lower cultural period origin, even though this layer was not represented in this location. Occupation on the hill behind had presumably released soil for downwash on to the dune below, including in one case a complete pot that had been washed with rocks and clay into square C10, presumably during a torrential downpour. This pot was of upper cultural layer affinity, but it is possible that the hill top was occupied during the lower cultural phase too. If the A-C/9-11 area at the base of the hill was actually occupied, and it has to be stated clearly that this is not proven in the absence of any stone house walls (cf. K-N/27-29 above), then the date of this occupation is generally late, presumably between 1000 and 600 BP according to the monochrome ceramics recovered throughout (no blue and white – Fig. 4.17). As stated, no coherent sign of the lower cultural layer 4 was observed in this trench, suggesting that occupation and jar burial at this time did not occur at the base of the hill. However, as far as our excavations were concerned this was by far the area of densest artefact accumulation of the upper cultural phase.

Figure 4.16. Savidug Dune Site KL/28-29, boulder house foundation in the upper cultural layer (layer 2), probably once holding in place an organic wall of bamboo or cogon grass. Date perhaps *c.*500 BP.

Source: Peter Bellwood.

Figure 4.17. Savidug Dune Site: monochrome Asian export ceramics from the upper cultural layer. Presumably, the dates for these focus on the Song and Yuan Dynasties.

Source: Peter Bellwood.

Excavation trench E1-G1/9-11

This trench was excavated on the seaward side of the road under the direction of Marc Oxenham, with the main intention being to understand the placement of the burial jars in the site. Luckily, four were discovered in this trench, with that in E_1 and that in the H_1 baulk being badly broken. The other two in the main part of the trench were well preserved and still standing upright, albeit with only poor bone preservation. The upper cultural layer in this trench had been badly disturbed by the digging of recent lime pits, and sherds were fairly few. The lower cultural layer, as an occupation rather than as a locus of jar burials, was virtually absent, although layer 4 was there as an old topsoil.

The complete burial jar shown in Figs 4.18 and 4.19, and reconstructed in Fig. 4.20, together with the other broken jars found in this trench, had its base embedded at the level of upper layer 4 and its body encased entirely in the sterile sand of layer 3. When the upper cultural layer 2 was laid down these jars would therefore have been already buried under sand, although some elsewhere might have been visible, or within easy reach of discovery. The burial jar illustrated is the most interesting one discovered so far. It had a badly broken small lid consisting of a red-slipped bowl placed upside down, partly removed in the photo to reveal the rim of the main jar below. The main jar has been drilled and chiselled from the inside to remove the upper part, like breaking off the top of a boiled egg - the line of this removal is clearly visible near the top of the jar in Fig. 4.19 and is marked in Fig. 4.20. The poorly preserved remains of an adult primary burial were then placed inside and the upper part of the jar was placed back on, perhaps with clay "glue" (we are not sure about this), and the lid put in place. This jar, and all the others, was then placed upright on the ground surface, perhaps in a small stabilising hollow, in the upper 30 cm or so of layer 4. The jar burial tradition at Savidug thus dates to the later part of layer 4, hence second half of the first millennium BC and early first millennium AD, according to the C14 dates to be discussed in chapter 5.

It should be stated that we have never found a single artefact in a burial jar at Savidug, except for a few sherds broken from rims and lids. Unlike jar burial sites further south in the Philippines, Indonesia, and central and southern Vietnam, where large numbers of small accessory vessels, ornaments, and so forth occur inside and around the burial jars (e.g. Tabon Caves on Palawan), the Batanes people appear to have used them only for burial, pure and simple. This was perhaps because the jars were placed deliberately above the ground surface in an open and exposed site, rather than being buried or placed in a hidden cave, thus visible and of course amenable to being ransacked. The nephrite *lingling-o* to be described later, found in trench QR/7-9, was apparently buried deliberately in a hole adjacent to the base of a burial jar.

Another interesting question concerns the origin of the sterile dune sand layer 3 that buries the jars and covers layer 4. Was this created by normal dune movement owing to wind? Or might there have been a tsunami from the cataclysmic eruption of Mt Iraya on Batan at *c.*1500 BP? If the latter, one wonders how the jars survived at all, and we have never seen any trace on Sabtang of the Iraya volcanic ash layer that mantles Batan Island. Slow dune migration seems the most likely possibility for the burial of layer 4 at Savidug Dune Site at present.

Excavation trench QR/9-11

This was by far the most prolific trench for the lower cultural layer 4, the upper cultural layer 2 being rather ephemeral here. The lower layer in the QR trench was more complex than elsewhere, with cultural material not only in the old topsoil layer 4, but also quite densely in the sand dune layer 5 below, that elsewhere was sterile (Fig. 4.13). As can be seen from Tables 6.6 and 8.1, layers 4 and the top of 5 in QR were 130 cm thick in combination, by far the thickest in the site.

Figure 4.18. Savidug Dune Site: two burial jars exposed in trench E1-G1/9-11, the right hand one already emptied.

Source: Peter Bellwood.

Figure 4.19. Savidug Dune Site: complete burial jar in E1-G1/9-11 with the lower part of its red-slipped lid still in place. The upper part of the vessel was removed in antiquity and put back, in order to contain a primary burial.

Source: Peter Bellwood.

top of jar deliberately removed
by chiselling around
the circumference
from within

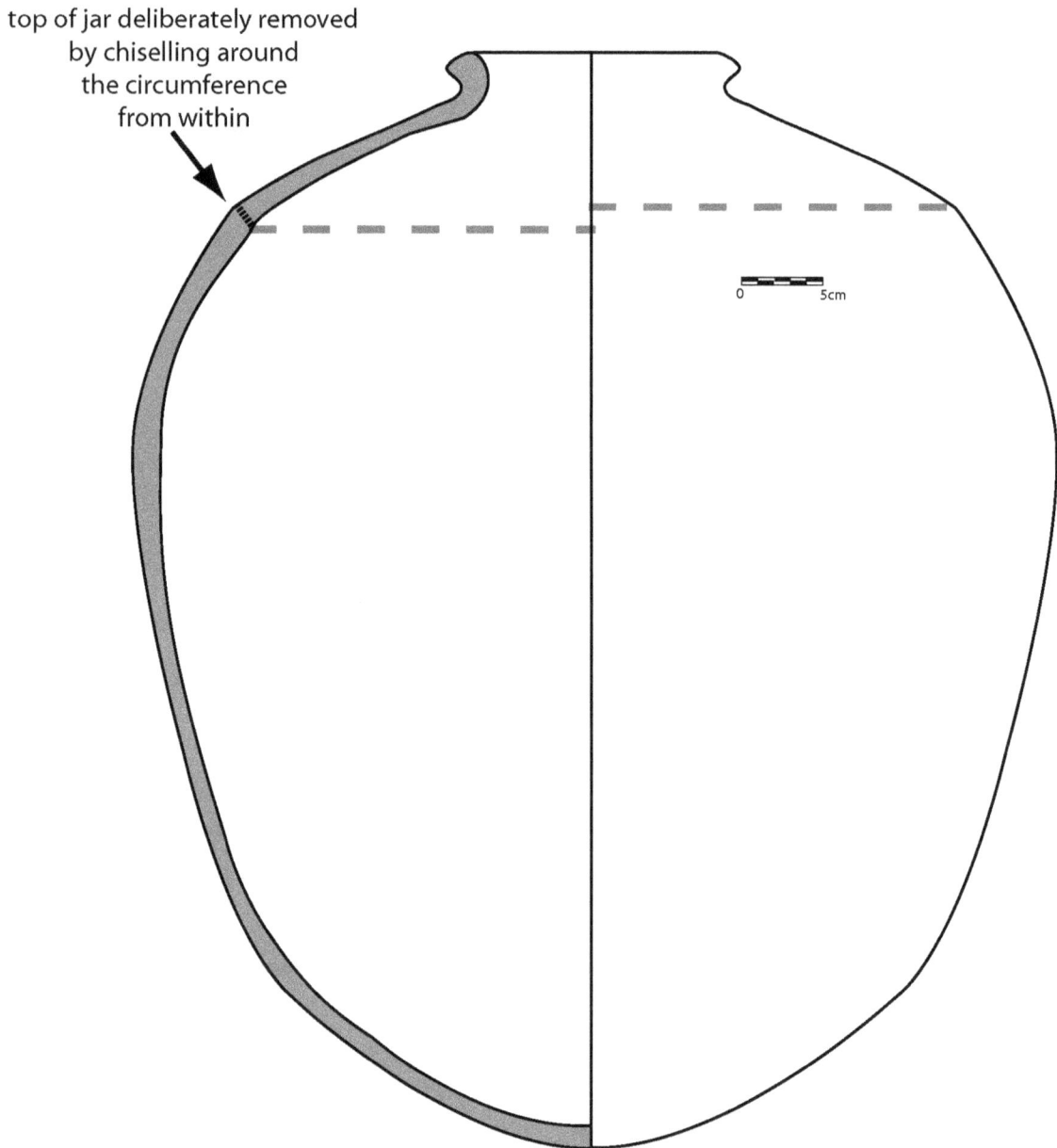

Figure 4.20. Savidug Dune Site: the jar in Fig. 4.19, showing the location of the deliberate break to lift the upper part of the jar to insert the body. The lid is not shown – it was too badly damaged to reconstruct, but was a red-slipped and presumably round-based open bowl.

Source: Peter Bellwood.

Pottery density is greatest at about 120 cm below the surface, which is where the bases of most of the burial jars were placed, suggesting that activity in the actual jar burial phase was rather intensive. However, pottery extends far below the jar burials, down to the two C14 dates (here and in the 2006 test trench) of c.1000 BC. So jar burial cannot be stated to have been an activity in the early years of occupation, and it perhaps commenced after 500 BC.

One complete and undisturbed burial jar was excavated at the north end of QR/7-9 (alas, like all the others, with no surviving artefacts). This is similar to the one described above from 2006 (Fig. 4.14), having a lower red slipped jar with its top cut off, and a lid made from the lower part of a similar vessel (Fig. 4.15). The nephrite *lingling-o* shown in Fig. 9.2 was buried just to one side of the base of this jar, with charcoal in the immediate vicinity dated by Wk 21809 to about 500-400 BC. This is one of the best dates for a nephrite ornament of this type in Island Southeast Asia, as discussed further in chapter 9. It can also be seen from Table 8.1 that a number of archaeologically informative artefact categories extend through layer 4, and also into layer 5 in QR7-9. These are discussed later.

3200 years of occupation at Savidug

Tables 6.6 and 8.1 indicate that Savidug Dune Site has two stratigraphic and cultural phases of usage: an upper cultural layer (layer 2) dated *c.*1000 to 600 BP, with imported ceramics and iron, and a lower cultural layer dated *c.*3200 to 2000/1500 BP (layers 4/5). The lower cultural layer can be divided into an earlier and a later phase. The earlier is associated with rare examples of circle-stamped pottery, dated 3200 to 2700 BP in the site and from some fairly precise parallels at Sunget and Anaro. The later phase, dated *c.*2700 to 2000/1500 BP, is associated with jar burial, Taiwan nephrite and possibly copper working.

The quantity of circle stamped pottery at Savidug is rather small compared to Sunget and Anaro, raising the possibility that it was imported from another Batanes location. Interestingly, the lattice pattern of stamped circles that is associated with nephrite working at Anaro is absent at Savidug, where the nephrite is mainly associated with plain pottery (see chapter 6).

Table 4.1 contains data on the ratios of smashed cowries to other shell species for upper cultural layer 2 (*c.*1000 to 600 BP) in the A-C and K-N squares at Savidug Dune Site. This table has been constructed from data counted at the time of excavation, and is therefore complementary to the post-excavation analytical data presented in chapter 12. In the A-C squares, there is a fairly consistent rise over time in the proportion of smashed cowries to other shell species in cultural layer 2 (except for the 100-110 cm depth, which has a small sample size). A similar but less regular pattern occurs in K-N. The point to note here is that this focus on small cowrie shells, broken open energetically to remove the contents, is highly emphasised in the upper cultural layer at Savidug Dune Site, as at Pamayan. It is also reflected in the intensive fragmentation of animal bones at Pamayan, as discussed in chapter 10. This could relate to considerable pressure on resources during that relatively late period in Batanes prehistory, corresponding with the stressful and feud-ridden lifestyle recorded by visitors such as Jirobei in 1669 and Dampier in 1687 (see chapter 1). This issue is also discussed from a slightly different and more ecological perspective in chapter 12.

Table 4.1. Weights and relative frequencies of smashed cowrie shells in the upper cultural layer at Savidug Dune Site.

Depth cm	2007 A-C/9-11 (3 by 3 m)			2007 K-N/27-29 (3 by 3 m)		
	Smashed cowrie gm (approx.)	Non-cowrie gm	Ratio cowrie to non-cowrie	Smashed cowrie gm (approx.)	Non-cowrie gm	Ratio cowrie to non-cowrie
0-20	Plough zone			268	305	0.88
20-40	2870	1420	2.02	1137	925	1.23
40-50	5447	3848	1.42	2220	1084	2.05
50-60	12,596	8185	1.54	2919	1167	2.50
60-70	2943	3882	0.76	688	1030	0.67
70-80	1075	1390	0.77	1305	1830	0.71
80-90	1000	1813	0.55	-	-	-
90-100	300	440	0.68	-	-	-
100-110	1200	210	5.7	-	-	-

5

The Chronology of Batanes Prehistory

Peter Bellwood and Eusebio Dizon

This chapter describes the radiocarbon dated chronology of all the sites excavated in the Batanes Islands, and groups the assemblages into four dated phases that cover the past 4000 years. The major sites excavated between 2002 antd 2007, on Itbayat, Siayan, Batan and Sabtang Islands, have been described in the previous three chapters. Here, it is necessary to consider absolute chronology as derived from C14 dates, to place each site in relative chronological order with respect to other sites, and to consider the issue of phases within Batanes prehistory. The latter are a little difficult to distinguish since most of Batanes prehistory was essentially "Neolithic", despite the rare presence of metal in some younger sites. The only stratigraphic boundary of a catastrophic kind was produced by the eruption of Iraya on Batan Island at about 1500 years ago, but the geomorphic results of this eruption are only visible in central Batan Island. It is clear, however, that Batanes prehistory witnessed some significant changes in pottery shape and decoration through its 4000 years of progression, and the same appears to be true for other artefacts of stone and shell, as well as for the presences of imported Taiwan nephrite and slate.

Do we need phases for Batanes prehistory? Bellwood and Dizon (2005) decided to avoid putting firm chronological boundaries on the cultural phases suggested earlier in the life of the project (Bellwood et al. 2003) owing to problems of overlap and dating uncertainty. Furthermore, there is absolutely no reason to suppose that the whole population of the Batanes Islands was ever replaced at any time in prehistory, even after the Iraya eruption. One basic problem is that, as more sites are discovered, excavated and dated, so one phase tends to blend into another. Eventually, their apparent signatures tend to disappear into a hazy background, although it can still remain the case that specific artefact categories have specific time ranges (see Fig. 5.3).

To circumvent this problem of overlap one might ignore phases altogether and just discuss each site as a completely independent entity. But the time always comes when a coherent presentation of Batanes prehistory is required, by general public and other scholars alike, that needs to be more than just a list of sites, assemblages and dates. Somewhere along the line, one has to attempt to write some coherent history for interested parties who are not archaeologists (e.g. the Batanes people themselves).

When our research began on Batan Island in 2002, it was fairly evident that three separate assemblages were present on this island, at least in terms of pottery. These were termed the Sunget Phase with its circle-stamped pottery dated 1200 to 700 BC, then the Naidi Phase with its plain and red-slipped pottery between 700 BC and AD 500, and finally the Rakwaydi Phase with its mainly plain and unslipped pottery postdating the AD 500 Iraya eruption (Bellwood et al. 2003:151). The Sabtang research produced a sequence matched most closely in Batan. But further work on Itbayat soon complicated matters, and it became necessary on this island to identify the Torongan, Anaro and Garayao phases, with the first-named having plain red-slipped pottery that predated the Sunget phase on Batan. Indeed, it soon became apparent that four pan-Batanes pottery phases were being foreshadowed in terms of typology. The first (Torongan) had plain red-slipped pottery, the second (Sunget and early Anaro) had circle-stamped pottery, the third (Naidi and later Anaro) saw a return to plain red-slipped pottery, and the fourth (Rakwaydi and Garayao) was focused on plain and mostly unslipped pottery.

By the end of the fieldwork in 2007, it was possible to characterise these four successive phases as follows, based on the distributions of pottery characteristics in all of the excavated sites, on all investigated islands, and considering regional trends further afield in southeastern Taiwan and in the Cagayan Valley of northern Luzon:

Phase 1: red-slipped plain wares: Torongan and Reranum caves on Itbayat only, with an added (and unique for Batanes) presence of fine cord-marked pottery in Reranum.

Phase 2: circle-stamped decorative patterns imposed over continuing red slip: Sunget (Batan), Anaro (Itbayat) and Savidug (Sabtang). Within Anaro there are two apparent sub phases, with older rectilinear and younger lozenge (net-like) emphases in the designs (described in chapter 6).

Phase 3: plain wares with continuing red slip, but no stamping: Naidi and Payaman (Batan), Mitangeb (Siayan), upper layer 4 at Savidug, and the middle layers at Anaro. This phase has shorter but cross-sectionally more complex rim forms than Phases 1 and 2, especially thickened rims.

Phase 4: similar to Phase 3, but with the appearance of imported Asian glazed ceramics in small quantities, grading upwards into the European contact phase. There seems little point in giving Phase 4 a precise termination date, although one could choose the late 17th century, when the first recorded observations of Batanes society were made.

The marker horizon represented by the AD 500 eruption of Mt Iraya on Batan is, of course, stratigraphically useful for correlation purposes. It does not in itself mark a phase boundary since there was no obvious change in artefact styles that occurred precisely around AD 500. However, by examining the date distributions for the Batan Island sites plotted in the two right hand columns in Fig. 5.1, it can be seen post-eruption occupation in central Batan, at least in terms of the available C14 dates, could have witnessed a hiatus to some degree between AD 500 and 1000. All of the C14 means from the pre-eruption occupations at Naidi, Payaman, Tayid and Mahatao predate AD 500, and one Payaman date (ANU 12086 – 1486 uncal. BP) corresponds virtually exactly with the presumed date of the eruption. Reoccupation, in the Mavuyok, Mavatoy and Dios Dipun rock shelters, did not apparently occur until after AD 1000.

We need now to give date ranges to these four phases defined by artefact changes, an exercise for which the raw data are given in Table 5.1. The 51 radiocarbon dates listed were produced by the Radiocarbon Laboratory at ANU, the Waikato Laboratory in New Zealand, and the Australian Institute of Nuclear Sciences and Engineering at Lucas Heights in Sydney. It should be remembered that there is absolutely no sign of any preceramic occupation in Batanes; everything found so far is Neolithic or later, despite the excavation of no less than seven separate cave and rockshelter sites (Reranum, Torongan, the Anaro 3 and 6 shelters, Dios Dipun, Mavuyok a Ahchip and Mavatoy). This seems to rule out chance as a major factor in the absence of pre-Neolithic settlement. If there ever was a Batanes Palaeolithic, it has been erased with astonishing efficiency from the landscape.

There is another factor connected with the radiocarbon dates listed in Table 5.1. This is that we have no charcoal dates from the oldest Batanes sites, these being Torongan and Reranum caves on Itbayat. The Batanes environment is generally subject to strong and seasonally-variable weathering conditions, such that ancient charcoal seems generally to have disintegrated and been washed through soil deposits by water movement, especially in the open sites subject to the direct impact of heavy monsoonal rainfall. Charcoal sometimes survives under protective covers such as large potsherds or rocks, but large concentrations were very rare in our excavations, except in very recent cave sites such as Mavuyok a Ahchip on Batan. Most of our early radiocarbon dates are from marine shells and food residues attached to sherds. The oldest dated charcoal comes from Savidug Dune Site, at only 2870 radiocarbon years (Wk 21810).

Marine shells require a variable marine reservoir calibration, and food residues can sometimes incorporate ancient carbon residues contained within potting clays, especially if sample removal in the laboratory was not sufficiently careful. We have potential problems here, as discussed by Anderson (2005), who favours extremely young dates for Batanes prehistory based on the limited results of our first two seasons of excavation in 2002 and 2003. In the case of Torongan Cave, however, it can be seen that the food residue and marine shell dates are very similar in range, back to beyond 2000 BC, which is reassuring. The marine shells come from a location within the cave that is about 150 metres from the sea, and about 13 m above sea level (Fig. 2.5). So it is very unlikely that the dated shells were simply washed there by high seas. Movement by hermit crabs is possible, as discussed in chapter 12, but the shells all appear fresh and not heavily rolled, so their role as dating material is not necessarily undermined. The Batanes dates overall, as presented in Table 5.1 and Fig. 5.1, give strong support to the claim that Batanes prehistory had commenced by 2000 BC. Further precision at the moment would be unwarranted.

Batanes Islands Phase 1, outer limits 2500 to 1000 BC

The most significant dates from Torongan and Reranum are illustrated in the two OxCal plots in Fig. 5.2. In Torongan, these all come from the zone of in-washed soil with red-slipped pottery between 40 and 60 cm in depth, and range from 2500 BC onwards to 1200 BC for two sherd residue and four marine shell samples. Reranum shows obvious disturbance. Sherds of fine cord-marked pottery occur throughout the very shallow deposit (maximum 50 cm) and these are very small in size compared to the bulk of the Reranum pottery, thus perhaps derived from an older deposit now destroyed. Such cord-marked pottery has not been reported before from any other site or time period in the northern Philippines (except for one surface-collected sherd from Anaro), although there is cord-marked pottery in the undated Tabon Caves sequence from Palawan (Fox 1970: Fig. 21). The disappearance of fine cord-marked pottery in southeastern Taiwan had occurred by about 2000/1500 BC (Hung 2005, 2008).

Batanes Islands Phase 2, outer limits 1300 BC to AD 1

The circle-stamped and red-slipped pottery in Batanes progressed through two sub phases, the earlier dominated by rectangular meander designs, the younger dominated by lozenge (fishnet) designs. The fishnet type of decoration is only reported in quantity from the squares with plentiful Fengtian nephrite excavated at Anaro 3 on Itbayat. The earlier pottery with rectangular meanders, also found with Fengtian nephrite but in smaller amounts and without the manufacturing debris associated with circular ear ornaments, is represented at Sunget, in the basal layers at Anaro, and at Savidug. Fig. 5.2 (bottom) shows the five C14 dates most relevant for this early rectangular meander sub phase, all on food residues on sherds, and all clustered between 1300 and 800 BC. The two younger dates from Sunget listed in Table 5.1 are considered to reflect post-occupation cultivation, and the very old date for OZH 776 clearly reflects the use of ancient resin for coating pottery.

The younger sub phase, with the lozenge/fishnet patterns, is found only at Anaro 3, where it is associated with the three dates OXJ 692, 693 and 695 (Table 5.1). These suggest a range between 700 BC and AD 1. The younger C14 dates from Anaro 3B, as discussed in more detail in chapter 6, belong to Phase 3 contexts. A clinching factor here is Wk 21971 from the site of Mitangeb on Siayan, which dates to about AD 1, yet is associated with absolutely no stamped pottery at all, and so postdates Phase 2 (see the plotting of these dates in Fig. 5.1).

Table 5.1. Radiocarbon dates for assemblages from Itbayat, Sabtang and Batan Islands, with selected dates for red-slipped pottery excavated in northern Luzon. Calibrations have used Oxcal 3.10, with a delta R for marine shells of 18±34 from coral core data, Xisha Island, Paracel Islands (Fiona Petchey, Waikato C14 Laboratory, pers. comm. 20/11/06).

LOCATION, SITE	CONTEXT	DATE BP	Δ13C‰	LAB NO.	OXCAL 3.10, 2 SIGMA
ITBAYAT ISLAND					
Torongan Cave	Food residue on sherd at 55-60 cm (base of cultural layer)	3860±70	not measured	OZH 771	2562-2066 BC
	Tectarius shell at 55-60 cm	3880±40	-2.0	OZH 772	2025-1721 BC
	Food residue on sherd at 55-60 cm	3320±40	-25.3	Wk 14642	1726-1503 BC
	Turbo shell at 55-60 cm	2496±37	+2.3	Wk 15795	339-47 BC
	Turbo shell at 50-55 cm	3352±35	+2.8	Wk 14641	1384-1095 BC
	Thais shell at 45-50 cm	3663±41	+2.0	Wk 15794	1737-1456 BC
	Marine shell at 40-45 cm	3470±50	+2.0	OZH 773	1522-1217 BC
	Food residue on sherd at 15-20 cm	520±70	-31.1	OZH 775	AD 1287-1613
Reranum Cave	Square A, 30-35 cm, Purpura persica marine shell	1798±37	+3.1	Wk 19716	AD 500-718
	Square A, 25-30 cm, Turbo argyrostomus marine shell	3253±47	+2.3	Wk 19715	1279-929 BC
	Square A, 15-20 cm, food residue on sherd	479±30	-27.1	NZA 26374	AD 1408-1452
	Square A, 10 cm, food residue on sherd	768±34	-26.6	Wk 19714	AD 1213-1285
	2A, 15-20 cm, food residue on sherd	1876±41	-26.0	Wk 14643	AD 53-238
	3, 90-95 cm, food residue on sherd	1360±39	-23.6	Wk 14645	AD 607-768
	3, 95-105 cm, food residue on sherd	2770±50	-23.6	OZH 774	1038-813 BC
	3A, 80-90 cm, food residue on sherd	2095±45	-25.2	OZJ 692	349 BC-AD 4
Anaro	3A, 100-110 cm, food residue on sherd	2475±45	-24.0	OZJ 693	767-414 BC
	3B, 65-70 cm, food residue on sherd	1280±45	-20.7	OZJ 694	AD 657-866
	3B, 70-75, food residue on sherd	2080±45	-26.3	OZJ 695	338 BC-AD 21
	3B, 85-90, food residue on sherd	1375±45	-25.9	OZJ 696	AD 583-768
	3B, 90-95, food residue on sherd	1510±60	-24.4	OZJ 697	AD 427-644
Siayan Island, Mitangeb	Turbo shell from Test Pit 1, 50-55 cm	1659±32	+2.6	Wk 14646	AD 662-866
	Food residue on sherd, A 50-60	1962±35	-20.3	Wk 21971	50 BC-AD 90
BATAN and SABTANG IS.					
Sunget Top Terrace	Layer 5, 15-20 cm within layer, resin coating on sherd exterior	5790±150	not measured	OZH 776	Not calibrated (fossil resin)

Table 5.1. Continued.

LOCATION, SITE	CONTEXT	DATE BP	Δ13C‰	LAB NO.	OXCAL 3.10, 2 SIGMA
ITBAYAT ISLAND					
	Layer 5, 20-30 cm within layer, food residue in pottery	2910±190	not measured	ANU 11817	1614-597 BC
	Layer 5, 15-20 cm within layer, food residue in pottery	2915±49	-26.0	Wk 14640	1286-941 BC
	Layer 5, 20-30 cm within layer, charcoal concentration	2630±30	-27.0	ANU 11693	837-774 BC
	Layer 5, 30-35 cm within layer, scattered charcoal fragments	2383±35	-25.9	Wk 15649	730-391 BC
	Squares A/D, layer 5, charcoal at 20-30 cm within layer	2000±140	-27.6	ANU 11707	378 BC–AD 322
Savidug Dune Site, 2003	Infant tooth enamel from burial jar exposed in road cutting	1755±25	-7.4	ANU 33938	AD 222-381
Savidug Dune Site, 2006	Layer 5, 180 cm below surface, charcoal with Sunget style pottery	2828±37	-26.7	Wk 19711	1114-901 BC
Savidug Dune Site, 2007	R7-9, Layer 5, 220 cm below surface, food residue on sherd	2870±30	-25.8	Wk 21810	1130-930 BC
	R7-9, Layer 5, 210 cm below surface, charcoal	2146±30	-26.9	Wk 21808	360-50 BC
	R7-9, Layer 4, 135 cm below surface, charcoal near jade ornament	2416±30	-24.6	Wk 21809	560-390 BC
Pamayan shell midden	Square A, 100-105 cm below surface (AMS)	418±41	-27.2	Wk 13170	AD 1420-1630
Savidug ijang	Below ijang, square C, 100-110 cm	740±180	not measured	ANU 12070	AD 850-1650
	Charcoal in A2, 0-10 cm within layer	2240±140	-26.7	ANU 11708	754 BC – AD 45
Naidi	Charcoal in road section	1590±210	-24.9	ANU 11694	36 BC – AD 886
	Charcoal in road section	2620±30	-25.0	ANU 11695	830-771 BC
Mahatao town	Charcoal in palaeosol below volcanic ash (with sherds)	2090±60	-27.8	ANU 11710	354 BC – AD 51
	Charcoal in palaeosol below volcanic ash (with sherds)	1829±180	not measured	ANU 12071	344 BC – AD 597
Payaman	North square, layer 3, charcoal at 10-25 cm within layer	1988±47	-26.9	Wk 13092	106 BC – AD 125
	South square, layer 3, charcoal at 20-25 cm within layer	1486±185	not measured	ANU 12068	AD 132-946
Tayid	Beneath main ash deposit, food residue on sherd	1842±215	not measured	ANU 12069	359 BC – AD 609
Mavatoy shelter	Square A, 25-30 cm below surface (Turbo shell)	682±49	+3.2	Wk 13336	AD 1282-1402
Dios Dipun shelter	Test Pit 2 at 175 cm below surface	500±260	not measured	ANU 11696	AD 1040-1954
	Extension trench, south end, 120 cm below surface	590±110	-27.6	ANU 11736	AD 1210-1530
Mavuyok a Ahchip cave	Square C, layer 2, 5-10 cm within layer	Modern	-26.4	ANU 11711	Modern
	Square C, layer 3, 0-5 cm within layer	550±70	-28.0	ANU 11712	AD 1290-1470
	Square B, layer 3, 25-30 cm within layer	750±80	not measured	ANU 11697	AD 1040-1400
	Square C, layer 3, 30-35 cm within layer	900±60	-26.9	ANU 11713	AD 1020-1260

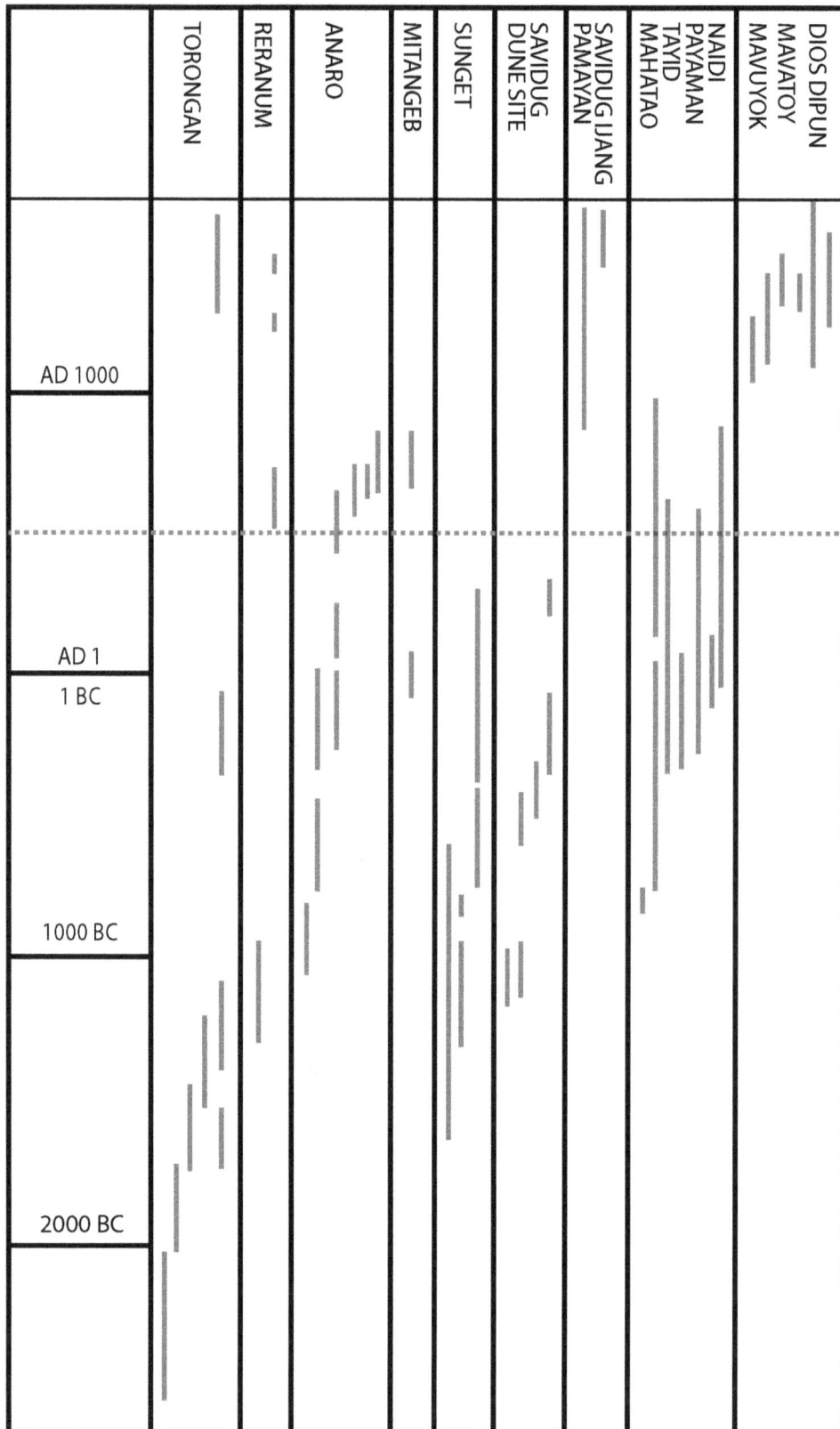

Figure 5.1. A plot of all the Batanes calibrated radiocarbon dates with their ranges, by site, as listed in Table 5.1. The dotted line represents the Iraya eruption.

Source: Peter Bellwood.

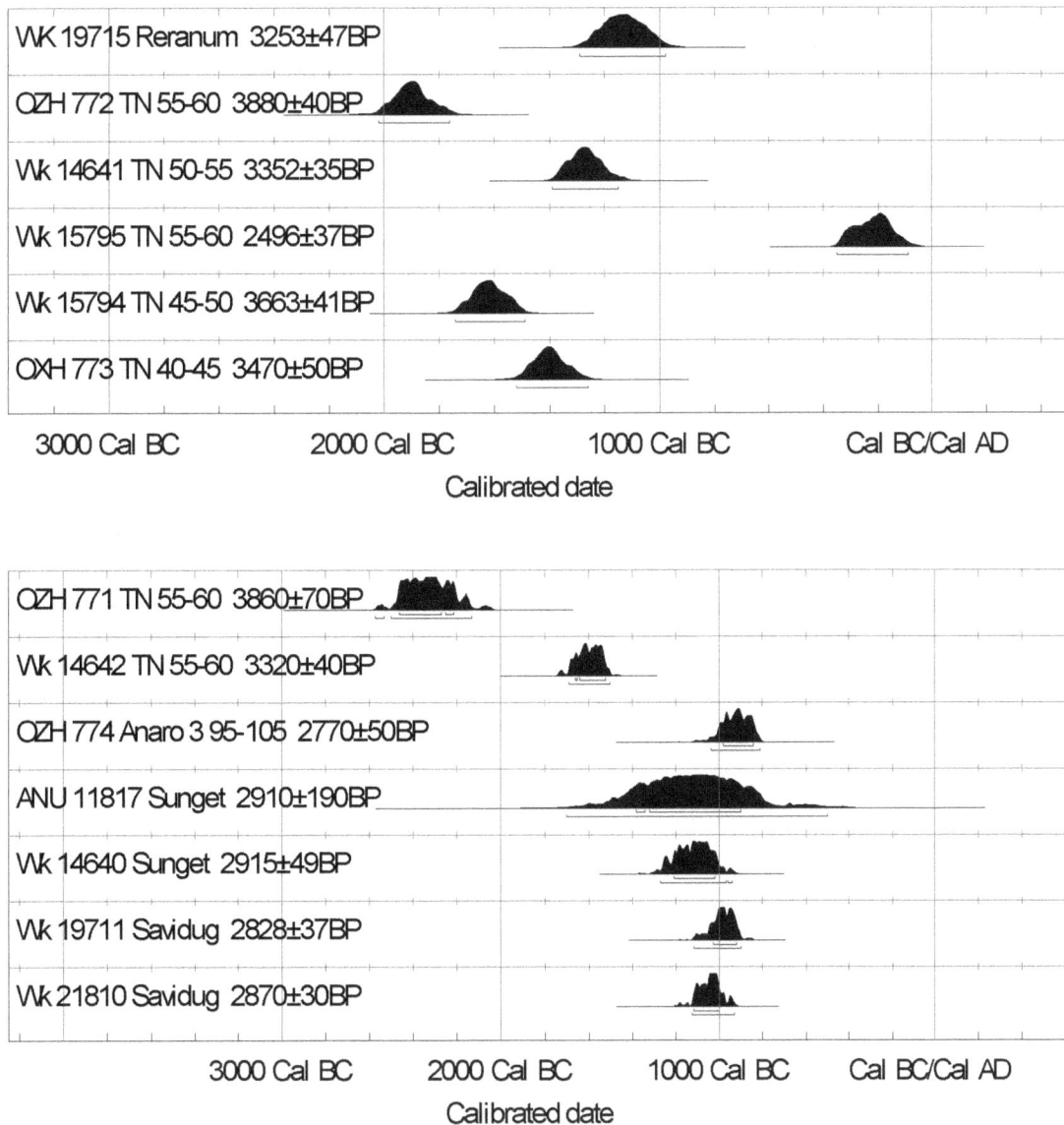

Figure 5.2. Top: Oxcal 3.10 plots of marine shell dates older than 2500 cal. BP (except for Wk 15795) from Reranum and Torongan (TN) Caves. Bottom: Oxcal 3.10 plots of food residue dates older than 2500 cal. BP from Torongan Cave (TN), Anaro 3, Sunget and Savidug Dune Site.

Source: Peter Bellwood.

Batanes Islands Phase 3, outer limits 500 BC/AD 1 to AD 1200

The upper 30-40 cm in the Anaro 3 squares, the site of Mitangeb on Siayan Island, the upper part of layer 4 at Savidug (with the jar burials), and the sites of Naidi, Payaman, Tayid and Mahatao on Batan belong in this phase, which lacks any pottery surface decoration apart from red-slipping. The Naidi dates from Batan are the oldest, potentially back to 800 BC (ANU 11695), but the sample from this site is so small that an absence of stamped pottery cannot be guaranteed. The Naidi pottery is very similar to that from Payaman in terms of rim shapes, and Payaman, like Naidi, lacks stamped pottery. Payaman dates from about AD 1 onwards (Wk 13092 in Table

5.1). The Mitangeb date Wk 21971, also c.AD 1, is significant because of the complete lack of any stamping in such a large sample, suggesting its true demise by this time. Additional dates for this phase come from Mahatao and Tayid.

Batanes Islands Phase 4, commencement c.AD 1200

This phase is marked by the appearance of imported ceramics, that are represented through excavation in layer 2 at Savidug and at Pamayan, both on Sabtang Island, although lots of recent sites with imported ceramics on Batan are reported in Koomoto 1983. As discussed in chapter 6, the ceramics found in the upper layer at Savidug are of monochrome types that many reports loosely categorise as "Song and Yuan", on the assumption that blue and white sherds denote the following Ming or Qing dynasties. The Batan Island cave sites of Dios Dipun, Mavuyok a Ahchip and Mavatoy also date to within the past millennium, but lack imported ceramics.

Further comments on chronology

One difficulty with attempting to establish a chronological sequence for the whole of the Batanes is that different islands might have had different sequences of changing pottery and artefact styles, although their geographical closeness and inter-visibility render absolute isolation and independence unthinkable. It is interesting, however, that cord-marked pottery has only so far been found in Reranum shelter, and lozenge shaped circle-stamped motifs only in Anaro, both on Itbayat. This raises the possibility that what might appear to be a continuous sequence of change is in fact made up of a large number of short term occupations revealed to us by those locations selected for excavation. Many times and places were not, of course, investigated by excavation at all, hence perhaps some of the apparent "gaps" and C14 ambiguities in the overall sequence.

Nevertheless, examination of the plot of C14 dates in Fig. 5.1 reveals that there was no obvious hiatus of non-occupation across the Batanes at any time in prehistory, despite the likelihood of an abandonment of parts of Batan after AD 500. Nothing in the record suggests a total population replacement at any time, and nothing refutes the suggestion that, in the Batanes Islands in general, the first arrivals at 2000 BC were at least partial ancestors for the inhabitants in AD 1687.

It is worth noting also that the general sequence proposed here, despite the gaps, matches well with pottery sequences published from Taiwan, northern Luzon, and even areas further south such as Sabah and eastern Indonesia (Bellwood 1988, 2007; Anggraeni et al. in press). Plain red-slipped pottery seems to predate stamped and incised pottery very widely in eastern Island Southeast Asia, and the latter often reverts to plain ware at some point during the Early Metal Phase. A possible exception to this generalisation could be the Cagayan valley on Luzon (Hung et al. 2011; Carson et al. 2013), where the punctate stamped pottery appears to be at the base of the sequence, although this is still a little uncertain.

Fig. 5.3 illustrates the four proposed phases for Batanes, together with likely chronologies for the excavated and C14-dated Batanes sites, and contemporary cultural manifestations in Taiwan and Luzon (see Bellwood 2011; Bellwood et al. 2011 for further discussion).

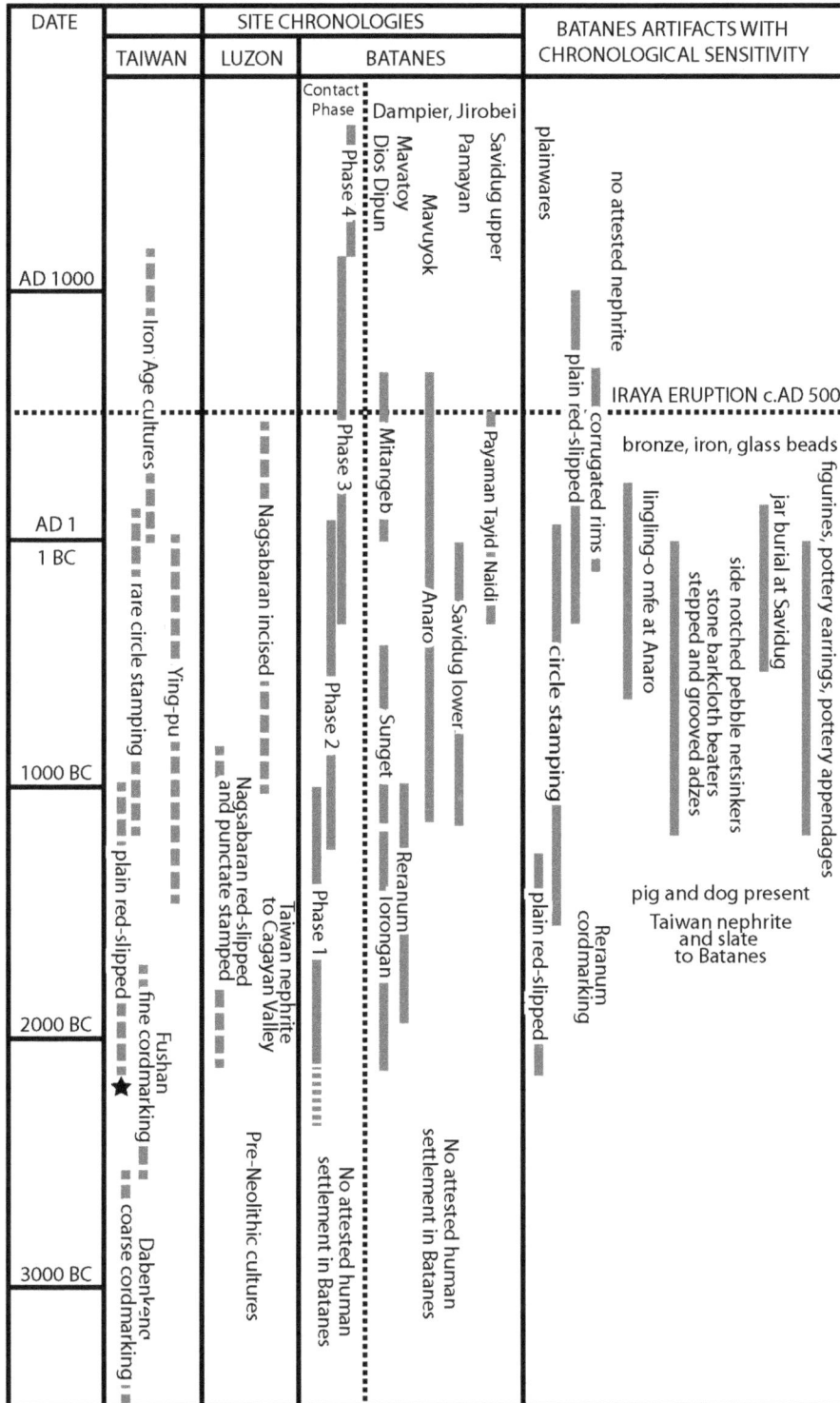

Figure 5.3. The four proposed phases for Batanes prehistory (4th column from left), together with radiocarbon chronologies for the excavated Batanes sites, and contemporary cultural manifestations in Taiwan and Luzon. This figure is repeated later as Fig. 13.1.

Source: Peter Bellwood.

6

The Batanes Pottery Sequence, 2500 BC to Recent

Peter Bellwood, Eusebio Dizon and Alexandra De Leon

This chapter describes the sequential changes that occurred in pottery shape and decoration during the 4000 years of recorded Batanes prehistory. The major assemblages discussed come from Torongan Cave, Reranum rockshelter and Anaro on Itbayat, Mitangeb on Siayan Island, Sunget on Batan, and Savidug Dune Site on Sabtang.

The sequence of change in pottery form and decoration presented here for Batanes, covering almost 4000 years, is only matched within the Philippines by the related sequence from the Cagayan Valley in northern Luzon, most recently analysed by Ogawa (2000, 2002), Mijares (2006) and Hung (2008; Hung et al. 2011; Carson et al. 2013). Greater understanding of Philippine prehistory from the Neolithic onwards will require a much stronger chronological framework for ceramic change than exists at present, extending through long periods of time and covering different regions of the archipelago. The famous Tabon Cave sequence described by Fox (1970) made a start in this regard, but was mainly concerned with surface decoration, in many cases of sherds from undated and disturbed jar burials in caves. The Fuga Moro Island (northeastern Luzon) study of Snow and Shutler (1985) was concerned only with sherds from very late prehistory, and thereby lacked significant time depth. The recent thesis on Batanes pottery by Alexandra de Leon (2008) is an important development in this regard, and some of her analyses of the pottery from Savidug and Anaro are incorporated in this chapter.

The Batanes landscape is liberally littered with sherds of pottery. In the central and northern parts of Batan Island, any surface sherds collected from locations buried by the AD 500 Iraya eruption can be virtually guaranteed to be less than 1500 years old, except where the ground has been disturbed by road cuttings, latrine pits and the like. In other areas unaffected by the eruption, much older pottery can sometimes be found in surface exposures, as for instance in vast quantities from 1200 BC onwards around the slopes of the Anaro hilltop site on Itbayat. But excavations of both deep stratigraphic profiles and well-integrated single-period assemblages, together with radiocarbon dating, are needed in order to place the different types of pottery in a time sequence. In this chapter, the pottery from Batanes is described in approximate chronological order from the excavated assemblages, beginning with assemblages from Itbayat, then Batan and Sabtang, before summarising the sequence as a whole. The burial jars from Savidug have already been described in chapter 4.

Torongan Cave, Itbayat (*c*.2000 to 1200 BC)

The Torongan pottery comes essentially from two contexts, the first being the well stratified and dated layer of in-washed topsoil concentrated between 40 and 65 cm depth in squares A-D, the other being the up-slope and shallow square X plus the scattered surface finds (Fig. 2.5). Only the former in-washed topsoil context can be considered reliably dated, but unfortunately the sherds from here are small and eroded.

Most of the roughly 3000 sherds recovered from Torongan cave are either plain or red-slipped. Unlike Reranum (below), no cord-marked sherds were recovered. Torongan does have three circle-stamped sherds with white lime or clay infilling, but these occur in the upper part of the excavated stratigraphy and appear to be relatively late in the sequence (Table 2.1; Fig. 6.1, top left).

Figure 6.1. Top left: Torongan: two circle-stamped and one incised sherd with white infill, identified in the latter sherd as white clay (not lime) by Alan Watchman. Remainder of photo: Reranum: red-slipped and white in-filled circle-stamped sherd (top centre) and 18 small cord-marked sherds.

Source: Peter Bellwood.

All the rim sherds from the in-washed topsoil that can be reconstructed below the neck come from pots with everted rims, 18-20 cm in diameter, with the rims having mostly unthickened profiles and rounded lips (Fig. 6.2, top). There is one foot ring fragment too small to draw. Three rim sherds from one vessel shown in Fig. 6.2 (square B 45-50 cm, 4th from top on left) have an outer thickening of the lip, paralleled in the Taiwan Middle Neolithic at sites such as Suogang, Nangang (both in the Penghu Islands), Niupu, Dazhuwei, Wanlijiatou and Fengbitou (Hung 2008:126). One rim shown in Fig. 6.2 (top right) has a flat lip, and some others have sharp internal neck angles similar to some rims excavated by Hung (2008) from Chaolaiqiao (2200 BC) in southeastern Taiwan (Fig. 6.2, middle). Some Torongan rims reveal faint traces of red slip, but insufficient survives for any precise statement to be made about the frequency of this surface finish.

Overall, the Torongan rim profiles match well with contemporary pottery (*c*.2000 BC) in Taiwan, including that from Chaolaiqiao and Donghebei near Taidong on the southeastern coast (Fig. 6.2, lower). Furthermore, like Torongan, Chaolaiqiao also has almost no cord-marked sherds, but it is precisely dated by two excellent AMS C14 samples to 2200 cal. BC (Hung 2008: chapter 5). Torongan and Chaolaiqiao thus have a strong chronological tie in this regard.

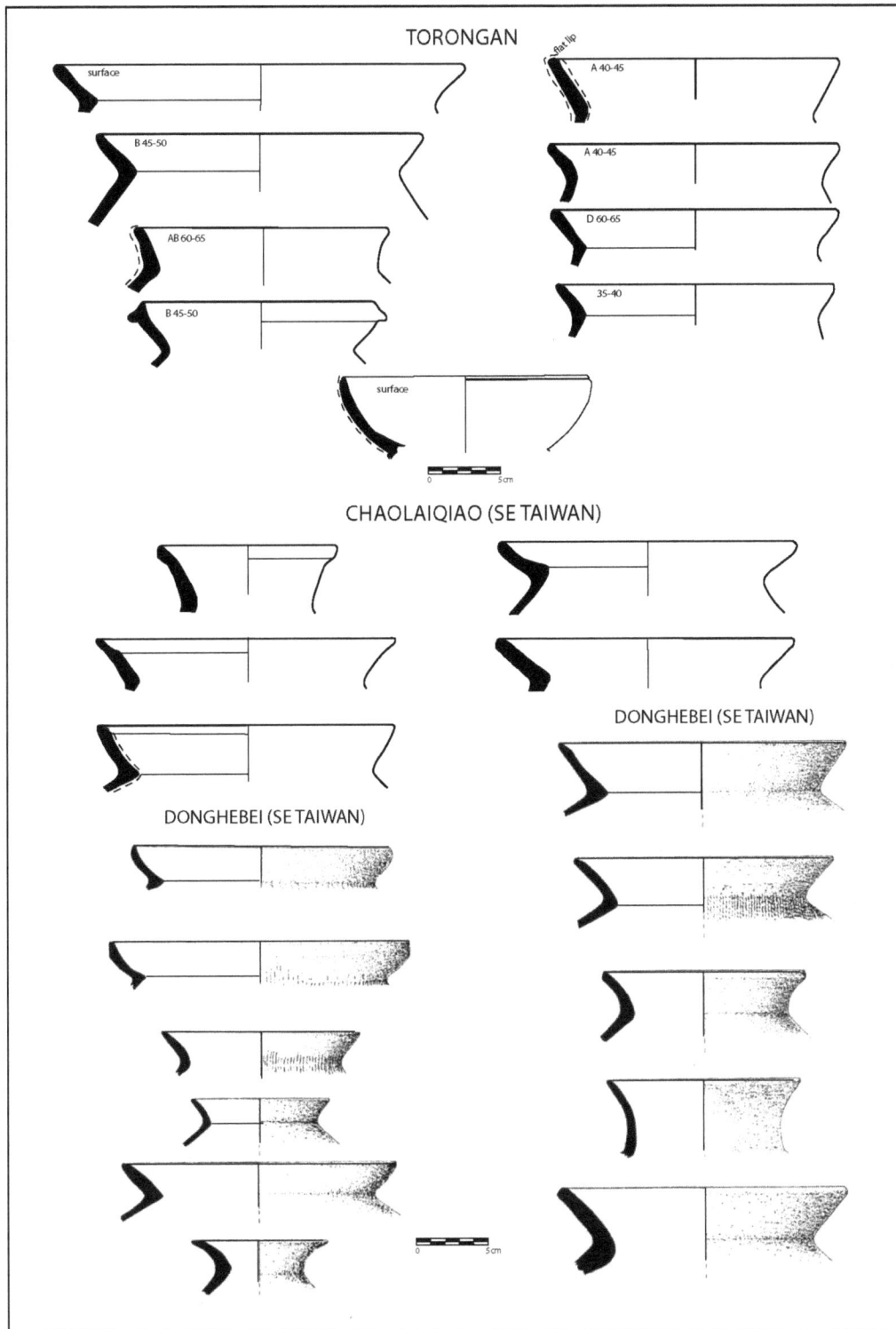

Figure 6.2. Top: rim forms from Torongan Cave. Dotted lines indicate visible traces of surface resin or red slip. Middle: comparable jar rims from Chaolaiqiao, southeastern Taiwan, 2000-2200 BC. Bottom: comparable jar rims from the site of Donghebei in southeastern Taiwan, after Chu (1990). Many of the Donghebei vessels are cord-marked, unlike those from Torongan and Chaolaiqiao.

Source: Peter Bellwood.

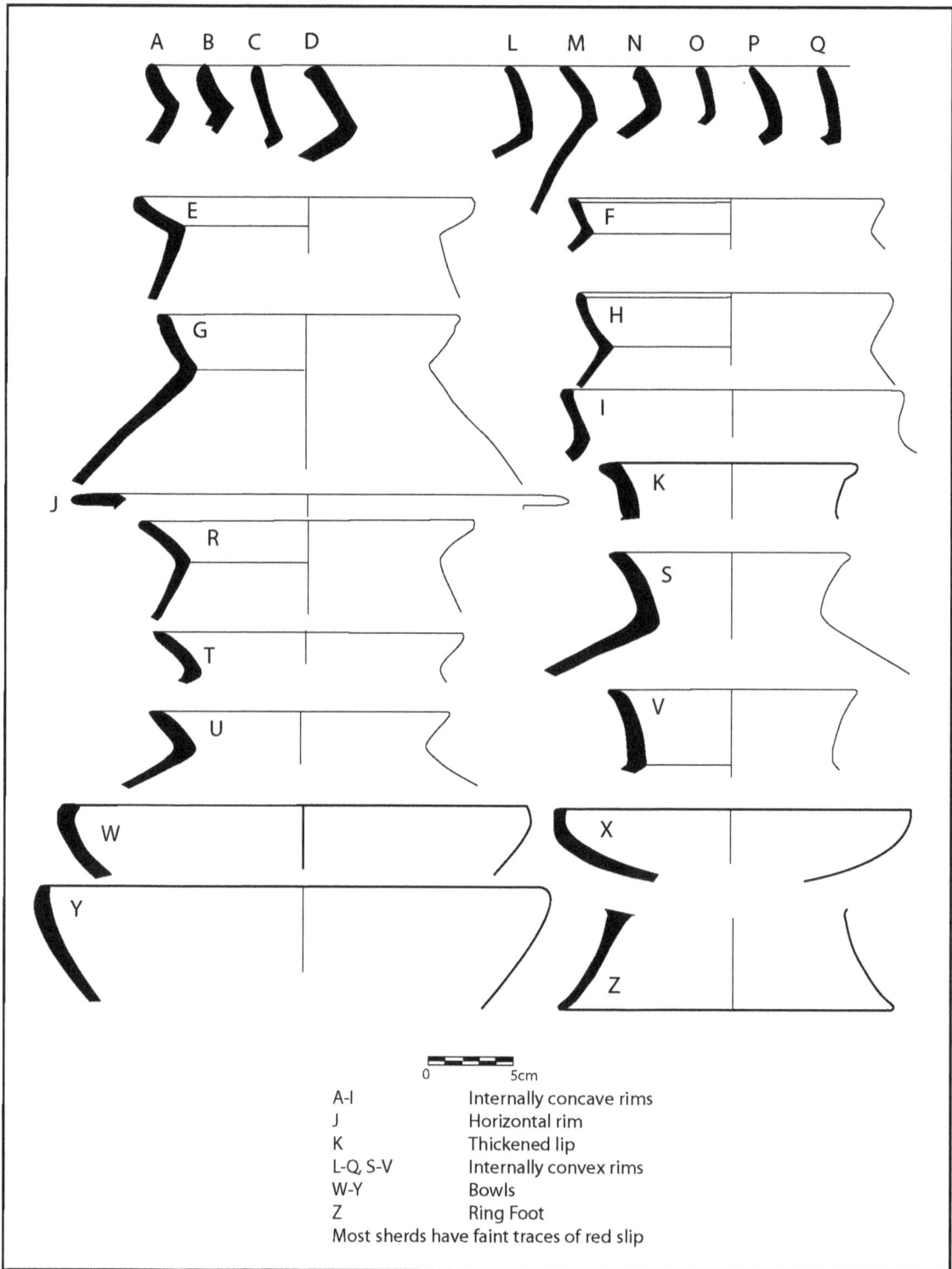

Figure 6.3. Jar rims from Reranum shelter. The top line contains sherds too small for diameter calculation. These sherds are from both excavated and surface contexts.

Source: Peter Bellwood.

The unstratified sherds from Torongan, including those from square X, also contain a few ring feet and a handle attachment, the latter possibly for some kind of loop handle. The surface finds also include sherds of open bowls with direct rims on ring feet (Fig. 6.2, above upper scale), although no certain sherds of open bowls occurred in the in-washed topsoil. To avoid confusion, it is best if these sherds are considered undated in the present state of knowledge about Torongan.

The total collection of everted rims from Torongan contains 53 measureable examples, of which 36 (68%) are over 30 mm tall above the neck externally, with a maximum height of 39 mm. Torongan absolute neck heights are noticeably shorter on average than those from Reranum. This "rim height metric" or "tallness value" is discussed further below.

Reranum shelter (second millennium BC)

Almost 2700 sherds were unearthed from the 3 square metres, maximum depth 50 cm, excavated in 2006 in Reranum shelter (not including the sample of large sherds thrown out of the shelter in the recent past) (Table 2.2). As at Torongan, most are plain, with sand tempers. Only 20 are decorated (0.007%), all cord-marked except for a single circle-stamped sherd from 15-20 cm (Fig. 6.1). Also like Torongan, many sherds have traces of red slip, again too fugitive to present useful statistics. Besides the rim and body sherds there are also parts of body carinations and ring feet, but no handles.

The cord-marked sherds are very small compared to most of the other sherds from the site, suggesting that perhaps they were derived from an older and more trampled deposit that no longer survives with any stratigraphic clarity. If this is so, then the majority of the Reranum plain rims could be younger than the cord-marked sherds, although younger by how much cannot be known. The only relevant radiocarbon date from the site, on a marine shell from 25-30 cm in square A (Table 5.1, Fig. 5.1), falls in the late second millennium BC. The cord-marked pottery would appear to be older than this, given its absence from any other sites in the northern Philippines (except for one surface sherd from Anaro, below) and its apparent disappearance in southeastern Taiwan by about 2000/1500 BC, as discussed by Hung (2005, 2008).

Regarding the Reranum vessel forms, a number of rim sherds, particularly from the surface finds outside the shelter, are sufficiently large to allow reconstruction of the upper shapes of the vessels (Fig. 6.3). As at Torongan, most are everted jar rims, with a few open and direct bowl rims. Reranum also has a fragment of a horizontally everted rim (Fig. 6.3J) of a type reported from a number of Middle Neolithic sites in Taiwan (Hung 2008: Fig. 3.7). These similarities mean that the Reranum assemblage fits well into a date range of 2000 to 1500 BC on Taiwan parallels. However, the Reranum rims are on average taller than those from Torongan, with 26 out of a total of 35 measurable examples (74%) being over 30 mm high, and with maximum external heights up to 63 mm as opposed to the 39 mm maximum at Torongan. Reranum also has 4 foot rings with complete profiles, with the highest being 72 mm (Fig. 6.3Z). The tallness of the rims suggests that the Reranum assemblage, minus the cord-marked sherds, could be slightly younger than that from Torongan (see below).

Comparative observations on the Torongan and Reranum pottery

The dominant unthickened and relatively tall everted rims with rounded lips from Torongan and Reranum are similar to the majority of rim forms from Middle Neolithic sites such as Donghebei and Chaolaiqiao (Fig. 6.2) in southeastern Taiwan, the latter dating to 2200 BC. In the case of Chaolaiqiao there is a predominance of red slip, with almost no cord-marking. Hsiao-chun Hung (2005, 2008) has compared the Reranum rims with these two Taiwan sites and notes strong similarities in the presences of fairly tall rims with unthickened concave or convex internal profiles. She also notes the presence in all these sites of a sharp angle on the insides of some lips.

Indeed, simple comparison of Figs 6.2 and 6.3 demonstrates how generically similar are the rims from Reranum, Torongan, Chaolaiqiao and Donghebei in terms of cross-section, rarity of thickening, and angle of eversion.

At present, there seem to be two possible differences between the Reranum and Torongan assemblages in terms of rim characteristics. The restricted vessels at Reranum have orifice diameters of two sizes, the majority between 18 and 20 cm as at Torongan, but there are also a few with diameters of only about 12 cm (Fig. 6.3, K, S and V). Torongan appears to lack the smaller diameter rims, that could have served as containers for liquids, but this could just reflect small sample size. Secondly, Reranum has taller rims on average than Torongan, and in this regard is more closely related to the assemblage of Sunget on Batan Island, which dates to *c.*1000 BC. However, Reranum, unlike Sunget and Anaro, lacks circle stamping (except for one sherd), and so seems to be older than either of these *c.*1200 BC and onwards assemblages.

The Torongan and Reranum pottery assemblages therefore establish a baseline for Batanes pottery evolution through prehistory, commencing at around 2000 BC with simple jar and bowl forms with red-slipped and plain surfaces, extremely rare cord-marking, and occasional foot rings and body carinations.

The Anaro and Mitangeb (Siayan Island) pottery sequences (*c.*1500 BC to recent)

Because Anaro and Mitangeb contain a number of separate excavation sequences, this section will consider first the pottery sequence excavated at Anaro 3, followed by Anaro 2 and Anaro 6, and then the site of Mitangeb on Siayan Island. The other squares excavated at Anaro were all too shallow to merit separate discussion. Then will follow a discussion of Anaro pottery surface finds, especially of stylistic elements such as lugs and figurines that are rare in the excavated collections. There is also a surface collection of "early" tall rim sherds from Anaro 5 that resemble the rims from Reranum and Sunget on Batan. Two major elements of pottery typology will be emphasised as they changed through time – rim profiles, and surface decoration - the latter mainly in the form of stamped circle motifs.

The distributions of pottery materials for Anaro 3, 2 and 6 respectively, by 10 cm spit (the site was dug in 5 cm spits, but 10 cm spits are sufficient for analytical purposes), are shown in Tables 6.1, 6.2, 6.4 and 6.5, together with the stratigraphic positions of radiocarbon dates. Most of the analytical detail comes from the squares Anaro 3 (dug in 2004) and Anaro 3A, 3B and 3C (dug in 2005). The pottery from 3B is dealt with by Sandy De Leon in more detail below. The diagnostic material from Anaro 3D, 3E and 3G (dug in 2006) was left in Manila and the body sherds from these squares were left on site. However, some information from notes on these squares is incorporated into the analysis.

Anaro 3 rim sherds are shown in Fig. 6.4, top left and top right, the former from above 40 cm, the latter from below 40 cm down to bedrock. As far as vessel body shapes are concerned, it is assumed that those with everted rims served as cooking pots, storage jars or vessels for storing liquids, and that those with direct rims (open bowls, presumably often on foot rings) functioned for food serving.

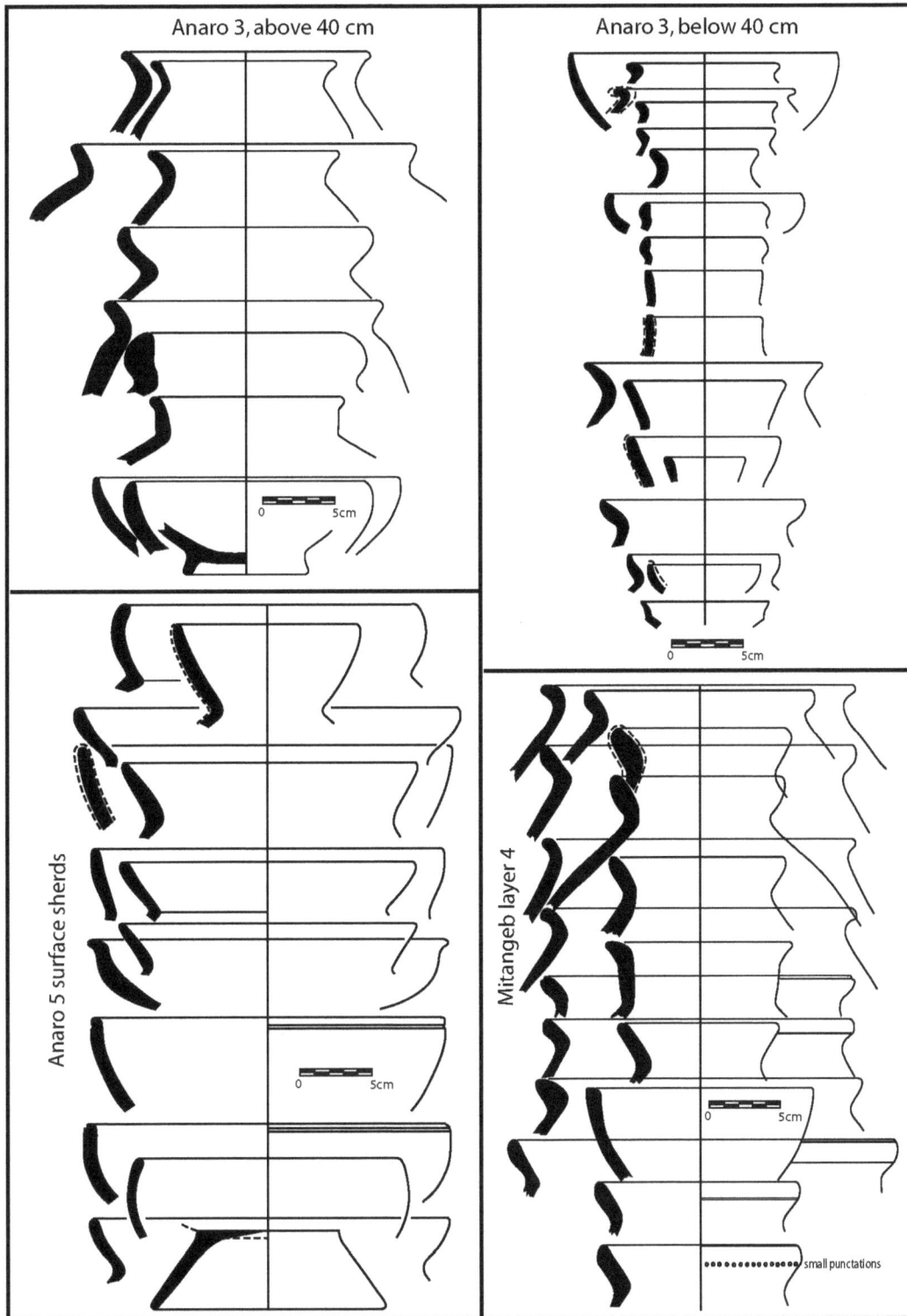

Figure 6.4. Undecorated rims from Anaro and Mitangeb. Top left: Anaro 3, above 40 cm. Top right: Anaro 3, below 40 cm. Bottom left: surface rims of Reranum affinity, including tall everted types, from Anaro 5. Bottom right: non-corrugated rims from Mitangeb layer 4. Dotted lines indicate red slip.

Source: Peter Bellwood.

As at Mitangeb (below), there seem to be two modal diameters for the vessels with everted rims, one around 10-12 cm, perhaps for liquids, the other larger at 16-20 cm, perhaps for cooking or solid storage. These can be differentiated very clearly in the drawings of the sherds below 40 cm from Anaro, as well as the sherds from Mitangeb portrayed just below in the same figure.

Tables 6.1 and 6.2 reveal a number of changes in the Anaro 3 squares through time. Only the lower layers have circle-stamped pottery. The sherds are generally bigger in the upper layers, the older sherds tend to be slightly thinner than the upper ones, and the older rims tend to be taller than the younger ones. We now examine each of these trends in more detail.

Firstly, there is a differentiation in all Anaro 3 squares at around 30-50 cm between the presence of circle-stamped pottery below this depth and its complete absence above. The C14 dates also form two groups, one in the first millennium BC, the other in the mid-first millennium AD and separated from the former by a 400 year gap. This differentiation is the main reason for separating the Anaro 3 rim sherd drawings into two groups, above and below 40 cm. However, apart from the disappearance of decoration there is considerable continuity in vessel and rim shapes from bottom to top of the Anaro site.

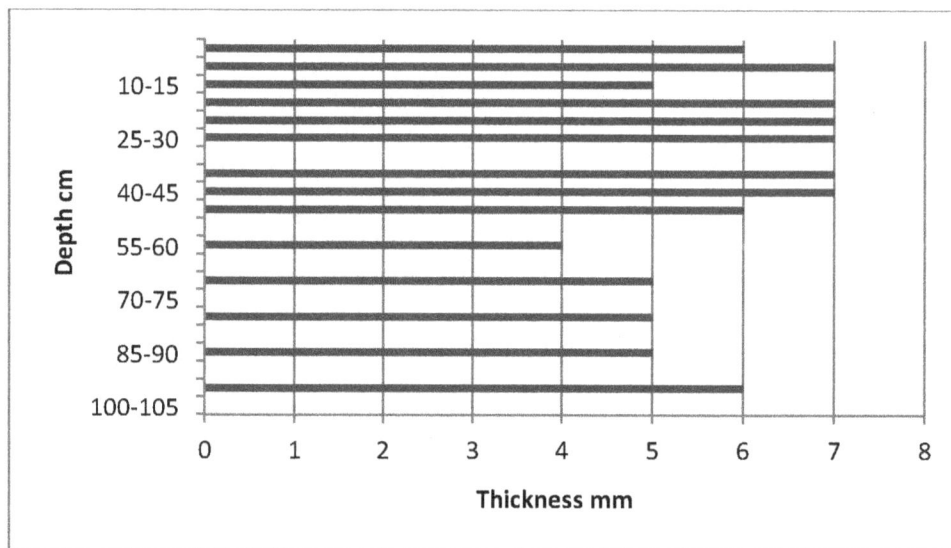

Figure 6.5. Modal body sherd thicknesses (mm) at Anaro 3 (2004) by depth from surface. Samples were not measured from missing spits.

Secondly, average single sherd weights in the top layers of all squares are much greater, sometimes by a factor of three, than in the lower layers. This could reflect the length of time they have spent in the ground (less time = less breakage and weathering?). Body sherd thickness does not seem to be a factor here since there is very little change in this from top to bottom of the site (Fig. 6.5). Regardless of the cause, this fairly smooth fall-off in sherd mass with depth is a very useful variable for identifying potential disturbance. For instance, in most squares the fall-off of average sherd size from top to bottom is fairly regular, except in 3B, where it can be seen from Table 6.1 that the bottom 70 to 90 cm depth has unusually large sherds. Three of the four C14 dates from this zone also conflict with the three older dates from squares 3 (2004) and 3A (Table 5.1). This might reflect disturbance in square 3B, involving a movement of younger material downwards in the profile, and had this circumstance been noted when we sent in the C14 samples to ANSTO in Sydney for dating we would probably have picked another square different from 3B. Hindsight, unfortunately, is rarely much help in such circumstances. In this regard it is important to note that 3A is inside the rockshelter, thus secure from tillage and tree root activity, and has two credible

C14 dates, whereas 3 and 3B are outside and more vulnerable in this regard. The better-protected 3A has a very even distribution of sherds and a regular fall off in sherd mass, suggesting that it has suffered little disturbance. The circle-stamped sherds in 3A are also remarkably homogeneous in their decorative motifs (to be described later), and show no signs of admixture with the other styles that occur in other parts of the Anaro site.

Thirdly, body sherd thicknesses were measured for several spits in the square Anaro 3 (2004). They range from 2 to 15 mm, with the vast majority being in the 5 to 10 mm range. The modal values do not vary sufficiently to hint at any significant change through time, although there is a tendency for older sherds to be slightly thinner, as can be seen in Fig. 6.5.

The modal value for body sherd thickness at Anaro 2 was also 5, similar to the lower levels in the Anaro 3 squares. But at Anaro 1A, where all the sherds appeared to be very recent, the mode was between 7 and 9 mm in all levels. So there probably was an increase in average body sherd thickness towards the end of Anaro and Itbayat prehistory, at a time when Chinese imports were available for food serving and local earthenware would probably have served more kitchen-based functions, thus needing to be thicker and heavier. As can be seen in Fig. 6.5, in Anaro 3 (2004), modes of 7 mm occur only in the top half of the stratigraphy.

Fourthly in this examination of trends, the external heights of the everted rims provide another useful variable for looking at change through time. This rim height metric has been discussed already for Torongan and Reranum. The external heights are measured from the vessel lip down the exterior of the rim to the point where the neck passes through verticality. In Tables 6.1 and 6.2 they are listed by percentage of everted rims over 3 cm tall for each layer in Anaro 3A, 3B, and 3C, and it is very clear that such rims do indeed become taller with increasing depth/age, even if the progression is slightly irregular. This value does not correlate with orifice diameter, and at Mitangeb the narrow-necked vessels that might have been used for liquids have taller necks then the wider cooking pots. It is clear that both time and function have their roles to play, but the metric appears to be useful as a time indicator, even if its exact functioning is not understood.

The importance of this tallness value can be seen in wider context. The percentages of rims over 3 cm tall for a number of other dated Batanes sites, apart from Anaro 3, are shown in Table 6.3, in each case from the whole measurable assemblage (i.e. rims that have adjoining necks). Despite minor fluctuations it is clear that there is a definite progression starting with the tall rims in the earlier sites of Torongan, Reranum and Sunget (with some up to 6 cm high in the latter two cases, but not at Torongan). We can add to this early phase the Anaro 5 undated but typologically early surface collection (1500-1000 BC? see Fig. 6.4 bottom left), and the Savidug Dune Site basal phase (Sunget and Savidug pottery is described below). This early tendency towards tallness is followed by a sharp decrease that seems to be fairly well marked by 500 BC (Savidug jar burial phase and Anaro 3). As noted, this can also be seen in the progressive decrease in percentages for this variable from bottom to top in the Anaro 3 squares (Tables 6.1 and 6.2) and the Savidug Dune Site trench QR/7-9 (Table 6.6). This shortening of rims through time can also be observed in the Sunget to Naidi sequence on Batan Island, and remarkably in the Neolithic pottery sequence from the sites of Minanga Sipakko and Kalumpang in the Karama valley in West Sulawesi, Indonesia (Anggraeni et al. in press). The significance of this observation involving Sulawesi need not be emphasised here, but in terms of broader Austronesian migration patterns it is of enormous importance. Interestingly, the Taiwan Middle Neolithic assemblages from Donghebei and Chaolaiqiao shown in Fig. 6.2 also have large proportions of eversions over 3 cm tall, linking them closely to Torongan and Reranum.

Table 6.1. Anaro 3: Pottery distributions by square and 10 cm spit, squares 3 (2004), 3A and 3B. For the Anaro circle-stamped type 1 vessels, the first figure refers to everted rim sherds with lozenge (fishnet) decoration, the second (following a plus sign) to body sherds with stepped double lines of circles.

Depths cm	Anaro 3 (2004)					Anaro 3A (2005)						Anaro 3B (2005)					
	Cal. C14 date	Body sherd no.	Body sherd average weight	Circle-stamped types 1	2A 2B	Cal. C14 date	Body sherd no.	Body sherd average weight	% of everted rims over 3 cm tall	Circle-stamped types 1	2A 2B	Cal. C14 date	Body sherd no.	Body sherd average weight	% of everted rims over 3 cm tall	Circle-stamped types 1	2A 2B
0-10		264	6.4	-	-	-	193	15.9	14	-	-		205	8.8	14	-	-
10-20		413	8.9	-	-	-	240	12.9	18	-	-		200	12.8	18	-	-
20-30		681	9.3	-	-	-	420	9.8	11	-	-		140	16.4	11	-	-
30-40		447	8.7	-	-	-	465	9.0	27	1+5	-		495	12.8	27	0+1	-
40-50		529	4.3	0+1	-	-	515	7.0	33	1+0	-		245	8.6	33	-	-
50-60		193	3.7	-	-	-	449	6.1	78	2+1	-		245	6.1	75	-	-
60-70		741	4.3	3+6	-	-	442	7.0	44	1+0	-	AD 657-866	371	6.0	44	-	-
70-80		1522	3.3	5+5	-	-	526	5.4	24	3+3	-	338 BC-AD 21	165	12.4	24	0+3	-
80-90		1062	4.2	2+8	-	349 BC-AD 4	374	5.0	40	3+1	-	AD 583-768	173	12.1	40	3+2	1
90-100	AD 607-768	308	2.9	1+1	2	-	601	5.2	56	5+2	-	AD 427-644	929	4.3	56	4+9	2
100-110	1038-813 BC		-	-	1	767-414 BC	415	3.6	50	4+4	-	-	-	-	-	-	-

Table 6.2. Anaro 3: Pottery distributions by square and 10 cm spit, squares 3C, 3F, and distributions of specific sherd classes. For the Anaro circle-stamped type 1 vessels, the first figure refers to everted rim sherds with lozenge (fishnet) decoration, the second (following a plus sign) to body sherds with stepped double lines of circles. A = incised sherds; B = sherd with parallel impressed ribs; C = corrugated rims (as at Mitangeb on Siayan); D = "phallic" lug; E = pottery figurine fragment; Fig. 6.9B.

Anaro 3C (2005)						Anaro 3F (2006)			All squares - specific classes				
Depths cm	Body sherd number	Body sherd average weight	% everted rims over 3 cm tall	Circle-stamped types		Body sherd number	Circle-stamped types		A	B	C	D	E
				1A	2A 2B		1A	2A 2B					
0-10	83	12	-	-	-	32							
10-20	284	11.3	-	-	-	59							
20-30	536	12.2	7	-	-	160							
30-40	518	6.6	8	2+2	-	235							
40-50	449	5.4	38	1+0	-	30					1		
50-60	1376	5.3	33	6+10	-	109	0+1						
60-70	835	5.1	40	3+11	-	97	0+1				1		
70-80	482	5.2	20	-	1	107	1+4	2	2	1		1	
80-90	30	4.1	no rims	-	3	93		3	1				1
90-100	-	-	-	-	-						1		
100-110	-	-	-	-	-				1				

Table 6.3. The decrease in the proportions of everted rims over 3 cm high in Batanes sites between 2000 BC and AD 600. See also the more detailed information on Anaro rim heights in Table 6.1, and the Savidug analysis by Alexandra de Leon, below.

Site and approximate date	No. everted rims	% over 3 cm tall
Torongan Cave, Itbayat, 2000 to 1200 BC	53	68
Reranum Cave, Itbayat, 2000 to 1000 BC	35	74
Sunget, Batan (1200-800 BC)	20	80
Savidug basal phase, Sabtang (1200-500 BC)	varies by spit	up to 83
Savidug jar burial phase, Sabtang (500-1 BC)	varies by spit	up to 30
Batan Island, Naidi Phase assemblages (200 BC–AD 500)	27 (Fig. 6.22)	23
Anaro 2, Itbayat, excavation and surface collection (500 BC-AD 500)	118	20
Anaro 6, Itbayat (AD 1-600)	134	10
Mitangeb, Siayan (AD 1-600)	51	8

The sequence of decorated (circle-stamped) pottery at Anaro

The situation with respect to decorated pottery in the Anaro 3 squares is most interesting. As can be seen in Tables 6.1 and 6.2, all decorated sherds are confined basically to the bottom half of each excavated square in this area, with first appearances always below 30 cm. Apart from a few rare incised sherds and one ribbed one, virtually all decoration in the Anaro 3 excavated squares is a standardised creation utilising rows of stamped circles, similar to the circle stamping at Sunget on Batan (described below), but also intriguingly different from Sunget in its preferred motifs. Enough large sherds, including rims, necks and bodies, survive from the excavated Anaro 3 squares to indicate that only one decorated vessel type existed during most of the time span represented by the deposits located in this area (Fig. 6.6 top), although this is certainly not true for the whole site. The Anaro 3 excavated rims, all everted and all over 3 cm tall, some with external lip grooves, have external lozenge or net-like lattice patterns built from single rows of circles. Upper bodies directly below the rims carry a pattern built from close-set parallel paired rows of circles, forming horizontal bands with low steps at intervals. We term this kind of vessel and decoration, in combination, *Anaro circle-stamped type 1*. Perhaps it was the signature style for the nephrite workers who clearly lived somewhere near this area of the site at the same time as this pottery was being made and the Anaro 3 deposits were being laid down. All Anaro circle-stamped type 1 rim sherds are everted, and no open bowls with direct rims appear to have been decorated in this exact style. Tables 6.1 and 6.2 present data on the distributions of circle-stamped pottery sherds in the analysed squares Anaro 3 (2004), 3A, 3B, 3C and 3F. In 3A especially, all the decorated sherds recovered, a total of 36, belong to Anaro circle-stamped type 1 vessels, all with everted rims.

However, the excavated layers at Anaro 3 clearly do not give the full sequence for the Anaro site as a whole, at least not according to the voluminous surface finds. There is another very common form of decoration which occurs in large quantities in the surface collections, and sometimes also very rarely at the base of the Anaro 3 excavated squares. This form of decoration, of single rather than parallel rows of circles creating especially meander and zigzag motifs, defines vessels of *Anaro circle-stamped types 2A* (everted rim vessels with round or carinated bodies) and *2B* (direct-rimmed open bowls). These motifs are quite different from the lozenge motifs and double rows of circles on the Anaro circle-stamped type 1 vessels. Many examples of circle-stamped type 2A and 2B vessels, all surface finds collected from below the eastern side of the hill (the opposite side from Anaro 3), are illustrated in the lower section of Fig. 6.6. In Table 6.1, columns headed 2A/2B, it can be seen that sherds of these two types occur only in very small numbers in the bottom layers of squares 3 (2004), 3B, 3C and 3F, suggesting a temporal priority for Anaro circle-stamped type 2A/2B vessels over the younger Anaro circle-stamped type 1.

Fig. 6.7 shows surface collected examples of a third class of rims, classified as *Anaro circle-stamped types 3A* (everted) and *3B* (direct), again all collected from the lower slopes of the north side of Anaro Hill, where remnants of early layers now destroyed have slid down and come to rest. These form a category of stamped circle designs which are neither of circle-stamped types 1 nor 2, so are hence defined as a kind of residual entity, but one that may be significant nevertheless. Absolutely no sherds of Anaro circle-stamped type 3 were found in the Anaro 3 excavated squares.

To summarise, three design styles of circle-stamped pottery with associated vessel types can be identified for Anaro, the first two being successive in time, as follows:

1. (Younger) This consists of the linked lozenge and double-row-of-circle designs that characterise the Anaro 3 excavated squares, and apparently the phase of the most intensive nephrite working at Anaro (Fig. 6.6 top). As noted, this style is termed Anaro circle-stamped type 1, and all recovered vessels have everted rims.

2. (Older) This consists of the single-row-of-circle open meander and zigzag designs that occur basally in very small numbers in the Anaro 3 excavated squares, mostly towards the base in Anaro 2, and very commonly in surface collections from AN2 and AN5 (Fig. 6.6 lower). This style incorporates Anaro circle-stamped type 2A (everted rim) and 2B (direct rim) vessels.

3. (Equivocal chronology, but probably older than Anaro circle-stamped type 1) This consists of unique designs, most so far found on single sherds found only on the surface at Anaro. Some of the multiple-row-of-circle designs, such as the two labelled A and B in Fig. 6.7, are paralleled very closely at Sunget on Batan and the Savidug Dune Site on Sabtang, both c.1200-800 BC. This style is present on Anaro circle-stamped type 3A (everted rim) and 3B (direct rim) vessels.

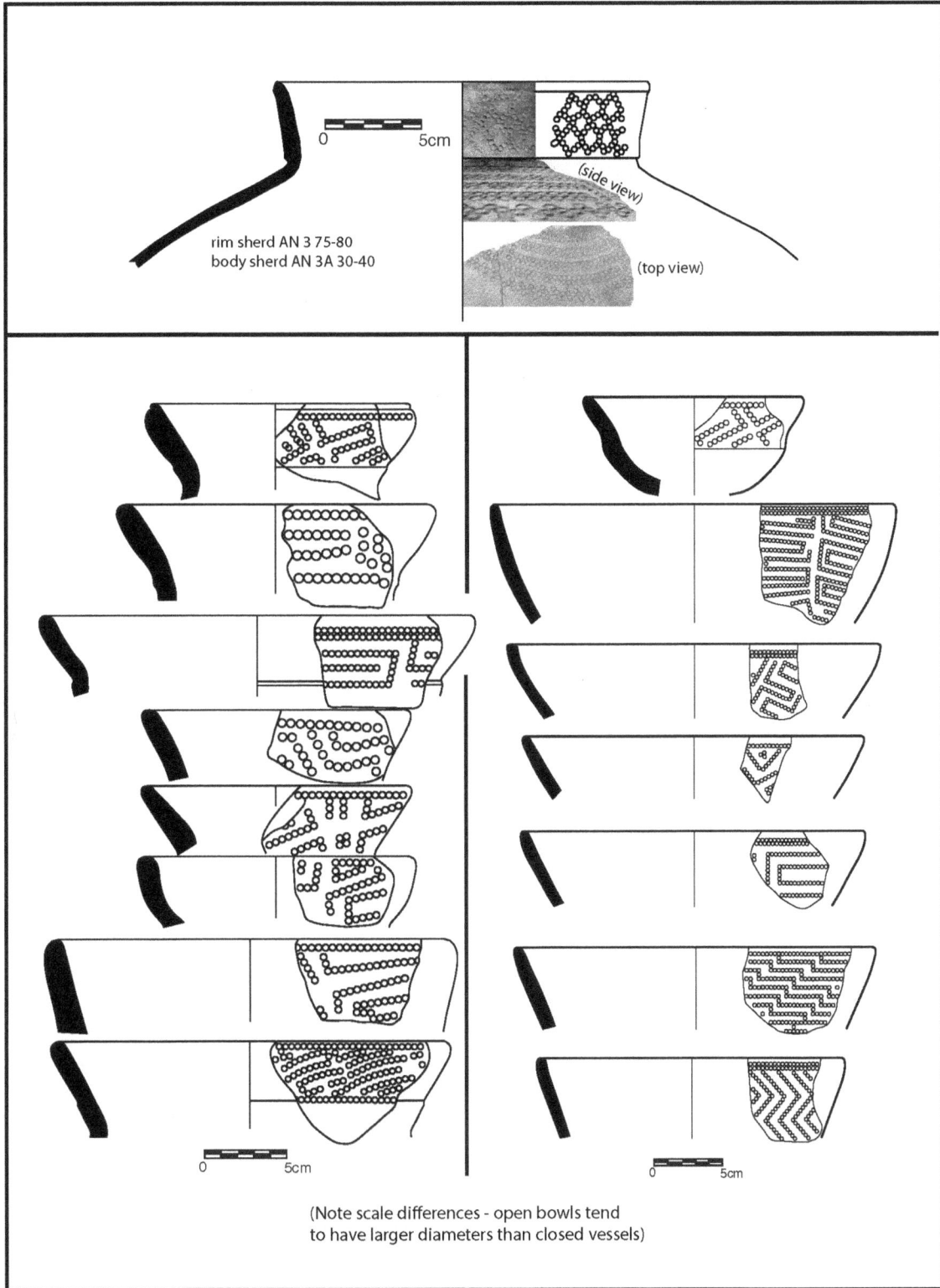

Figure 6.6. Top: reconstruction of an Anaro circle-stamped type 1 vessel, the type found in close association with nephrite working in the lower layers of Anaro 3. Lip diameter 21 cm. Bottom: surface finds of rims of Anaro circle-stamped types 2A and 2B, with rectangular meander designs.

Source: Peter Bellwood.

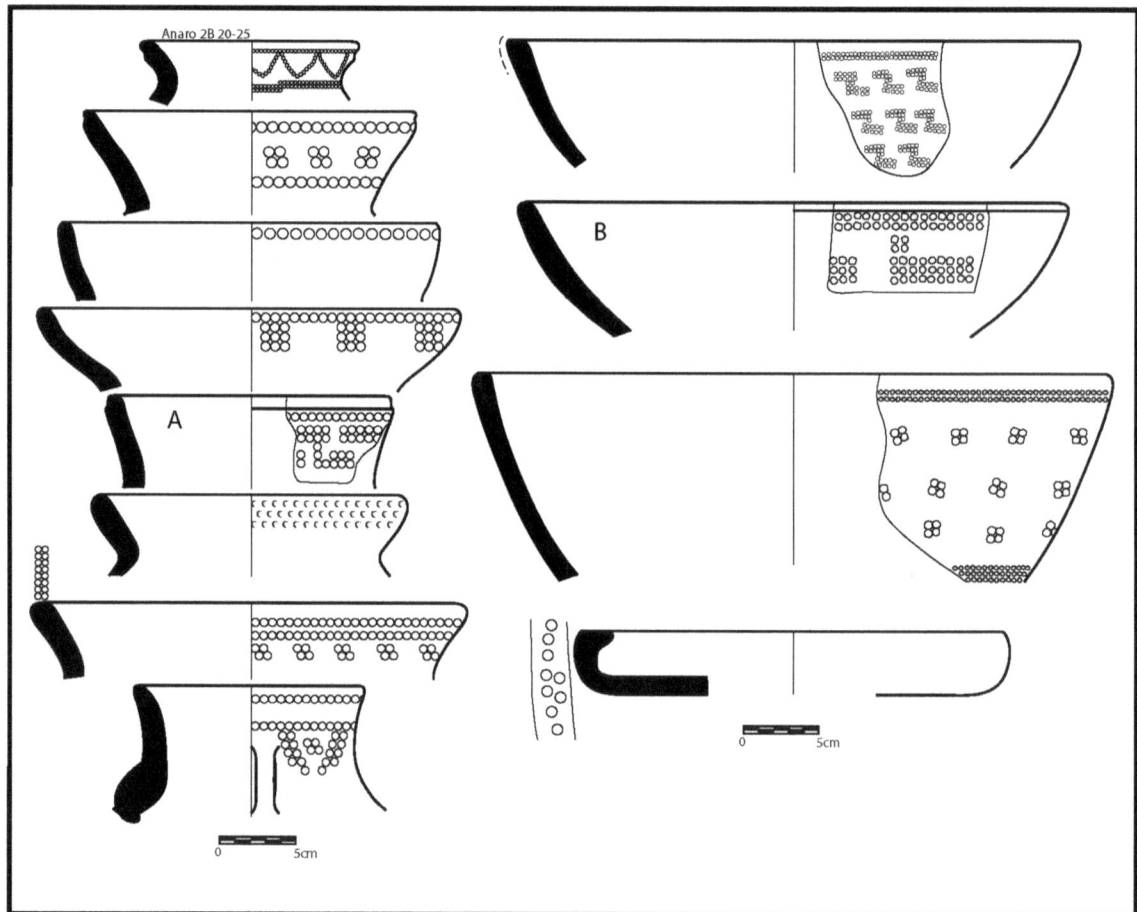

Figure 6.7. Surface finds of rims of Anaro circle-stamped types 3A and 3B, with varied designs. Fifth down on the left hand side is paralleled in the Sunget assemblage from Batan. The example at top left was excavated in Anaro 2.

Source: Peter Bellwood.

One implication of the above distribution is that the surviving excavated archaeological layers on the terraces and top of Anaro contain pottery dating only to the past 3000 years at the most, given the rarity of types 2A and 2B and the total absence of type 3A and 3B sherds in the excavations. Once-existing older layers and their contained pottery were perhaps eroded off these areas prior to this date. These older materials can now be found only as surface finds down the hill slopes.

As will be discussed below, "phallic" shaped lugs are common in surface collections from Anaro (Fig. 6.8) and are sometimes decorated with the same stamped circle motifs as Anaro circle-stamped type 2A and 2B vessels. Their rarity in the excavated layers in the Anaro 3 squares is therefore not surprising (only one was found), since they may be older in date. The single human figurine arm from the base of Anaro square 3F has tattoo decoration of rows of single circles (Fig. 6.9 B), relating it to the Anaro circle-stamped types 2A and 2B rather than the Anaro circle-stamped type 1 vessels.

The Anaro 2 pottery

Anaro 2 was only a 3x1 m excavation, quite shallow, and contained what appeared to be mixed deposits (doubtless cultivated) above and below a single C14 date of AD 53-238 (Table 6.4). The sherds in general are very small and eroded, with low average weights. Most of the occupation deposit that once existed here has been eroded away down the side of the hill, and in the fields cleared for cultivation below the Anaro 2 excavation in 2004 we found large numbers of quite large rims, decorated sherds, stone adzes and pieces of slate. Anaro 2 has a mixed assemblage of decorated sherds, unlike the far more homogeneous Anaro 3, with Anaro circle-stamped type 1 and 2A/2B sherds represented throughout. Anaro 2 is thus unlikely to represent a single phase of occupation. However, the Anaro circle-stamped type 1 rims do appear to have a higher stratigraphic centre of gravity than the Anaro circle-stamped type 2 rims (Table 6.4), and this situation in general accords with that in Anaro 3. For instance, 10 of the 15 Anaro circle-stamped type 2A/2B rims occur below the C14 dated level of AD 53-238.

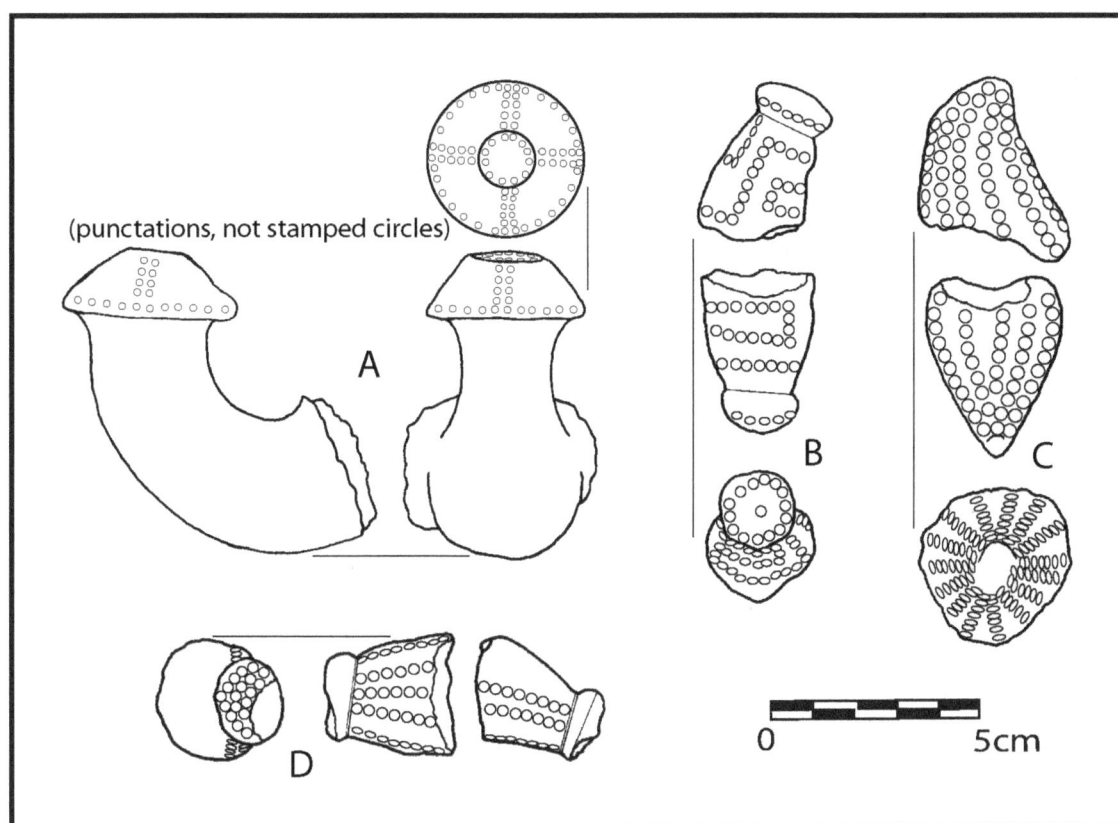

Figure 6.8. Examples of decorated pottery appendages from Anaro, all surface finds.

Source: Peter Bellwood.

Table 6.4. Pottery distribution by 10 cm spit at Anaro 2. For the Anaro circle-stamped type 1 vessels, the first figure refers to everted rim sherds with lozenge (fishnet) decoration, the second following a + sign to body sherds with stepped double lines of circles.

Anaro 2	Cal. C14 date	Body sherd number (Excavation squares Anaro 2A and 2B only)	Body sherd average weight	% everted rims ove	Circle-stamped types		Incised sherds
					1	2A 2B	
0-10		767	4.8	29	0+2		1
10-20	AD 53-238	2879	3.9	9	0+1	5	1
below 20		1959	3.7	18	1+1	10	1

terra australis 40

The Anaro 6 pottery

Anaro 6 was a 1 by 1 m excavation in a cave that produced a large amount of pottery, from the surface down to about 120 cm, very similar to that from Mitangeb on Siayan Island (to be described below). Anaro 6 has similar corrugated rims to Mitangeb, but like Mitangeb lacks vessel knobs and figurines, nephrite and slate. Four Anaro circle-stamped type 1 decorated body sherds were found, but in a total of 2381 body sherds these are rather negligible. Interestingly, three monochrome Chinese sherds (Song or Ming, probably) were also found between 30 and 60 cm. It is not clear how the latter relate to the date of the assemblage as a whole, given that absolutely no Chinese sherds were found at Mitangeb. Anaro 6 clearly does not have a great deal of stratigraphic integrity and average sherd weights in fact become greater with depth (Table 6.5), suggesting perhaps a degree of stratigraphic inversion reflecting erosion and redeposition inside the cave of an uphill deposit from the surface downwards.

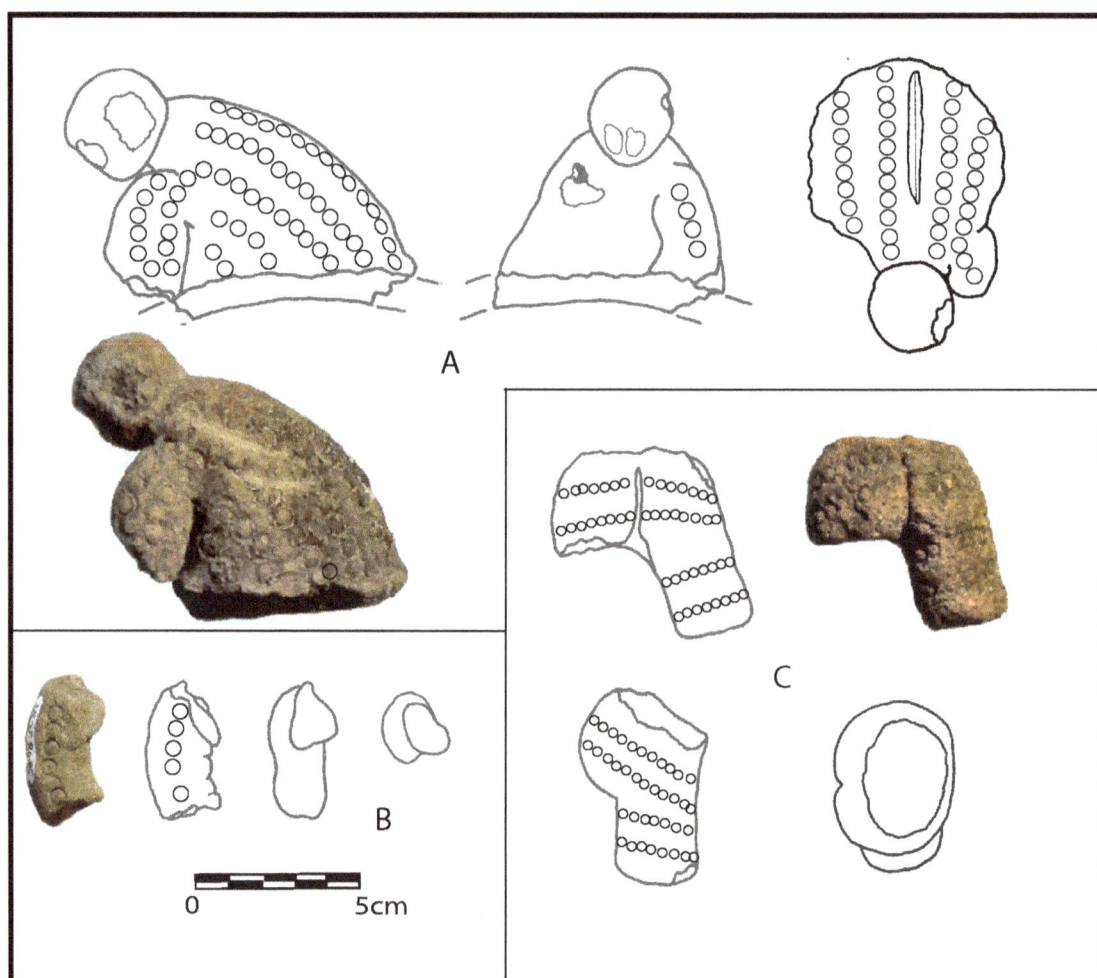

Figure 6.9. Decorated human figurine fragments from Anaro. A was clearly affixed to a pot as a handle (surface find). B is an arm similar to that attached to A, excavated from Anaro 3F 80-85 cm, and thus perhaps 2500-3000 years old. C is a tattooed buttocks area and upper right leg (surface find).

Source: Peter Bellwood and Cathy Fitzgerald.

Table 6.5. Pottery distribution by 10 cm spit at Anaro 6.

Anaro 6	Body sherd number	Body sherd average weight	Circle-stamped type 1	Chinese
0-20	140	6.4	1	
20-30	285	6.3		
30-40	129	8.2		1
40-60	115	8.4	1	2
60-70	258	7.8	1	
70-80	277	10.5		
80-90	385	7		
90-100	426	10.1	1	
100-110	228	10.9		
110-120	119	9.2		
120-130	22	6.6		

The Mitangeb pottery (c.AD 1-600)

The reconstructable rims excavated from Mitangeb, with sufficient circumference to determine diameter and rim height, are illustrated in Figs 6.4 (bottom right) and 6.10. It is obvious that there are two classes in terms of rim diameter, one about 12 cm across the mouth and perhaps for storing liquids, the other about 16 cm. The corrugated rims shown in Fig. 6.10 all belong to the smaller diameter group. Most of these vessels have short everted rims – only 18% are longer than 2 cm and only 8% longer than 3 cm. This distinguishes this assemblage very clearly from the earlier and taller rims from sites such as Torongan, Reranum, Savidug on Sabtang and Sunget on Batan.

The remarkable similarity with contemporary vessels from Anaro suggests that the Mitangeb pottery was perhaps taken to Siayan from Itbayat, containing food and water for use on the island by groups engaged in some exploitative activity such as fishing or catching turtles. Surprisingly, the whole Mitangeb assemblage has only one example of a direct-rimmed open serving bowl, shown in Figure 6.4. Such vessels are very common in sites on the larger islands, and this situation may indicate that elegant food serving was not considered a priority in the difficult circumstances of life on Siayan.

Mitangeb is of great interest because it has absolutely no examples of full circle stamping, apart from the rather different horseshoe stamps shown on the top left sherd in Figure 6.10. Red slipping is present, as it is through the whole Batanes ceramic sequence, but it is also quite rare in this site – Figs 6.4 and 6.10 show only two red-slipped rims, one corrugated. Figure 6.10 also shows a corrugated foot ring from a surface location below Anaro 2, together with some excavated examples from Anaro 3 and 6. The foot ring is added to show that such vessels sometimes had them, even though none were found at Mitangeb.

At this point it can be noted that the Mitangeb site offers a clear and unambiguous time horizon lasting for a short period during the early first millennium AD, perhaps AD 1-600, by which time circle stamping was completely absent, but corrugated rims identical to those in the middle layers at Anaro 3 were present. Mitangeb also has no Taiwan slate or nephrite artefacts. Anaro 6 has almost identical pottery, again with corrugated rims, but almost no circle stamping and no nephrite. Whether this apparent absence of nephrite at this time reflects reality, or just small sample size, remains unclear, and perhaps much should not be made of this observation. There is actually no reason to assume that nephrite movement ceased at this time.

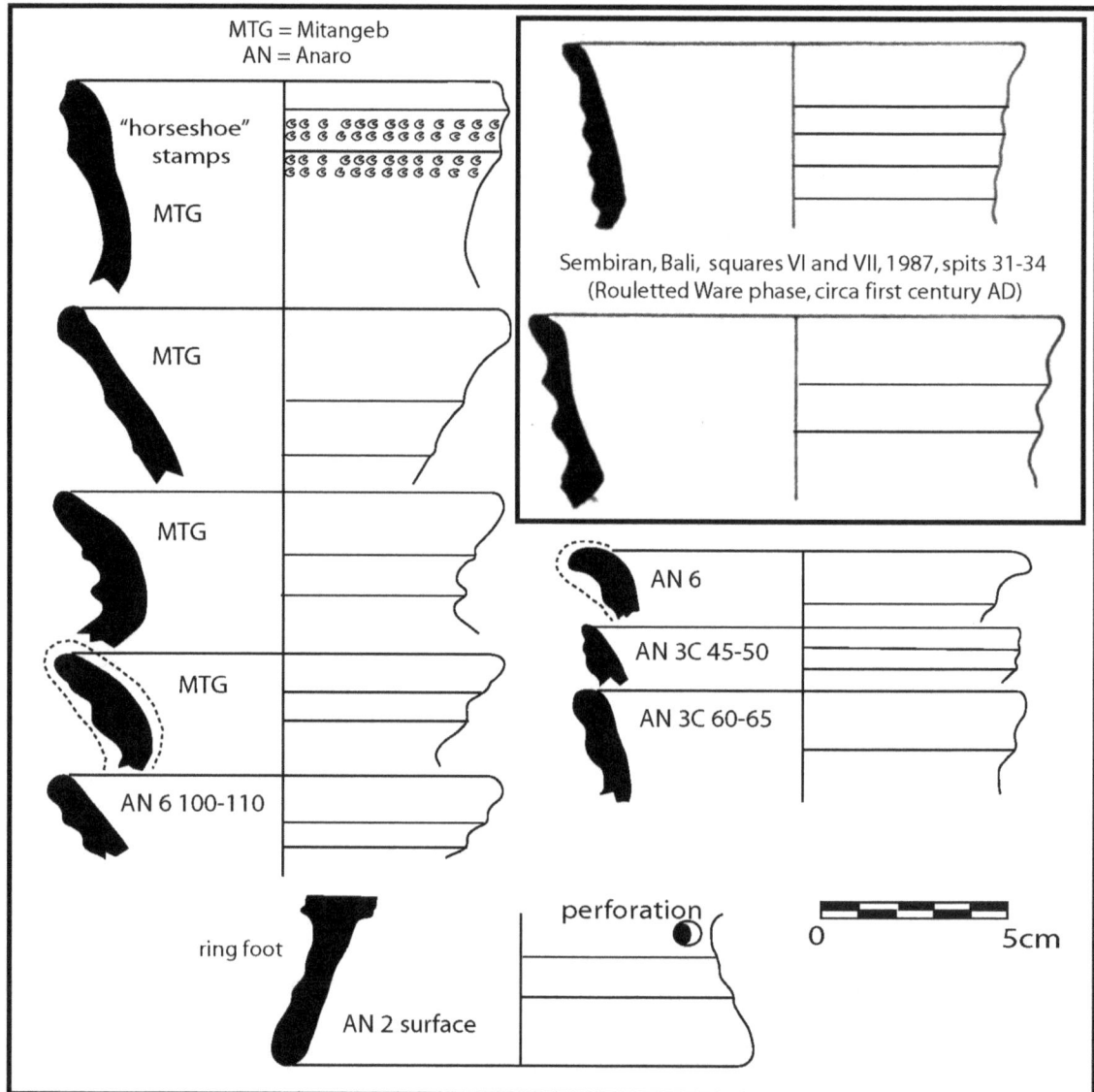

Figure 6.10. Left side: Mitangeb and Anaro corrugated rims, all 12 cm diameter and probably from water jars. Dotted lines around rims = red slip. Right side: rims and a whole pot from Sembiran, North Bali, from Ardika 1991, Fig. 5.4.

Source: Peter Bellwood.

The corrugated rims, in fact, require a further commentary since they could be very significant markers of a time range between AD 1 and 500. They occur in the early Indic-contact phase sites of Sembiran and Pacung in northern Bali, dating generally to around 2000 years ago (Ardika and Bellwood 1991), and a series drawn in the unpublished PhD thesis of I Wayan Ardika (1991, page 98) are reproduced here in Figure 6.10. More have been recovered from these two very important sites during current research by Ambra Calo (pers. comm.). Corrugated rims and even red-slipped and circle-stamped pottery are known also to come from the site of Ying-pu in western Taiwan, according to the collections of the National Museum of Natural Science in Taiwan, but in this case the dating is not clear.

The corrugated rim form is easy to recognise, and seemingly concentrated in its occurrence to layers in Batanes and Bali dating from the early first millennium AD. Is it a reflection of inter-island contact during the early period of trade stimulated by contacts with India? Corrugated rims of the exact Mitangeb and Sembiran types do not seem to be present in India, although it is impossible to check every museum collection and published report. But corrugation is present on rims and necks from the famous site of Arikamedu in Tamil Nadu (e.g. Wheeler et al. 1946: Fig. 27 no. 63b, and various examples in Figs 34 and 35). Whether this is all coincidence remains to be seen, but at least the resemblances are worthy of comment. Could it be that they reflect in some way the trade in Taiwan nephrite to be described by Hsiao-chun Hung in chapter 9 (allowing, of course, that Taiwan nephrite has not yet been positively identified in either India or anywhere in Indonesia, or for that matter in Anaro 6 or Mitangeb)?

The Anaro pottery surface finds

The surface finds made at Anaro have been quite staggering in quantity, spread like a carpet over the steep slopes that surround the limestone summit and especially visible whenever fields are cleared for planting. Many finds were made by the field teams, others by the family of Rodobaldo Ponce, owner of some of the land on the eastern side of the hill. Non-pottery artefacts such as adzes, nephrite and slate, together with spindle whorls, are described in chapters 7 to 9. This section is concerned only with the pottery sherds.

The richest lower-slope collection areas are labelled on Fig. 2.13 as AN1, AN5, AN2/4, and KX 2-4 (Kaxanggan is the land name for the western side of the hill). The most coherent and concentrated collections came from AN 2/4 and 5, the former partly fallen down from the terrace area excavated at Anaro 2 in 2004. Much of the material from AN 2/4 obviously resembles that from the Anaro 2 excavation, and some sherds from above and below, albeit weathered, look as if they could be from the same pots. Unfortunately, the shallowness and evident disturbance of the Anaro 2 excavation stratigraphy by cultivation makes it difficult to regard the material from here as a single chronological assemblage.

AN 5, however, was especially interesting because many of the rims from there resemble those from Torongan, Reranum and Sunget, i.e. sites with ages in excess of 3000 years. Some are shown in Fig. 6.4, at bottom left. These rims are tall, often internally concave, and some vessels had high foot rings, as at Reranum. Large numbers of decorated sherds were collected from AN 2/4 and 5, of which the vast majority belong to Anaro circle-stamped types 2A and 2B. Anaro circle-stamped type 1 vessels, so common at Anaro 3, are rare, but never totally absent. It is difficult to give statistics for surface collected materials since we never collected absolutely everything that was visible (car boot-loads would have resulted), and so the relationship between a collected sample size and the background universe cannot be precisely known.

Anaro pottery handles and other appendages

Mostly surface rather than excavated finds, the vessel handles and/or appendages at Anaro consist of the following categories:

1. Cylindrical projections, possibly handles, that have a variety of "phallic" shapes. Some of these have single rows of circle-stamped decoration like that on the Anaro circle-stamped 2A and 2B sherds (Figs 6.8 B, D; 6.11 middle row).

2. Human figurines with single rows of tattoo-like circle-stamped decoration (Fig. 6.9). An arm of one of these was excavated from Anaro 3F, 80-85 cm (Fig. 6.9B).

3. Handles, of both loop and lug forms, the former resembling handles from Sunget (1200-800 BC) (Fig. 6.11 top row). One is associated with circle-stamped decoration (top right).

4. A variety of blunt, fat and round projections, some with single rows of circle-stamped decoration (Fig. 6.8 C, 6.11 bottom row).

Chronologically, these appendages would appear in general to be older than 500 BC at Anaro, given the similarities in decoration with Anaro circle-stamped sherds of types 2 and 3. They are absent in the AD 1-600 site of Mitangeb, and contemporary or later Anaro 6 has only a single undecorated phallic knob, at 60-70 cm depth.

The Itbayat pottery sequence: Anaro and Mitangeb through time

To build up a cultural chronology for Anaro and Mitangeb, it is necessary to work from known and well-dated assemblages into the relative unknown. Thus, commencing with Mitangeb in the early first millennium AD, we have a well-defined phase with plain pottery with short everted rims, two categories of diameter (for liquid storage and cooking?), almost no red slip, no surface decoration, and a common presence of the important chronological marker category of corrugated rims. Nephrite and slate are both absent, although the Mitangeb excavation was small and there is no reason to assume a total absence of contact with Taiwan at this time. Allied with Mitangeb we also have most of the contents of Anaro 6, plus the middle layers of Anaro 3 (albeit rather indistinctly in this case). The four C14 dates that range from AD 400 to 900 from Anaro 3 and 3B presumably relate to this phase, despite the fact that all of them are in stratigraphic situations that suggest disturbance. All are on food residues from inside the bases of pots, by definition a vessel location that was never decorated, thus making it impossible to know if the sherds came from pots that ever carried decoration (this is a problem with all food residue AMS dates from pottery, for obvious reasons).

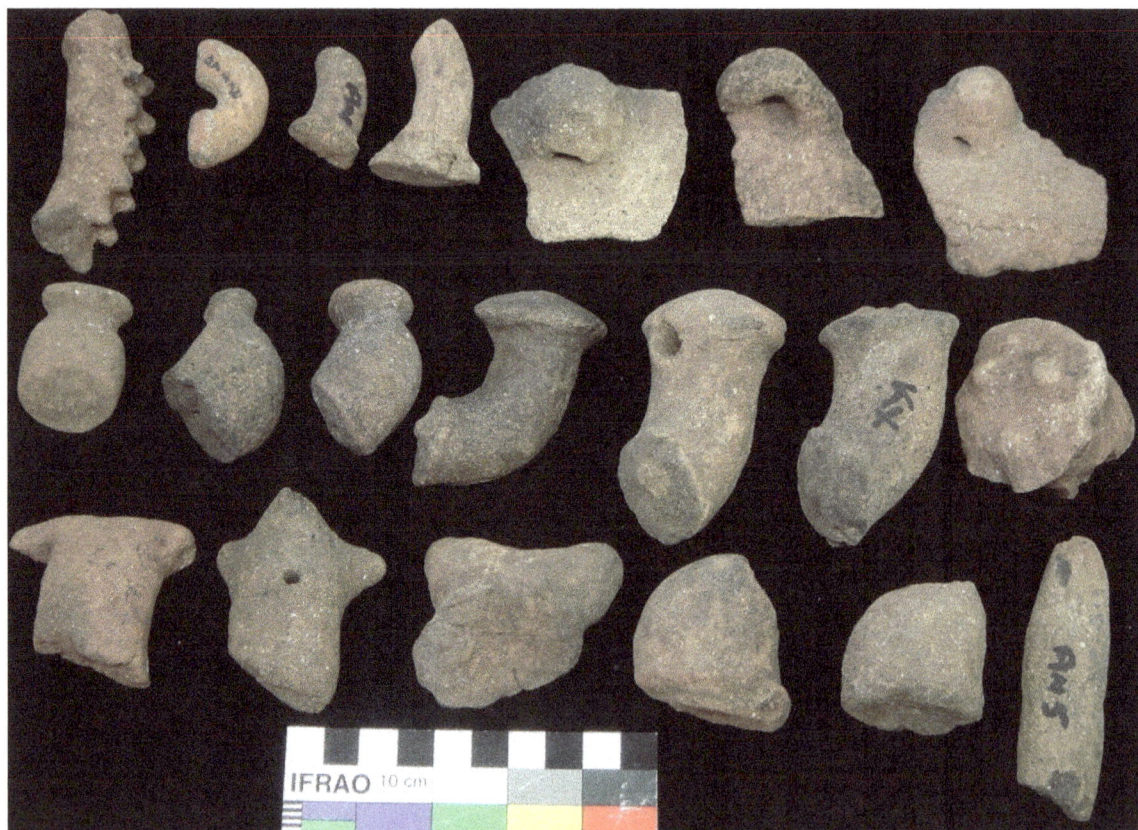

Figure 6.11. A range of pottery appendages from Anaro, all surface finds. Top row: handles (loop and lug), specimen on right on a circle-stamped sherd. Middle: knobs of roughly "phallic" shape, the two at right with subsidiary distal bumps. Bottom: angular, round and fat projections, presumably pottery handles.

Source: Peter Bellwood.

If we then move to the Anaro 3 excavated sequence, we come to an immediately older phase with Anaro circle-stamped type 1 pottery, nephrite and slate, associated with three C14 dates between 500 BC AD 1. This date range is supported by the date of 400 BC (Wk 21809, Table 5.1) for a green Fengtian nephrite *lingling-o* from Savidug Dune Site on Sabtang Island, probably similar to ones that the nephrite debitage suggests were being made at Anaro. Other *lingling-o* dates from Thailand and Vietnam also fall between 400 BC and AD 1 (Hung et al. 2007).

Prior to this phase, with its typical sherds of Anaro circle-stamped type 1, comes an even earlier phase with the sherds of Anaro circle-stamped types 2A and 2B, and presumably also types 3A and 3B. Some of the latter (Fig. 6.7, sherds labelled A,B) have stepped decorative motifs very similar to those dated to c.1200 – 800 BC from Sunget on Batan and Savidug on Sabtang. The basal date of *c.*1000 BC from Anaro square 3 (2004) relates to this material.

Finally, a single sherd of fine cord-marked pottery was found in surface collections from Anaro, although no occupation level that belongs to this period has yet been found in the excavations. It is similar in fabric and temper to fine cord-marked sherds from Middle Neolithic eastern Taiwan, but future study is needed to confirm its source.

The above observations allow an overall ceramic chronology for Itbayat to be formulated, following on from the discussion in chapter 5:

1. Phase 1, outer limits 2500 to 1000 BC: plain pottery of the types present at Torongan and Reranum Caves. Fine cord-marked sherds were still present at Reranum and possibly Anaro. Red slip was common.

2. Phase 2a, outer limits 1300 to 500 BC: circle-stamped pottery appears at Anaro, initially of types 2 and 3 defined above. Baked clay figurines and spindle whorls (chapter 7) were also present at this time, according to their circle-stamped decoration. Taiwan nephrite and slate were probably present.

3. Phase 2b: outer limits 500 BC to AD 1: Anaro circle-stamped type 1 vessels. Taiwan nephrite and slate were now being worked at Anaro.

4. Phase 3, outer limits AD 1 to 1200: Mitangeb and Anaro plain ware, with no surface decoration at all and no appendages. Corrugated rims are present, as in early Indic contact phase sites in Bali. Iron appeared, but nephrite and slate are not so far reported.

5. Phase 4, commencement AD 1200: plain wares with short rims became universal, as in the top 50 cm in the Anaro 3 excavated squares. Chinese imports and glass beads also belong in this phase.

The Sunget pottery, Batan Island, 1200 to 800 BC

The two Sunget sites (Top and Main Terraces), located on the ridge above Mahatao township on Batan, were excavated three times, in 2002, 2003 and 2004, as described in chapter 3. The materials recovered on each occasion were clearly part of a single assemblage, and identical to the materials recovered by the Kumamoto University team in the road cutting immediately below the Main Terrace in 1982. These two Sunget localities, as well the road cutting location, were occupied only for a short time between 1200 and 800 BC, when the present town site of Mahatao was occupied by a marine bay. This was about 1500 years before the major Iraya eruption that filled the bay and provided the large area of flat land upon which Mahatao township sits today. Since about 800 BC, the Sunget Ridge has only been used for agricultural purposes, not occupation, and this means that the whole assemblage from 1982 onwards can be ascribed to one short phase of prehistoric activity.

The pottery discovered at Sunget in 2004 was essentially identical to that recovered in 2002-3, described in Bellwood et al. 2003 (pp. 151-3 and Figs 11-15). Within the Batanes Islands, its closest relationships in shape, but not decoration, are with the assemblage from Reranum Cave on Itbayat, particularly in its preferences for tall rims (80% over 3 cm high – see above) on restricted vessels, and for quite tall ring feet. Sunget, however, unlike Reranum, lacks sherds of cord-marked pottery.

The Sunget pottery (Figs 6.12 to 6.14), like that from Torongan and Reranum, was probably once mainly red-slipped, to judge from surviving traces on sherds. The profiles shown are virtually identical to those published by Koomoto (1983: Figs 15-17) and are dominated by globular vessels with tall everted rims, the majority being internally concave. The Japanese team also published a number of loop handles and phallic-like appendages, similar to those from the contemporary occupation at Anaro on Itbayat. There are also a few carinated body sherds, flat-topped or knobbed lids, and open bowls decorated with multiple-rowed zones of Z-shaped stamped circle motifs, paralleled but rare at Anaro and Savidug Dune Site. Koomoto (1983) reconstructed some of these open bowls as being on pedestals, and some of the globular restricted vessels were also on ring feet. The stamped circle decoration was originally filled with a white substance (Fig. 6.13), either clay or lime. One example from an incised sherd was identified by geologist Alan Watchman as white clay, presumably added deliberately by the potter.

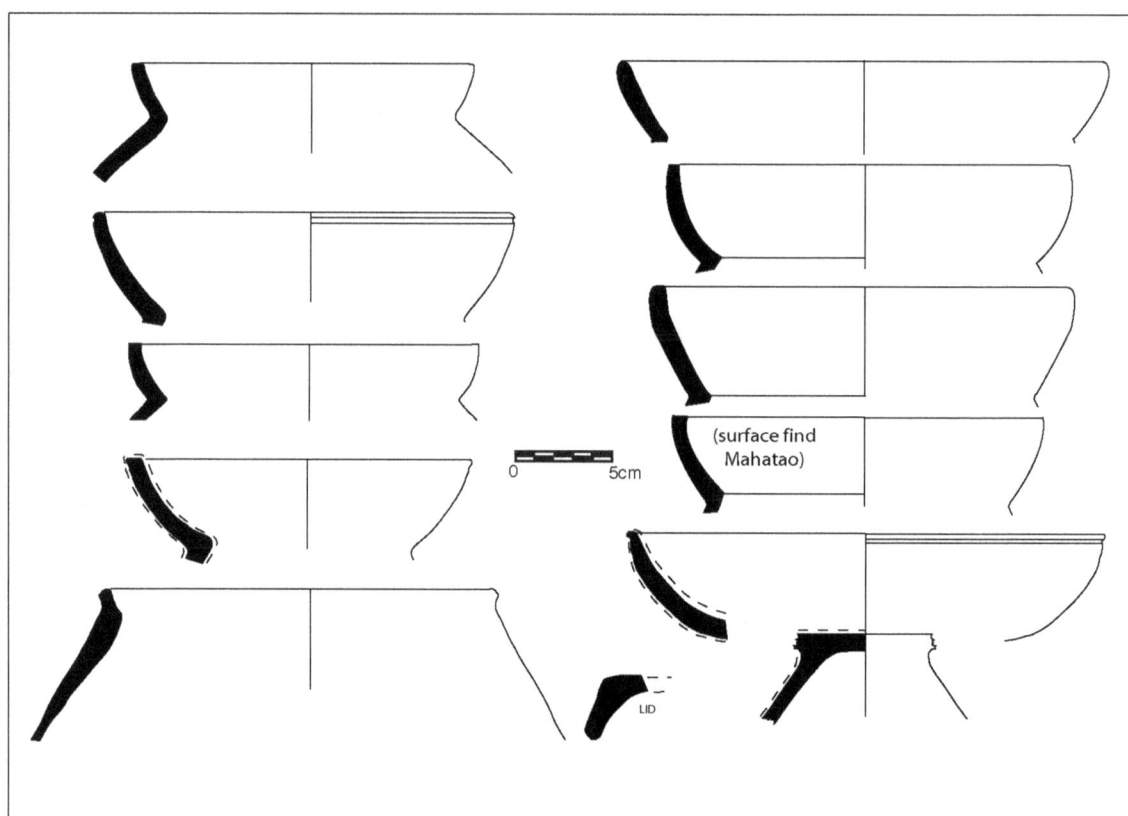

(surface find Mahatao)

0   5cm

LID

Figure 6.12. Profiles of Sunget pottery excavated between 2002 and 2004, from the Top and Main Terraces. Dotted lines indicate visible red slip, although most might have been slipped originally.

Source: Peter Bellwood.

Some further points about the Sunget pottery are worthy of note. Firstly, several vessels, both restricted and unrestricted, have a shallow groove just below the outer edge of the lip (Fig. 6.12), a feature paralleled in much of the pottery from the contemporary lower layer of Savidug. There are also many everted rims that are internally concave, like many of the rims from Reranum (Fig. 6.3). As noted, there is no cord marking at Sunget, and therefore the assemblage must post-date the period of cord-marking dominance in southeastern Taiwan, a dominance that was already on the wane by 2000/1500 BC according to the evidence from Chaolaiqiao (Hung 2005, 2008). The corollary of this is that Sunget does not have occupation from the initial settlement phase on Batan. Such might lie beneath the deep ash mantle that buried the original coastal Neolithic settlement in Mahatao itself, just downhill from the Sunget sites (see discussion in chapter 3), but this material was too deeply buried for us to reach by excavation.

The lower occupation in Savidug Dune Site, Sabtang Island (1200 BC to AD 1)

As noted in chapter 4, the lower cultural layer in the Savidug Dune Site can be divided into

a) an earlier phase associated with red-slipped and rare circle-stamped pottery, with Sunget and basal Anaro parallels, dated 1200 to 700 BC;

b) a later phase, dated *c.*700 BC to the early centuries AD, associated with jar burial, Taiwan nephrite, and possibly copper working.

Figure 6.13. Left: circle-stamped sherds from the Sunget excavations. The top two are open bowl rims, the lower red-slipped piece appears to abut a carination. The middle sherd still has white infill. Right: two loop handles (one red-slipped) and a lid knob from Sunget.

Source: Peter Bellwood.

Savidug Dune Site was uninhabited through most of the first millennium AD, but occupation started again in late prehistory, with a different local pottery style associated with Chinese ceramic imports and intriguing evidence for a heavy impact on reef resources (chapter 12). This later pottery assemblage will be described separately towards the end of this chapter.

The basic distribution of sherdage throughout most of the Savidug Dune Site excavations is shown in Table 6.6. The 2006 test trench had an upper cultural layer (layer 2) with very sparse pottery, then a rich lower cultural layer (layer 4) beneath the sterile sand layer 3. This lower assemblage contained many very large sherds and appeared to represent a relatively short period of cultural activity that was quickly buried under encroaching sand. The sherds excavated in 2006 from this lower layer are shown as a group in Fig. 6.15, and were stratified just above the radiocarbon date of *c*.1000 BC (Wk 19711, Table 5.1). The vessel forms are mostly red-slipped, and the Savidug sand dune appears to have been a favourable environment for preservation in this regard. Everted rims tend to be tall, and some have grooves externally just below the lip (Fig. 6.15 A, B, D, E, K), similar to the Sunget assemblage. There is also a small carinated red-slipped vessel (Fig. 6.15 L), and a red-slipped everted rim with an appliqué band around the external neck (Fig. 6.15 I), impressed repeatedly with what appears to have been a small round stick. We will meet these forms again in Sandy De Leon's analysis of Savidug rims (below). One sherd, Fig. 6.15 E, has horizontal parallel lines on its upper surface suggesting use of a slow wheel in manufacture.

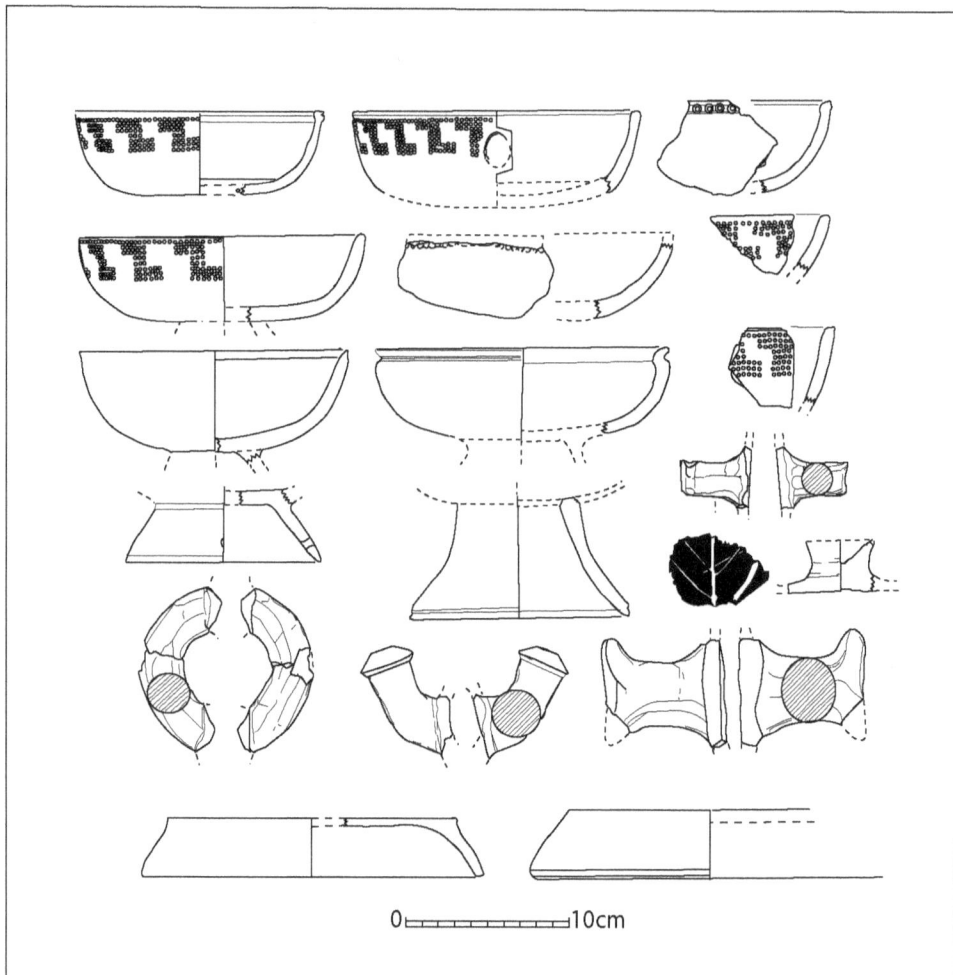

Figure 6.14. Open bowls with stamped circle decoration, handles, knobs and lids from Sunget.

Source: From Koomoto 1983, reproduced with permission.

Overall, the Savidug rims are similar in shape and size to those from Sunget, except in the rarity of circle-stamping and the absence of the everted and internally concave rim which dominates the Sunget assemblage. The total of four excavated circle-stamped sherds from Savidug are shown in Fig. 6.16. Sherds C (QR7-9 170-180 cm) and B (2006, 180 cm) are both from the basal layer in the site and carry the Z-shaped Sunget circle-stamped design, but since the circles are of different sizes they probably come from separate vessels. The same design occurs on the rim fragment D with a broken handle attachment from QR/7-9 170-180 cm, and this has the same profile as rim B. Rim A, a surface find, looks like an Anaro circle-stamped type 1 rim, except that the pattern is a zigzag rather than a lattice. Rim and handle combination E has double rows of stamped circles that might also be of the Sunget design. Overall, these few stamped sherds indicate occupation at Savidug throughout the general life span of circle stamping in Batanes, from perhaps 1200 BC to AD 1. It is quite possible that some of the sherds were imported from Batan Island, since some appear similar to Sunget pottery fabrics in having quite dense small black inclusions.

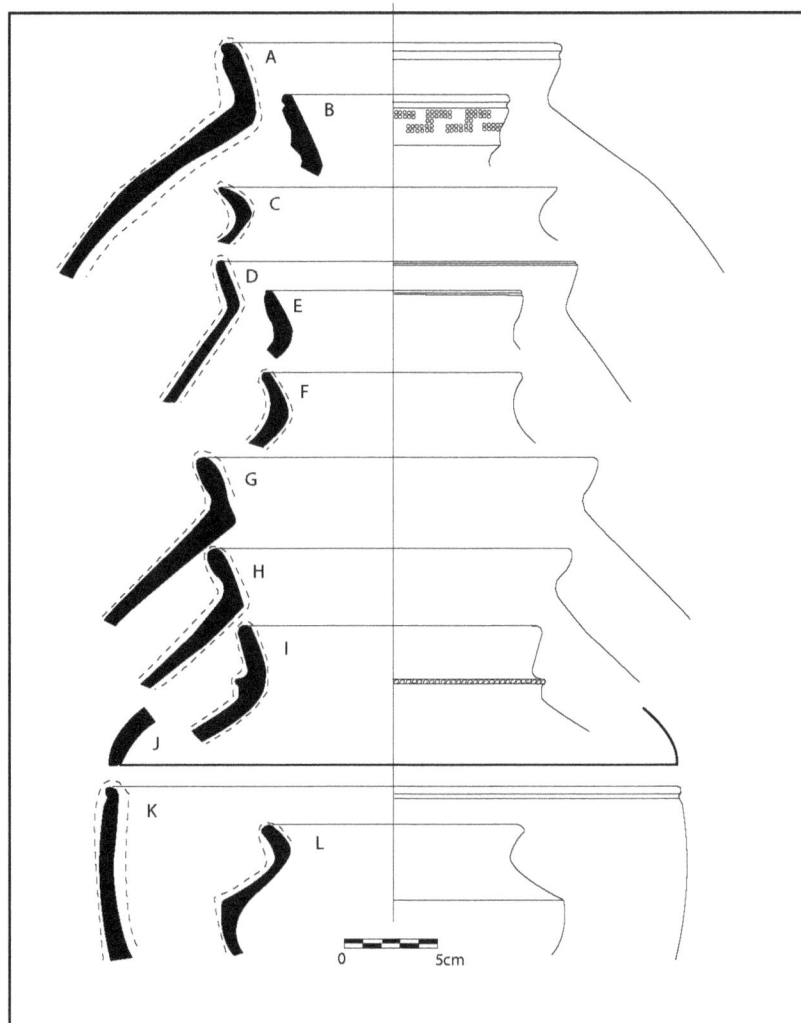

Figure 6.15. Vessel group excavated from layer 4 in the Savidug Dune Site test trench in 2006, stratified above a C14 date of c.1000 BC. Item B is also shown as Fig. 6.16 B.

Source: Peter Bellwood.

From the 2007 excavation, Trench K-N/27-29 had very limited remains from layer 4 (the lower cultural layer), which had here virtually disappeared. Trench QR/7-9 was much more prolific, and the pottery from here is described in more detail by Sandy De Leon below. Table 6.6 indicates that the pottery in layers 4 and 5 in QR/7-9 occurred with two sharp peaks in sherd numbers at about 120 and 170 cm. Average sherd weights at Savidug are quite high compared to those at Anaro, suggesting that protective burial was quite rapid in the soft sand dune environment. In

QR/7-9, the percentages of everted rims over 3 cm tall increase fairly regularly downwards from top to bottom of the lower cultural layer, placing this early Savidug assemblage between Sunget and Mitangeb in time from a typological perspective.

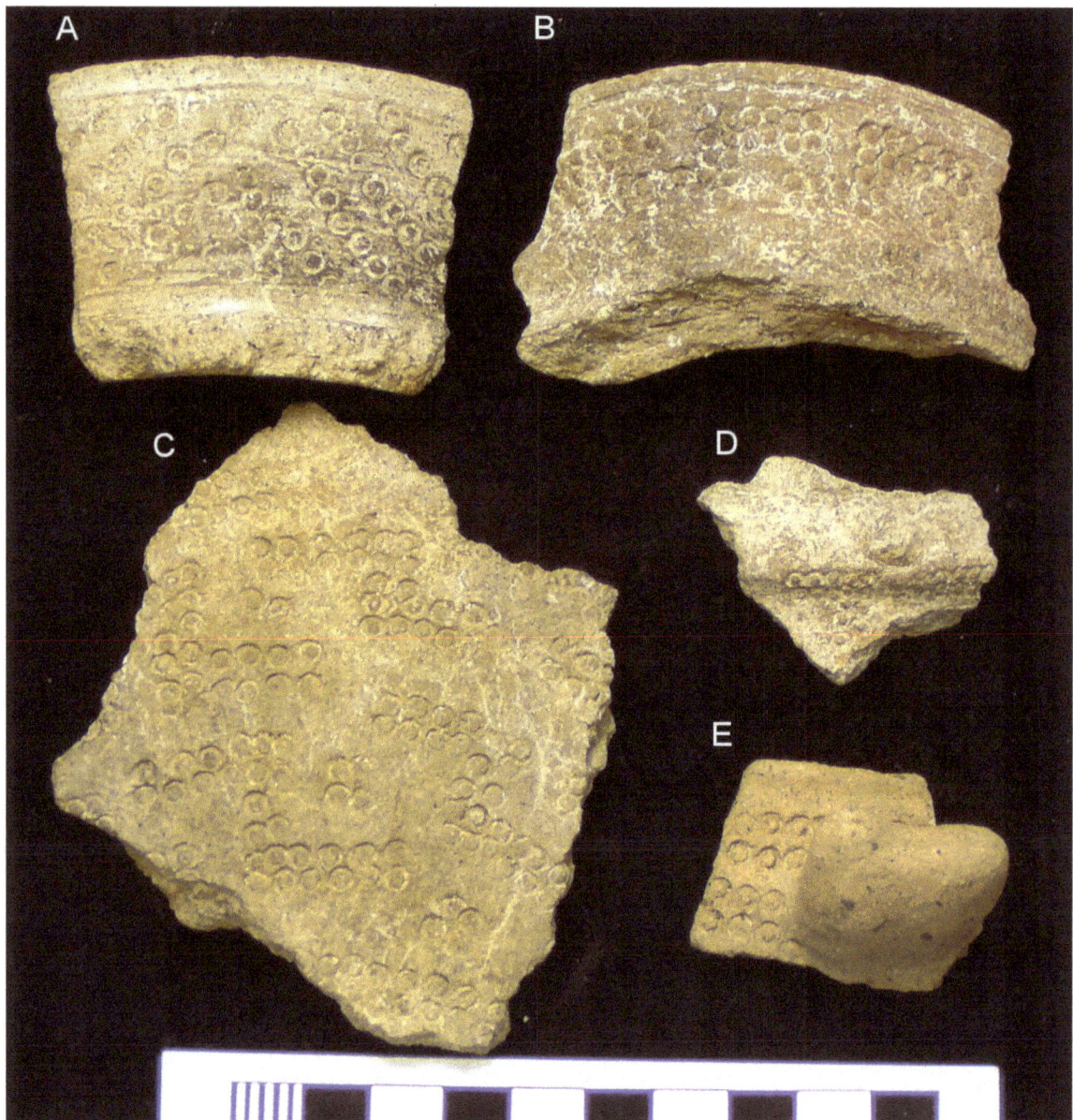

Figure 6.16. Circle-stamped sherds from the Savidug Dune Site. A: rim from road cutting with Anaro circle-stamped type 1 shape and pattern. B. Rim with Sunget-style decoration from the 2006 trench at 180 cm (basal layer 4). C: Body sherd with identical pattern from QR/7-9 170-180 cm. D: rim fragment with broken handle attachment, very similar to rim B, from QR/7-9 130-140 cm. E: surface find of an apparent bowl rim with a lug and decoration of double rows of circles.

Source: Peter Bellwood.

Savidug Dune Site and Anaro: A comparison of pottery attributes (by Alexandra De Leon)

In 2008, a University of the Philippines thesis on the pottery excavated in 2007 from Savidug Dune Site was completed by Alexandra De Leon, who compared 335 diagnostic sherds from layers 4 and 5 (lower cultural layer) in Savidug trench QR/7-9 with 250 sherds from the excavated square Anaro 3B on Itbayat. The objective of this research was to identify similarity or variation within and between the two assemblages in order to address issues of interaction between the two islands. The focus of the comparison was on rim sherds. First to be described is the Savidug sample.

Savidug

In Savidug trench QR/7-9, pottery occurred throughout the 130 cm thick lower cultural layer, dated to the first millennium BC, between 90 and 220 cm below the present ground surface (Table 6.6). Rim sherds from this sample were first of all refitted where possible, leaving rims belonging to 256 separate vessels for analysis. These rims can be categorised as belonging to bowls (Fig. 6.17, left side), hole-mouthed vessels (Fig. 6.18, left side), and jars with everted rims (Fig. 6.19, left side). Within the QR/7-9 lower cultural layer sample there are 30 bowl rims (12%), 10 hole-mouthed rims (4%) and 216 everted jar rims (84%).

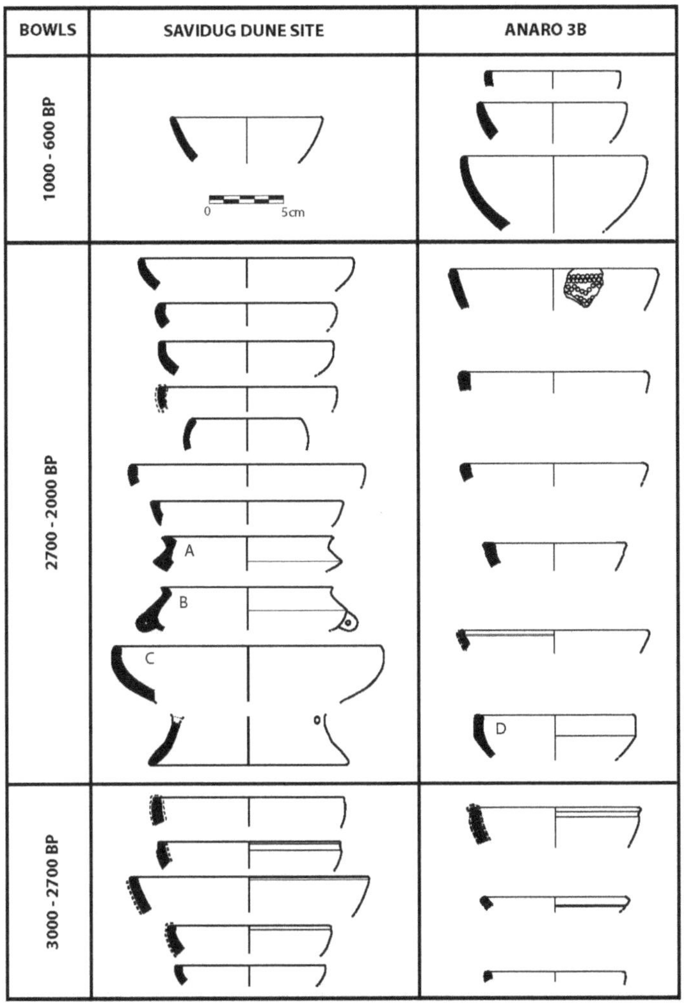

Figure 6.17. Bowl sections compared from Savidug QR/7-9 and Anaro 3B.

Source: Alexandra De Leon.

Table 6.6. Pottery distribution by 10 cm spit at Savidug Dune Site.

Depths cm	Test trench 2006 (2X1m)			A-C/9-11 (3x3 m)			K-N/27-29 (3x3 m)			QR7-9 2007 (3X1.75 m)				F1-G1/9-11 (3X2 m)
	Cal. C14 date	Body sherd number	Body sherd average weight gm	Area exc. m2	Body sherd number	Body sherd average weight gm	Body sherd number	Body sherd average weight gm	Cal. C14 date	Cal. C14 date	Body sherd number	Body sherd average weight gm	% everted rims over 3 cm tall	Body sherd number
0-20	Plough zone			Plough zone			353	8.3		Plough zone				51
20-30				9	1280	4.9	264	4.3						188
30-40							649	5.3						202
40-50		43	17.7	9	1543	6.6	953	4.8			240	14.3	0	414
50-60		15	16	6	4179	5.2	980	4.8		Layer 3, archaeologically sterile				
60-70		39	5.6	4.6	1422	6.2	280	3.5						430
70-80		25	4.8	3	663	5.0	181	6.7						
80-90		14	7.1	3	567	7.6	Layer 3, archaeologically sterile				210	7.6	0	82
90-100		2		2	221	9.6					445	7.4	0	26
100-110	Layer 3, archaeologically sterile			1	115	17.3					1088	10.9	14	6
110-120				Archaeologically sterile							735	9.5	3	sterile
120-130											394	9.7	21	
130-140										560-390 BC	376	11.3	0	
140-150		322	6.4				11	30			323	11.4	44	
150-160		16	6.9				15	5.3			294	12.0	60	
160-170		156	19.1				29	6.9			968	9.7	27	
170-180		130	14.5				77	15.1			120	12.5	50	
180-190	1114-901 BC	8	7.5				Layer 5, archaeologically sterile							
190-200	Layer 5, archaeologically sterile													
200-210										360-50 BC	67	9.3	50	
210-220										1130-930 BC	28	5.0		

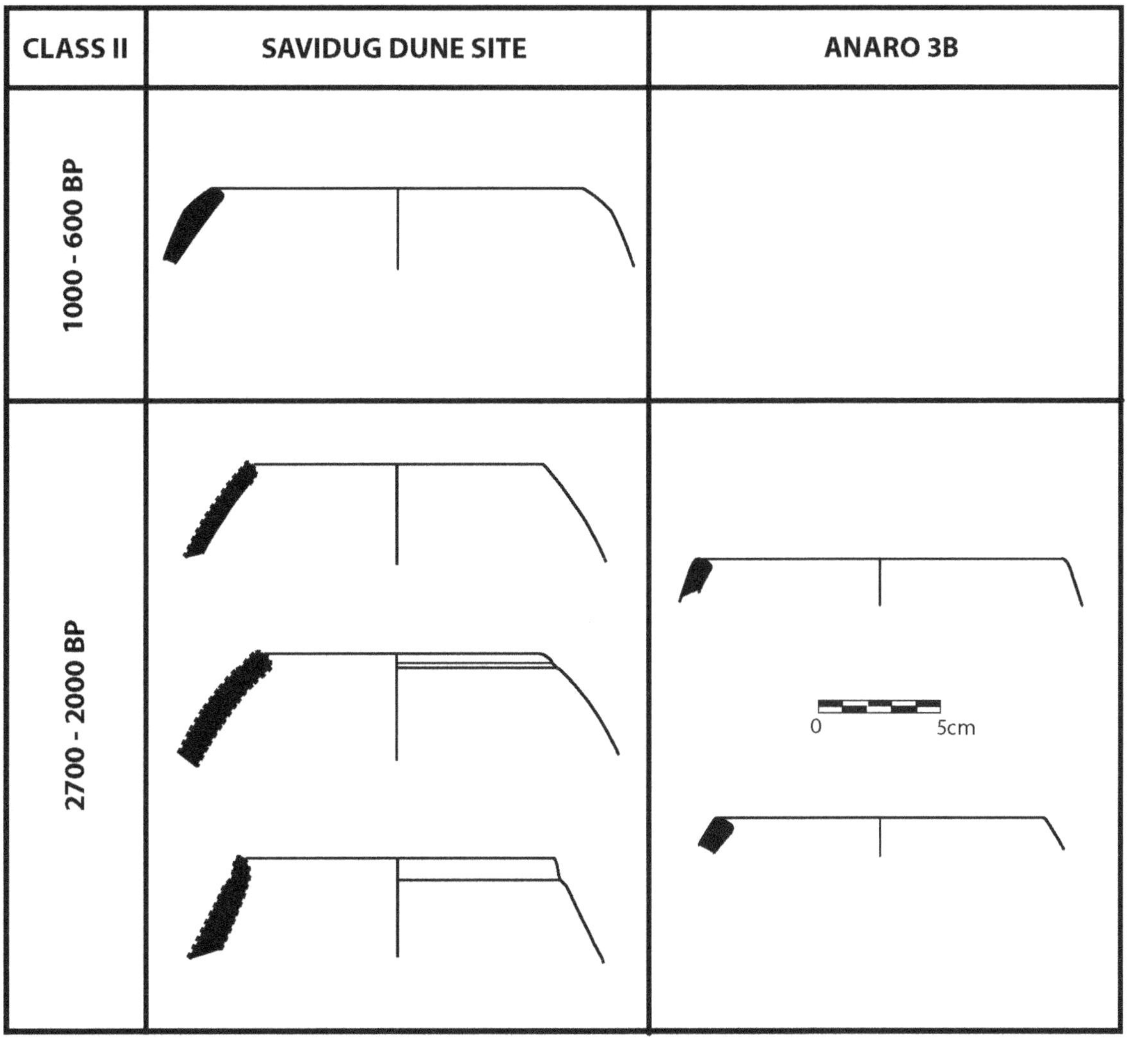

CLASS II	SAVIDUG DUNE SITE	ANARO 3B
1000 - 600 BP		
2700 - 2000 BP		

Figure 6.18. Hole-mouthed rim section compared from Savidug QR/7-9 and Anaro 3B.

Source: Alexandra De Leon.

Savidug bowl rims can be unrestricted (open), or restricted and carinated. Some bowls were probably on pedestals. The rim profiles of the open bowls are mostly parallel-sided and rounded at the lip, but below 140 cm they sometimes have outer grooves below the lips, like Sunget pottery. Open bowls vary in mouth diameter and can be grouped into small (11-12 cm) and large (17-26 cm) classes, the latter being in the majority. Red-slipping was used more frequently to finish vessels in the earlier spits. It continues in the upper spits, but polished and smoothed bowls here become more common.

Restricted and carinated bowls comprise only 3 specimens, found between 90 and 150 cm. Two are similar, with short, pointed and out-curving rims (6.17 A, B), but belonged to different vessels. One has a lug attached just below the carination (6.17 B). Both are 18 cm in mouth diameter. The bowl reconstructed as having a pedestal in Fig. 6.17 C is larger, at 27-28 cm diameter.

The second, hole-mouthed, form in the QR/7-9 pottery assemblage has an unthickened inverted rim which forms a round hole-mouth (N=10, or 4% of the assemblage) (Fig. 6.18). They occur only in the upper and middle portions of the QR/7-9 lower cultural layer, between 110 and 170 cm. Some of the earlier examples have an external groove below the lip, like the bowls (above), and again paralleled in the Sunget assemblage (although this kind of hole-mouthed vessel has not been recognised at Sunget).

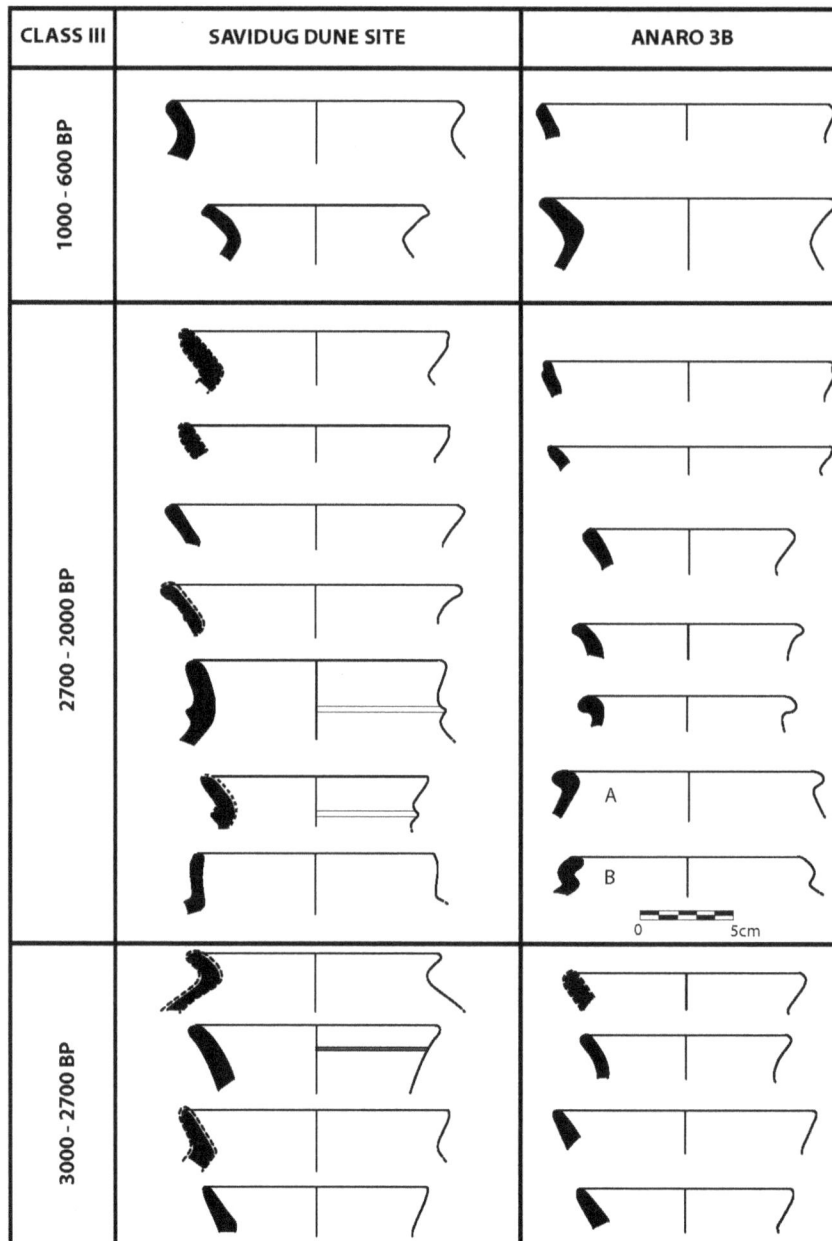

CLASS III	SAVIDUG DUNE SITE	ANARO 3B
1000 - 600 BP		
2700 - 2000 BP		
3000 - 2700 BP		

Figure 6.19. Jar rims compared from Savidug QR/7-9 and Anaro 3B.

Source: Alexandra De Leon.

In some cases, these hole-mouthed rims could have belonged to large carinated bowls, but such forms can no longer be reconstructed so they are identified as a separate class for the purposes of this analysis. Mouth diameters range from 8 to 17 cm, with the earlier ones tending to be larger than the later. Hole-mouthed vessels have a surface finish that is either red-slipped (60%) or polished black. Red-slipping is more common in the lower levels.

Everted jar rims (Fig. 6.19) are the most common form at Savidug, representing at least 216 vessels, or 84% of all rims from the lower cultural layer. They occur throughout from 90-220 cm, but are especially dense at the 110-130 cm level. Most rim profiles are unthickened and parallel, but a few also converge towards the lip. As with the other vessel forms, red-slipping is more common in the lower levels. The mouth diameters of these simple everted jar rims range from 9-25 cm, with no clearly differentiated categories, perhaps due to wide variation in function. External grooves below the lips also occur only in the lower half of the profile, below 140 cm.

One important variety of jar rim that is common at Savidug has an applied band around the external neck, in many cases impressed with what appears to have been a small round stick (as discussed above for the 2006 assemblage for the site) (Fig. 6.20). In QR/7-9 they occur in the upper part of the lower cultural layer above 150 cm, except for one from the 180-200 cm level. Many are red-slipped. It is interesting that the single example found in 2006 (Fig. 6.15 I) was also from the top of the lower cultural layer as excavated in that season, suggesting that this form was most favoured after c.700 BC.

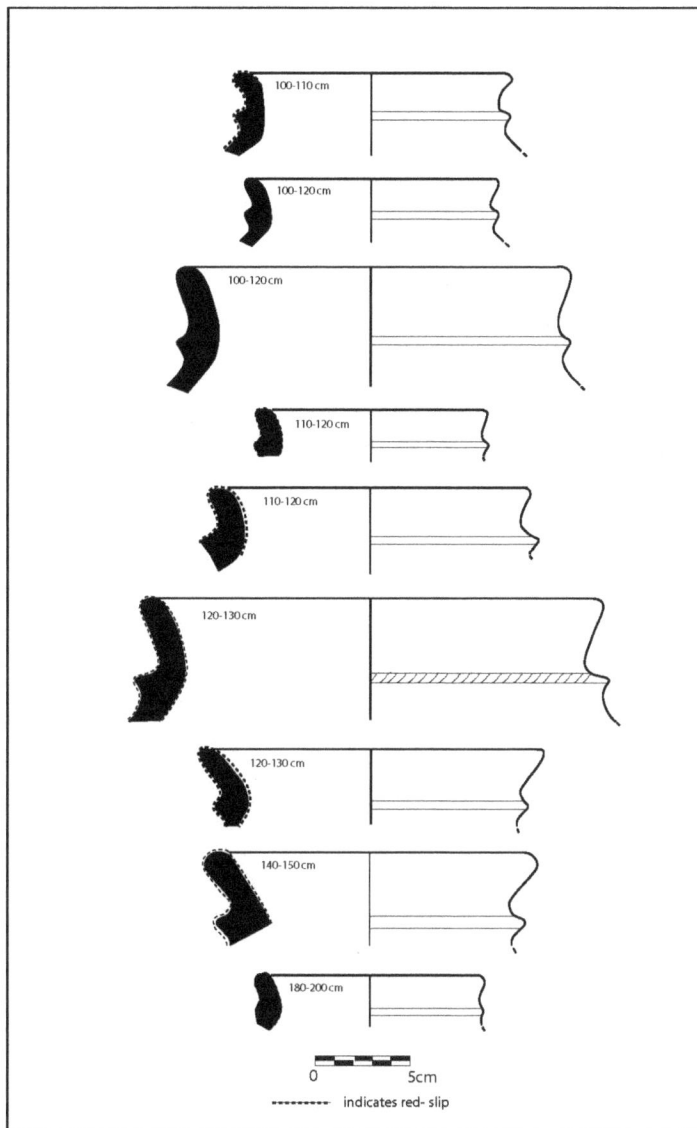

Figure 6.20. Jar rims with external applied bands from Savidug QR/7-9.

Source: Alexandra De Leon.

Rim heights for the total of 200 everted jar rims from QR/7-9 have been measured, and provide extra detail to the discussion presented above (Table 6.3). Using the percentages of rim heights over 3 cm per 10 cm spit, a statistic that is more informative than average rim height, we see the following trend with depth:

90-100 cm	14% (N=7)
100-110 cm	20% (N=20)
110-120 cm	31% (N=51)
120-130 cm	30% (N=30)
130-140 cm	48% (N=21)
140-150 cm	47% (N=17)
150-160 cm	59% (N=22)
160-220 cm	62% (N=21)

The lowest 60 cm has been treated as one spit to maintain a rough parity of sample size, but the general trend is still very obvious, and is paralleled almost exactly at Anaro (Tables 6.1 and 6.2).

There remains one very important sherd from QR/7-9 110-120, not analysed in Manila since it was sent to Canberra after the excavation in 2007. In is shown in Fig. 6.21, and is an inflected bulbous rim of what might have been a water jar, red-slipped on the exterior, slightly concave on the interior, and of a smooth pale brown fabric with a very fine temper. The red-slipping and fabric relate this vessel to the red-slipped carinated jar shown as Fig. 6.15 L, and several similar carinated sherds were found in the 2006 excavation, all with the pale brown fabric that appears to be foreign to the rest of the Savidug assemblage. The rim does not match any specific carinated sherd, but it is not difficult to imagine that it was once attached to a carinated pot like Fig. 6.15 L, at the top of a vertical spout. Should this seem far-fetched, two vessels of such a shape, from the site of Gunung Piring on Lombok Island, central Indonesia (Gunadi et al. 1978; Bellwood 2007: Plate 60), are likely to be contemporary with Savidug QR/7-9 and late first millennium BC in date. Although Gunung Piring yielded extended burials and Savidug has jar burials, the question arises whether this rather striking kind of red-slipped pouring vessel was widely traded in the islands of Southeast Asia. To determine this, we need analysis of pottery fabrics.

Anaro 3B

250 diagnostic sherds were studied from Anaro square 3B, excavated from 0-120 cm below the present surface. The sample includes 202 rims, 32 decorated body sherds, 8 carinated sherds, 7 foot rings and one ear/lug, belonging to at least 187 vessels. The basic vessel forms are the same as at Savidug - bowls, hole-mouthed vessels, and jars. Samples are shown down the right hand sides of Figs 6.17 - 6.19 for comparison with Savidug.

As mentioned in chapter 2, it was discovered after this analysis had commenced that the radiocarbon dates for Anaro 3B did not correlate with those from Anaro 3A, perhaps due to erosional and disturbance factors in the case of 3B. The Anaro 3B assemblage is therefore studied here mainly for comparative purposes with Savidug, rather than to establish chronological markers.

Bowl forms (Fig. 6.17) with direct rims make-up 20% of the Anaro 3B assemblage, as opposed to 12% at Savidug. They can, as at Savidug, be categorized as open bowls and (slightly) restricted and carinated bowls, and some were possibly on pedestals. They tend to have parallel-sided rims with mostly flat lips, although there is some variation. External rim grooves and circle-stamped designs tend to be concentrated in the lower spits, as already noted. The three carinated bowls from Anaro 3B, found between 60 and 70 cm, have flat lipped parallel-sided rims with slightly incurving tendencies (Fig. 6.17 D). All are polished and plain.

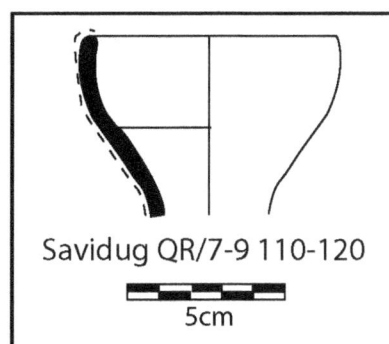

Figure 6.21. Bulbous spout of a vessel for holding liquids from Savidug Dune Site QR/7-9.

Source: Peter Bellwood.

Anaro 3B has only two potential examples of the hole-mouthed vessel form (Fig. 6.18), found in the middle spits between 65 and 80 cm. The everted jar rims (Fig. 6.19) from Anaro 3B belong to at least 139 vessels (either cooking pots or storage jars) that represent 71% of the analysed assemblage. Rims of this type are mostly out-curving, parallel-sided in profile and round lipped. Below 60 cm, however, some everted rims exhibit unique profiles, such as the squat and rounded and S-profiled rims shown as Fig. 6.19 A and B. Externally grooved rims are again restricted to the lower spits. The heights of the rims range from 1.0 to 5.0 cm, with an average of 1.96. However, short rims (under 1 cm) and tall rims (over 4-5 cm) occur only below 60 cm (see also Table 6.1).

A comparison of trends through time at Savidug and Anaro

Were the inhabitants of Sabtang and Itbayat islands in contact during prehistory? Since the islands are intervisible this seems very likely. To assess the likelihood, the pottery assemblages from the two sites have been compared in terms of rim form and surface decoration. Results of a petrographic analysis of sherd thin sections from both sites are also presented below.

Generally, vessel shapes at both Savidug and Anaro are similar. Jars with everted rims dominate both assemblages. Ancillary features such as lugs, carinations and foot rings are present in both sites. Rim attributes are similar, but by no means identical.

Amongst the bowls, the fairly standard open form occurred throughout both sites, largely characterized by flat lipped, parallel-sided rims that are either straight or incurving. As noted, external grooves just below the lip occur in both Savidug Dune Site (in several levels below the jar burials) and in the lower levels of Anaro 3B, and this form also exists at Sunget on Batan island. However, the carinated bowls of Savidug and Anaro are rather different, with slightly more complex rim forms at Savidug (Fig. 6.17). Moreover, the pedestals/foot rings from Savidug are rather wide and tall, having foot diameters of 15 to 25 cm and heights of 4.5 to 5.5 cm. The foot rings from Anaro are smaller and shorter, 8 or 9 cm in diameter and 1 to 2.5 cm in height. It should be mentioned that indeterminate fragments of foot rings occur in the lower levels at both Savidug and Anaro, suggesting that this form appeared early in both sites.

Hole-mouthed vessel rims make up the smallest portion of the pottery assemblages at both Savidug and Anaro. They appear at the same time in both sites, perhaps between 700 BC and AD 1, in the upper to middle spits of the Savidug QR/7-9 lower cultural layer and the middle to lower levels of Anaro 3B.

The earliest everted jar rims at Savidug and Anaro are mostly parallel-sided and round-lipped, with either straight or incurving courses. They have diameters that range from 10-21 cm and rim heights from 1 to 4 cm. Again, external grooves are typical in the lower spits in both assemblages. Squat and S-profiled rims appeared uniquely at Anaro, but rims with external appliqué bands around their necks occur only at Savidug.

As discussed above, both sites have stamped-circle decorative motifs, although much more commonly at Anaro. Incision occurs but is rare in both sites. Neither has cord-marking, apart from a single undated surface find at Anaro.

Fabric analysis

Thin section analysis was carried out on 15 sherds from Savidug and Anaro in order to define the nature of the mineral inclusions in the pottery from both sites, and to identify any movement of pottery between islands. Samples were analysed in Manila and only included plain sherds, since the decorated sherds were in Canberra at the time of the analysis. Petrographic analysis was carried out by Dr Balangue Tarriela and Mr Adrian Fernandez at the University of the Philippines National Institute of Geological Science. This showed that the inclusions in the sherds from both sites are mainly grains of plagioclase. Other minerals associated with volcanic or igneous rocks, such as amphibole, biotite, pyroxene and quartz, occur at varying frequencies. Organics and mineral oxides also occur. The Savidug pottery on average has more frequent plagioclase grains and a large proportion are coarse in size. At Anaro, the minerals are weathered (detrital) and the plagioclase and other grains are finer in size. Almost all samples show poorly sorted grains. No calcite grains occurred in the sherd samples in either site, which may be significant considering that Anaro is located in a karstic environment and Savidug is located in a coastal area with both living and raised coral. In terms of soil chart colours, the overall matrices of Savidug pottery in cross polar light are gley, while those of the Anaro pottery are reddish orange.

In sum, the petrographic analysis indicates that both the Savidug and Anaro pottery assemblages were composed of similar volcanic minerals. However, despite the similarities in mineral composition, the characters of the minerals present in each site vary. This indicates that the raw materials came from different geological sources. The locations of these sources are not a subject of this study, but the large plagioclase grains which occur in the thin sections from Savidug are consistent with the character of the Sabtang island volcanic rocks, while the weathered minerals, oxides and the mostly reddish nature of the Anaro thin sections also coincide with the nature of Itbayat volcanic geology. This suggests that pottery was produced locally in both islands, and not traded between islands in large quantities. A similar conclusion concerning pottery fabrics was also reached by William Dickinson (2006), after his petrographic examinations of sand tempers in sherds from Taiwan, Batanes and Luzon that were under analysis by Mary Clare Swete Kelly for her ANU PhD thesis (Swete Kelly 2008). Needless to say, further sourcing studies should be undertaken to determine specific sources of raw materials to fully understand the nature of pottery production in prehistory.

At this point, the continuing similarities through time in rim forms and decoration can best be explained by cultural interaction rather than pottery trade between the occupants of the two sites, and the Batanes Islands in general. However, the possibility of some inter-island trade in unusual and specialised vessel forms has been raised above, and further research on this topic is clearly needed.

Post-Sunget assemblages on Batan, prior to the Iraya eruption (200 BC to AD 500)

A number of sites belonging to this phase on Batan were investigated in 2002 and 2003, especially at Naidi, Mahatao (through augering), Pamayan and Tayid (Fig. 3.1). These so-called " Naidi Phase" pottery assemblages on Batan (after Bellwood et al. 2003) are heavily red-slipped but have no other form of decoration such as stamping or incision (Fig. 6.22), and in particular no trace of the Anaro circle-stamped type 1 pottery style that was clearly so important in connection with nephrite working at Anaro between 500 BC and AD 1. Neither do any of these later Batan sites have any nephrite. For this reason, the radiocarbon dates for the Batan sites of this phase (Naidi, Mahatao, Payaman and Tayid in Table 5.1 and Fig. 5.1) are taken more or less at face value and presumed to indicate a time span between the end of the first millennium BC and the mid first millennium AD, or Phase 3 in the Batanes sequence presented in chapter 5. All the sites predate the Iraya eruption, which provides a terminus ante quem of about 1500 years ago (chapter 3).

The closest parallels to these Naidi Phase assemblages discussed so far lie in the lower cultural layer at Savidug Dune Site and at Anaro, but the absence of stamped circles clearly places the Naidi pottery later than the Phase 2 material from these two sites. A range of Naidi rim forms is illustrated in Fig. 6.22. The same vessel forms continue as previously – bowls with direct rims and jars with everted rims – although the hole-mouthed forms are absent. External grooves just below lips continue on many everted rims, and carinated vessels occur that are similar to those from Savidug. The Payaman rims in Fig. 6.22 are well dated to the early first millennium AD. But some of the Naidi rims could be a little older. Mahurohuron and Disvayangan are close to Mahatao, with surface finds also illustrated in Fig. 6.22.

Vessel rims within the Naidi phase assemblages are generally shorter vertically than at Sunget. Of the 26 vessels shown in Fig. 6.22 that have everted rims, only 6 (23%, mostly at the top of the figure) are greater than 3 cm in external height. Lips are quite often rolled or thickened externally, as shown in several examples in Fig. 6.22. This type of squat and rolled rim shape also occurs in contemporary assemblages from Savidug and Anaro, as noted in Alexandra De Leon's analysis above. Some of these rim forms are also closely paralleled in the Cagayan Valley on Luzon, for instance with the Neolithic assemblage from Irigayen (Ogawa 2002). Payaman has a number of small perforated pottery lugs that clearly belong to a separate and presumably later tradition than the large handles from Sunget.

So far, pottery of the Naidi Phase seems to be very widespread, occurring certainly beneath the major AD 500 ash fall in sites all over central Batan, both coastal and inland, such as Disvayangan (unstratified), Mahatao Town (in a septic tank pit), Buyabuy (surface finds), Mahurohuron, Mahatao Patio, Payaman, Chatavayan, Tayid, San Vicente Holiday Camp, and possibly in three other sites (K1, K6 and K41 on Fig. 3.1) recorded by Koomoto (1983). This suggests that a large population was already in occupation on Batan by this phase.

Recent pottery

Pottery from the past 1500 years can be found liberally scattered all over the Batanes landscape. No detailed study has been made of this material, although some recent rims are illustrated in Fig. 6.23 for Batan. The practice of applying red slip to pottery vessels declined after AD 500, but it never disappeared entirely and in 2003 this surface finish was still being applied using a hematite-rich clay by one of the last individuals producing pottery at Itbud on Batan. Red-slipped vessels were also common at *c*.AD 1500 or younger at Pamayan on Sabtang. Basically, the recent pottery continued existing trends in rim length reduction, decreasing red slip and thicker vessel walls, but there was a basic continuity in vessel shapes from early to late throughout the Batanes sequence. As stated already, there is no point in the Batanes sequence where a whole new replacement pottery style can be identified as an introduction from outside.

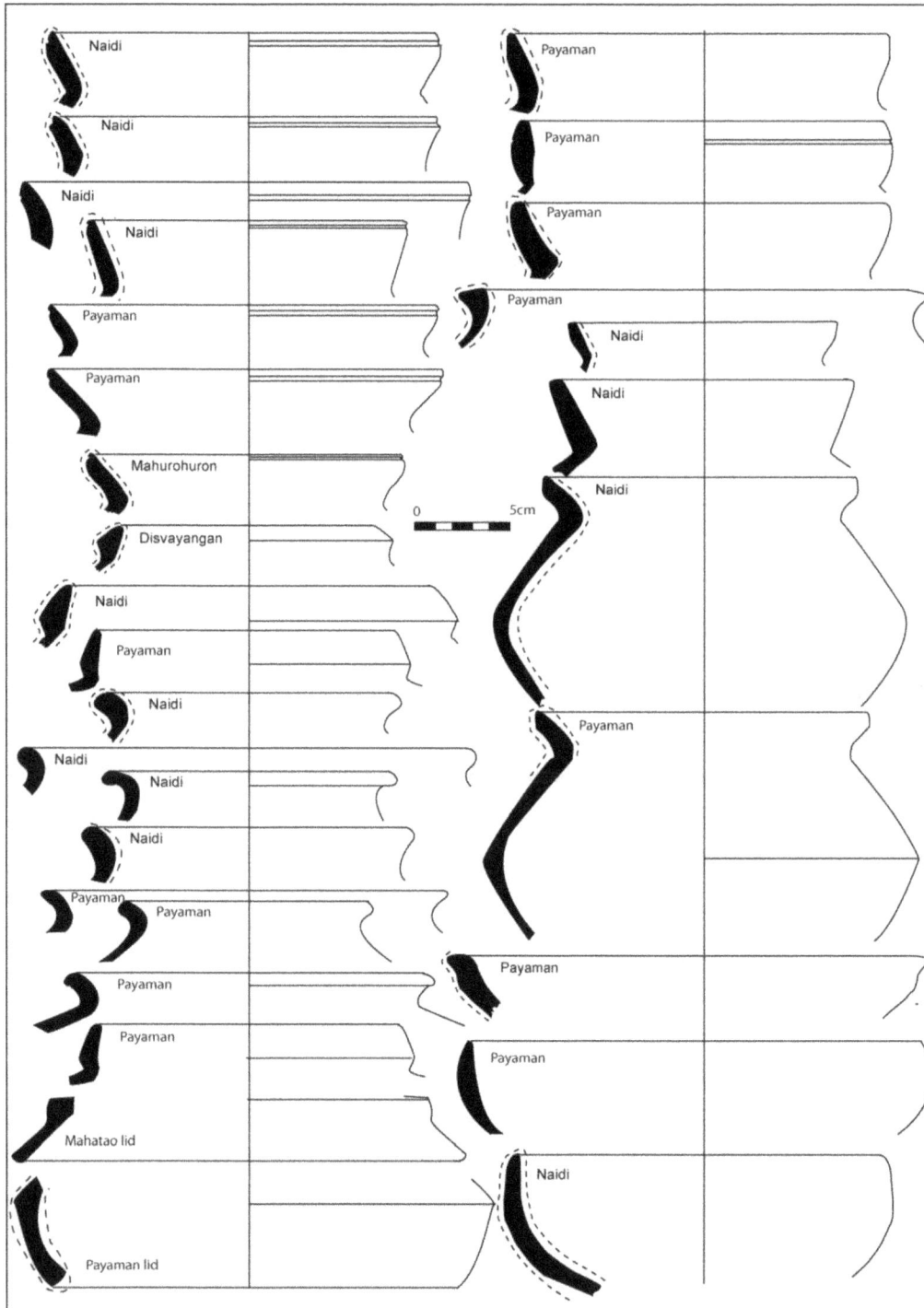

Figure 6.22. Naidi phase pottery from Batan sites: Naidi (dates uncertain), Payaman (AD 1 to 600), Mahurohuron, Disvayangan and Mahatao (surface finds).

Source: Peter Bellwood.

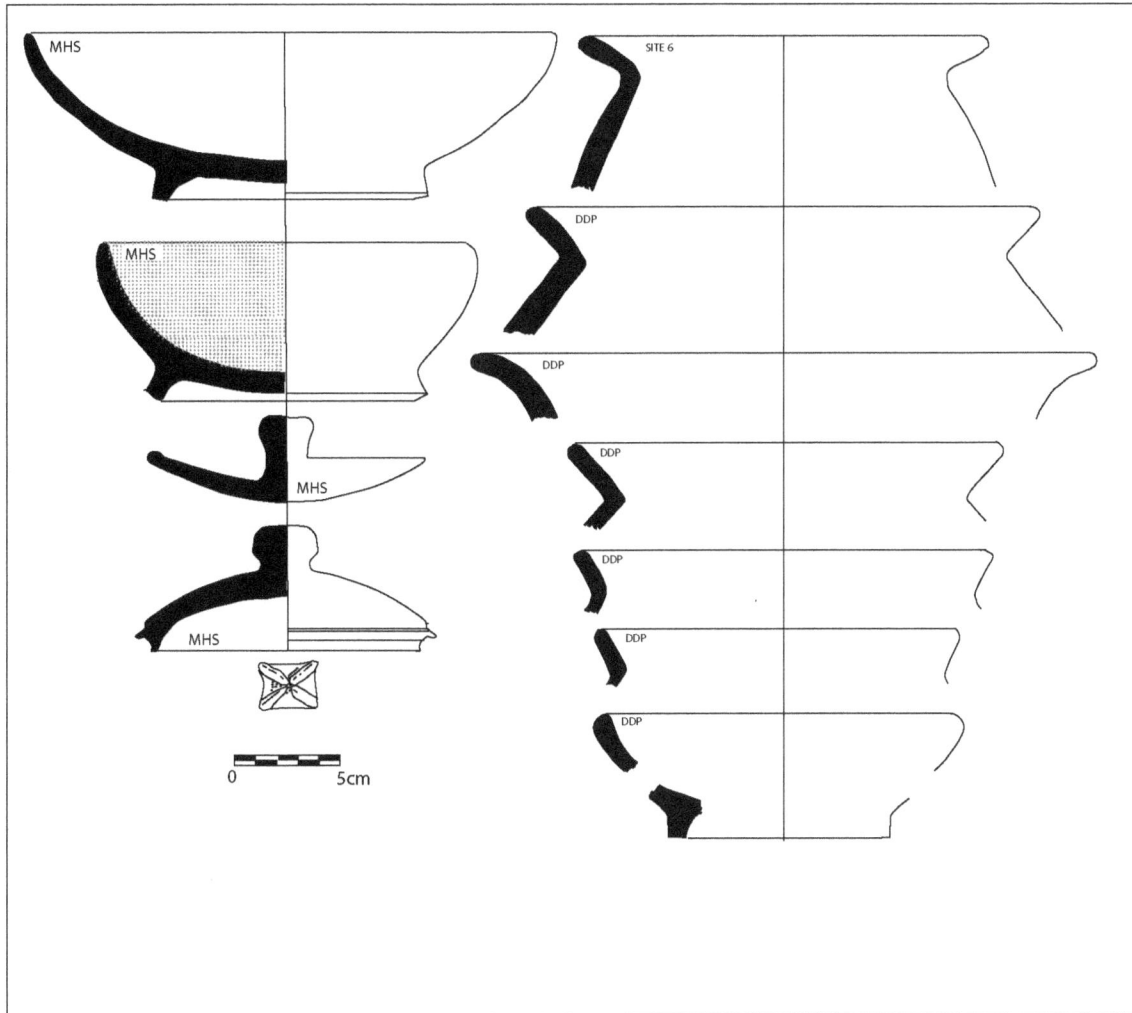

Figure 6.23. Two complete footed bowls and two lids of presumed ethnographic date kept in Mahatao High School (MHS), together with excavated late phase pottery from the Mavuyok a Ahchip (MAA) and Diosdipun (DDP) rock shelters. The bowl shown second down on the left is internally red-slipped.

Source: Peter Bellwood.

7

The Spinning Tools from Sunget, Anaro and Savidug

Judith Cameron

This chapter describes the spindle whorls recovered from the sites of Sunget, Anaro and Savidug Dune Site. The majority belong to the period between approximately 1200 BC and AD 1.

The technology of textiles revolves around the preparation of fibres to produce thread suitable for loom weaving. During the Neolithic period in South China, a simple device called the hand spindle was developed for this purpose. Comprised of a weight (whorl) and a shaft (rod) designed to keep the weight vertical, the hand spindle twists fibres mechanically to extend their length before being woven on looms. While the length of plant fibres can also be extended manually through hand twisting or knotting, the hand spindle twists fibres much faster and more efficiently. Spinning also increases the tensile strength of fibres ensuring that woven threads neither break nor unravel. For these reasons, the invention of the hand spindle in many parts of the world has been heralded as a Neolithic revolution in textile technology.

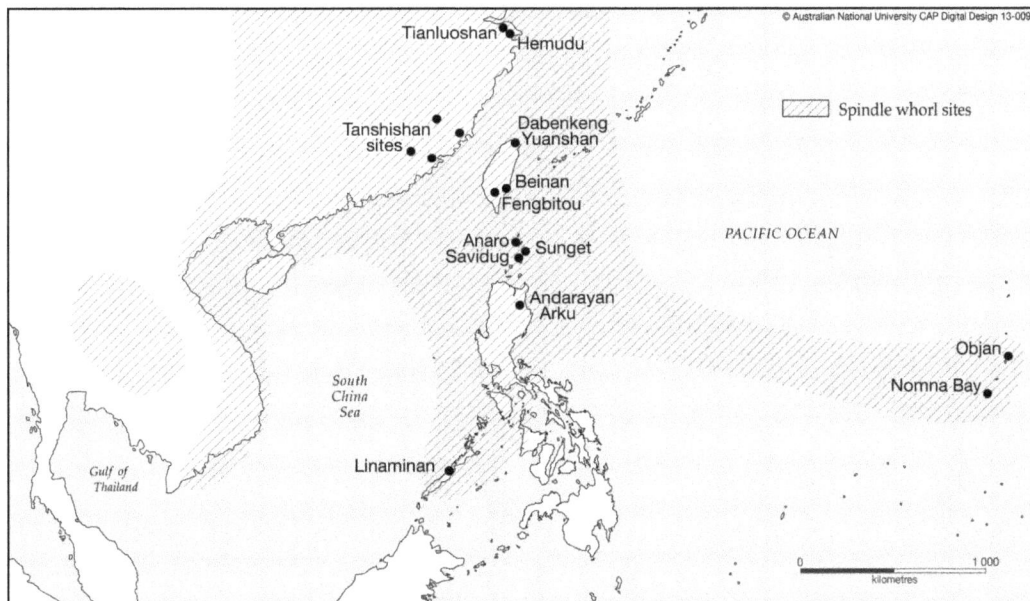

Figure 7.1. The archaeological distribution of spindle whorls in Neolithic Southeast Asia (updated from Cameron 2001: Fig.1).

Source: Map preparation by ANU College of Asia and the Pacific, CartoGIS.

Table 7.1. Functional attributes of biconical pottery spindle whorls from Anaro, Savidug and Sunget.

Site	National Museum Accession No.	Context	Weight (g) (complete whorls only)	Height cm.	Diam. cm.	Central hole diam. cm.	Description	C14 date range calibrated BP
							Decorated whorls	
Sunget	II-2002-N-38	Top Terrace, layer 5, 2002	-	>3.2	5.8	missing	Biconical fragment, decorated with 2 horizontal rows of small stamped circles above and 2 below the greatest diameter. Fig. 7.2E.	3200-2800
Anaro	II-2004-I-2810	Anaro 5 surface	-	3.7	5.0	0.8	Sub-biconical fragment, decorated with horizontal and vertical rows of small stamped circles. Fig. 7.2G.	3200-2500 on decoration
Anaro	II-2005-I-Q-74	Anaro 4 surface	-	3.9	5.0	0.6	Biconical fragment decorated with lines of tiny stamped circles 0.15 cm diameter, resin coated. Fig. 7.2I.	3200-2500 on decoration
Anaro	II-2005-U-113	Kaxanggan surface	-	4.5	c.5.0	0.7	Biconical fragment, decorated with horizontal rows of large (5 mm diam.) stamped circles. Fig. 7.2F.	3200-2500 on decoration
Anaro	-	Surface find 2010	-	~3	3.6	0.5	Biconical fragment decorated with parallel horizontal rows of fingernail impressions	uncertain
Savidug	II-2006-T-399	A9 60 cm (upper cultural layer)	-	>3.4	5.8	0.7	Sub-biconical fragment, decorated with horizontal and vertical rows of linear incisions. Fig. 7.2H.	<800
							Undecorated whorls	
Sunget	II-2002-N-302	Top Terrace 31-35 cm, 2003	98	4.2	5.5	0.8	Biconical complete whorl, undecorated and resin coated. Fig. 7.2A.	3200-2800
Anaro	II-2005 Q-71	Anaro 4 surface	58	3.1	4.8	0.4	Biconical complete whorl, undecorated. Fig. 7.2 C.	uncertain
Anaro	II-2004-I-2809	Anaro 6 60-70 cm	25	2.5	3.2	0.6	Biconical complete whorl, undecorated. Fig. 7.2 B.	uncertain
Anaro	-	Surface find 2010	24	2.5	3.2	0.5	Biconical complete whorl, undecorated (identical to Fig. 7.2B).	uncertain
Anaro	II-2004-I-4440	Anaro 3G 70-80 cm	-	2.1	4.0	0.6	Biconical fragment, undecorated	<2500
Anaro	II-2004-I-4565	Anaro 3 70-75 cm	-	2.7	4.0	0.4	Biconical fragment, undecorated	<2500
Anaro	II-2004-I-2808	Anaro 3B 35 cm	-	3.0	3.0	0.4	Spherical fragment, undecorated	uncertain
Anaro	II-2005-V-35	Kaxanggan surface	-	>3.5	3.8	0.6	Conical fragment, undecorated	uncertain
Savidug	II-2006-T-422	K-N layer 4	-	2.8	5.0	missing	Biconical fragment, undecorated	3200-2800
Savidug	II-2006-T-414	QR7-9 120-130 cm	-	2.3	3.3	0.5	Biconical fragment, undecorated	2500-2000
Savidug	II-2006-T 413	QR 7-9 110-120 cm	-	>3.9	5.0	0.7	Sub-biconical fragment, undecorated	2500-2000

Previously, I have traced the prehistoric origins and movement of spinning technology from Southeast China into Taiwan, Island Southeast Asia and the Marianas (Cameron 2001, 2002). This research showed the distribution and dramatic decline of spinning data south of Taiwan. Although a small number of whorls have been found in northern Luzon, only a very few isolated examples have been found further south in Island Southeast Asia (Fig. 7.1). This can be explained by two inter-related environmental factors. Firstly, the hot and wet tropical climate south of Luzon was not conducive to the cultivation of some of the fibre-producing plants upon which textile technology developed. Secondly, these tropical islands hosted species such as *Curculigo latifolia* (lemba) and *Musa textilis* (abaca), whose fibres were knotted or twisted, rather than spun, before being woven on looms.

This chapter provides the results of an analysis of a small assemblage of spindle whorls from the Batanes sites of Sunget, Anaro and Savidug. The functional attributes of the tools in the assemblage were measured (Table 7.1), and decorative elements were recorded where present (Fig. 7.2). The results are compared with excavated parallels from Taiwan and the Cagayan Valley in Luzon. Because of the strategic position of the Batanes between Taiwan and the Philippines, the Batanes whorls provide insights into the introduction of textile technology into Island Southeast Asia.

The largest number of whorls found in Batanes come from the site of Anaro on Itbayat Island. Significantly perhaps, the oldest Itbayat assemblages, from Torongan and Reranum caves (2000-1000 BC), were devoid of whorls, although these sites both have very small artefact assemblages so this could just be sample size bias. In total, four complete whorls and seven fragments were found at Anaro. These ranged in size from 3.0 to 5.0 cm in diameter, which is within the range of prehistoric Chinese and Southeast Asian whorls. All items were made from the same type of fired earthenware as the other pottery from the site. Many of the whorls from Anaro (as also at Sunget and Savidug) are biconical in shape, although one is sub-conical with a slight tendency to a tear-drop shape, one is conical, and another is spherical. The majority were decorated, either with fingernail impressions, incised lines, or stamped circles. One resin coated whorl (Fig. 7.2 I) is similar to the resin coated undecorated whorl from Sunget shown in Fig. 7.2 A. The stamped circle motifs at Anaro and Sunget could have been applied using stems of *Calamus mollis* (rattan), or bamboo.

Unfortunately, the decorated specimens from Anaro were all surface finds, but their zoned stamped circle motifs relate them to the lowest cultural phase at Anaro (Phase 2, older subphase, as defined in chapter 5), between 1200 and 500 BC and thus contemporary with the whorls from Sunget. Interestingly, the three biconical specimens found in the excavations at Anaro were all plain, and date stratigraphically from the younger subphase of Phase 2, after 500 BC.

Sunget on Batan Island produced three whorls, one fragment being decorated with four rows of stamped circles around the greatest diameter (Fig. 7.2 E). The resin coated specimen from 31-35 cm in the top terrace (Fig. 7.2 A) has a high mineral content with traces of quartz.

Savidug Dune Site on Sabtang Island produced four whorls, three plain biconical examples from the lower cultural layer, and one (Fig. 7.2 H) from the upper cultural layer decorated with short incisions. Interestingly, this younger specimen has the same layout of decoration as the presumed much older specimen shown in Fig. 7.2 G from Anaro 5. This suggests they both belong to a continuing technological tradition. But, by the time of the Savidug upper layer, the stamped circle fashion had completely died so a different kind of short incision was preferred.

Savidug is also located near a stream which was probably used in fibre preparation. As bast fibres need to be washed many times during fibre processing, proximity to fresh water is important. Surprisingly, no whorls were found inside the burial jars that characterize the Savidug site.

Figure 7.2. Baked clay spindle whorls from Sunget, Anaro and Savidug. The 5 cm scale only refers to the four complete whorls at top left (A to D). The others have been enlarged to show their decoration (dimensions are given in Table 7.1).

A. Sunget Top Terrace, 31-35 cm;

B. Anaro 6, 60-70 cm;

C. Anaro 4 surface;

D. sub-biconical whorl from Andarayan, Cagayan Valley;

E. Sunget Top Terrace with 4 rows of stamped circles;

F. Anaro surface (Kaxanggan) with very deeply impressed circles;

G. Anaro 5 surface with paired vertical rows each with 4 small stamped circles;

H. Savidug A9 60 cm (upper cultural layer) with horizontal and vertical rows of linear incisions;

I. Anaro 4 surface with resin coat and horizontal and vertical rows of small stamped circles.

G, H and I have the same design structure, even though H is about 1000 years or more younger in date.

Discussion

Can these prehistoric spinning tools from the Batanes be linked to any prehistoric groups?

This analysis clearly shows that the whorls recovered during the Batanes excavations belonged to a prehistoric textile technology tradition that had roots in South China. The most diagnostic functional attribute of the Batanes whorls is shape. Significantly, most of the whorls in the assemblage are biconical or sub-biconical. Although some basic spindle whorl types are generic, Cameron (2002) previously demonstrated that biconical spindle whorl shapes are so specific culturally that they can be used to trace the movement of prehistoric groups into various parts of Southeast Asia. In Mainland Southeast Asia, this distribution is entirely in keeping with the dispersal of rice, as established by Higham and Lu (1998).

Until recently, biconical whorls were defined as atypical for China, belonging to the Tanshishan culture, a relatively late Neolithic culture in southeast China (Kuhn 1988; Cameron 2001, 2002, 2007). However, recent excavations in the upper layers of the early Neolithic site of Tianluoshan (5000-2500 BC) in Zhejiang Province, which belongs to the Hemudu culture, have also produced biconical whorls, as well as evidence for the some of the oldest rice fields in China (Zheng et al 2009; Fuller et al. 2009). Biconical whorls then continued in the archaeological record in the above-mentioned Tanshishan sites (Fujian Province) and in many Neolithic sites in Taiwan. Despite the fact that prehistoric spindle whorls are relatively rare in the archaeological record of the Philippines, biconical types have also been found on Luzon at Arku Cave (Thiel 1986-7a), Magapit (Aoyagi et al. 1993) and Nagsabaran (Cameron in Hung 2008), and at Linaminan on Palawan Island (Cameron 2007).

Other morphological features link the whorls in the Batanes assemblage to Neolithic examples from the Philippines. For example, the complete whorl from Anaro 4 (Fig. 7.2 C) compares favourably in material composition, size and weight with a sub-biconical whorl excavated by Shutler from the Neolithic site of Andarayan in the Cagayan Valley, Luzon (Fig. 7.2 D). The Andarayan site also produced evidence for a presence of rice chaff in pottery (Snow et al. 1986).

The stamped decorative technique that distinguishes the whorls in the Batanes assemblage first occurs on spindle whorls from Tianluoshan, and continues in the archaeological record on whorls from the type site of Hemudu (Cameron 2002). While the meaning of the stamped motifs remains obscure, it seems far from coincidental that stamping was also used to decorate biconical whorls at Tanshishan sites in southeast China and across the Taiwan Straits in late Neolithic Beinan phase sites on Taiwan. The elaboration of this technique into configurations of stamped circles also distinguished the decorated Batanes pottery (1200-500 BC) found at Anaro, Savidug and Sunget.

Significantly, most whorls found in Batanes belong to Phase 2 of the Batanes sequence, where they occur with nephrite and slate from Taiwan. The relatively small number of whorls at the sites discussed does not indicate intensification of textile production for trade or exchange, but implies domestic production at the household level.

Can the prehistoric spindle whorls from Batanes be linked to any contemporary ethnographic groups?

Although the Philippines are better known for traditional textiles woven using knotted or reeled fibres from *Musa textilis* (abaca) and *Ananas comosus* (pineapple), or imported pre-spun cotton, spindle whorls have also long been used by several ethnographic groups. The Banaue people of Ifugao Province use the drop spindle to spin bark fibres (Milgram 2007). The National Museum of the Philippines houses a biconical whorl from Abra Province which belonged to Tinguian spinners. The usage of the hand spindle by these groups was also recorded ethnographically (Cooper-Cole 1915), and historical records also indicate that Bontok Igorots spun tree cotton (probably kapok from *Ceiba petandra*) with hand spindles (Jenks 1905). Significantly, these recent and contemporary spinning groups (Banaue, Igorot, Tinguian) are wet-rice cultivators from provinces close to the Cagayan Valley, where prehistoric spindle whorls have been found. There can be little doubt from the ethnographic and archaeological evidence that spinning was introduced into the northern Philippines Provinces (Batanes Islands and the Cagayan Valley) with rice during the Neolithic period.

What fibres were spun with these prehistoric tools?

The question concerning the fibres that were spun remains hypothetical. The only extant archaeological textile found to date in the Philippines is a 12th century unspun abaca cloth from Banton Island currently being analysed by Quizon and Cameron (2009). Previously, it has been suggested (Cameron 2002; Cameron in Bellwood et al. 2003; Cameron and Mijares 2006) that fibres from *Musa sp.* could also have been spun with the prehistoric whorls found in the Philippines. There were several reasons for this suggestion. During fieldwork, the author's informants stressed that spinners are extraordinarily pragmatic and use a wide range of fibres with choice contingent on availability. Textiles woven from *Musa textilis* (abaca) have been known in South China for more than 2000 years (Kuhn 1988). Interpretation is difficult because this fibre is not spun with whorls in the Philippines today, being simply twisted or knotted, processes which represent a different stage in the development of textile technology. However, *M. textilis* is reeled in Iloilo province (Krieger 1942: Plate 9.2), using a simple reeling machine of the type which replaced the spindle whorl in China during the Han dynasty (206 BC-AD 220). In addition, Navarette reported the usage of *M. textilis* (Manila hemp) for black "hemp" rigging and cables on the island of Mindoro in the 17th century (Cummins 1962:81). Known as Manila hemp, this fibre's tensile strength makes it the world's premium natural cordage fibre for maritime purposes. Moreover, experiments conducted with abaca by contemporary craft persons in other parts of the world have demonstrated that the fibres spin very well.

We know with greater certainty that *Pueraria thunbergiana* (bean creeper) was an important fibre-producing plant during the prehistoric period in South China. Shanghai textile scholars have identified the species in archaeological textiles dating back to the 4th millennium BC. Considered to be native to East Asia, its wild progenitor, *Pueraria thomsonii*, grows prolifically in the southeast coastal provinces of China (Kuhn 1988). The author has also observed this species growing near the archaeological site of Hemudu in Zhejiang Province, where evidence is first found for the back strap loom that is represented throughout Southeast Asi.

Another fibre-producing plant that may have been used in the Batanes is *Broussonetia papyrifera* (paper mulberry). In southern China, paper mulberry fibres were obtained and processed in the same way as abaca - stripped, boiled, and split before being spliced and spun. The origins and early distribution of the paper mulberry is well documented (Matthews 1996), and the species was central to Austronesian dispersals in Island Southeast Asia and Polynesia (Bellwood 2007). But discussion of it is usually confined to the manufacture of beaten bark cloth (Cameron 2006, 2008). However, Milgram's (2007) research has clearly established that contemporary Banuag from Ifugao use paper mulberry for both beaten bark cloth and spun and woven textiles.

The fibre-producing plant *Hibiscus tiliaceae* has also been identified in the Batanes Islands, as well as along seashores and tidal estuaries in the Philippines generally. Given the range of possibilities, Neolithic spinners may have introduced a range of suitable textile fibres into Island Southeast Asia during this period.

Previously, the author has suggested that *Boehmeria nivea* (ramie) could have been spun using biconical whorls. During the prehistoric and early historic periods in South China, ramie was the dominant textile fibre, whereas *Cannabis sativa* (hemp) was the fibre of the north. Extant remains of ramie textiles have been found at sites in southeast China (Kuhn 1988) and Vietnam (Cameron 2008), and in association with biconical whorls at Tanshishan sites in Fujian Province (Cameron 2000, 2002). I have observed the usage of biconical whorls to spin ramie fibres on Hainan Island, and botanical research in Batanes has also revealed the presence there of wild ramie, *Maoutia setosa* Wedd. (Valerio 1995-1997).

The spindle whorl data provide unequivocal evidence for the movement of textile technology into the Batanes from southeast China and Taiwan during the late prehistoric period, around or before 1200 BC, and enable us to link the Batanes spinners to specific prehistoric and contemporary cultures. The absence of pottery whorls south of Luzon militates against any introduction of this technology from further south in Island Southeast Asia. The parallels in the spinning data are interpreted as archaeological evidence for population movement rather than as evidence for independent invention, or trade and exchange. Had spinning been invented independently in the Batanes, basic whorl types (flat discs) would be represented rather than biconical forms. Because biconical whorls have a higher moment of inertia than basic types, and spin faster than basic forms, they indicate a presence of spinners with technical knowledge and skill, not novices.

8

Other Portable Artefacts from the Batanes Sites

Peter Bellwood and Eusebio Dizon

This chapter describes the many portable artefacts found during the Batanes investigations, with the exceptions of pottery (chapter 6), spindle whorls (chapter 7) and nephrite (chapter 9). The main categories discussed in this chapter are ground, polished and hammer-dressed stone, baked clay (for earrings), shell, bone, and other relatively young archaeological materials such as glass and metal.

The portable artefacts from the Batanes archaeological sites come from both excavated and surface contexts. Surface finds came from all sites investigated, perhaps most prolifically from the site of Anaro on Itbayat. The surface finds from here are difficult to date individually since Anaro was occupied for perhaps 2000 years or more (1000 BC to later than AD 1000), and everything has become mixed up in falling down the slopes around the site. The material collected by the Kumamoto team from Sunget on Batan in 1982 was also mostly surface-collected from a road cutting, although in this case only a single occupation dating between 1200 and 800 BC is attested from our subsequent excavations at Sunget, so it seems reasonable to assume that the artefacts collected in 1982 also belong to this period. At Savidug Dune Site, many important surface finds were recovered from the road cutting next to the excavations, but most came clearly from the lower layer in the site (1200 BC to AD 1), since the upper cultural layer is ephemeral in this location. Table 8.1 shows the distributions of specific classes of non-pottery artefact by depth and trench at Savidug and Anaro.

In terms of raw material, the portable artefacts fall into several categories: stone, metal (rare in Batanes), glass (for beads), bone, baked clay (a bracelet and several penannular ear ornaments), and shell. This chapter uses raw material rather than presumed function as the primary classifier for artefacts.

Stone artefacts

These fall into 7 major classes: adzes with asymmetrical bevels (axes with symmetrical bevels do not occur in Batanes), flaked and hammer dressed "hoes", bark cloth beaters, sawn and ground Taiwan slate points and knives, grindstones, pendants, and side-notched pebble sinkers. Surprisingly, definite examples of stone beads were not found.

Table 8.1. Distributions of chronologically diagnostic excavated artefacts by square and depth at Savidug Dune Site and Anaro.

Anaro 3, all squares, depths in cm.

Depth (cm)	Baked clay penannular ear ornaments	^Spindle whorl *baked clay bracelet	Stone bark cloth beater	Tridacna adzes	Iron	Glass bead	Slate and exotic siliceous rocks	Nephrite	Dates (asterisked dates are presumed to reflect disturbance)
0-10									
10-20									
20-30		1^							
30-40					2			1	
40-50				1	2	1			
50-60	1			1			1		
60-70	1	1*					1	2	AD 657-866
70-80				1			1	5	338 BC-AD 21
80-90				1	1		1	1	349 BC-AD 4, AD 583-768*
90-100							4	2	AD 607-768*, AD 427-644*
100-110									1038-813 BC, 767-414 BC

Sample size very small

Anaro 2, all squares, depths in cm.

Depth (cm)	Stone bark cloth beater	Slate and exotic siliceous rocks	Nephrite	Dates
0-10				
10-20		1	1	AD 53-238
Below 20	1	2	1	

Savidug Dune Site, all squares, depths in cm.

Depth (cm)	Iron	Sherds with internal fabric impressions	Imported stoneware, celadon	Baked clay penannular ear ornaments	Circle stamped pottery	Biconical baked clay spindle whorls	nephrite lingling-o	Taiwan slate knife	Double side-notched pebble sinkers	Turbo marmoratus pendants	Conus bracelets	Trochus niloticus bracelets	Turbo marmoratus edge-chipped opercula	Dates
0-10			5											
10-20														
20-30			2											
30-40	1	4	7											
40-50	1		3							2	2			
50-60	1	2	1*							3	2			
60-70		2	1							3	1			
70-80	1	1								4				
80-90		1								1				
90-100			1							2	1			
100-110									3			4		
110-120				1		2			8					
120-130				3		1			18	1				
130-140				2	2		1	1	4			1		560-390 BC
140-150				2					3				1	
150-160									5					
160-170					1				2			1		
170-180					1				6				1	
180-190									4					1114-901 BC
190-200									4					
200-210									1					360-50 BC
210-220									1					1139-930 BC

*Chinese coin

What is most surprising is the lack of a flaked stone industry (excluding the side-notched pebble sinkers and flakes struck from polished adzes) in all the Batanes sites. The unground flaked cores, flakes and blade-like flakes that occur in many Palaeolithic and Neolithic contexts in islands to the south and east – the main Philippines, Indonesia, western Oceania – are virtually absent in Batanes, apart from a 12.5 cm long blade-like flake of volcanic rock from Torongan (square D, 50-55 cm), and a similar one from Anaro (3A, 0-10 cm), this last virtually a surface find. Anaro also produced one chert flake at 70-80 cm in square 3A, and a few tiny chips of crystalline rock were found at Payaman on Batan Island (c.AD 1-500). The rarity of flaked stone in Batanes could reflect lack of suitable raw materials, since the Batanes Islands only have coarse volcanic rocks and raised coral, with no chert, obsidian or fine-grained metamorphics. However, local volcanic rocks were sometimes used for adzes in Batanes (see below), and purely flaked lithics are also rare in Neolithic and later sites in Taiwan and southern China (see Jiao 2007 for Fujian). So there is a possibility that the absence could reflect a cultural choice for ground and polished tools, rather than simple lack of suitable stone.

Indeed, it is quite possible that a pre-Neolithic preference for purely flaked stone tools was imported as a cultural substratum into the Neolithic stone repertoire as it spread through Luzon and beyond towards the south and east, from resident native (preceramic) populations who were not present in Batanes. The southern Chinese Neolithic cultures from which the Island Southeast Asian Neolithic cultures were ultimately derived specialised in stone working by sawing (as in nephrite and shell working), hammer dressing and grinding/polishing, rather than by flaking alone, even though the latter was of course practised during the preliminary shaping of many subsequently-ground stone tools.

Figure 8.1. Lithic artefacts collected from Sunget, Batan, in 1982.

A. Stepped adze of metamorphic rock (two views).

B. Adze segment of metamorphic rock, probably reworked (two views).

C. Segment of trapezoidal-sectioned adze of metamorphic rock.

D. Small untanged trapezoidal-sectioned adze of metamorphic rock.

E. Metamorphic rock adze of shouldered shape, although this could have been present in the original blank (two views).

F. Polished adze-shaped stone pendant with an evenly drilled hole, but drilled from both sides.

G. Another pendent with an hourglass-shaped hole drilled from both sides, of Taiwan slate or schist.

H. Part of a Taiwan slate perforated point (worked into a stone saw?).

I. A piece of coarse laminated Taiwan slate with a lenticular cross-section, similar in raw material to many slate artefacts from SE Taiwan.

Source: Peter Bellwood.

Stone adzes

In general terms, the Batanes adzes can be described as having trapezoidal cross-sections, but ranging through many intermediate shapes between rectangular and triangular extremes. Those with the most sharply rectangular cross-sections are from Anaro and of Fengtian nephrite (eastern Taiwan), shown in Fig. 9.3 and discussed by Hsiao-chun Hung in chapter 9. The only certain hafting modifications are either a horizontal groove or a step on the front of the adze, on the opposite side away from the bevel and the handle (Figs 8.2, 8.3, below). The front of the adze is always the widest edge of the trapezoid, and the closest Duff (1970) forms are 1A and 3. No definite shouldered adzes have yet been found in Batanes.

Most adzes are of metamorphic rocks which are not native to Batanes, although at present we cannot be sure whether the metamorphic raw materials (apart from nephrite) came from Taiwan, Luzon, or both locations. Only detailed geological sourcing research could ever provide certainty in this regard. So far, the only sourcing research with positive tracking results has been that on Fengtian nephrite by Yoshiyuki Iizuka at Academia Sinica in Taipei, as discussed in chapter 9. There are nine Fengtian Taiwan nephrite adzes from surface contexts at Anaro on Itbayat, and one from Sunget on Batan. Taiwan, in particular, has a long and well-dated sequence of stone adze manufacture with many different raw materials and shapes, extending back to before 3000 BC (Hung 2004). Many of the Batanes adzes match very closely with counterparts in Taiwan, and some forms also extend into Luzon.

The Sunget adzes

Because of their significance in terms of date we begin with the adzes collected from Sunget on Batan Island in 1982. As discussed in chapter 3, all indications are that the Sunget occupation dates between 1200 and 800 BC, and it is reasonable to assume that these artefacts are of similar date. Unfortunately, no stone tools apart from notched pebble sinkers were found during the Sunget excavations in 2002-4.

Fig. 8.1 A-E are five adzes found at Sunget, all of metamorphic rock (Koomoto 1983: Plate 35). A is a stepped adze of Duff type 1A, minus its butt; B is a fairly indeterminate segment of an adze, probably reused; C and D have the same trapezoidal cross-sections as many specimens from Anaro and the Cagayan Valley on Luzon (see below); and E is a possible shouldered form, although the shape could be fortuitous (and no shouldered adzes were otherwise found in Batanes, even though they do occur rarely in Taiwan).

This Sunget assemblage is important because it establishes a presence of the stepped adze (Duff type 1A, mainly) in Batanes at 1200-800 BC. Duff (1970: 115) illustrates stepped adzes from Luzon and from the Neolithic site of Yuanshan in Taipei, northern Taiwan (c.1000 BC – Fig. 8.3 H), and Chang (1969:165) illustrates a much older example from the basal layer at Dabenkeng in Taiwan, probably older than 2000 BC. In nearby Fujian Province, stepped adzes occur in large numbers in the sites of Tanshishan and Huangguashan (Fig. 8.3 I and J), dated to between 3000 and 1500 BC by Jiao (2007). Heading south, their distribution goes at least as far as Ha Long Bay in northern Vietnam (Nguyen 2007). The direction of movement of this stepped form into Batanes from Fujian via Taiwan is fairly clear, and it is probably not coincidental that the 3rd millennium BC site of Tanshishan in Fujian has also produced red-slipped pottery, some with stamped circles. Another Fujian site, Damaoshan (3000-2300 BC), lacks tanged adzes, but it has yielded punctate-stamped biconical spindle whorls like those in Batanes (see chapter 7) (Jiao 2007:154).

Sunget is also important because of the presence of a small adze of identified Fengtian nephrite, shown in Fig. 9.2 A and discussed in the next chapter.

The Anaro adzes and their parallels

Figs 8.2, 8.3, 8.4 and 8.5 detail the main elements of the Anaro adze assemblage. A total of well over 100 adzes and adze fragments have been recorded from this site, most broken and small (local people find them all the time, so an exact total is elusive). But of the total, 10 are complete enough to be recognised as grooved adzes, and 7 as stepped adzes (Figs 8.2, 8.3). Nine untanged adzes are of Taiwan nephrite (see chapter 9).

Most of the recovered stone adzes from Anaro are surface finds, but the site also produced four specimens from excavation. A fragment of a battered and possibly stepped adze was found in Anaro 4a at a depth of 60-70 cm; Anaro 6 produced a fragment of a trapezoidal-sectioned adze from 30-40 cm; Anaro 7 produced the stepped adze shown as Fig. 8.3 E from a depth of 5-10 cm; and Anaro 3C yielded an indeterminate fragment of a possible adze from a depth of 55-60 cm, in association with Anaro circle-stamped type 1 pottery (chapter 6) dated between 700 BC and AD 1.

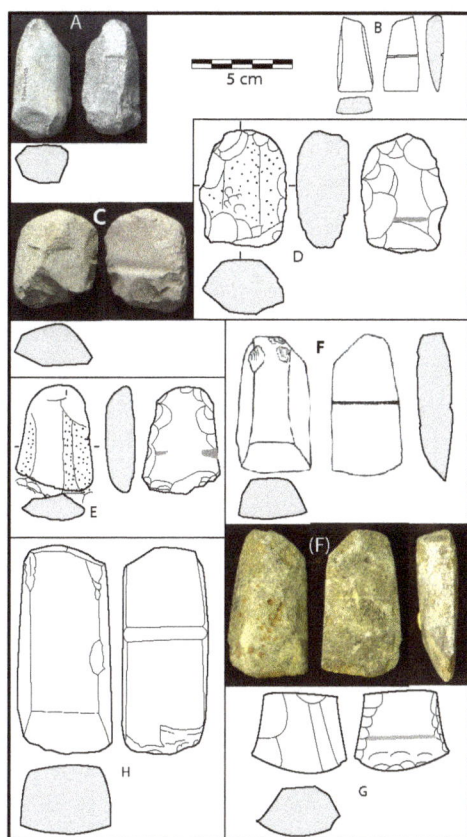

Figure 8.2. Grooved (scarfed) adzes from Anaro and Taiwan.

A. Anaro, surface.

B. Anaro, surface.

C. Kaxanggan (west side of Anaro), surface, probably metamorphic.

D, E. Below Anaro 4, surface.

F. Lagnaani (east side of Anaro), dark grey local volcanic rock that contains iron oxide, ilmenite, clinopyroxene, orthopyroxene, plagioclase and apatite, identified by Yoshiyuki Iizuka at the Institute of Earth Sciences, Academia Sinica, Taipei, using a low-vacuum scanning electron microscope equipped with an energy-dispersive x-ray spectrometer.

G. Kaxanggan (west side of Anaro), surface.

H. Taipei City, redrawn from Duff 1970:116.

Source: Peter Bellwood.

Fig. 8.2 illustrates seven of the grooved adzes from Anaro, all surface finds. This type of adze was referred to as "scarfed" by Duff, and he illustrated similar examples from Luzon and Taiwan, in the latter case from Yuanshan and "Taipei City" (Fig. 8.2 H) (Duff 1970:116, 137). The Neolithic Yuanshan culture in northern Taiwan, with its red-slipped pottery and stepped and shouldered adzes, is loosely dated to between 1500 and 500 BC by Tsang (2000:48). Chang (1969: Fig. 34/3, Plate 96) also illustrates grooved adzes from his "Lungshanoid" phase at Fengbitou in SW Taiwan. De la Torre (2000: Fig. 13, no. 11) illustrates one from Irigayen in the Cagayan Valley, dated to 1400-1000 BC (lower layer), and Ogawa (2002:100) illustrates two from the site of Magapit, also in the Cagayan Valley. It thus seems reasonable to assume that this form was widely distributed in the northern Philippines by around 1500 BC. Specimen F in Fig. 8.2 from Anaro is of a volcanic rock that is probably local to Batanes, according to Yoshiyuki Iizuka of Academia Sinica in Taipei. All of these adzes have cross-sections that are basically trapezoidal, some modified by damage. Thiel (1986-7a, 1986-7b) also illustrates stone adzes with trapezoidal cross-sections from Cagayan sites, but none appear to be stepped or grooved.

Fig 8.3 illustrates 6 stepped adzes from Anaro, again all surface finds. Item C is from the track going to Torongan Cave, and is of the same pale grey metamorphic rock as Fig. 8.5 C, and indeed many of the adzes from both Anaro and the Cagayan Valley. It appears to have been sawn into shape. Apart from D and E, these stepped adzes have quite thin trapezoidal cross-sections, although this may just reflect their small size. D and E have been damaged by use, E apparently as a hammer stone. Fig. 8.3 H to J are similar forms from Yuanshan in Taiwan and Huangguashan in Fujian (Jiao 2007: 122), the latter possibly predating 2000 BC. Chang (1969: Plates 94-5) also illustrates several examples of stepped adzes from Yuanshan. Duff (1970:137-8) illustrates undated specimens from Luzon, and Fig. 8.5 D from Magapit has a likely antiquity of 1500-500 BC. This stepped form is therefore presumably contemporary with the grooved form, and contemporary with the widespread Neolithic use of red-slipped pottery.

Fig. 8.4 illustrates a number of other butt and blade fragments from Anaro, three identified as being of exotic metamorphic rocks by Yoshi Iizuka. Fig. 8.4 K is a broken adze blade that has been used as an awl, found on the flat summit of the next hill to Anaro, called Pivalan, today denuded of soil.

Fig. 8.5 is a compilation of special and interesting stone adze finds. It shows two complete specimens of large but untanged trapezoidal sectioned adzes, one of a local volcanic rock from the surface of Taripan cave in northwest Itbayat, another found during construction activities in Mahatao on Batan and now kept in the High School there. Neither can be dated, but the Mahatao one is likely to be from the Sunget period of occupation. The other items C to G in Fig. 8.5 have been selected to illustrate potential parallels for the Anaro assemblage within the rest of the Austronesian-speaking world. C shows a butt and blade from Anaro, from different adzes but made of the same pale grey metamorphic rock. D is a stepped adze from Magapit that appears to be of exactly the same rock; the step of this adze can be seen at the top of the right hand photograph (the adze front). Adzes of this pale grey metamorphic rock are quite common in the Cagayan Valley, so this suggests that a possible source for this raw material exists somewhere in northern Luzon.

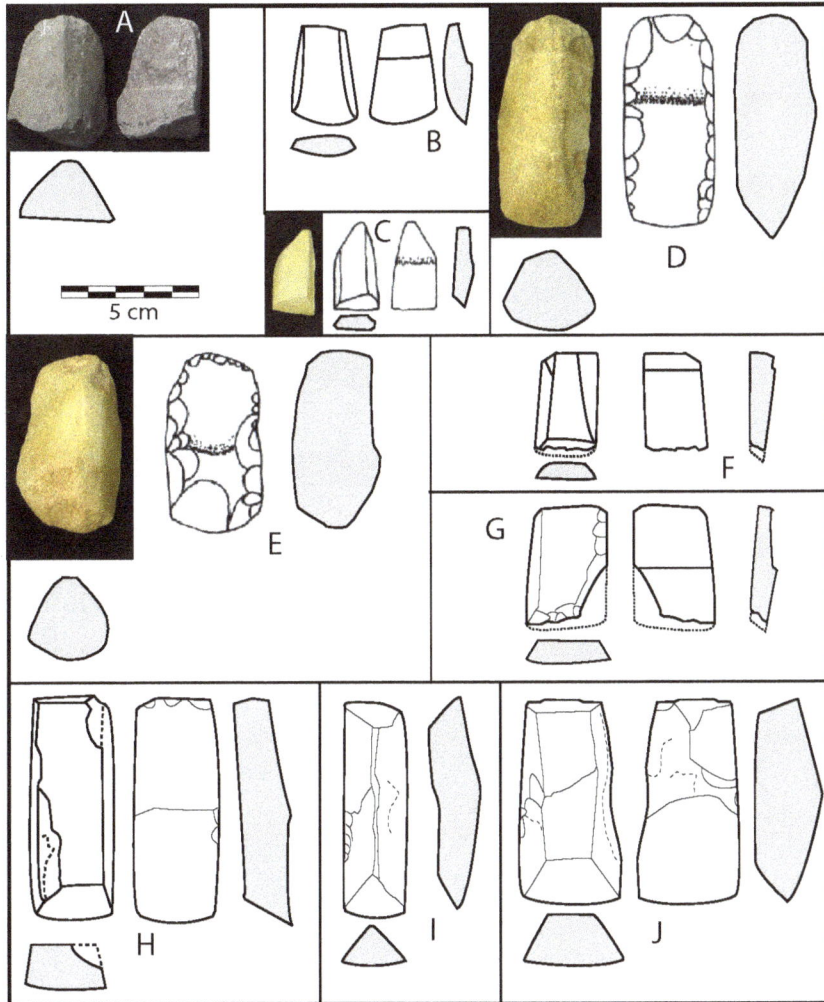

Figure 8.3. Stepped adzes from Anaro, Taiwan and Fujian.

A. Below Anaro 4, surface, triangular to trapezoidal in cross-section, with a shallow hammer-dressed step.

B. Anaro surface.

C. Found on track to Torongan Cave. Light grey metamorphic rock similar to Fig. 8.5 C and D. Sawn into shape, similar to nephrite working

D. Below Anaro 2, surface. Thick and fairly triangular cross-section, cf. Duff 1970: sheet 32 lower right, from Taipei City (Yuanshan?).

E. Excavated from Anaro square 7 at a depth of 5-10 cm, although this square was too shallow to give any precise idea of dating, and the adze need not have been *in situ*. Very similar to item D.

F. Below Anaro 4, surface, fairly thin trapezoidal cross-section and sharply cut tang.

G. Kaxanggan, similar to item F.

H. Yuanshan, Taipei, Taiwan, redrawn from Duff 1970, sheet 32 lower left, *c.*1000 BC?

I, J. Two tanged adzes with triangular and trapezoidal cross-sections from Huangguashan, Fujian Province, China, redrawn from Jiao 2007: Fig. 19. Jiao dates this site from 7 AMS C14 samples to about 2300-1500 BC.

Source: Peter Bellwood.

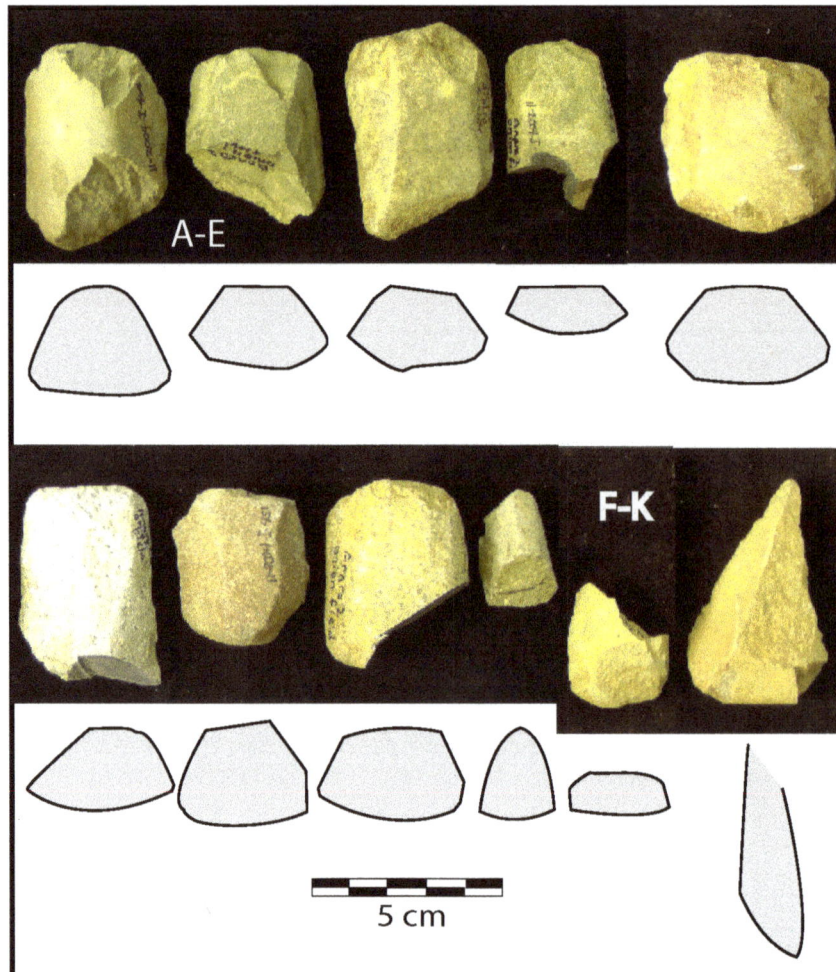

Figure 8.4. Broken adze butts and blades, all apparently from untanged forms, from Anaro surface collections. Three are of metamorphic rocks exotic to Batanes. Cross-sections vary from triangular to thick trapezoidal.

A, B. Below Anaro 2.

C. Kaxanggan.

D. Below Anaro 2. Grey exotic metamorphic rock that contains iron oxide, titanite, epidote, plagioclase, amphibole, quartz and garnet (pyrite), identified by Yoshiyuki Iizuka.

E. Kaxanggan.

F. Below Anaro 2. Grey exotic metamorphic rock that contains iron oxide, titanite, epidote, plagioclase, albite, amphibole, quartz and garnet (chalcopyrite), identified by Yoshiyuki Iizuka.

G. Below Anaro 2.

H. Below Anaro 2. Brown exotic metamorphic rock that contains iron oxide, titanite, plagioclase, amphibole and quartz, identified by Yoshiyuki Iizuka.

I. Kaxanggan – note small triangular cross-section (chisel?).

J. Below Anaro 2.

K. Adze bevel made into a drill, Pivalan (a limestone hill adjacent to Anaro), surface find.

Source: Peter Bellwood.

Figure 8.5. Complete (and other) adzes from the Batanes Islands and other locations.

A. Trapezoidal cross-sectioned adze without tang, possibly of local volcanic rock, from Taripan rockshelter, NW Itbayat (private collection of Mrs Faustina Cano).

B. Trapezoidal to triangular cross-sectioned untanged adze, probably of basalt or other fine grained volcanic rock, from Mahatao, Batan. Surface find, in possession of Mahatao High School – see Fig. 3.6, find place M8, for location.

C. Butt and blade of a very similar pale grey metamorphic rock from Anaro.

D. A very similar adze to the items in C, of identical metamorphic rock in appearance, from Magapit, Cagayan Valley, Luzon (c.1000 BC). This adze was either tanged or grooved.

E, F, G and H: Four chisels of very similar size, shape and rounded cross-section, but of different rocks, from the furthest limits of the Austronesian linguistic region; E, Savidug Dune Site square 29M 30-40 cm; F,: Anaro surface; G, Uattamdi, Kayoa, Maluku Utara (1300-1000 BC); H, Pitcairn Island, Polynesia (courtesy of the Harry Maude collection).

Source: Peter Bellwood.

The roughly circular cross-sectioned chisels, items E to H, come respectively from Savidug Dune Site (from square 29M at a depth of 30-40 cm, thus from the upper cultural layer), Anaro (surface), Uattamdi in the northern Moluccas (c.1000 BC), and Pitcairn Island in Polynesia (undated;

see also Bellwood 2007, plate 34, top right). Because of their relative rarity, it is interesting to speculate whether chisels of this type are linked by cultural transmission, or resemble each other purely by chance. The Anaro specimen is unfortunately rather battered, and the Savidug specimen is only a butt, interestingly stepped, and perhaps not found in its original place of deposition. But the overall shapes and dimensions of all these chisels are remarkably similar. De la Torre (2000: Fig. 13 no. 12) illustrates another one, 7.1 cm long, from the lower layer with red-slipped pottery beneath the Irigayen shell midden in the Cagayan Valley, dated *c.*1400-1000 BC (Ogawa 2002: Table 1).

Hoe-like flaked and hammer-dressed tools

These artefacts are not especially common in Batanes, but when they do occur they resemble a large class of flaked hoe-like tools reported extensively from Neolithic sites in Taiwan, for instance by Li (1983) for Oluanbi and Tsang et al. (2006) for the Early Neolithic site of Nanguanli near Tainan. The Batanes specimens are made of local volcanic rocks, rather than the finer and presumably exotic metamorphic rocks preferred for adzes. Item A in Fig. 8.6 was excavated from just above the pottery-bearing layer in Torongan Cave on Itbayat (square B, 30-35 cm), and thus has an age approaching 1500-2000 BC. The other four specimens are all surface finds from Anaro, but item D is particularly interesting and unique because of the splayed shape of its blade. Sung et al. (1992: Plate 85) illustrate two similar waisted forms with splayed blades from Lanyu (Jiranweina site), but unfortunately these are undated. As a group these artefacts have much stronger parallels in Taiwan than in the main Philippines. All show heavy use damage, consistent with hoeing rather than woodworking.

In terms of all the above-discussed categories of stone artefacts, the volcanic and metamorphic rocks identified by Yoshiyuki Iizuka are listed in the relevant figure captions. Basalts and andesites are very common in the Taiwan-Luzon Arc, particularly in eastern Taiwan, Batanes and the northern Philippines. Their geochemical fingerprints (age, trace elements and isotope compositions) might be similar in different localities, and the three specimens identified as volcanic in origin (Fig. 8.2 F and 8.6 B and D) could possibly be from Itbayat. The metamorphic specimens (Fig. 8.4 D, F and H) are not from Itbayat, but are otherwise hard to source since similar rocks occur widely in both Taiwan and Luzon.

Bark cloth beaters

Four specimens were recovered from Anaro, all broken. The most important is the working area of a "horned" beater of what appears to be a local volcanic rock from Anaro 2 (Fig. 8.7 D), recovered during excavation on the limestone bedrock, sealed below a C14 date of AD 50-240 (Wk 14643). As discussed in chapter 6, the stamped pottery from Anaro 2 agrees with a commencement date for occupation of this location around 1000 BC, so this beater could be of a similar antiquity. It is therefore significant that the handle end of a similar beater, albeit without the end that might once have carried a "horn", was recovered during the excavations at Nanguanli, an early Neolithic site dating to 2500-3000 BC in southwestern Taiwan (Tsang et al. 2006: 91). This Nanguanli beater is perhaps the oldest dated specimen of its type from Island Southeast Asia, and specimens of similar antiquity occur in Guangdong (Cameron 2006).

Figure 8.6. Hoe-like tools from Anaro.

A. Waisted hoe of volcanic rock from Torongan Cave, square A, 50-55 cm, hammer dressed and flaked into shape. The margins all show heavy wear. c.2000-1500 BC.

B. Butt end of a hoe flaked from local Batanes volcanic rock that contains iron oxide, ilmenite, clinopyroxene, orthopyroxene and plagioclase, identified by Yoshiyuki Iizuka. From Anaro, surface find.

C. Flaked and partially ground mid-segment of a hoe of volcanic rock, Anaro surface find.

D. Splayed blade of a flaked and ground hoe of a local volcanic rock with the same identified composition as item B. Heavily battered on the cutting edge. Anaro surface find. Sung et al. 1992: Plate 85, show a similar but complete example from Jiranweina on Lanyu Island, off SE Taiwan.

E. Bifacially-flaked hoe with a lenticular cross-section from Anaro (Kaxanggan).

Source: Peter Bellwood.

Figure 8.7. Bark cloth beaters from Anaro.

A. Hammer dressed object of volcanic rock, hammer dressed into the shape of a bird's head and similar in shape to the distal end of the horned bark cloth beater illustrated as item D. The photos are of the right hand side, at two different exposures, and from the top. The left hand side has the same decoration as the right. Anaro surface find.

B. Segment of the working area of a bark cloth beater of volcanic rock, surface find from Anaro. This is similar in shape to the corresponding portion of item D.

C. Fragment of another beater, shape indeterminate. Anaro surface find.

D. Distal end of a horned bark cloth beater with 8 working grooves from Anaro square 2B, found in a small pocket on the limestone bedrock below 20 cm, below a C14 sample dated to c. AD 100.

Source: Peter Bellwood.

Also from Anaro, as a surface find, is a segment of the working area of another bark cloth beater of volcanic rock (Fig. 8.7 B). This is almost identical in shape to the relevant portion of the above specimen from Anaro 2B, and presumably came from a similar beater. Another beater fragment shown as Fig. 8.7 C, also of volcanic rock, has an indeterminate original shape.

Another remarkable surface find from Anaro, shown as Fig. 8.7 A, is the hammer dressed object of volcanic rock in the apparent shape of a bird's head and similar in profile shape to the distal end of the horned bark cloth beater from Anaro 2B. The photos are of the right hand side, at two different exposures, and from the top. The left hand side has the same decoration as the right. This rather beautiful object cannot be proven to have been the end of a bark cloth beater, but this remains a possibility.

Sawn and ground Taiwan slate points

In excess of 50 fragments of Taiwan slate knives and projectile points (mostly broken butts and points), together with a few other items of siliceous rock that appear to be non-native to the

Batanes Islands, were collected as surface finds around Anaro by land owner Mr Rodobaldo Ponce and given to the research team. As with the adzes, local people find these fragments all the time so an exact total of finds is elusive. A small number of items were also recovered from the Anaro excavations (Table 8.1). As will be discussed in chapter 9, Anaro clearly served as a locus for working Taiwan nephrite using a sawing and drilling technology (Hung et al. 2007), and many of the recovered slate items clearly functioned as part of this industry for sawing stone. The remarkable site of Pinglin close to the Fengtian nephrite source in eastern Taiwan has yielded many such points and knives as surface finds, in many cases with cutting edges that actually fit into grooves in discarded nephrite slabs.

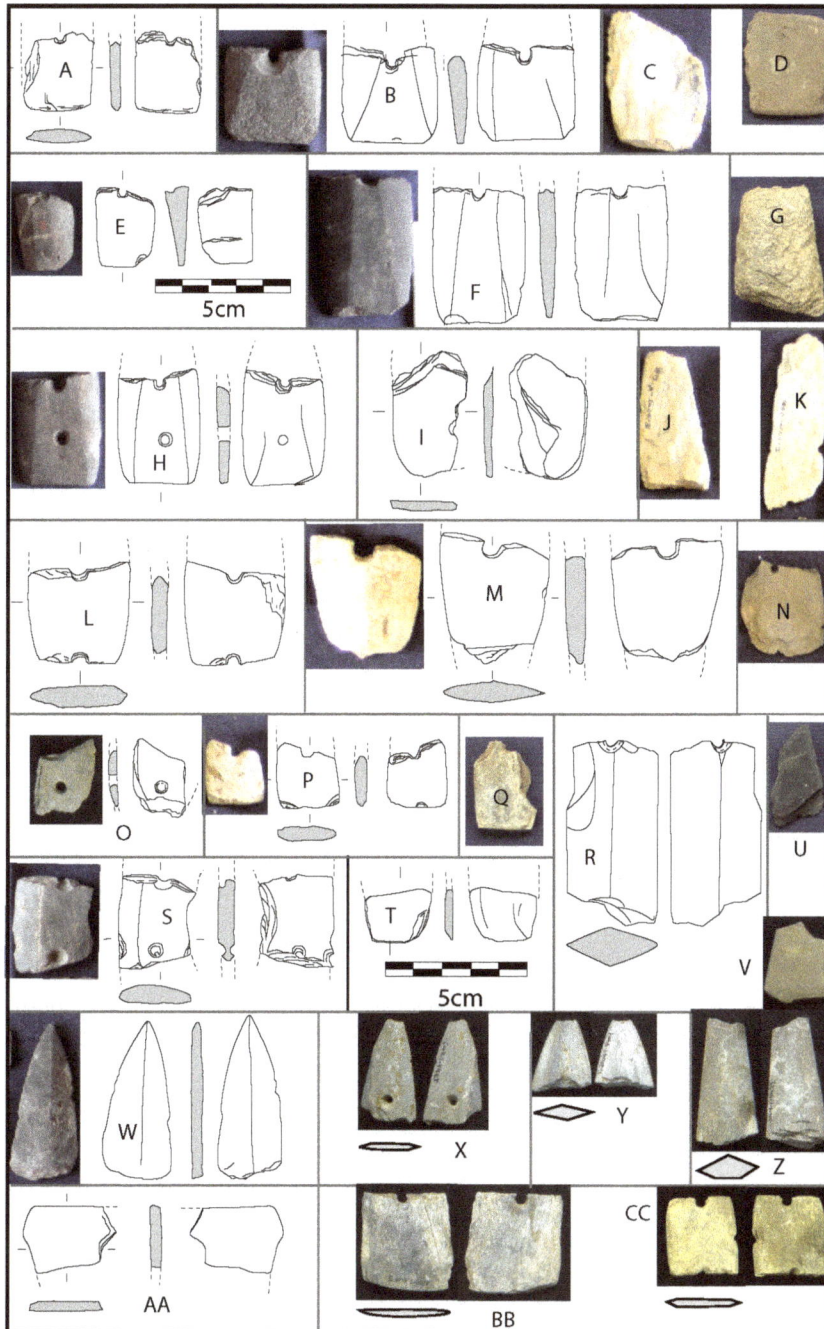

Figure 8.8. Taiwan slate points, point butts and knives from Sunget and Anaro.

Source: Peter Bellwood.

The Anaro slate items are mostly both the points and the butts of projectile points, all broken (not a single complete one was found), many with one or two surviving perforations. At least one (Fig. 8.8 S) had an unfinished perforation. All perforations are hourglass-shaped in cross-section, drilled from both sides. There are also a few knife-like specimens, usually with one or more worn and rounded edges. Fig. 8.8 D shows one of these, excavated from Anaro 3(2004) at a depth of 85-90 cm and thus of first millennium BC date. It appears to be one end of a stone "reaping knife", perhaps similar to the perforated complete examples illustrated by Li (1983: Plates 69-70) from Oluanbi Phase III (c.1000 BC) at the southern tip of Taiwan, also by Chang (1969: Plate 76) from his "Lungshanoid" phase at Fengbitou, and by Tsang et al. (2006:146-7) from the Niuchouzi phase (2000 BC) in the Tainan area in southwestern Taiwan. No such complete perforated knives have ever been found in Batanes.

It is interesting to note that all the points and knives were broken prior to discard. Were they imported complete into Batanes, and then broken during use? This seems unlikely, since Batanes had no large mammals that could have been hunted with the points (unless they hunted humans), and rice has never been a significant crop there, thus removing two of the suggested functions as projectile points and harvesting knives. It seems more likely that these items were all broken and discarded in Taiwan, and then brought to Batanes by people who possibly scavenged them from abandoned archaeological sites. Let us not forget that the archaeological sites that survive in Taiwan today would have loomed much larger in the landscape soon after they were occupied, when they were perhaps strewn with thousands of discarded items just lying on the surface of the ground. A use-wear study of the Anaro slate items would perhaps throw some light on questions of function, but even the naked eye can see that many have the kind of rounded edge wear that we would expect from the sawing of nephrite using quartz grit and water, exactly like the edges on many of the slate saws from the Pinglin nephrite workshop in eastern Taiwan.

The item of coarse slate shown in Fig. 8.8 G is of interest. This seems too laminated and crumbly to have served as a useful sawing tool, but this kind of coarse slate is a raw material common in sites in southeast Taiwan, such as Beinan, where it was used for architectural features including large items identified as house ladders (one is on display in the Beinan excavation park in Taidong). This is the only piece of this particular raw material from Anaro. The large diamond cross-sectioned slate rod shown in Fig. 8.8 R has a trace of a perforation at one end, and is of interest because of the evident large size of the complete original. Fig. 8.8 Z also seems to be a fragment of a relatively narrow and elongated point.

The eight most significant slate specimens (excluding tiny fragments) recovered from the Anaro excavations are as follows:

- Anaro 3, 85-90: the end of a rectangular slate knife, already discussed above (Fig. 8.8 D);

- Anaro 3, 90-95: a slate fragment with one straight ground edge (Fig. 8.8 U);

- Anaro 3B, 90-95, a knife-like fragment of siliceous rock (Fig. 8.8 V);

- Anaro 3F, 60-65, a knife-like fragment of siliceous rock (not illustrated);

- Anaro 3E, 40-50: a slate point (Fig. 8.8 Y).

- Anaro 2A, 10-15, a slate fragment with one ground and one sharp edge (not illustrated here, but see Bellwood and Dizon 2005: Fig. 17 F);

- Anaro 2A, 20-25, a siliceous fragment with one sharp but damaged edge (not illustrated here, but see Bellwood and Dizon 2005: Fig. 17 I);

- Anaro 2B, 20-25, a tip of a slate projectile point (not illustrated here, but see Bellwood and Dizon 2005: Fig. 17 G).

If we exclude the C14 dates from the disturbed square Anaro 3B, these excavated items all come from the earlier part of the Anaro sequence, prior to 2000 years ago. They equate well with the evidence for nephrite working on the site during the first millennium BC. Two slate items were also collected at Sunget on Batan, with a similar chronology, shown as G and H in Fig. 8.1. One is a small perforated pendant, the other a fragment of a slate point that seems originally to have been bi-perforated. As noted, the Sunget items also date close to 1000 BC.

Parallels for these slate points and knives in Taiwan are prolific, from the beginning of the Neolithic onwards (Dabenkeng culture) through into the first millennium BC. In specific terms they include Chang 1969: Plates 16, 23, 76, 77, 98 (Fengbitou, Dabenkeng and Yuanshan); Li 1983: Plates 69-70 (Oluanbi III); Tsang et al. 2006: 90-91, 112, 146-7 (Nanguanli and Youxianfang); and Lien and Sung 1989: Plates III, IV (Beinan). It will be noted that these parallels come from all over Taiwan, and it is impossible to point to one location as a primary source for all the slate items from Anaro.

Body ornaments of stone

Surprisingly perhaps, given the stony nature of the Batanes landscape, personal ornaments of stone were remarkably rare in all sites. Fig. 8.1 F and G are two perforated stone pendants from Sunget on Batan, item G of Taiwan slate. No stone beads were ever found in Batanes, and none of carnelian or nephrite. It would be true to say that we found very little evidence for any kind of body ornamentation in Batanes prehistory.

Side-notched pebble sinkers

This is an important artefact type that occurs in Taiwan from the earliest Neolithic onwards (e.g. Tsang et al. 2006:113 for Nanguanli, Tainan, c.2800 BC). In Batanes, they were particularly common in the lower layer of Savidug Dune Site (first millennium BC), and in the excavations at Sunget (1200 to 800 BC). Only four were ever found on Itbayat, surface finds from the vicinity of Anaro. This could reflect the nature of the Itbayat coastline, surrounded entirely by cliffs with no shallow water. Such an environment would be difficult for using nets, and indeed the only people we ever saw fishing off the coast of Itbayat were swimmers with spear guns. Net fishing, however, involving several men using boats, was observed on several occasions in sheltered bays off the western coast of Batan (Yang 2006).

The Sunget pebble sinkers were the subject of a MA thesis at ANU completed by Shawna Hsiu-ying Yang in 2006. Adding the examples collected in 1982, Sunget has produced a total of 81 of these items, averaging 3.3 cm long (range 2.1 to 5.3 cm). Fig. 8.9 shows in its upper three rows the 36 complete examples recovered from the 2002-2004 excavations, together with (next row down) a number of unworked pebbles found in the site that appear to have been carried there from nearby beach or river bed sources for manufacturing purposes.

Shawna Yang also surveyed the occurrence of sinkers of this type (A1 in her classification) in Taiwan. This was the only shape present in early Neolithic sites of the Dabenkeng culture, before 2500 BC, both in western Taiwan (e.g. Nanguanli – above) and in the Penghu Islands. Although this form continues in later sites as well, this observation opens the possibility that the initial settlement of Batanes from Taiwan might have occurred during the latter part of the Dabenkeng phase, possibly even prior to 2000 BC. If so, the first settlers brought the A1 sinker form only, and continued to use it until about 2000 years ago. No sinkers have been found in well-dated younger contexts in Batanes, for instance in Phase 3 sites such as Payaman and Naidi on Batan Island.

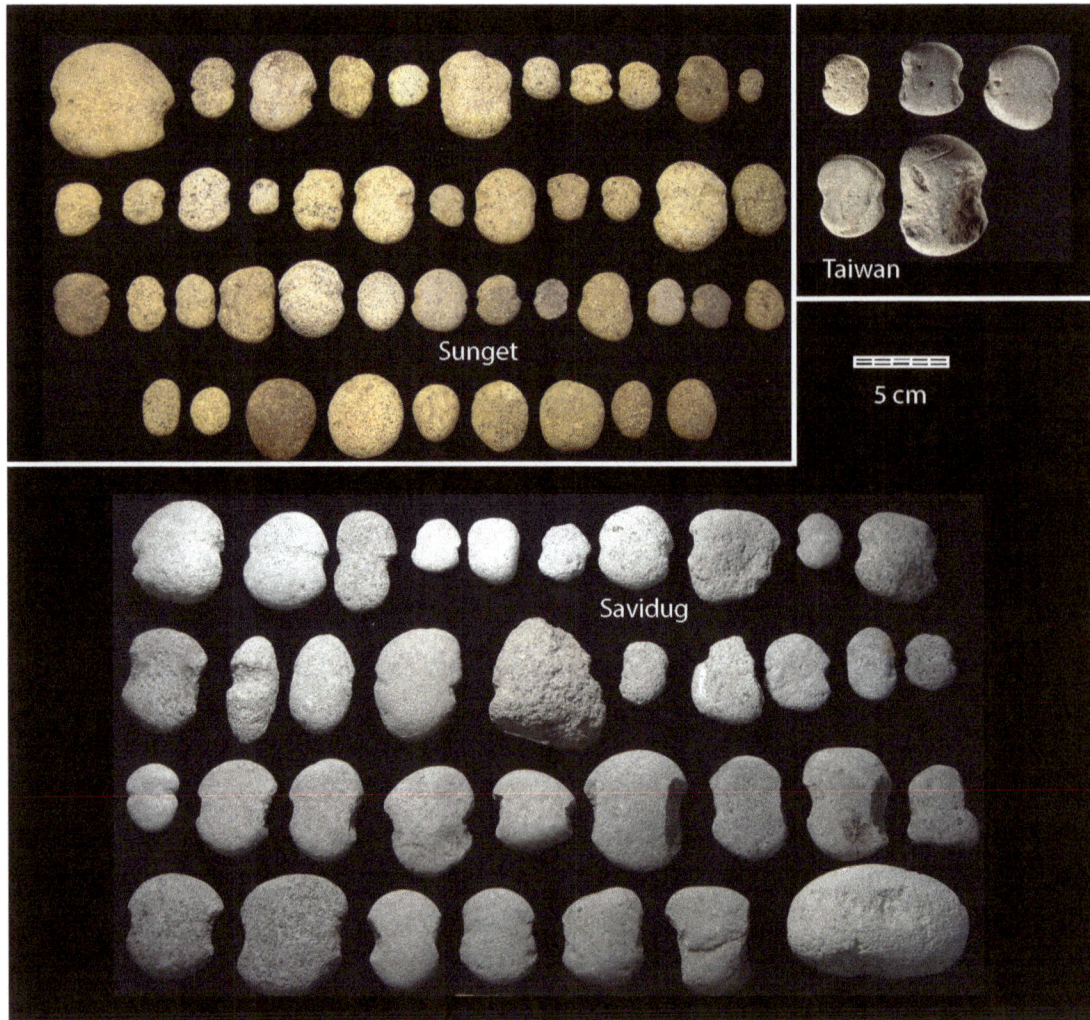

Figure 8.9. Side-notched pebble sinkers from Sunget, Savidug Dune Site, and Taiwan. Top left: 36 side-notched pebble sinkers from the cultural layer at Sunget (Top and Main Terraces) on Batan, together with nine unworked river pebbles, a sample of many found in the Sunget excavations that were carried up to the site, presumably to make sinkers when needed. Top right: 5 notched pebbles of the same type from Suogang, Penghu Islands, *c.*2500 BC; Kending, Southern Tip, *c.*2000 BC; and Guishan, southwestern Taiwan. Bottom: A sample of 26 side-notched volcanic rock pebble sinkers, part of a total of 59 from the lower cultural layer in Savidug Dune site.

Source: Peter Bellwood.

In Savidug Dune Site, a total of 59 of these A1 sinkers were found (Fig. 8.9, lower), identical in shape to those from Sunget, mostly in the lower cultural layer of trench QR7-9 (1100 BC to late first millennium BC; Table 8.1). A total of 29 were clustered in two small areas of trench QR7-9 between 100 and 120 cm, suggesting that one or more fishnets had been discarded there with their sinkers still tied on.

Grindstones

These occur in most sites, and form a category that is not particularly amenable to time and space sorting. Many have coarse siliceous structures and could have been used for various polishing activities (Fig. 8.10).

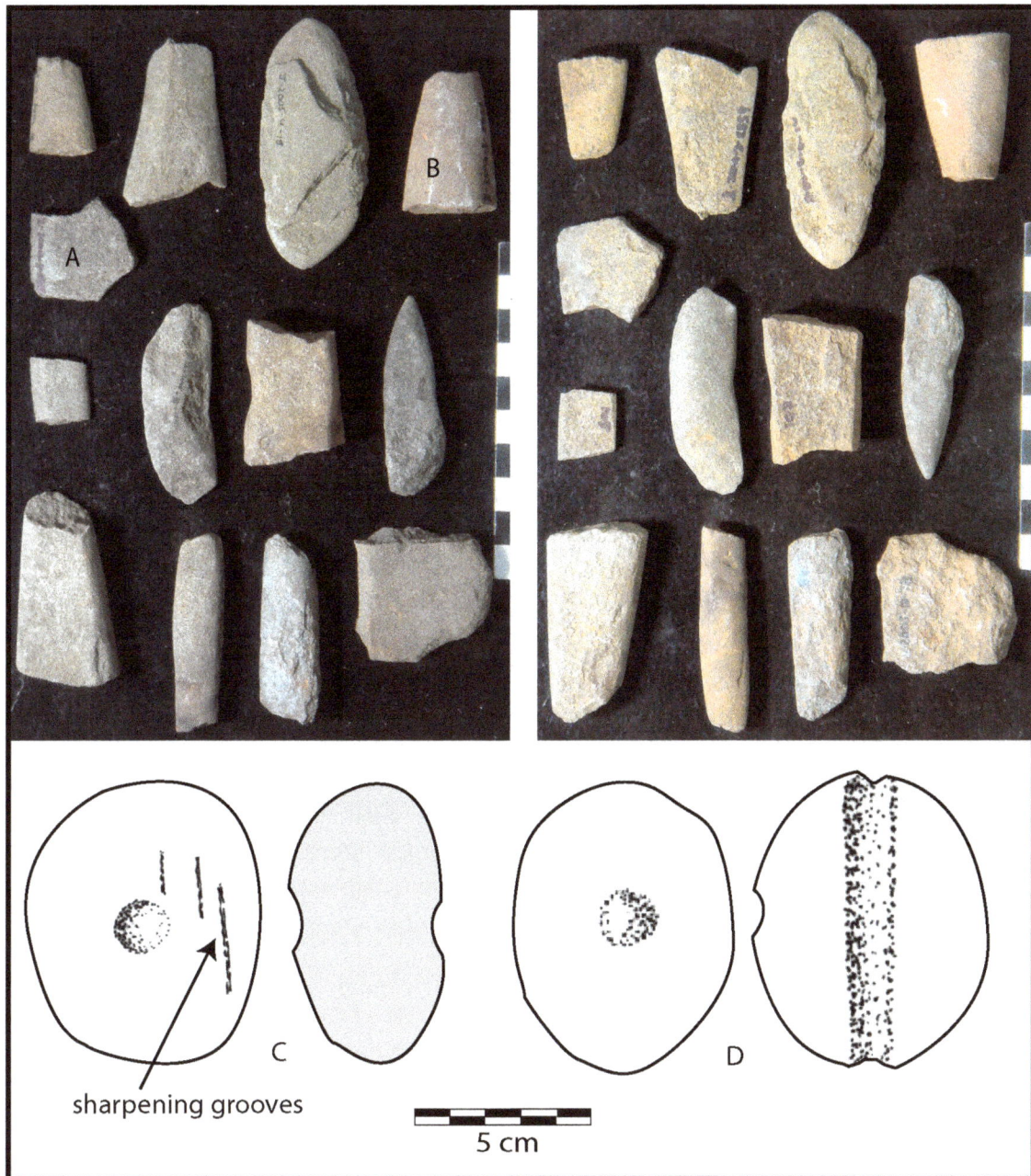

Figure 8.10. Grindstones and polishing stones. Upper: These 13 specimens all come from Anaro on Itbayat. A was excavated from Anaro 3C, 55-60 cm, and B from Anaro 3C, 50-55 cm. All are turned over for the right hand photograph. Scale in cm. Lower: Pitted stone anvils: (C) Savidug Dune Site, lower cultural layer; Savidug Ijang; (D) Mitangeb trench B, top of layer 5.

Source: Peter Bellwood.

Pitted anvil stones

Three of these were found, one from layer 5 at Mitangeb on Siayan Island (Fig. 8.10 D) and two from Savidug Dune site at 80 and 150 cm depth, thus within the lower cultural layer. Fig. 8.10 C shows the Savidug specimen from 80 cm, which has three additional sharpening grooves on its surface. That from 150 cm is almost identical, with an anvil pit on each side, but is not illustrated. Pitted anvils are a type of artefact that seems to have occurred across much of Island

Southeast Asia from Pleistocene times onwards, examples being found, for instance, in sites in the northern Moluccas and there termed "canarium anvils", since local informants told us they were used for cracking *Canarium* sp. (*kenari*) nuts (Bellwood et al. 1998: Fig. 4a, Table 3, Table 5). The example from Mitangeb seems to have been modified into a fishing sinker of Shawna Yang's (2006) type B, reported from southern China, Taiwan and Japan (Jomon Period), but not previously from Batanes. Recorded drift voyages from Japan to Batanes are discussed in chapter 1.

Metal artefacts

These were rather rare in the Batanes excavations, in accord with Dampier's 1687 statement to the effect that iron was scarce (see chapter 1). A few pieces were found in the excavations at Savidug Dune Site and Anaro, in all cases but one (from Anaro at 80-90 cm) in upper layers, and probably dating well after AD 500. The specimens from Savidug are highly corroded and are not illustrated, but 4 pieces from Anaro together with a piece of probable iron slag are shown in Fig. 8.11. From left to right these are respectively from Anaro 5, 0-5 cm; Anaro 3C, 40-50 cm; Anaro 3A, 80-90 cm; and Anaro 6, 70-80 cm. All are clearly blade- or knife-like objects with flat thin cross-sections, all too corroded for former cutting edges to be definitely identified. The piece from Anaro 3A, 80-90 cm (Fig. 8.11 C), is particularly interesting because of its rod-like shape. Was this part of a drill used for boring holes in stone, especially nephrite?

A small piece of copper was found in the road cutting through the Savidug Dune Site. This had a lead isotope signature not consistent with a Thai origin (neither Khao Wong Prachan Valley nor Phu Lon, according to Oli Pryce, pers. comm.), but its exact source remains unknown. It almost certainly came from the Savidug lower cultural layer since the cutting passes near trench QR7-9, where the upper cultural layer was virtually absent. More interesting was the finding in the same place of one fired clay valve of a bivalve casting assembly for what appears to have been a socketed axe (Fig. 8.11 F). This demonstrates conclusively that copper/bronze casting was carried out in Batanes in prehistory, albeit probably using imported scrap metal as raw material. Another casting mould fragment, also of fired clay, was found in 1982 at Tayid, a site shown to date to about 1850 years ago when investigated in 2003 (see chapter 3 and Fig. 8.11 G). Between them, these finds suggest that cupreous metallurgy was present in Batanes by around 2000 years ago, if not before.

Artefacts of glass and bone

Glass beads from recent layers, all apparently dating within the past 1500 years, are shown in Fig. 8.11 (bottom). Most are blue, suggesting perhaps that the Batanes Islands had access mainly to only one source of beads, wherever that might have been. A few pottery examples are shown as well, but the general lack of shell beads in Batanes is interesting given their common occurrence in Neolithic sites elsewhere in Island Southeast Asia. Only two are shown in the figure.

Bone artefacts are also rather rare. The perforated pig tusk pendant from Savidug QR7-9 120 cm (*c.* 500 BC to AD 1: Fig. 8.11 I) is unique. Bone points and the pig canine fishing gorge (Fig. 8.11 J and K) are paralleled in southern Taiwan (Li 1983: Plate 102 for Oluanbi III at *c.*1000 BC; Tosca Chang pers. comm. for new excavations at Oluanbi; C-H. Tsang et al. 2006:175) and at Nagsabaran in the Cagayan Valley (also *c.*1500-1000 BC, Philip Piper pers. comm.). As well as the illustrated bipoint, two other bone unipoints (or broken bipoints) were found in the same general horizon at Anaro (square 3, 70-75 and 80-85), suggesting a first millennium BC date. The carved bone human ornament comes from Anaro 3C at 50-55 cm.

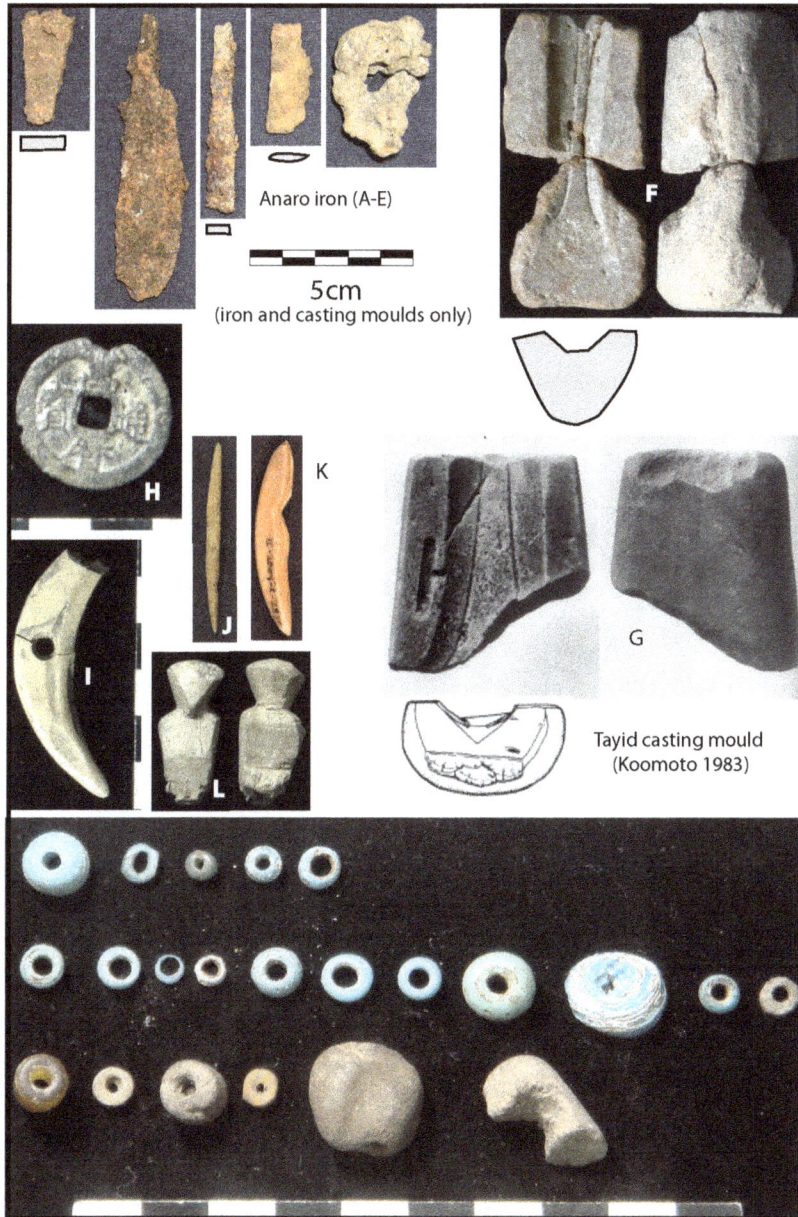

Figure 8.11. Metal, bone and glass artefacts from Batanes sites.

Source: Peter Bellwood.

A-E: four iron items and a piece of iron slag (A-E) from Anaro (see text for locations). F: fired clay casting valve from Savidug. G: fired clay casting mould from Tayid. H: coin of the Ming ruler Wan Li (AD 1583-1620) from Torongan Cave, 0-5 cm.

I-L: Bone artefacts, all to one scale (attached to item I). I: Perforated and carved pig tusk pendant from Savidug QR7-9 120 (500 BC to AD 1 approx.). J: bone bipoint, Anaro 3A 80-90. K: pig canine fishing gorge, Anaro 3C 60-65. L: a carved bone human ornament from Anaro 3C 50-55 cm.

Bottom: Beads (mainly glass) from Batanes sites, with a baked clay *lingling-o* hook at bottom right (see Fig. 8.12). Top row from left: Torongan Cave surface; Garayao (Itbayat) surface (2 beads); Torongan A, 0-5 cm; Anaro surface. Middle row from left: Anaro 5, 10-15; Anaro 5, 0-5 (3 beads, the white one is shell); Anaro surface; Anaro 3G, 10-20; Anaro 3E, 30-40; Anaro 9, 0-5; Anaro surface (shell). Bottom row from left: Torongan 0-5 (brown tubular glass); Anaro surface; Anaro surface, probably pottery; Savidug Dune Site KL29, 70-90 (pottery?); Anaro 3A, 0-10 (sub-spherical clay); Savidug QR7-9, 120-30, baked clay *lingling-o* hook.

Baked clay body ornaments

Fig. 8.12 A shows a pottery bracelet fragment decorated with stamped circles from Anaro 3C, 60-65 cm, set in a zig-zag motif similar to that in the bottom row of shoulder decoration in the Anaro circle-stamped type 1 vessels. Stratigraphically and stylistically, this dates between 500 BC and AD 1. Also shown in Fig. 8.12 are ten very diagnostic clay *lingling-o* ear ornaments, eight from the lower cultural layer at Savidug Dune Site (first millennium BC), and two from between 55 and 70 cm in Anaro 3C, probably also late first millennium BC.

The eight Savidug ear ornaments are so similar that they were probably made by the same artisan. All have lenticular cross-sections and are between 2 and 2.5 cm thick, and all have remnant stubs of broken-off hooks for attachment through the earlobe. A complete but broken-off hook is shown in Fig. 8.11, bottom right. The two Anaro specimens have different cross-sections, more angular and thinner than those from Savidug.

The reason why this form is so significant concerns its further distribution far beyond Batanes, in the Cagayan Valley of Luzon, the Tabon Caves on Palawan, and in central and southern coastal Vietnam. Large numbers of baked clay earrings with inner openings larger than those from Batanes come from contexts with red slipped pottery at Magapit, Nagsabaran and Lal-lo in the Cagayan Valley (Ogawa 2002:100; Thiel 1986-7a: Fig. 4). Others, closer to the Batanes specimens in shape, come from Irigayen and Arku Cave (de la Torre 2000: Fig. 13, 6-8; Thiel 1986-7b: Fig. 5). In Irigayen they occur at stratigraphically ambiguous intermediate depths in association with C14 dates that could extend earlier than 1000 BC or to as recently as AD 500 (Ogawa 2002:95 lists the Irigayen dates), but in Arku they are more tightly enclosed within the first millennium BC. As noted, a date for the Batanes type closer to 2500/2000 than 3000 years ago would perhaps be more likely, but there is no reason why the form should not be older in Cagayan. None were found at Sunget, which perhaps rules out their occurrence in Batanes in the period 1200-800 BC. The Tabon specimens come from Duyong and Pagayona Caves (Fox 1970: Fig. 43a), and were attributed by Fox to his Early and Developed Metal Ages, 500 BC to AD 200. This overlaps the likely date range for these items in Batanes.

The long-distance significance of this type of ear ornament lies in the observation that dramatically similar ones occur in sites such as Giong Ca Vo in coastal southern Vietnam, and in Sa Huynh and pre-Sa Huynh sites such as Binh Chau and Thach Lac in central Vietnam. These occurrences could date back as far as 800 BC at Binh Chau and Thach Lac, and are discussed in more detail by Hung et al. (in press) and Bellwood (in press). Given the occurrence of seemingly earlier examples of these objects in Cagayan sites such as Nagsabaran and Magapit, and their corresponding absence in Vietnam Early Neolithic (second millennium BC) sites such as An Son and Rach Nui (Long An Province) and Man Bac (Ninh Binh Province), a Philippine origin currently seems most likely. Future discoveries could of course change this, but these artefacts are carrying information that could be very important in determining the origins and cultural affinities of Malayo-Polynesian (Chamic subgroup) settlement in central Vietnam.

Figure 8.12. Baked clay ornaments from Anaro and Savidug Dune Site.

A. Pottery bracelet fragment decorated with a zigzag design of stamped circles on each side. Anaro 3C, 60-65 cm.

Main figure: baked clay ear ornaments. Top two rows from Savidug Dune Site (from top left: road cutting surface find; 2006 150 cm; L28 145 cm; QR7-9 110-120 cm; QR7-9 120 cm (2); QR7-9 120-130 cm; QR7-9 130 cm). Bottom row from Anaro (3C 65-70 cm, 3C 55-60 cm). Two sides of each specimen are shown.

Source: Peter Bellwood.

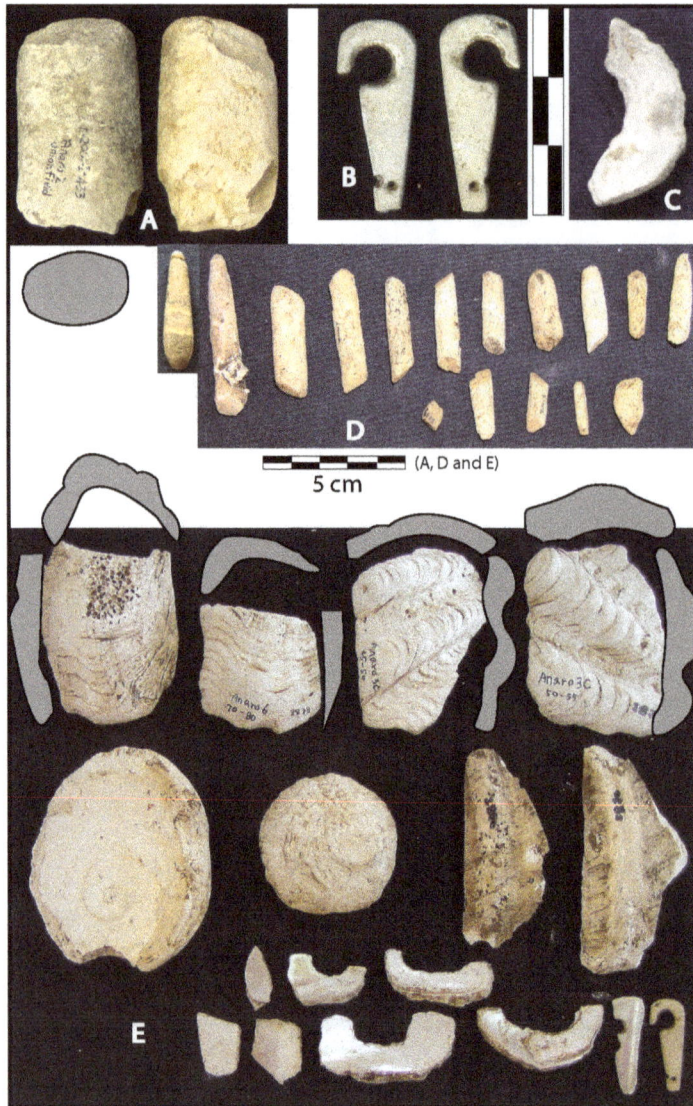

Figure 8.13. Shell artefacts from Anaro (note that B and C share a different scale from the other items).

A. Hammer dressed poll of a shell adze, from weight and appearance perhaps of fossil shell from the uplifted reef limestone at Anaro.

B. Hook-like shell ornament, possibly a pendant or ear ornament, from Anaro 3, 100-110 cm. Stratigraphically, this piece dates to c.1000 BC and it is paralleled closely by a stone example from Magapit in the Cagayan Valley (Ogawa 2002:100).

C. Shell ring or fishhook fragment, Anaro 3, 65-70 cm.

D. 16 worked sea urchin spines from Anaro. 7 of these came from excavated contexts, mostly between 20 and 65 cm, and have ground ends, sometimes with two facets. Example at left is grooved around one end and comes from Anaro 6, 110-120 cm.

E. Top row: four presumed adzes (all are damaged) that retain the dorsal surfaces of *Tridacna* shells. From left: Anaro 3B, 85-90 cm; Anaro 6, 70-80 cm; Anaro 3C, 45-50 cm; Anaro 3C, 50-55 cm. The two at left still retain possible curved cutting edges (see longitudinal sections), while the two at right appear to be broken body segments without blades. See also chapter 12 for further discussion of these items.

Middle row: 2 chipped opercula of *Turbo marmoratus* from Anaro 3B, 75-80 cm and Anaro 6, 10-20 cm respectively. At right are two pieces of *T. marmoratus* shell (external view), perhaps worked.

Bottom row: various pieces of worked shell from Anaro 3A 40-80, the round ones presumably from fishhooks (chapter 12). At right is the ornament shown above at B, and to its left a similar but less complete piece from Anaro 3A 30-40 cm.

Source: Peter Bellwood.

Shell artefacts

Anaro shell artefacts

Fig. 8.13 shows a range of shell artefacts from Anaro. These are described in the caption, but a few further comments are necessary. It is possibly that the adze butt of fossil shell (item A) could be from a large *Tridacna* adze similar to those illustrated by Fox (1970: Fig. 19) from Duyong Cave on Palawan. So far, this specimen is unique in Batanes, but the Anaro limestone massif contains a lot of fossil shell.

The perforated hook-like shell item of presumed personal decoration shown as item B in Fig. 8.13 (and again in the bottom right corner) is paralleled by a stone example from Magapit (Ogawa 2002: 100). It is also a form that can be seen in a number of nephrite ornaments from the Beinan burials in southeastern Taiwan, as shown by Lien (2002: Fig. 3, especially her forms IIIB1, IIIB2 and IV4). The precise date range for the Beinan assemblage is uncertain, but available dates fall within the period 1500 BC to AD 1.

The Anaro sea urchin spine "files" are a form widespread in Pacific archaeology, but little mentioned in Taiwan or Island Southeast Asia, presumably because their status as artefacts is not always obvious. These Anaro specimens seem to have been held and used like pencils since the faceting is on their ends.

The four *Tridacna* adzes with dorsal surface configurations come from the middle and lower parts of the Anaro sequence (Fig. 8.13 E). The two at left show signs of grinding and have cutting edges with markedly gouge-like profiles. They are rather similar to *Tridacna* adzes excavated in Golo Cave in the northern Moluccas (Bellwood 1997: Plate 25), originally dated to the late Pleistocene (Bellwood et al. 1998) because of their association with C14-dated food shells of this time period. However, direct AMS dating of Golo shell adzes has since shown that some were made of fossil shell, and they were probably also cached in holes dug in the cave floor. A date for these Golo Cave shell adzes well within the Holocene now seems very likely. The other two Anaro specimens at right are not so clearly worked and might just be debitage.

The two chipped *Turbo marmoratus* opercula are a form that is common across Southeast Asia from preceramic times onwards, being for instance quite numerous in OLP Phase I at Oluanbi in southern Taiwan (Li 1983: Plate 31). Szabo et al. (2007) note the use of *T. marmoratus* opercula for making artefacts as early as 30,000 years ago in the northern Moluccas, Indonesia. Their use presumably continued until recent times.

The worked ring-like pieces at the top right (item C) and bottom of Fig. 8.13 are presumed to be from fishhook roughouts (cf. the similar roughout pieces of one-piece bait hooks illustrated by Kirch and Yen 1982: Figs 94-95, from the Polynesian Outlier of Tikopia, Solomon Islands). Nevertheless, we found no complete shell fishhooks in Batanes. Shell one-piece bait hooks, however, do occur at Oluanbi in southern Taiwan (Li 1983: Plate 94).

The shell artefacts from Anaro, and Savidug (below), are discussed in further detail by the authors of chapter 12.

Savidug Dune Site shell artefacts

The shell artefacts shown in Fig. 8.14 are quite remarkable in the stylistic differentiation that they reveal between the two cultural layers that are separated by sterile sand in the Savidug Dune Site. As noted in chapter 4, these two layers are about one millennium apart, the older dating from the first millennium BC, the younger from the second millennium AD. Such a high level of stratigraphic separation is especially important since it lowers the chances of unnoticed mixing and disturbance that occur so commonly in shallow rock shelters and single component open sites. Batan Island has similar situations, where archaeological deposits are securely buried and protected beneath volcanic ash, as at Sunget.

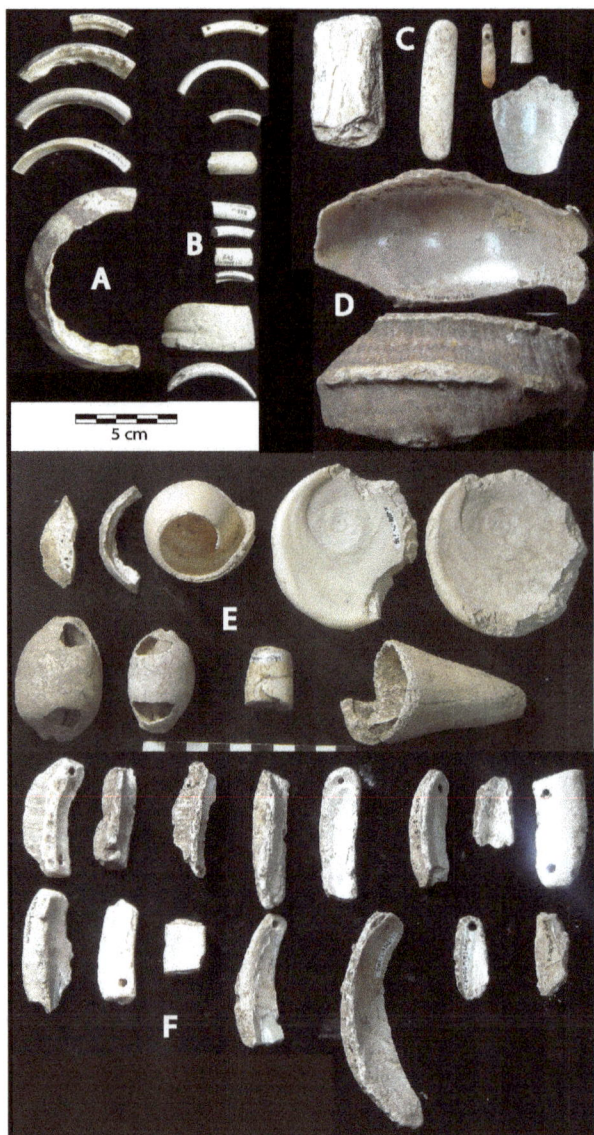

Figure 8.14. Shell artefacts from Savidug Dune Site. (UCL = upper cultural layer; LCL = lower cultural layer).

A. Bracelet fragments of *Trochus niloticus*, including a large rough-out, all from the LCL (first millennium BC) in QR7-9 (110-170 cm).

B. Ring or bracelet fragments (the lower three are shown from two views each) that appear to be mostly of *Conus* sp. shell, except for the top bi-perforate example that appears to be made of *Trochus* shell. These all come from the UCL (45-100 cm).

C. At left, worked shell adze or knife, B9 70-80 cm (UCL). Next is a smooth scraper-like tool or polisher of shell from burial jar 3 in F1 (LCL). At right are two perforated sea urchin spines from QR7-9, LCL.

D. This large shell "spoon" of *Turbo marmoratus* is a remarkable piece found in the road cutting and most probably from the LCL that outcrops at this point. To top right is the distal end of another one, excavated from QR7-9 130-140 and thus firmly of LCL date (first millennium BC).

E (above scale). Various items of worked shell, including (top row from left) part of a bracelet core (UCL), *Trochus* bracelet rough-out (LCL), *Conus* shell subjected to direct percussion (LCL), and two chipped *T. marmoratus* opercula (LCL). Bottom row: 2 bi-perforate cowry shells (LCL - possibly scrapers), sawn gastropod tube, possibly *Terebra* sp. (UCL), *Conus* shell subjected to direct percussion (UCL).

F. Uni- and bi-perforate long units made of *T. marmoratus* shell, all from the UCL except for the fragment at bottom right (QR7-9 120-130), that is indeterminate in shape.

Source: Peter Bellwood. Descriptions E and F incorporate comments from Katherine Szabó.

The bracelets offer the clearest chronological separation. *Trochus* shell bracelets (Fig. 8.14 A) occur only in the lower cultural layer at Savidug. *Trochus* bracelets were also an important form in Oceania from Lapita times onwards, as was the use of *Tridacna* for making adzes, also seen at Savidug (Leach and Davidson 2008: 310). However, *Conus* rings or bracelets of smaller diameter (Fig. 8.14 B), together with uni- and bi-perforated long units of *Turbo marmoratus* (Fig. 8.14 F), occur only in the upper cultural layer. During excavation we suspected that these *Turbo* long units might have been pendants, but in fact it seems possible that they could have served as shanks for composite fishhooks, especially given the presence of large pelagic carnivores such as the dolphinfish (*Coryphaena hippurus*) amongst the fishbones in the upper Savidug layers. No obvious shell points for such hooks were found, but it might have been possible to use thorn or bone points for this purpose. The evidence for exploitation of dolphinfish at Savidug and Pamayan is discussed in detail in chapter 11.

Apart from these enigmatic long units, whether parts of ornaments or fishing equipment, other interesting shell artefacts are two "spoons" or scoops (Fig. 8.14 D), the larger one a surface find but almost certainly from the lower cultural layer, as definitely was the other fragment illustrated just above it. These artefacts have very close parallels in Oluanbi Phase III (Li 1983: Plate 93) in southern Taiwan, and in the Tabon Complex in Palawan (Fox 1970: Fig. 42). The Oluanbi specimen is better finished on its dorsal surface than that from Savidug, but appears to be made also from a *Turbo marmoratus* shell and is presumably of first millennium BC antiquity. The Tabon specimens illustrated by Fox are evidently on different shell species, but the general idea still comes through. These are also Metal Age in Fox's terminology (500 BC to AD 200).

Non-ceramic artefacts: A review

The most remarkable point about the artefacts described above is their wide range of parallels, taking in Taiwan, Luzon, Palawan, and central Vietnam. These parallels no doubt reflect the progress of archaeological research – points of light in a vast fog of obscurity – but they are undeniable and of great import. The strongest parallels are undoubtedly with Taiwan, in nephrite, slate, stone adzes (stepped, grooved, some of Taiwan nephrite), flaked hoes, bark cloth beaters, pebble sinkers, spindle whorls, and a number of shell items. Even the possible shell lure shanks from Savidug are well-paralleled in stone from many sites in Taiwan. Many parallels occur also with Luzon, especially the Cagayan Valley, presumably because we have a good archaeological record from there. These parallels in Cagayan again include stone adzes (stepped and grooved, trapezoidal cross-sections, pale grey metamorphic raw material), bark cloth beaters, Taiwan nephrite (but apparently not Taiwan slate), baked clay ear ornaments, spindle whorls (e.g. Arku Cave; Thiel 1986-7b: Fig. 7), and some shell items, although the Cagayan sites, being inland, are not rich in shell artefacts.

Pottery connections also go both ways – the red-slipped surfaces and many vessel forms occur in both Taiwan and Cagayan, but the use of circle stamping alone (without punctate or dentate stamping) that was so specific to Batanes has only Taiwan parallels (e.g. Lanyu Island, Kending in the south, Yuanshan in the north, Yingpu near the west coast), and not Luzon as yet. The Cagayan sites, as well as those in the Mariana Islands and western Melanesia (Lapita), specialized in related but slightly different modes of decoration based on punctate and dentate stamping, with a lesser occurrence of circle stamping that was used mainly for zone boundaries rather than actual motifs (Hung et al. 2011; Carson et al. 2013). Further parallels in baked clay penannular earrings, in Palawan and central and southern (but not northern) Vietnam, are even more interesting. In the latter case they could perhaps relate to the major phenomenon in Austronesian history of Chamic colonization of the central Vietnamese portion of the Asian mainland, from somewhere in the Philippine-Borneo region during the middle or late first millennium BC (Hung et al. in press).

In recent years, many archaeologists, especially those who do not favour a role for Taiwan in the spread of Neolithic communities into Island Southeast Asia, have suggested that Taiwan to Luzon sailing would always have been impossible because of the existence of the south to north flowing Kuroshio current. In chapter 1, it was noted that although the Taiwan to Luzon route lay partly in the face of this current, there have been recorded drift voyages from Japan to Batanes, and also good reasons why longitudinal course shifts, counter currents and variations in intensity should not have allowed periodic movement to occur from Taiwan southwards. That such movement did occur is, of course, demonstrated without the slightest doubt by many of the artefacts described above. The Batanes Islands were clearly not settled only by people moving north from Luzon, unless someone can one day demonstrate the existence of unprecedentedly-large quantities of Taiwan artefacts in currently undiscovered Luzon sites. The sheer extent of the Cagayan Valley archaeological sample makes this most unlikely. Contacts with Taiwan occurred over more than 3000 years of prehistory, and they probably occurred many times. This issue is raised again for discussion in the concluding chapter, where a specific instance of contact around 2500 to 2000 years ago between the Batanes Islands and Lanyu Island, to the southeast of Taiwan, is highlighted.

Finally, attention should be drawn to the recent demonstration of very close parallels in red-slipped and decorated pottery forms between the Batanes and Cagayan Neolithic sites on the one hand, and the two sites of Minanga Sipakko and Kamassi in the Karama Valley of West Sulawesi, Indonesia, on the other (Anggraeni et al. in press). These two central Indonesian sites date to between 1500 and 500 BC, and thus fit perfectly with a model of Neolithic expansion southwards through the Philippines into central Indonesia.

9

The Batanes Nephrite Artefacts

Hsiao-chun Hung and Yoshiyuki Iizuka

Nephrite (jade) ornaments, especially ear-ornaments, are among the most attractive artefacts in Southeast Asian archaeology. As Loofs-Wissowa stated (1980-81: 57): "Ear-ornaments in general seem to have played, and are still playing in some societies, a greater role in Southeast Asia and parts of South Asia than almost anywhere else in the world....." Because of the beautifully wrought shapes and enchanting translucent colours of nephrite or jadeitite ornaments, generations of archaeologists have asked who made them, during which time period, with what kind of manufacturing process, using which trading networks, and for what purpose.

The study of nephrite in Philippine archaeology

In the Philippines, several thousand tools of a white variety of nephrite, especially adzes and chisels, were discovered during the 1930s and 1940s by H. Otley Beyer in Batangas, Rizal and Laguna Provinces in southwestern Luzon (Beyer 1948: 44-71). During the 1960s and 1970s, Robert Fox (1970: 127-135) excavated about 350 green nephrite ornaments, including *lingling-o* earrings, bracelets and beads, from sites on Palawan Island, particularly from the Tabon Cave Complex on Lipuun Point. Besides these findings, more nephrite artefacts have been found in other parts of the Philippines during the past decade, especially from the Batanes Islands, as described here.

Where were the geological sources for these nephrite artefacts found in the Philippines? H. Otley Beyer (1947: 249) noted: "Equally intriguing is the origin of the Batangas nephrite. The great quantity of artefacts found led us to seek diligently for some possible local source of the material, but the results so far have been wholly negative...". Over 20 years later, Robert B. Fox (1970: 131) commented on the same issue: "... there is no question that nephrite was worked extensively ... in the Philippines, notably in Batangas Province where the writer believes a local but still undiscovered source of nephrite was known and worked...".

Seeking nephrite sources has been a major preoccupation in Philippine archaeology, important not only for understanding these objects of art but also for studies of cultural interaction, trade, and the development of craft specialisation. Since the 1940s, archaeologists in Southeast Asia have noted the widespread occurrence of nephrite ornaments with similar characteristics and have postulated various opinions about their possible dispersal histories. Kano Tadao (1946: 233) was the first to discern at least four types of penannular nephrite earring with circumferential projections in Southeast Asia. He believed that they originated in northern Vietnam, whence they spread northwards to Hong Kong and Taiwan. He believed as well that they could have reached Taiwan via northern Luzon (in the case of his types 2, 3 and 4) (see Hung et al. 2006, Fig. 20.1). In these early studies, researchers explored cultural contacts and exchange only from a typological perspective. However, the data that may be derived from such an approach will be extremely limited without knowing the sources of the raw materials.

The past decade of research

Because nephrite is a rare mono-mineralic rock, formed only under specific geological conditions, it is highly amenable to geochemical compositional analysis for fingerprinting the sources used for those artefacts that eventually were transported to distant locations. From geological information, there are about 120 known nephrite deposits in the world, distributed in roughly 20 countries (Harlow and Sorensen 2005). In East Asia, nephrite deposits are located in Siberia, Mainland China, Korea, Japan, and at Fengtian in eastern Taiwan. So far, no green nephrite sources have been reported from Island Southeast Asia, although there are separate white nephrite sources that exhibit different mineralogy in southern Luzon and probably Vietnam (Hung et al. 2007). Therefore, the geological source(s) of the green nephrite artefacts found in the Philippines and other Southeast Asian sites present questions of great interest.

Recent developments in archaeology, in partnership with earth sciences, have provided us with a uniquely informative way to combine the typological comparative methods of archaeology with applications of mineral and chemical analysis, in order to source nephrite artefacts in the Philippines and other Southeast Asian countries. Since 2000, a number of sourcing techniques have been applied by various colleagues working in collaboration with us. Chih-ming Wang Lee has performed X-ray diffraction (XRD) in the Department of Geology, National Taiwan University, in Taipei. Stable oxygen isotope analysis has been undertaken by Tzeng-fu Yui of the Institute of Earth Sciences, Academia Sinica, also in Taipei. Most recently, Yoshiyuki Iizuka has developed an approach using electron probe micro-analysis (EPMA) and low vacuum type scanning electron microscopy (LV-SEM), equipped with energy dispersive X-ray spectrometry (EDS), in the Institute of Earth Sciences at Academia Sinica. The technicalities behind these techniques have been described in our other publications (Hung et al. 2004; Iizuka and Hung 2005; Iizuka et al. 2005, 2007; Hung et al. 2007).

Between 2003 and 2004, our studies began to focus mostly on the Philippines, primarily working with collections in the National Museum of the Philippines in Manila. In 2004, Peter Bellwood and Eusebio Dizon discovered the Anaro nephrite workshop on Itbayat Island in Batanes, which has provided the bulk of the artefacts described here. In this chapter, we review all discoveries and sourcing results of nephrite and jade-like remains in the Batanes Islands, finishing with a broader cultural interpretation of the Batanes nephrite materials in the context of Southeast Asian archaeology.

Nephrite and other jade-like artefacts from Batanes

Since 2004, excavations at Anaro (Itbayat Island) have recovered many drilled-out disc-shaped and cylindrical cores, pelta-shaped pieces, and grooved-and-cut nephrite debris, all strongly indicative of the former existence of a nephrite workshop on the site. The Anaro chronology is discussed in more detail in chapters 2 and 5, where it was noted that the majority of the nephrite pieces belonged to Batanes Phase 2, subphase 2b, dating between 500 BC and the early centuries AD. They were found mostly in association with Anaro circle-stamped type 1 pottery sherds.

So far, most of the nephrite and jade-like cut fragments and artefacts have been discovered predominately as surface finds from the Anaro workshop. Currently, there are 58 samples from

Anaro, two from Savidug, and one from Sunget. After testing by Yoshiyuki Iizuka of all of the pieces from the total project, each has been confirmed as falling within the geochemical ranges of Fengtian nephrite from eastern Taiwan, except for one piece of mica and another two of quartz schist (Fig. 9.1).

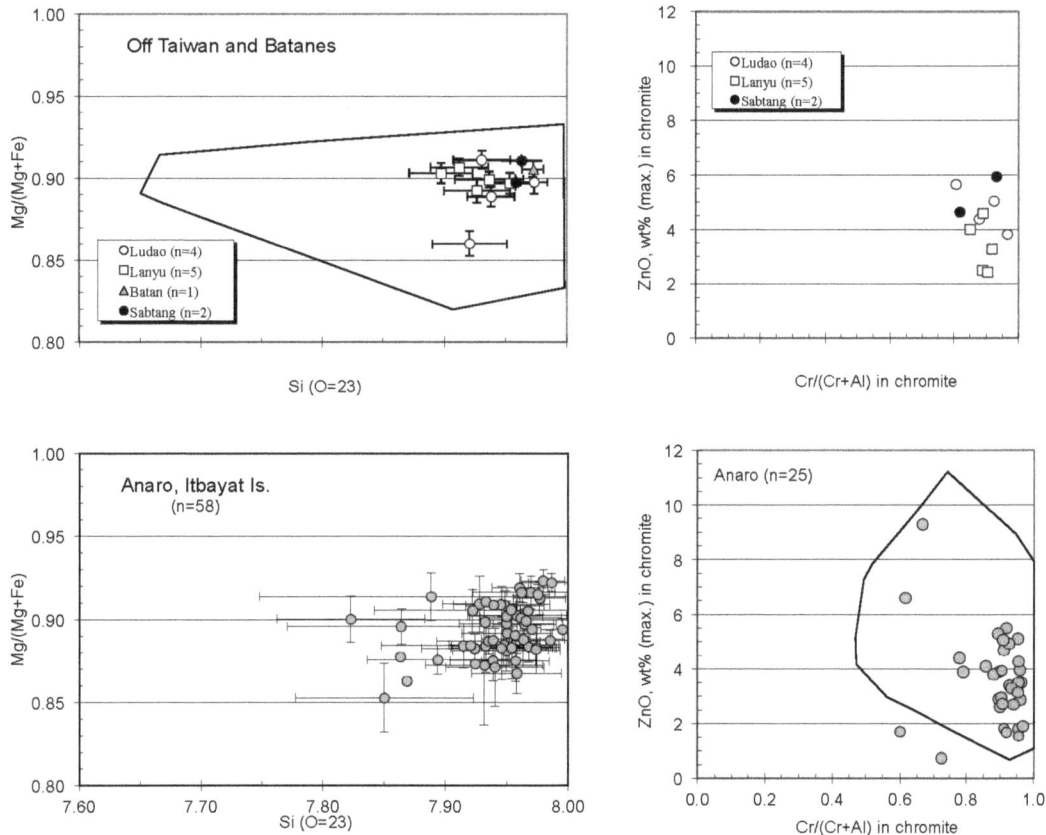

Figure 9.1. Left side: Chemical compositions of nephrite artefact matrices. The X- and Y-axes represent Si (atoms per formula unit) and Mg/(Mg+Fe) ratios, respectively, of Ca-amphibole Ca2(Mg,Fe)5(Si8O22)(OH)2. The chemical boundary between tremolite and actinolite is 0.90 in the Mg/(Mg+Fe) ratio (Leake et al. 1997). The enclosed areas in each plot contain the chemical compositions of source nephrite samples from the Fengtian mine area in eastern Taiwan (8-hand specimens and 262 analysis points) and a nearby riverbed (9-hand specimens and 385 analysis points) (after Iizuka and Hung 2005). n: numbers of analysis spots by the non-invasive LVSEM-EDS technique. Right side: Chemical compositions of zinc-bearing chromite ([Mg,Fe,Zn][Al,Cr]2O4) inclusions in the surfaces of nephrite artefacts, analysed by the non-invasive LVSEM-EDS technique. Symbols represent the value for zinc oxide (ZnO in wt %) and the Cr/(Cr+Al) ratio for each artefact. Because the chromite in Fengtian nephrite bears significant amounts of zinc (2 to 11 wt % in ZnO) (Iizuka and Hung 2005) in comparison with the other possible green nephrite (actinolite/tremolite) sources tested (Chara Jelgra, Siberia and Nanshan, Gansu), the Zn content provides a good clue for the identification of Fengtian nephrite. Enclosed areas contain the chemical compositions of Fengtian nephrite samples.

Source: Yoshiyuki Iizuka.

Batan Island

A nephrite adze (Fig. 9.2 A) from Sunget was first reported by Koomoto (1983: 61; Fig. 25: 48) as a small miniature stone axe. We examined this artefact in 2006, and confirmed it as an adze of Fengtian (Taiwan) nephrite, of a type very common during the Taiwan Neolithic. In Taiwan itself, nephrite adzes first appeared in the Early Neolithic (c.3000 BC) and were made and used extensively through the Late Neolithic (Hung 2004: 58), even continuing into the Iron Age. As discussed in chapters 3 and 5, Sunget is dated between 1200 and 800 BC, contemporary with the Late Neolithic in Taiwan.

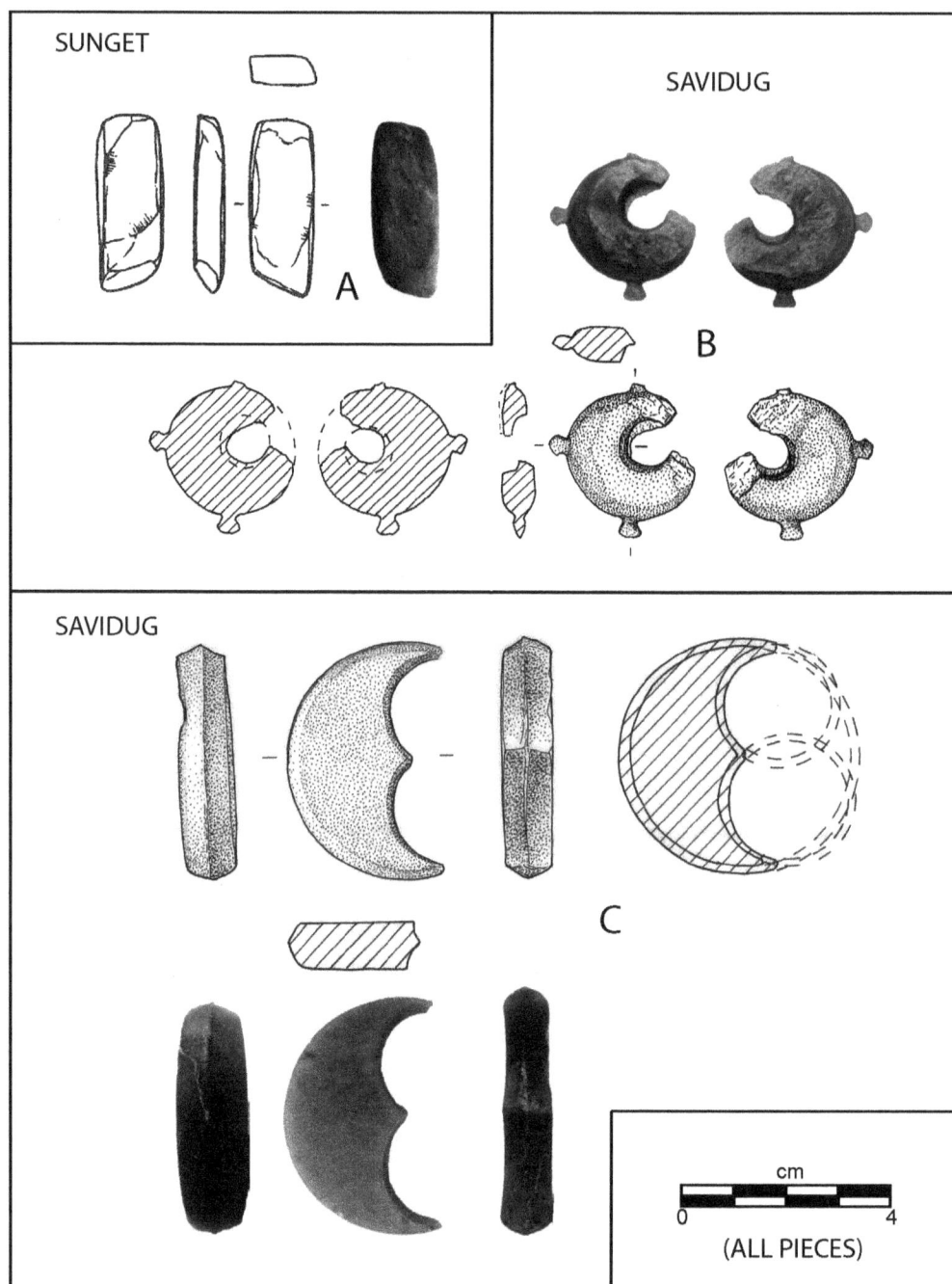

Figure 9.2. (A) Nephrite adze from Sunget. (B and C) Three-pointed *lingling-o* and pelta-shaped nephrite segment from Savidug (NB: the term *pelta*, used in European archaeology, refers to an object shaped like an ancient Greek light shield).

Source: Hsiao-chun Hung.

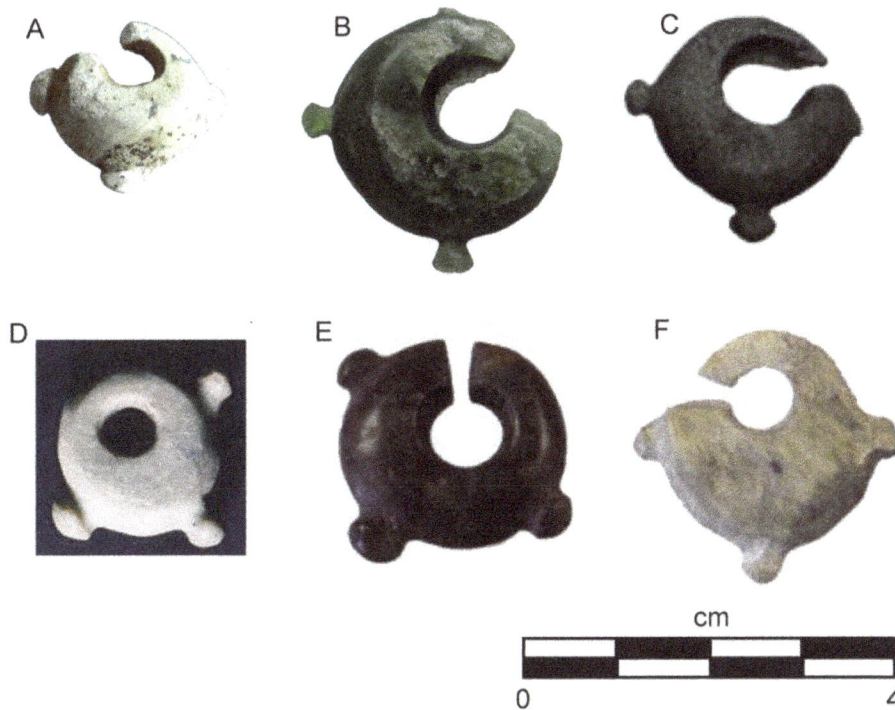

Figure 9.3. Possible nephrite prototypes for the *lingling-o* type of penannular earring with three pointed circumferential projections (see examples in Fig. 9.10), from:

(A) Hengchun, southern tip of Taiwan - courtesy National Museum of Prehistory, Taiwan;

(B) Savidug Dune Site, Sabtang (see also Fig. 9.2 B);

(C and D) Lanyu Island - courtesy National Museum of Prehistory, Taiwan;

(E and F) Arku Cave, Cagayan Valley - courtesy National Museum of the Philippines.

Source: Hsiao-chun Hung.

Sabtang Island

During the excavation of Savidug Dune Site, a Fengtian nephrite *lingling-o* with three rounded projections (Fig. 9.2 B) was found close to the base of a burial jar, in a layer dated to 590 to 390 BC (Wk 21809: Table 5.1). It is slightly different from the more numerous *lingling-o* earrings found in the Philippines which have three sharply-pointed projections (Fig. 9.10). As can be seen in Fig. 9.3, this Savidug specimen is paralleled by other examples from Hengchun in southern Taiwan (Hung and Bellwood 2010: Fig. 2.1), Lanyu Island (Hsu 2008: Fig. 34.9; Li 2010), and in nephrite and shell from Arku Cave in the Cagayan valley, northern Luzon (Thiel 1986-87: Fig. 5). The rounded knobs in these specimens are similar to those on the four-knobbed earrings of the Late Neolithic of Taiwan (see type IIA in the Beinan classification of Lien 2002). It is suggested here that they might have been ancestral to the *lingling-os* with more sharply-pointed projections from a wide range of sites in Taiwan, the Philippines, Sarawak, Vietnam, Thailand and Cambodia (Hung et al. 2007). Most of these sharply-pointed examples are of Iron Age date, and presumably younger than the *c.*500 BC date that might apply to the Savidug specimen discussed here.

The burial jar in Savidug trench QR/7-9, close to the base of which the *lingling-o* was found, had a red-slipped surface and its top had been intentionally removed (Figs 4.19, 4.20). Similar burial jars are very common in the Hualian region of eastern Taiwan, at sites such as Huagangshan and Yanliao, where nephrite production was also rather well developed. They belong to the Huagangshan culture, dated most reliably at Yanliao to 2953±78 (NZA6102) and 2846±82 uncal. BP (NZA6101) (Ye 2001:96).

A pelta-shaped discard of Fengtian nephrite (Fig. 9.2 C) was also found in the Savidug road cutting, hence unstratified but quite probably from the same layer as the *lingling-o*. This had an original outer diameter of 4.9 cm, and is 10 mm thick. The two drill-hole remnants have diameters very similar to that of the body (without the projections) of the Savidug *lingling-o*. We suspect that this pelta-shaped piece was debitage from *lingling-o* manufacture, since it is similar in shape to, but larger than, the specimens to be described below from Anaro and the site of Rusarsol on Lanyu Island (Hsu 2008: Fig. 34.1). Such pieces have never been found in other locations in Southeast Asia. Suggestions of how such pelta-shaped pieces, both large and small, could be produced by drilling out two discs offset from the diameter of an original circular blank of Fengtian nephrite are offered in Figs 9.2 and 9.7.

Within the same cultural layer at Savidug and from the same depth (130-140 cm) as the *lingling-o*, many double side-notched pebble sinkers of eastern Taiwan character were also found (Fig. 8.9, lower). All this evidence strongly suggests that the inhabitants of Savidug Dune Site had strong cultural relations with Taiwan, possibly with the Huagangshan sites around the mouth of the Hualian River in eastern Taiwan, and also with Lanyu Island. Some Huagangshan sites, such as Yanliao, have yielded large amounts of worked nephrite, associated with slate knives (Ye 2001).

Itbayat Island

Nine nephrite adzes were recovered as surface finds at Anaro (Fig. 9.4), of which at least five narrow specimens might be considered as chisels. Most have quite sharply rectangular cross-sections, unlike the Anaro trapezoidal-sectioned adzes and circular-sectioned chisels of other raw materials described in chapter 8. This rectangular-sectioned type of Taiwan nephrite adze/chisel was very common in the Middle (2500-1500 BC) and Late (1500-300 BC) Neolithic phases in Taiwan (Hung 2004), and some even continued to be used into the Iron Age. The largest Anaro nephrite specimen measures 7.1 cm in length, 4.9 cm in width, and 3.9 cm in thickness (Fig. 9.4, bottom left). Two parallel grooves occur on its surface, and we presume from this that some of the larger nephrite adzes taken to Anaro were eventually cut or drilled into smaller pieces and recycled for manufacturing ornaments.

The five fragmentary circular nephrite specimens from Anaro shown in Fig. 9.5 are from either half-finished or finished but broken ornaments, presumably rings, bracelets or earrings. Two of them (A and B) are from bracelet-like ornaments with off-centre perforations. Two others (D and E) are small ring-shaped fragments presumably broken during manufacture, since the insides retain very clear drilling marks. The fifth perforated specimen (C) came from a finished ornament, but it is uncertain whether it was a bracelet or an earring.

In total, ten primary cores drilled out from the centres of circular ornaments were discovered from Anaro. Most were surface finds, except for two excavated from Anaro 3 at 65-70 cm (Fig. 9.6 A) and 70-75 cm (Fig. 9.6 D) respectively, They can be grouped into two types. Four (Fig. 9.6 A-D) are roughly conical or biconical in shape as a result of drilling from one or both sides of a thick blank. They are smaller in diameter than the second disc type to be described next. The two biconical specimens (A and B) are both 0.8 cm in diameter, and we believe they were drilled from the central holes of the popular three-pointed type of *lingling-o* shown in Fig. 9.10, although none of these finished ornaments were actually found at Anaro, perhaps because all were exported for use elsewhere.

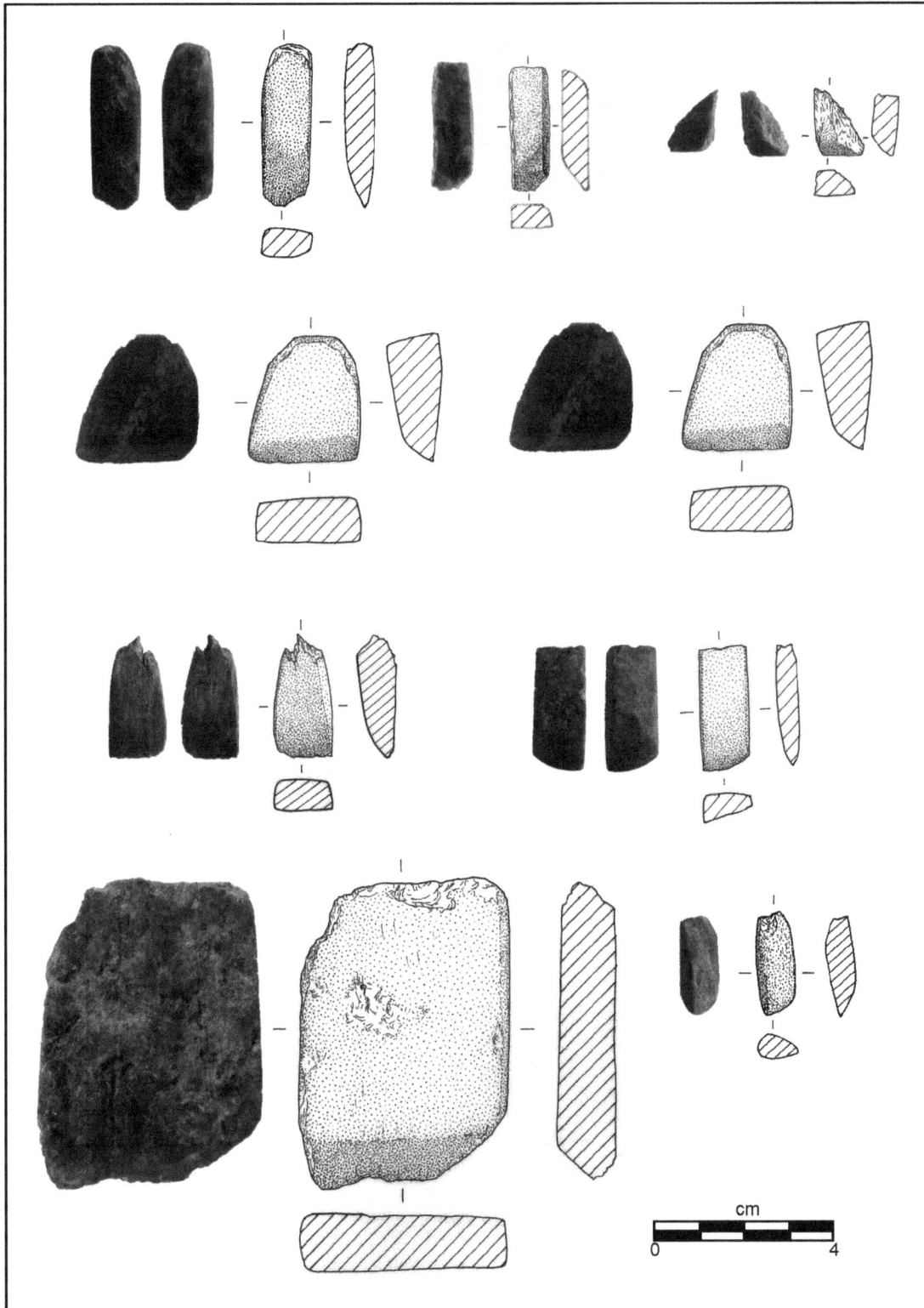

Figure 9.4. Nephrite adzes from Anaro.

Source: Hsiao-chun Hung.

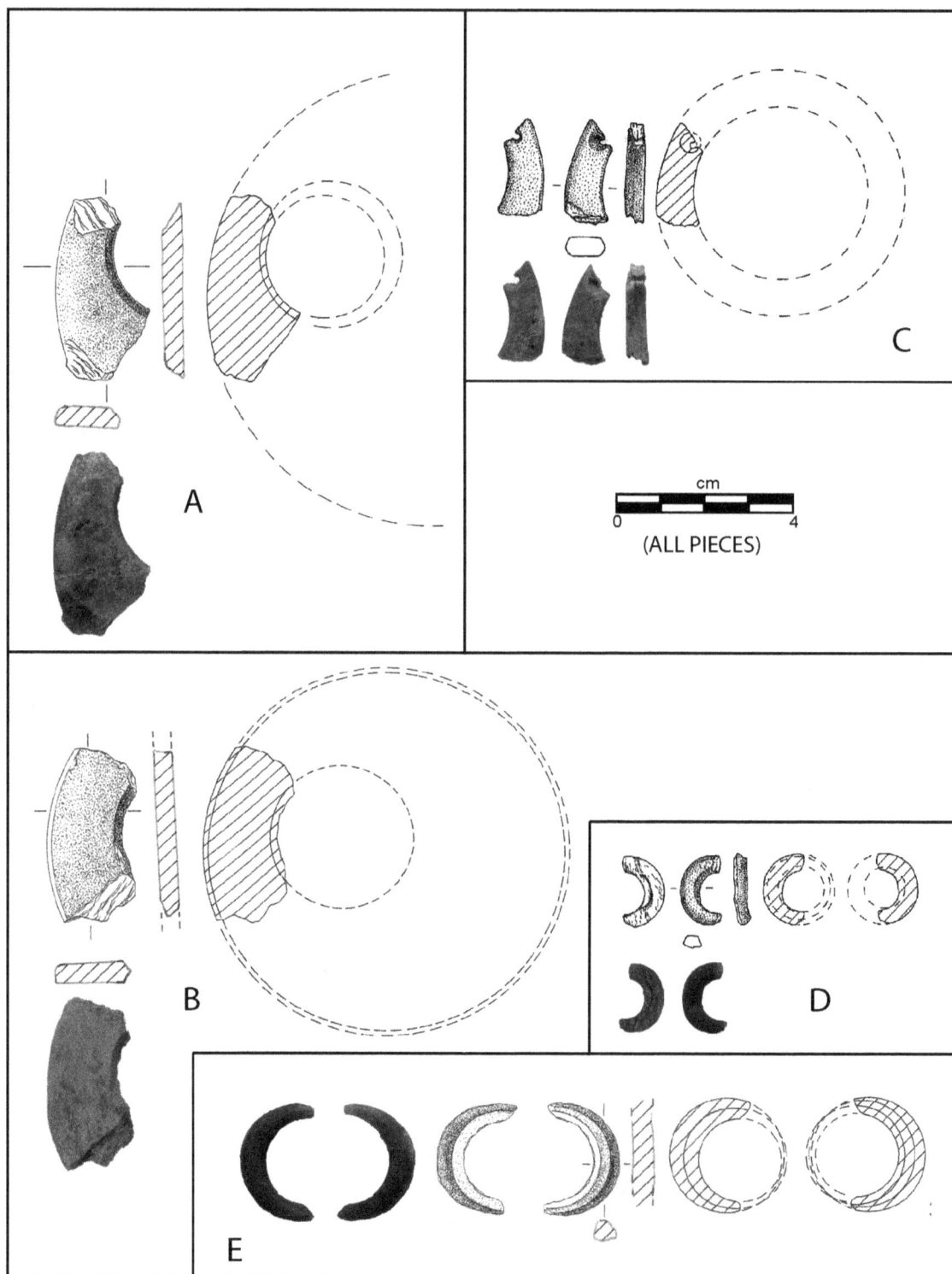

Figure 9.5. Fragments of circular ring-shaped nephrite ornaments from Anaro.

Source: Hsiao-chun Hung.

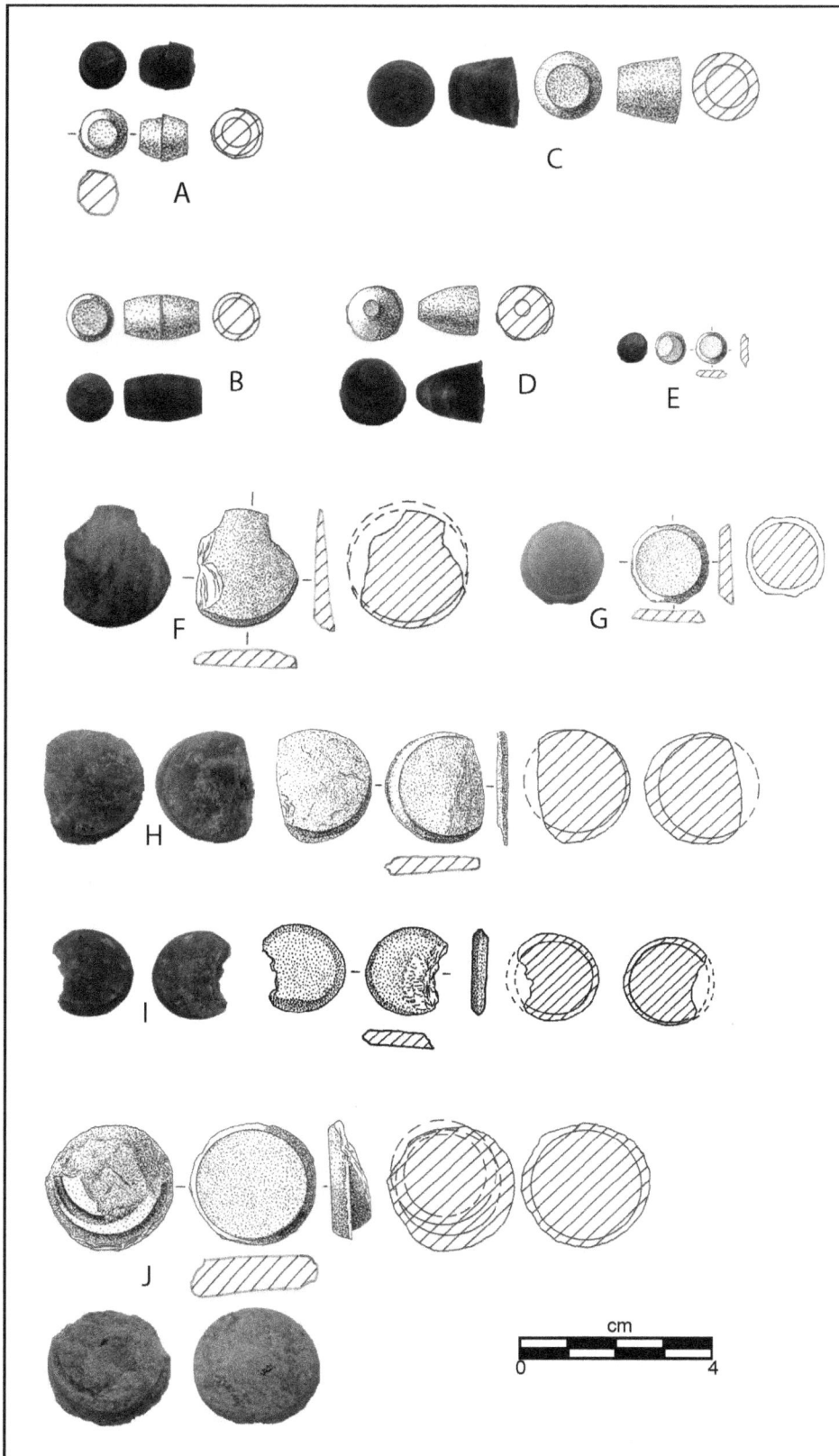

Figure 9.6. Drilled-out nephrite biconical and conical cores, and flat circular discs, from Anaro.

Source: Hsiao-chun Hung.

terra australis 40

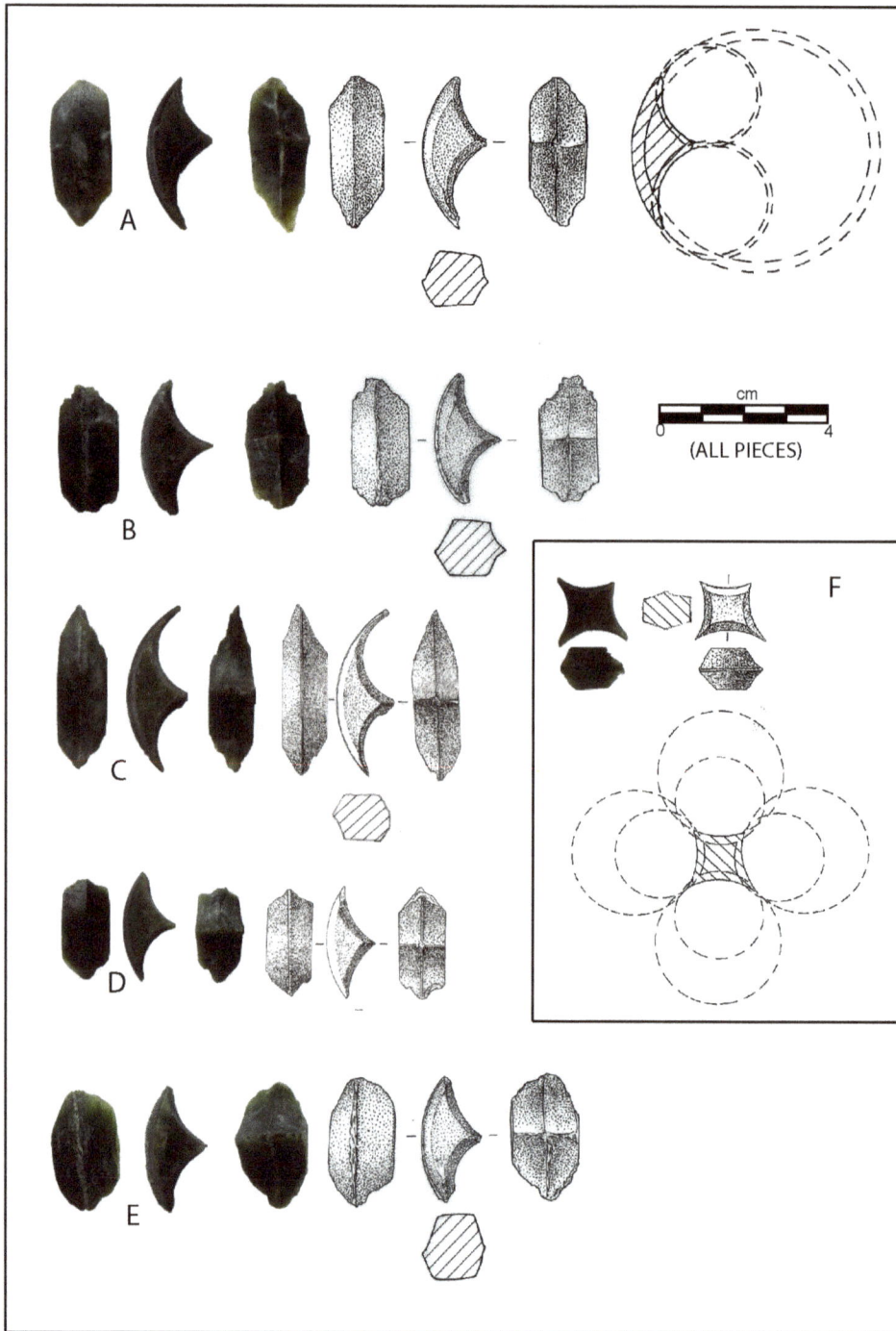

Figure 9.7. Pelta-shaped nephrite segments (A-E) and star-shaped central discard (F) from Anaro.

Source: Hsiao-chun Hung.

The six disc-shaped specimens (Fig. 9.6 E to J) are much thinner, about 2.0-2.7 cm in diameter (except for the much smaller specimen shown in Fig. 9.6 E), and 0.3-0.8 cm thick. These perhaps resulted from the manufacture of simple earrings similar to types found in the Late Neolithic or Iron Age of Taiwan, types IA and IIA of the Beinan classification of Lien (2002). At least five identical flat circular discs have been excavated from the site of Rusarsol (Lanyu High School), on Lanyu Island, as discussed further below (Hsu 2008: Fig. 34).

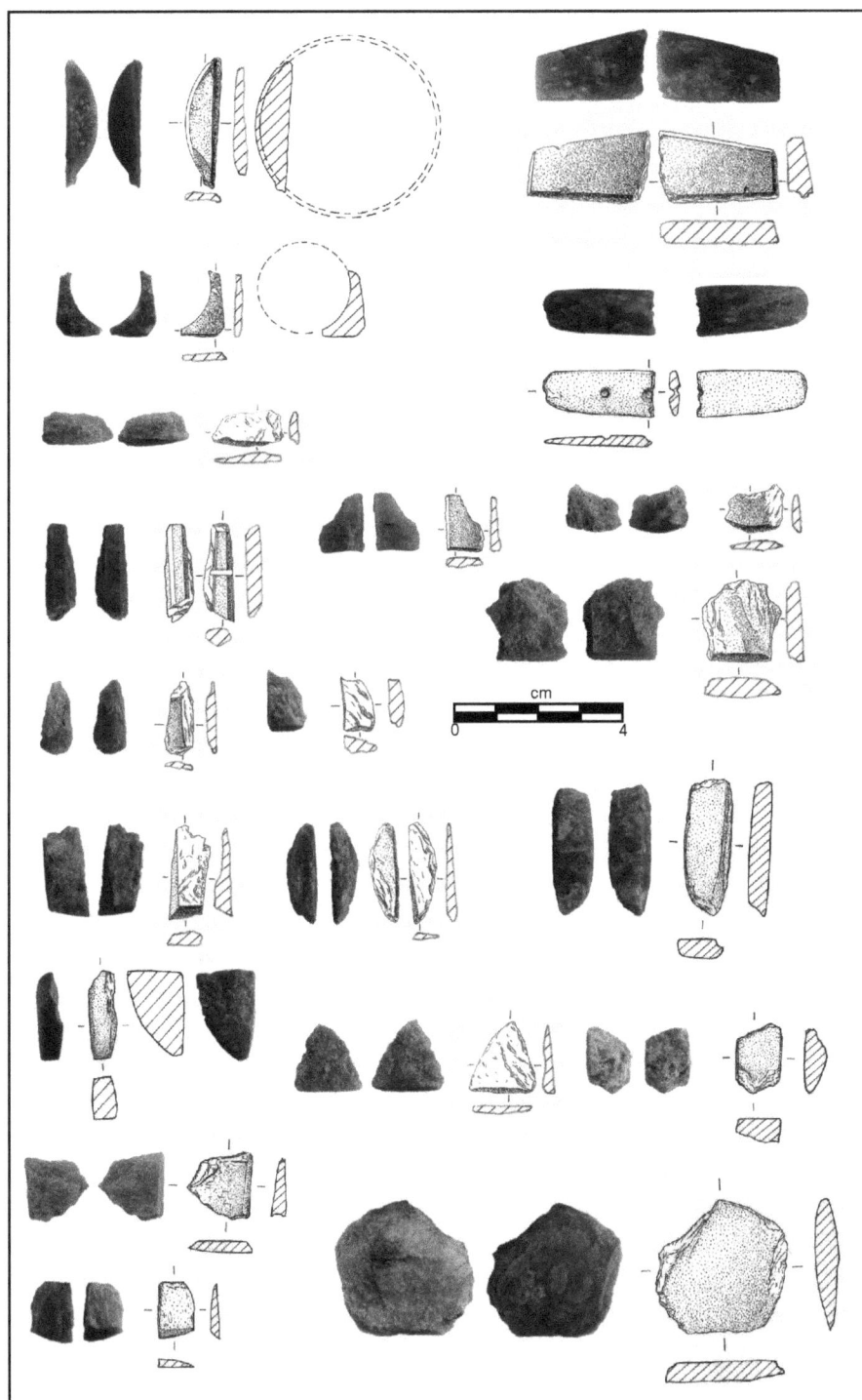

Figure 9.8. Other worked fragments of nephrite from Anaro.

Source: Hsiao-chun Hung.

Five pelta-shaped peripheral fragments resulting from double or quadripartite drilling into a large circular blank were found at Anaro (Fig. 9.7). These are similar to but smaller than the Savidug pelta-shaped specimen described above, and again one example of this precise form has been excavated at Rusarsol on Lanyu (Hsu 2008: Fig. 34.1 and 2). Four were surface finds, but that shown as Fig. 9.7 B was found at 10-15 cm in Anaro 5, a shallow square dug on the flat limestone top of the hill. The star-shaped specimen shown as Fig. 9.7 F is the only one of this shape found so far in Batanes, or elsewhere in Southeast Asia, and it appears to be the central remnant left after drilling out four circular cores from a large circular blank, with the pelta-shaped pieces coming from the outer periphery. We can observe clearly from the profiles of all of these specimens that they were drilled from both sides of their blanks, perhaps using bamboo bow drills and sand. The holes were originally hourglass-shaped in section.

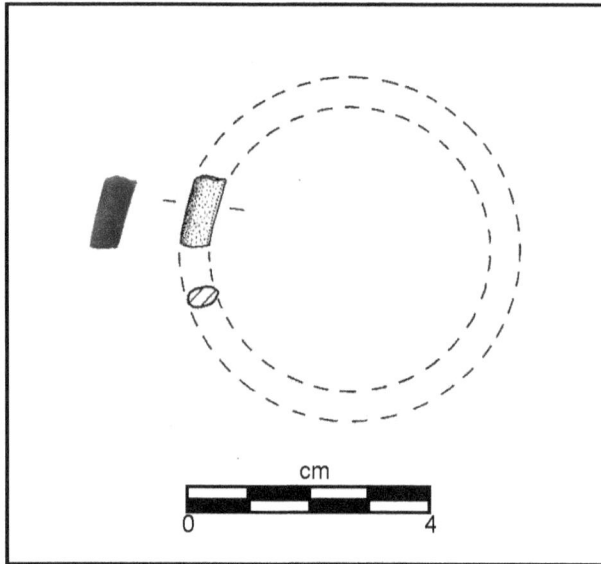

Figure 9.9. A fragment of a muscovite bracelet from Anaro.

Source: Hsiao-chun Hung.

In total, 20 other worked nephrite fragments of rectangular, curved or irregular shapes were also collected from Anaro (Fig. 9.8). Most grooves and drilling marks were made from both sides of the blanks, and in the case of grooving the usual procedure seems to have been to cut in from both sides until a thin ridge was left, which could be snapped prior to polishing and finishing.

Anaro is the most important nephrite workshop found so far in the Philippines, as it illustrates what appears to be the full production sequence for making circular rings and ear ornaments, including possibly the widespread type of *lingling-o* with three projections (Hung et al. 2007). Many slate pieces, probably used as knives since many were formed from broken projectile points, were also found here with the nephrite fragments (Fig. 8.8). We suggest they were used with sand and water for grooving the nephrite prior to snapping, as in the nephrite workshops at Pinglin, near the Fengtian nephrite source, in Taiwan. As mentioned, these slate tools were imported to Batanes from Taiwan, where such knives and points are very common.

Beside nephrite materials, one green muscovite fragment, cylindrical in cross-section, was also found on the surface at Anaro (Fig. 9.9). It probably came from a broken bracelet or ear pendant. This muscovite is called "Mindoro jade" in the Philippines and is smooth and greenish in colour (Hung et al. 2005), not as hard as nephrite, and of a paler green. A number of jade-like *lingling-o* earrings and beads in the Philippines were manufactured of this material (see below for further discussion).

The Batanes green nephrite and muscovite artefacts in the context of Philippine and Southeast Asian archaeology

After examining the specimens of nephrite and similar raw materials in the collections of the Philippine National Museum, we suggest that several types of raw material, namely green nephrite, white nephrite, green Mindoro muscovite, and other greenish raw materials (such as green quartz schist, talc and steatite) were used to manufacture stone ornaments during the Neolithic and Iron Age of the Philippines.

Figure 9.10. Green nephrite *lingling-os* and double animal-headed ear pendants from the Tabon Caves, Palawan.

Source: Hsiao-chun Hung.

Most of the green nephrite artefacts examined in the Philippines (including those from Batanes) are translucent green in colour, with black inclusions. All specimens tested by Yoshiyuki Iizuka are of Fengtian nephrite, and most were manufactured by sawing, drilling and polishing to produce body ornaments such as beads, bracelets, and double animal-headed and *lingling-o* earrings (Fig. 9.10). Very few adzes of green nephrite occur in the Philippines, except in the Batanes Islands. So far, more than 400 green nephrite ornaments have been discovered in the Philippines, at about 20 different sites (Fox 1970: 135; Hung 2005, 2006) including the following (Fig. 9.11):

1. Anaro, Sunget and Savidug in Batanes, as described here;

2. Nagsabaran, Lanna, Arku Cave and Lattu-Lattuc Cave in the Cagayan Valley, northern Luzon (Barbosa 1979);

3. Dimolit in Isabela, northeastern Luzon;

4. Calatagan and Kay Daing in Batangas, western Luzon;

5. Bato Cave in Sorsogon, southern Luzon;

6. Kalanay Cave on Masbate Island;

7. Leta-Leta and Ille Caves in northern Palawan;

8. Duyong, Manunggul, Uyaw, Guri, Bubulungun and Rito-Fabian Caves (all within the Tabon Caves complex) central Palawan.

According to our previous studies, all examined Taiwan nephrite artefacts, and the Fengtian geological source rocks themselves, are composed of nephrite (tremolite-actinolite amphiboles) with zinc-bearing chromite inclusions. The results suggest that Fengtian was the major source for all of the nephrite artefacts so far analysed from Taiwan itself. Outside Taiwan, more than 100 artefacts from more than 10 sites in Southeast Asia have been confirmed by Yoshiyuki Iizuka as made of Fengtian nephrite. These sites occur in the Batanes Islands, Luzon, Palawan, Sarawak, central Vietnam, southern Vietnam and southern Thailand (Iizuka et al. 2006; Hung et al. 2007). No Fengtian nephrite has yet been reported from northern Vietnam.

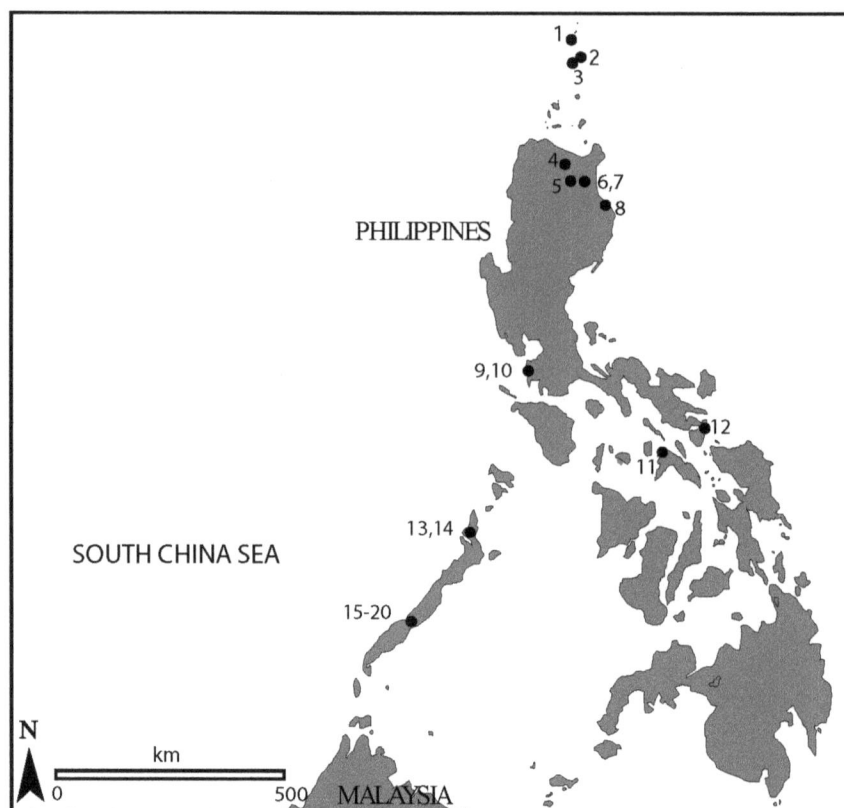

Figure 9.11. The distribution of green nephrite ornaments in the Philippines. 1. Anaro; 2. Sunget; 3. Savidug; 4. Nagsabaran, Cagayan Valley; 5. Lanna, Cagayan Valley; 6. Arku Cave, Cagayan; 7. Lattu-Lattuc Cave, Cagayan; 8. Dimolit, Isabela; 9-10. Calatagan and Kay Daing, Batangas; 11. Kalanay Cave, Masbate Island; 12. Bato Cave, Sorsogon; 13-14. Leta-Leta and Ille Caves, northern Palawan; 15–20. Duyong, Manunggul, Uyaw, Guri, Bubulungun and Rito-Fabian Caves, central Palawan.

Source: Hsiao-chun Hung and Mike Carson.

In addition to the numerous artefacts of Fengtian nephrite found in the Philippines, a single adze blade fragment with an exceptional green colour was found in 1994 by Armand Mijares in Tinokod Cave, Abra de Ilog, Occidental Mindoro (Mijares 1996: 33). The adze had been manufactured by flaking and polishing into a quadrangular shape with a trapezoidal cross-section. Its matrix component is actinolite/tremolite amphibole, consistent with nephrite of a chemical composition comparable to Fengtian nephrite. However, the inclusion minerals of this piece are different. Therefore, it was not derived from Fengtian, and its source remains unknown.

White nephrite adzes in Luzon

Philippine white nephrite artefacts (Figs 9.12 and 9.13) are usually milky on the surface, sometimes with reddish-brown, black or green bands. Almost all were manufactured by flaking and polishing into adzes with trapezoidal cross-sections, including some that were stepped for hafting. So far, we have seen only adzes, axes, chisels and gouges in this white nephrite, and have not encountered any ornaments made of this material (Hung et al. 2005). Although a large number of white nephrite adzes and similar tools were collected by Beyer in the 1930s and 1940s in southern Luzon, he left insufficient information about the contexts of the finds. The sites of Beyer's primary explorations were in Bulacan, Rizal, Laguna, Batangas and Quezon provinces. In the past decade, more white nephrite adzes have been found in the Baha and Ulilang Bundok open sites in Calatagan (de la Torre 2003), at Ille Rockshelter in northern Palawan, and possibly on Siargao Island in Surigao del Norte, eastern Mindanao (Cecilio Salcedo, National Museum Manila, pers. comm.). None have ever been found in Batanes. Although the exact number of white nephrite adzes found by Beyer is unknown, his publications (Beyer 1947, 1948) and the National Museum of the Philippines collections indicate that several thousand were discovered in southern Luzon, a quantity much greater than the total of green nephrite artefacts found in the Philippines.

Figure 9.12. Examples of white nephrite adzes from the Philippines (Beyer collection, courtesy: National Museum of the Philippines).

Source: Hsiao-chun Hung.

Mineralogical and geochemical analyses of 15 white nephrite adzes and two preforms from the Beyer collection, and one adze from Ulilang Bundok, show that the raw materials are tremolitic amphibole, or tremolite. Their chemical compositions clearly differ from the green (actinolite) nephrites, such as that from the Fengtian source (Iizuka and Hung 2005). The oxygen isotope ratios of the white nephrite adzes are the highest of all known tremolite sources in East Asia (Iizuka and Hung 2005; Hung et al. 2005; Hung et al. 2007), and given the large numbers in southern Luzon and their apparent absence in Batanes, it is likely that the raw material came from somewhere in southern Luzon, perhaps from a geological zone where marble and/or muscovite occur. However, this source so far has not been found.

Green Mindoro muscovite, or "Mindoro jade"

This raw material was also used for making earrings and beads in the Philippines. A Neolithic example of a "Mindoro jade" earring was found with red-slipped pottery at Irigayen in the Cagayan Valley (de la Torre 2000: 128); this specimen curiously mimics a style of earring common at Beinan (Late Neolithic of eastern Taiwan, c. 1500-300 BC). It has been tested by Yoshiyuki Iizuka and confirmed as highly similar in composition to Mindoro muscovite. Several other ornaments from Calatagan in Batangas, such as two disc beads from Ulilang Bundok (Fig. 9.14), and four disc beads from Ngipe't Duldug cave on Palawan, all green in colour, were also found to be made of this kind of muscovite.

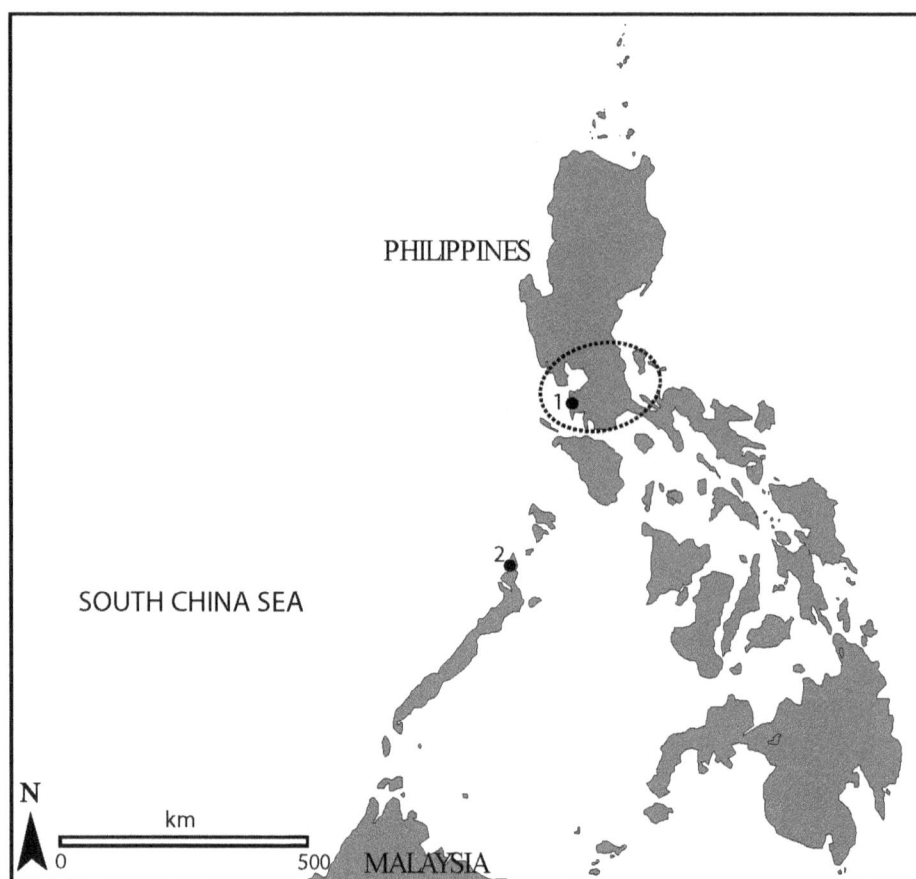

Figure 9.13. The distribution of white nephrite adzes in the Philippines; the shading marks the primary region of Beyer's discoveries in central Luzon. 1. Baha and Ulilang Bundok, Calatagan, Batangas; 2. Ille Cave, El Nido, northern Palawan.

Source: Hsiao-chun Hung and Mike Carson.

In July 2005, Hsiao-chun Hung examined a number of nephrite artefacts in private collections in Manila. Several ornaments in the collections of Richard Lopez and Ramon Villegas appeared to be made of Mindoro jade, including 14 *lingling-o* earrings with three pointed projections and 7 cylindrical beads. Based on these, and other observations, most Mindoro jade artefacts have apparently been found in Cagayan, Batangas and Palawan (Fig. 9.15), together with the muscovite bracelet fragment (Fig. 9.9) discovered at Anaro and mentioned above. Presumably, ancient people sometimes selected this material as a local substitute for green nephrite.

One of the known sources of muscovite is located at Arakaak, Santa Cruz, Mindoro Occidental (Mary Jane Bolunia and Rey Santiago, National Museum of the Philippines, pers. comm.). We cannot be certain that this type of muscovite occurs only in Mindoro, but we are unaware of any other source in the Philippines. From our analyses, the geological raw material from Arakaak, and the ornaments from Irigayen, Calatagan and Ngipe't Duldug Cave, have all been confirmed as muscovite of the Mindoro type (Hung et al. 2005). At present, it is likely that Mindoro Island was the source for these muscovite ornaments, but this material is more difficult to source with precision than nephrite.

Figure 9.14. "Mindoro jade" (muscovite) disc beads from Ulilang Bundok, southern Luzon, excavated by Amalia de la Torre. Courtesy: National Museum of the Philippines.

Source: Hsiao-chun Hung.

Elsewhere in Island Southeast Asia, a perforated pendant of probable Mindoro jade has been discovered in a Neolithic context at Bukit Tengkorak in Sabah, dated to *c.*1300 BC (Peter Molijol, Sabah Museum, pers. comm. to Peter Bellwood). This piece has been analysed by Iizuka and confirmed as the same muscovite raw material. However, no Fengtian nephrite has ever been found in Sabah. Muscovite artefacts have been found in other parts of Southeast Asia (but not yet in Taiwan), often co-occurring with objects made of Fengtian Taiwan nephrite, as in Guri Cave on Palawan, and in coastal Vietnam and Peninsular Thailand. Therefore, we suspect that the muscovite was traded through the same networks as the Fengtian nephrite.

Green quartz schist

Quartz schist, talc and shell were also shaped by drilling, sawing and polishing into beads, bracelets and earrings in the Philippines. These artefacts exhibit strong similarities with the green nephrite ornaments, in terms of both manufacturing technology and style. The green quartz schist was used specifically for making disc-shaped beads, found in more than 10 Philippine sites. Most are either fresh green on the surface and similar to green nephrite in colour, or weathered grey. Their distribution in the Philippines is very wide, including northern and southern Luzon and Palawan, but not yet Batanes.

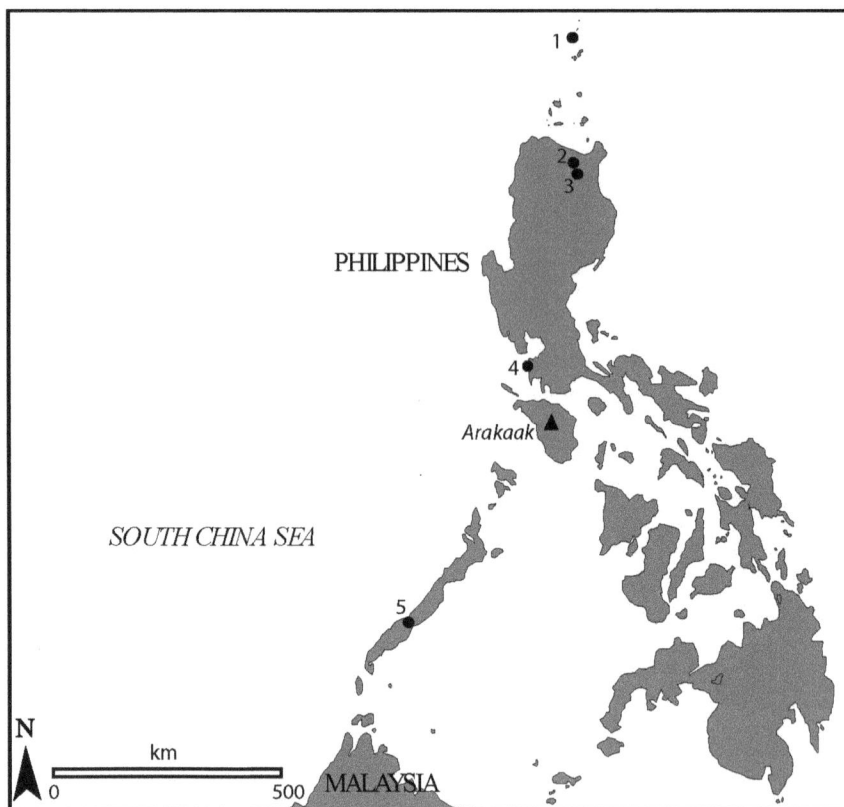

Figure 9.15. The distribution of "Mindoro jade" (muscovite) ornaments in the Philippines; 1. Anaro, Itbayat Island; 2. Irigayen, Cagayan Valley; 3. Magapit, Cagayan Valley; 4. Ulilang Bundok, Calatagan, Batangas; 5. Ngipe't Duldug cave, Quezon, Palawan. The triangle marks the possible Mindoro jade (muscovite) source at Arakaak on Mindoro.

Source: Hsiao-chun Hung and Mike Carson.

Geologically, green quartz schist is common in metamorphic regions. Although we have not yet been able to trace the source of the raw material, southern Luzon is a potential area because so many quartz schist beads have been found there. They show a high level of standardization, implying specialized production (Hung 2008: 178-179).

Nephrite workshops in Taiwan, and on Ludao and Lanyu Islands

In Taiwan, workshop sites utilising Fengtian nephrite have been discovered at Pinglin, Chongguang and Yanliao, all in Hualian Province in eastern Taiwan and close to the Fengtian source (see Fig. 1.1 for locations). Offshore, they have been found at Youzihu on Ludao Island, and at Rusarsol (Lanyu High School) on Lanyu Island. Tested nephrite artefacts from Guanyindong on Ludao (n=4) and Rusarsol on Lanyu (n=5) have all been confirmed as Fengtian nephrite. Outside the Philippines, worked Fengtian nephrite has been found at Giong Ca Vo on the coast of southern Vietnam near Ho Chi Minh City (Dang et al. 1998), and at Khao Sam Kaeo in southern Thailand (Hung et al. 2007: 19749).

On Ludao, the Youzihu site was first excavated in 1929 by Tadao Kano (1946), who collected a green nephrite bracelet with incised crossed line decoration similar to one found in the Tabon Caves, two drilled-out nephrite discs 4-5 cm in diameter and 1.5 cm thick, long beads, pendants, and several types of *lingling-o* earring. The latter included *lingling-o* with four pigeon-tail projections and hook-shaped forms (Kano 1942). According to the quantity of drilled-out discs from Youzihu, this site probably served as a nephrite workshop, but at an uncertain date. The site has produced red-slipped pottery with circle-stamping like that made in Batanes Phase 2, and a shell "spoon" like that from Savidug Dune Site (Fig. 8.14 D), supporting a date during the first millennium BC. Other artefacts from Youzihu (Liu et al. 1995) indicate a date possibly prior to 1000 BC, contemporary with the Late Neolithic Beinan cultural phase in southeastern Taiwan, but the relevance of this for dating the nephrite remains uncertain.

Kano (1946) also described several types of nephrite earring from Lanyu, including a *lingling-o* with three projections, two *lingling-o*s with four pigeon-tail projections, and simple penannular rings. He noticed that some small discs from Lanyu, like those from Anaro (Fig. 9.6 E-J), were less than 2 cm in diameter and about 0.4 cm thick. In 1980, nephrite *lingling-o*s with three or four pigeon-tail or knuckle-shaped projections, nephrite bracelets, grooved nephrite debris and many drilled-out cores were found in association with jar burials and glass beads at Rusarsol (Lanyu High School). In addition, several house owners in this area found nephrite ornaments during property construction in 1997-1998, including two bracelets and one more *lingling-o* with four knuckle-shaped projections. In typology and size, most of the Lanyu *lingling-o*s are similar to those from Philippine Iron Age contexts, such as those from Arku Cave in northern Luzon and the Tabon Caves in Palawan.

Hsu's (2003, 2008) findings at Rusarsol are particularly important. She reported 19 nephrite specimens from there, including a pelta-shaped segment identical to the five from Anaro (Fig. 9.7 A-E), small secondary drilled-out cores like those in Fig. 9.6 E-J, and unfinished three-pointed *lingling-o*s. This worked nephrite assemblage has some remarkable similarities to that from Anaro, and both sites were clearly in direct communication and involved in the manufacture of similar types of ornament.

Although a radiocarbon date of 1200±40 BP comes from one of the Rusarsol jar burials (Tsang 2005), and Hsu (2008) accepted this age for the workshop, we argue that the date of the nephrite assemblage is earlier than 1200 years ago, given the much older date range for *lingling-o*s in the Philippines and Vietnam (Hung et al. 2007). Rusarsol also has pottery with circle stamping similar to the Anaro circle-stamped type 1 pottery from Itbayat, dated between 500 BC and AD 1.

According to the general similarities between Lanyu and the Batanes in pottery decoration, nephrite ornaments and jar burial practices (de Beauclair 1972; Bellwood and Dizon 2005, Hsu 2008), we suggest that the Neolithic and especially the Early Iron Age inhabitants of these islands shared close contacts, and probably created new fashions in nephrite artefacts, such as the *lingling-o* earrings, different from the shapes most favoured on the Taiwan mainland.

Conclusions

In Southeast Asia, the most numerous and geographically widespread penannular nephrite earrings of *lingling-o* type have three pointed circumferential projections (Fig. 9.10). They occur in southern Taiwan, the Philippines, Borneo, southern Vietnam and southern Thailand, and are mostly dated between 500 BC and AD 1. Both Anaro and Rusarsol yielded small disc-shaped drilled-out cores and pelta-shaped segments, and Anaro also yielded conical and biconical drilled-out cores. All of these items seem to have resulted from the manufacture of annular rings or penannular earrings, including possibly those of the *lingling-o* type with projections. The specific pelta and star shapes in nephrite are not known from other workshops outside Batanes and Lanyu.

We suspect that one likely prototype *lingling-o* had three rounded rather than pointed projections, like the specimen from Savidug, dated to *c*.600-400 BC (Fig. 9.2 B; Fig. 9.3). As noted, similar specimens have been found in southern Taiwan, Lanyu and the Cagayan Valley, and the rounded rather than pointed projections on all of them find parallels in earrings from Beinan Late Neolithic contexts in southeastern Taiwan.

Regardless of the Late Neolithic and Iron Age manufacture of nephrite ornaments in Lanyu and Batanes, we must remember that Fengtian nephrite was utilised as early as 3000 BC in Taiwan itself. It was already being exported outside Taiwan by 2000-1500 BC, as shown by two nephrite bracelet fragments found in the lower deposits with circle and punctate stamped red-slipped pottery at Nagsabaran in the Cagayan Valley (Hung 2008; Hung et al. 2011). The oldest Fengtian nephrite in Batanes could be as early as 1200 BC, from Sunget and Anaro, but apart from adzes it is not clear what other kinds of artefact were in use at this time, or if nephrite was actually worked in Batanes then.

We might ask finally why Fengtian nephrite workshops were located on small and rather inhospitable islands such as Lanyu and Itbayat? These islands have little land suitable for intensive agriculture and neither supported very much rice growing in prehistory, or even now, although Lanyu does support extensive areas of wet taro cultivation today (Kano 1952). Therefore, it seems likely that the boat technology that these islanders must have relied upon for survival in prehistory was a crucial element behind the nephrite working tradition, since it would have enabled them to reach the desired sources of nephrite in eastern Taiwan, and to travel back home with the raw materials afterwards. Thus, the inhabitants of Lanyu and Itbayat were seemingly importing raw materials, and exporting finished nephrite goods. What they received in return for the latter remains unclear, but perhaps we can imagine other scarce subsistence and technological resources such as the animal hides and iron referred to by Dampier (see page 6).

One major question remains. How did the Lanyu and Itbayat workshops interact and communicate, if at all, with the other nephrite workshops identified in southern Luzon, central and southern Vietnam, and southern Thailand? The nephrite itself certainly travelled far. But did the artisans?

10

The Terrestrial Vertebrate Remains

Philip J. Piper, Noel Amano Jr., Shawna Hsiu-Ying Yang and Terry O'Connor

This chapter describes the analysis and interpretation of the terrestrial vertebrate remains from the islands of Itbayat and Sabtang. The results indicate that pigs were present in the islands from the earliest recognised phases of colonization and were the only large mammal resource during the prehistoric period, from at least 1200 BC until after AD 1000, when the goat was introduced into the islands. Dogs appear to be present by at least 500 BC, as well as a species of civet cat from a similar or slightly earlier date on Itbayat, that has now been extirpated from the island.

Methods

In total, 3557 fragments of terrestrial vertebrate (including marine turtle) remains were recovered during the excavations at the sites of Anaro, Torongan, Savidug Dune Site and Pamayan. Dry sieving using a 5 mm mesh was undertaken at all sites except Sunget, where the hardness and high clay content of the archaeological deposits made it virtually impossible to pass them through a sieve. Bulk wet sieving was ruled out by the lack of any available water. This use of a fairly coarse sieve mesh has influenced the amount of information recoverable on pre- and post-depositional processes acting upon the vertebrate assemblages, and on the community structure and composition of the animals present. This was especially the case for taxa within the classes of small terrestrial vertebrates and fish. Nevertheless, considerable amounts of meaningful information about human subsistence were recovered from the animal bone assemblages.

For the purposes of this study, taphonomic terminology follows Piper (2003), modified from Lyman (1994). Important taphonomic alterations, some teeth, and other selective elements were photographed and archived using a Pentax M20 digital camera. The more interesting natural and anthropic modifications were also studied using a digital camera attached to a trinocular microscope, and butchery patterns of special interest were photographed. These marks were identified in morphological terms according to the conventions established by Potts and Shipman (1981), but we acknowledge that materials other than stone (the only material studied by Potts and Shipman) could potentially have been used during butchery. In this study, cut marks are identified as single, or multiple sub-parallel, linear incisions into the cortical surface of the bone, typically displaying regular V-shaped profiles. Chop marks are generally wider and deeper, and vary in their morphologies dependent on the direction and angle of strike.

The maximum length of each bone fragment was measured, unless there was modern breakage. This allowed us to identify varying rates of fragmentation between sites. Distinctive fragments of mammal and reptile bone were all identified to the highest taxonomic level possible, using the comparative assemblages housed in the Department of Archaeology, University of York, and the zooarchaeology laboratory at the University of the Philippines.

Most of the criteria for biometric analyses of suid and caprid post-cranial elements follow von den Dreisch (1976). However, due to the fragmentary nature of the bone assemblage, a number of alternative measurements have also been used. These measurements are archived and available for future study if requested.

For teeth, a standard length measurement was taken, and then the breadth of each molar column was measured. To interpret possible body-size changes in relation to domestication and animal management, the dimensions of the Batanes dp4s (deciduous 4th premolars) and 1st (M1s) to 3rd molars (M3s) have been compared with modern comparative specimens from China (data collected by J. Ochoa and P.J. Piper, Table 10.1) and Taiwan (unpublished data kindly provided by Keith Dobney, University of Aberdeen). Similar measurements were used for the length and breadth of caprid teeth. As few comparative data for caprids currently exist, and since no previous research has been carried out into body-size changes within Mainland and Island Southeast Asian caprine populations, these measurements are compared with the only other dataset currently available, from the 14th – 17th century AD East Timorese sites of Vasino and Macapainara (Amano and Piper 2011; Piper and Amano 2011). All references to tooth wear stages reported in the text and tables are from Grant (1982), and relative ages of pigs are from Bull and Payne (1982).

Linear enamel hypoplasia (LEH) is a defect acquired during the developmental stage of molars that manifests itself as rows of pits and linear depressions in the enamel surface. These defects are considered to indicate physiological stress, and in particular nutritional deficiency, during the early growth of an animal (Dobney et al. 2007). LEH is not randomly located on teeth, but occurs at specific heights on the molar crown. It has been suggested that birth and weaning are the direct causal effects of two distinctive peaks in LEH on the 1st permanent molar. Other defects on the 2nd and 3rd permanent molars are possibly related to the effects of nutritional stress during the animal's first and second winters respectively (Dobney and Ervynck 1998). Studies show that there are strong differences in the frequencies of stress-induced LEH that are useful indicators of former husbandry practices and environmental conditions (Ervynck and Dobney 1999). Importantly, there also appear to be marked differences in the levels of stress suffered by domestic pigs in comparison to their wild counterparts, and these can be used to differentiate between the two (Dobney et al. 2007). All pig molars were studied under a low-powered microscope for any LEH defects.

Taphonomic observations

Anaro: Taphonomy

Anaro produced the largest bone assemblage recovered from Itbayat, with a total of 1316 identified terrestrial vertebrate remains and a further 10 indeterminate fragments. Due to logistical problems of access to freshwater and the compact, sticky nature of the clay substrate the deposits from Anaro were dry-sieved through a 5 mm mesh. This has inevitably had a serious impact on the recovery of small bone fragments, and selective hand collection probably explains, at least in part, the low percentage of indeterminate fragments recovered (i.e. there was selective recovery of bones deemed identifiable by the archaeologists).

Table 10.1. The length and breadth measurements (mm) of the maxillary and mandibular dp4s to M3s from China held in the Field Museum of Natural History, Chicago (data P.J. Piper and J. Ochoa). Measurements in brackets for the M1s and M2s were taken at the occlusal surface, those without brackets are measurements at the enamo-root junction. None of the individuals were adult and the M3 was unerupted. L = length, Ba = breadth of anterior cusps, Bm = breadth of middle cusps (dp4 and M3 only), Bp = breadth of posterior cusps.

Accn No.	Locality	Sex	dp4L	dp4Ba	dp4Bm	dp4Bp	P4L	P4B	M1L	M1Ba	M1Bp	M2L	M2Ba	M2BP
Mandible														
39326	Shanxi, China	F	17.43 (18.19)	5.05	6.99	8.66	-	-	15.36 (16.66)	10.1	11.43	-	-	-
31799	Laos, Pong Saly	M	-	-	-	-	13.43	10.26	16.48 (17.77)	12.83	13.18	19.95 (20.61)	17.33	16.98
39327	Szechwan, China	?	18.04 (19.21)	6.54	7.98	8.9	-	-	15.9 (16.91)	-	-	-	-	-
31791	Annam, French Indo-China	M	-	-	-	-	14.71	12.29	17.75 (18.32)	13.8	13.7	22.91	19.16	18.42
Maxilla														
39326	Shanxi, China	F	12.37 (13.8)	10.42		11.15	-	-	16.03 (16.98)	13.6	13.4	-	-	-
31799	Laos, Pong Saly	M	-	-		-	12.78	14.44	15.71 (17.74)	15.99	15.77	20.82 (23.94)	20.55	19.9
39327	Szechwan, China	?	12.75 (13.35)	10.58		11.41	-	-	16.02 (16.98)	13.17	13.37	-	-	-
31791	Annam, French Indo-China	M	-	-		-	13.81	16.51	17.15 (19.15)	16.61	17.77	22.87 (25.31)	21.5	22.4

Table 10.2. The skeletal elements of goat, pig and bird that demonstrate different modifications associated with butchery, identified in the Anaro assemblages. Sq. = Square number; L = Left; R = Right.

Square	Depth	Taxon	Element	Side	Part of Element	Modification Type
3E	30-40	Capra aegagrus hircus	Humerus	L	Distal end and Shaft	Multiple cut marks on the antero-medial margins of the medial epicondyle, the antero-lateral margins of the lateral condyle and the antero-medial surfaces of the shaft above the medial epicondyle.
3F	50-55	Sus scrofa (domestic)	Radius	R	Shaft	Chop mark on the postero-medial surface
3C	30-40	Sus scrofa (domestic)	Femur	L	Proximal end of the diaphysis	Multiple cut marks and deliberate shattering of the long bone for marrow extraction.
3D	40-50	Bird	Coracoid	?	Proximal end fragment	One transverse cut mark
3D	60-70	Bird	Tibiotarsus	R	Proximal end	Oblique cut mark on postero-lateral surface

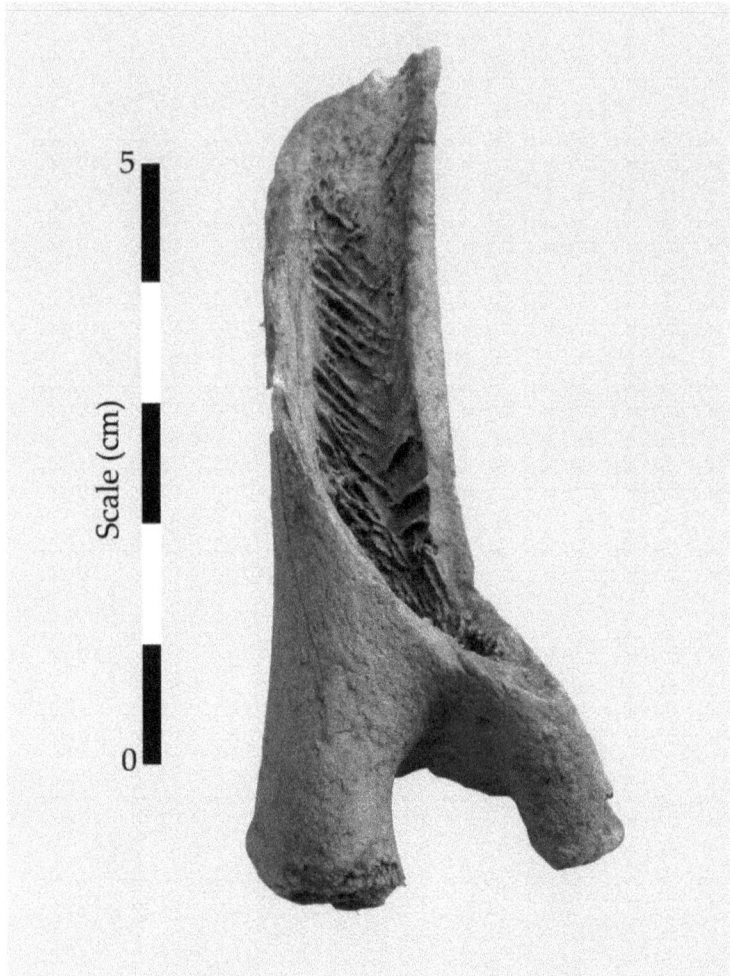

Figure 10.1. A pig right humerus from Savidug B11 (60–70 cm) demonstrating a spiral fracture and 'tearing' that has caused the loss of the posterior and lateral surfaces of the bone whilst it was still green and fresh.

Source: Philip Piper.

In terms of spatial distributions, the small rock shelter of Anaro 3 produced the highest number of animal bones, and discussion will primarily focus on this site. Close examination of surfaces and internal (cross-sectional) structure showed that most fragments were in relatively good condition, demonstrating little diagenetic breakdown of cortical bone matrices. The large- and intermediate-sized mammal bones consisted primarily of isolated teeth and bone fragments between 20 and 50 mm in length, indicating quite intensive fragmentation. Most breaks were either transverse, irregular transverse, or irregular, and occurred following discard when the bones were old and dry. Some fractures, however, were associated with impact scars and negative flake scars characteristic of deliberate human breakage - this type of butchery is commonly associated with marrow extraction (Johnson 1985; see Fig. 10.1 for an example from Savidug Dune Site).

Abrasion and rounding of articular ends and fracture surfaces indicate some degree of subsurface and post-depositional movement (Marshall 1989). Longitudinal cracking and splitting of cortical bone surfaces indicate extensive subaerial weathering and possibly trampling of most bone fragments from each grid square (Behrensmeyer 1978). For example, with the exception of two burnt bones from Anaro 3D, all the bone shows various stages of weathering, indicating that there was possibly some delay between deposition and eventual burial. Furthermore, surfaces were often pitted and root etched, implying quite shallow incorporation, i.e. burial within the active root-zone (Olsen and Shipman 1988).

Nineteen fragments of bone from six different skeletal elements demonstrate single or multiple cut marks and/or chop marks close to articular ends, associated with butchery (Tables 10.2 and 10.3). For example, the distal end (fused) and shaft of a goat left humerus from Anaro 3E (30–40 cm) possesses cut marks on the antero-medial margins of the medial epicondyle, the antero-lateral margins of the lateral condyle, and the antero-medial surfaces of the shaft above the medial epicondyle (Fig. 10.2). Cut marks in these locations suggest that the humerus was severed from the radius and ulna. In addition, several parallel cut marks were identified on the inferior surfaces of the diaphysial shaft, below the proximal articular end (unfused), of a pig left femur (Anaro 3C: 35–40 cm). The cut marks indicate that the femur was physically removed from the pelvis during butchery. Yet again, the proximal end of a chicken-sized avian right tibiotarsus (although not a chicken) from Anaro 3D (60-70 cm) possessed a single oblique cut mark on its postero-lateral surface. A proximal end fragment of chicken-sized coracoid also has a single transverse cut mark across its surface. These records clearly demonstrate that the local inhabitants of Anaro were hunting and butchering the local and/or introduced avifauna on Itbayat Island.

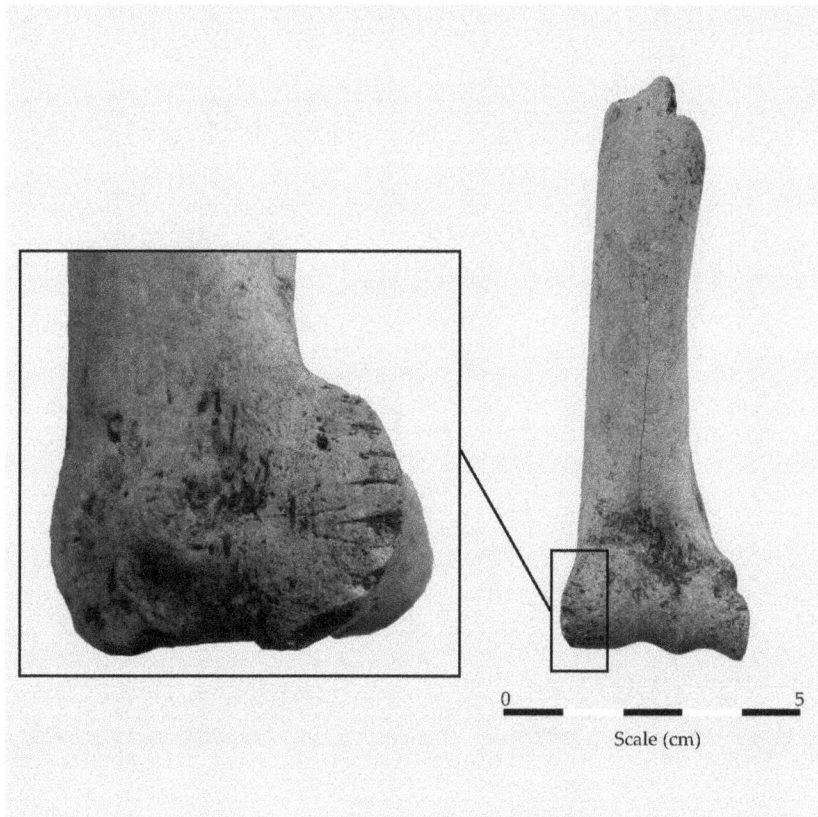

Figure 10.2. Close up of the cut marks on antero-medial margins of the medial epicondyle of a goat left humerus from Anaro 3E (30-40 cm).

Source: Philip Piper.

The vertebrate assemblage also contains several bones that exhibit parallel patterned grooving across articular surfaces and along shafts, both characteristic of rodent gnawing. These types of modification were observed, for example, on the distal end of a pig femur (Anaro 5: 0–5 cm). They feature narrow, contiguous shallow scrape marks across their surfaces and articulations.

terra australis 40

The breadths and depths of the incisor grooves are consistent with those produced by murids, probably rats, a modification also observed in the Savidug and Pamayan assemblages on Sabtang Island (see Fig. 10.3 for an example from Savidug Dune Site).

A single fragment of the neck and blade of a pig scapula (Anaro 3C: 60–65 cm) demonstrates shallow indentations around the periphery of the fracture margins and slight thinning of the breakage edges. These are features characteristic of carnivore gnawing (Lyman 1994: 206-216).

Torongan Cave: Taphonomy

The bone assemblage from Torongan demonstrates very different biostratinomic and post-depositional modifications from those identified at Anaro and Sunget. Many bone fragments are slightly or moderately eroded, causing shallow pitting and the smoothing and rounding of surfaces and fracture margins (Piper 2003). These modifications are characteristic of animal bones that have been subjected to reworking and re-deposition as a result of fluvial action. This interpretation is supported by the occurrence of isolated pieces of bone from similar depths that vary considerably in their state of preservation, with some appearing mid to dark brown in colour and highly weathered and eroded, whilst others have the appearance of being of more recent origin. This supports the sedimentary analysis and archaeological interpretation that these deposits represent in-washed soil from above the cave (chapter 2).

Savidug Dune Site: Taphonomy

In total, 1454 bone fragments of terrestrial vertebrate were recovered from all the layers identified at the Savidug Dune Site. Of these, 1190 (82%) could be identified as mammal, reptile or bird, with another 264 (18%) being indeterminate small fragments. 546 bones were securely provenanced to cultural layer 2, dating to AD 1000–1500 based on the trade ware pottery recovered. Another 406 were recorded in the lower cultural layer 4 at 90 to 150 cm, dated to between 560 and 390 BC (WK 21809). Just 47 bones were recovered from layer 5 (below 150 cm), correlated with a charcoal date of 1130-930 BC (WK 21810) (Chapter 5).

Table 10.3. The skeletal elements, not confidently identified to taxon, that demonstrate modifications associated with butchery from Anaro.

Square	Depth	Element	Modification Type
9	10-20	rib	One transverse cut mark
14	30-40	long bone fragment	One oblique cut mark
3G	30-40	long bone fragment	Two transverse chop marks
3D	40-50	long bone fragment	One transverse cut mark
3F	50-55	long bone fragment	Four transverse cut marks
3D	50-60	long bone fragment	Two Transverse cut marks
3G	50-60	long bone fragment	Transverse cut mark
3D	60-70	humeral shaft fragment	Transverse cut mark
3G	70-80	long bone fragment	Transverse chop mark and oblique cut mark
1C	0-10	Rib	Two dorso-ventrally orientated cut marks across the surface of the bone.
1C	10-20	Rib	Single cut mark on the medial surface.
3	40-45	Rib	Two chop marks of the lateral surface
3A	40-50	Rib	Two transverse cut marks on the lateral surface.
3	30-35	Indet.	Multiple transverse cut marks across the bone surface.

The bone accumulations in layers 2 and 4 are further spatially differentiated, with the layer 2 assemblage predominantly located in Trenches A-C and K-N. The highest layer 2 concentrations occur in the B and C squares and account for 698 (78.9%, including fish) of the recorded bone fragments. Bones below 90 cm (layers 4 and 5) are almost exclusively from Trench QR 7-9, with

1080 (99%, including fish) of the 1091 fragments recorded. Only six fragments of bone were recorded in QR 7-9 above 90 cm, suggesting that cultural layer 2 was almost completely absent from this trench in terms of bone deposition.

Figure 10.3. Fragment of bone from Savidug Dune Site B9 (80-90 cm) demonstrating the parallel grooving along a fracture margin characteristic of rodent gnawing (demarcated by the arrows).

Source: Philip Piper.

Bone fragment size in large mammals and reptiles is consistent across trenches and depths, with none of the excavated spits or layers having substantially larger or smaller bones than the average. A remarkably high proportion of the bones demonstrate surface weathering. In layer 2, the highest proportion of weathered and abraded mammal bone, with the greatest severity of modification, comes from the upper 20 cm (75%). Below this level the bones are characteristically around 40–50% weathered and abraded. In layer 4 the 90-100 cm spit has just 36% of weathered and abraded bones, but succeeding spits have increasing numbers of slight or moderately weathered fragments. Below 140-150 cm almost all bone fragments show some evidence of slight, moderate or severe levels of weathering.

Two long bone shaft fragments from Trenches C9 (40–50 cm) and B10 (50–60 cm), and a pig left calcaneus (B10 50–60 cm), radial shaft fragment (C11 60–70 cm), shaft of a 3rd or 4th metapodial (B9 80–90 cm), and basal medial phalanx (QR 7-9 110–120 cm), all display the characteristic parallel patterned grooving at fracture margins or along edges associated with rodent gnawing. The size and morphology of the grooves would suggest that rat-sized or smaller rodents were responsible for inflicting the observed damage (Fig. 10.3). The concentric pitting and localised thinning of bone around the fracture margins at one end of a left pig humeral shaft fragment from B11 (50–60 cm) is tentatively identified as possible dog gnawing.

Forty-eight fragments of bone from 11 different skeletal elements demonstrate various modifications associated with butchery (Tables 10.4 and 10.5). The evidence consists primarily of fine transverse or oblique parallel cut marks on bone surfaces, often close to articular ends. For example, a pig left femoral shaft fragment from close to the distal end in C11 (60-70 cm) possesses several small cut marks on the postero-lateral margins, and a fragment of unfused right ilium in C9 (40–50 cm) has four transverse cut marks on the dorsal surfaces. In addition, a few bones such as the distal end and midshaft of a pig right femur from C11 (60–70 cm) have been hacked through, presumably to facilitate marrow extraction. The spiral fracturing and longitudinal flaking of a pig right humeral shaft from B11 (50-60 cm) is also a good indication of deliberate fresh bone breakage for marrow extraction (Fig. 10.1). Overall, the butchery evidence suggests systematic dismemberment of carcasses and some long bone breakage for marrow extraction. In addition, 35 fragments of burnt bone were recorded throughout the bone assemblages, but specific concentrations could not be identified.

Overall, the taphonomic analysis would suggest that the Savidug Dune Site bone assemblages represent the remains of animals butchered and discarded by humans. The high incidence of bone surface weathering and rodent gnawing is consistent with bones that were not deliberately buried, but discarded on the ground surface. Their burial took an extended period of time after disposal.

Pamayan: Taphonomy

Of the 762 bone fragments excavated from Pamayan, 264 (34.6%) were recorded as mammal, 14 (1.8%) as bird, and there was one worked piece of turtle plastron. The other 483 (22.7%) fragments were recorded as indeterminate, although many fragments were probably small pieces of mammal bone.

The average fragment length in mammal and bird bone was just 2.7 cm, demonstrating the severity of fragmentation that has restricted identification in all classes of vertebrate. Similar observations were made in chapter 4 concerning the high levels of fragmentation of shells, especially small cowrie shells, in this site, which dates to the end of prehistory in Batanes. Within the mammals, even the pig and goat teeth were heavily fragmented. Almost all fragments of bone demonstrate varying stages of weathering indicating that they were left exposed on the ground surface prior to burial.

Butchery is rare in these very heavily fragmented assemblages, but the proximal end of a goat left femur from 65 - 70 cm possesses two transverse cut marks on the lateral margins. This same fragment also has evidence of rodent gnawing along the antero-lateral margins, a further indication that the bones remained on the ground surface prior to burial.

Table 10.4. The skeletal elements of pig and dog (in italics) that demonstrate different modifications associated with butchery, Savidug Dune Site. Sq. = Square number; L = Left; R = Right.

Square	Depth	Element	Side	Part of element	Modification Type
B10	20-40	Tibia	R	Shaft	Chopped at the proximal end of remaining shaft: single small transverse cut mark close to the proximal end
C9	20-40	Humerus	L	Distal shaft fragment	Shallow transverse cut marks on antero-medial margins
C9	40-50	Tibia	R	Proximal end of shaft-midshaft	Remains of a cut mark on the antero-medial surface at the break
C9	40-50	Ulna	L	Proximal end and shaft – fails the olecranon process	Cut marks on the lateral surface close to the dorsal break
C9	40-50	Ilium	R	Fragment of acetabulum	Four transverse cut marks on the dorsal surface
B10	50-60	Calcaneus	L	Fragment	Chop mark on the postero-lateral surface close to proximal break
B11	50-60	Humerus	L	Shaft towards distal end	Spiral fracture and longitudinal flaking
C10/11	50-60	Radius	R	Shaft fragment	Two tiny cut marks on the lateral surface
C11	50-60	Humerus	L	Proximal shaft – longitudinally split fragment of the postero-medial surface	14 cut marks on the postero-medial surface
C11	50-60	Humerus	R	Shaft fragment	Transverse and oblique fine cut marks on the medial, lateral and posterior surfaces
N29	50-60	Humerus	R	Distal shaft fragment	Oblique cut marks on the medial surface
A9	60-70	Lumbar vertebra		Fragment of right body and neural arch	Two transverse cut marks on ventral surface of the lateral process
C11	60-70	Femur	R	Distal shaft fragment	Hacked through the midshaft – cut mark on the postero-lateral margin
C11	60-70	Femur	L	Distal – midshaft fragment (no distal end)	Small cut marks of the postero-lateral margins
C11	60-70	Femur	R	Distal shaft fragment	Large (7.5cm and 7.3) cut marks on the antero-lateral and postero-lateral margins
C11	60-70	Radius	?	Distal shaft fragment	Cut marks on the posterior surface near the break possibly associated with marrow extraction
M27	70-80	Maxilla	R	Fragment containing partial canine alveolus	One oblique cut mark on the buccal surface
A9	90-100	Zygomatic	L	Body	Four dorso-ventral orientated cut marks on the medial surface
A9	90-100	Lumbar vertebra	L	Fragment of the neural arch	Two transverse cut marks on the right hand side of the dorsal spinous process; 3 x cut marks on the interior dorsal margins of the neural arch at the caudal end.
C10	100-110	Humerus	L	Almost complete distal end	Three small transverse cut marks on the antero-medial surface just above the condyle
R7-9	120-130	Oscoxa	L	Complete acetabulum	Two oblique cut marks on the dorso-lateral surface
R7-9	120-130	Tibia	L	Proximal end and partial shaft	Three oblique cut marks on the posterior surface
R7-9	110-120	*Mandible*	R	*Mandibular condyle*	*Eight transverse cut marks on the lateral aspect of condylar neck*

Table 10.5. The skeletal elements that could not be confidently identified to taxon demonstrating modifications associated with butchery from Savidug Dune Site.

Sq.	Depth	Element	Modification Type
M27	40-50	Rib	One cut mark on the medial surface
B10	50-60	Rib	Four transverse cut marks on the lateral surface of the shaft
B10	50-60	Indet.	Three transverse cut marks
C11	50-60	Indet.	Chop and cut marks
C11	60-70	Long bone shaft	Transverse chop marks
C11	60-70	Long bone shaft	Transverse cut marks
A9	90-100	Rib	Single transverse cut mark on the ventral surfaces close to what would have been the proximal articular end
B10	90-100	Vertebra - transverse process	Four transverse cut marks, 3 on one side and one on the other
KN29	130-150	Indet.	Several cut marks
R7-9	100-110	Long bone shaft	One transverse cut mark
R7-9	110-120	Long bone shaft	Transverse and oblique cut marks
R7-9	110-120	Long bone shaft	One Transverse cut mark
R7-9	110-120	Long bone shaft	Several oblique and transverse cut marks
R7-9	110-120	Long bone shaft	Four oblique cut marks
R7-9	110-120	Long bone shaft	One oblique cut mark
R7-9	110-120	Long bone shaft	Three transverse cut marks
R7-9	110-120	Long bone shaft	Oblique cut marks
R7-9	120-130	Indet.	Two transverse cut marks
R7-9	120-130	Long bone shaft	One oblique cut mark
R7-9	120-130	Long bone shaft	Two transverse cut marks
R7-9	120-130	Long bone shaft	Three transverse cut marks
R7-9	140-150	Long bone shaft	Transverse chop marks
R7-9	140-150	Long bone shaft	Spiral fracture

Taxonomic identifications

Anaro: Taxonomy

Of the 1316 bone fragments from Anaro, 307 (23.3%) could be identified to family or a lower taxonomic level. The highest proportion of identifiable skeletal elements was recovered from Anaro 3 (N=220; Table 10.6). The absence of goat below 50 cm in most trenches of Anaro 3 would seem to be consistent with the radiocarbon dating (chapter 5), which shows that the basal deposits pre-date the introduction of caprines, extending from *c.*1000 BC to beyond AD 500.

The pig was the most frequently occurring taxon (N=224) and was present at all depths from 110 - 120 cm in Anaro 6 to the subsurface in many trenches. In Anaro 3 there was a slight concentration of pig bones between 50 and 80 cm, perhaps indicating more intensive deposition of bone during this period, which most likely preceded the introduction of the goat towards the end of the 1st millennium AD (see below).

Both male and female pigs are represented at Anaro and can be distinguished by their canine morphologies. It is difficult to ascertain with any confidence whether the remains of entire carcasses were deposited at Anaro, due to the dispersed nature of the faunal remains. Certainly, the small compact extremities and loose teeth have survived the best (NISP = 155/224). Nevertheless, fragments of most body parts are present. Beyond those illustrated in Fig. 10.4, several small pieces of vertebrae and rib are almost certainly from pigs, especially below 50 cm where the goat is absent. Overall, it would seem that most major skeletal elements were discarded at Anaro.

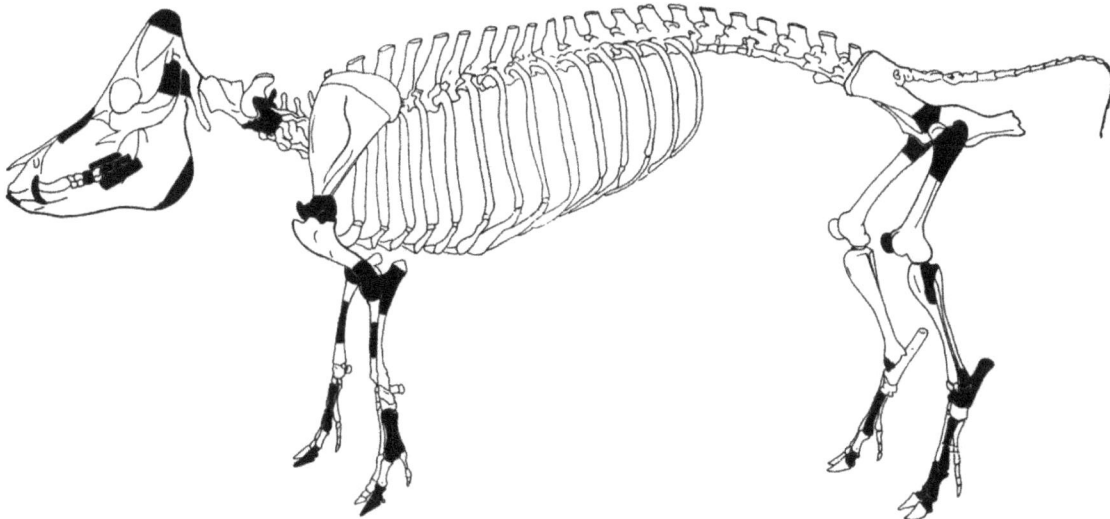

Figure 10.4. The pig body part representation (shaded) from Anaro.

Source: Philip Piper.

Table 10.6. The identifiable terrestrial vertebrate remains from Anaro 3 recorded as numbers of identifiable specimens (NISP) and depth (cm).

Depths (cm)		0-10	10-20	20-30	30-40	40-50	50-60	60-70	70-80	80-90	90-100	100-110
Reptiles	Serpentes indet.		1		1	1						
Birds	Bird indet.				1	3		2				
Mammals	Rat-sized murid		1	1		1		1				
	Rattus sp.		1		1							
	Viverridae				1	1	1	2	1	1		
	Sus scrofa (domestic)	3	5	8	12	6	25	30	43	5	7	6
	Capra aegagrus hircus (domestic)	2	9	11	18	5		4				

Table 10.7. Length and breadth measurements (mm) of the maxillary and mandibular dp4s to M3s, together with tooth wear stages (A to N), of pigs recovered from Anaro. All measurements for molar length are the greatest length of each tooth. L = length, Ba = breadth of anterior cusps, Bm = breadth of middle cusps (dp4 and M3 only), Bp = breadth of posterior cusps, D = damaged, un. = unerupted.

Square and max. depth		Side	Biometrics Maxilla														Toothwear				
			Dp4L	Dp4 Ba	dp4 Bm	dp4 Bp	M1L	M1 Ba	M1 Bp	M2L	M2 Ba	M2Bp	M3L	M3Ba	M3 Bm	M3Bp	dp4	P4	M1	M2	M3
3B	40-45	L	13.88	10.19		10.25											B				
3A	75-80	L	14.04	10.65		11.29											F				
3C	50-55	R					17.92	13.77	14.69	22.75	17.15	17							C	B	
3C	55-60	R					17.57	14.95	14.81										D		
3F	70-75	L					19.07	15.04	15.13										C		
9	10-20	L					15.4	11.69	11.44									A	B		
3E	60-65	R					18.52	13.36	13.67										C		
1B	0-5	L					18.31	13.56	13.98										Un.		
3B	40-45	L					17.79	15.28	14.68											E	
3A	105-110	R								23.01	17.82	18.26								B	
3C	50-55	L								21.9	15.39	18.57								Un.	

Table 10.7. Continued.

		Biometrics														Toothwear				
Square and max. depth	Side	DpaL	Dp4 Ba	dp4 Bm	dp4 Bp	M1L	M1 Ba	M1 Bp	M2L	M2 Ba	M2Bp	M3L	M3Ba	M3 Bm	M3Bp	dp4	P4	M1	M2	M3
3D	50-60	R								18.41									B	
3G	70-80	R							24.01	D	18.46								A	
3F	70-75	L							23.97	D	17.61								A	
4A	35-40	L										39.59	21.26	19.27	13.19					A
Mandible																				
1C	20	R	18.45	6.5	7.36	8.38										B				
3	20	R	17.18	5.92	7.26	8.31										D				
3	60-65	L	D		7.28	8.32										A				
3F	70-75	L	19.95	6.96	8.67	9.87										D				
3	20-25	R					16.85	10	10.98										A		
3C	70-75	R					18.88	13.25	13.34										C		
3C	55-60	L					17.97	11.22	12.19										D		
3G	70-80	?					15.92	11.96	12.02										N		
3A	75-80	R								19.65	13.78	13.89								C	
14	30-40	L								23.75	15.85	16.26								A	
1E	80-85	R											37.85	17.24	16.84	14.68					A
3B	65-70	L													16.22	15.93					Un.

Stages of epiphysial fusion suggest that pigs from a variety of ages are represented at Anaro. For example, a left ulna from 3E (60–65 cm), a left humerus from 3D (60–70 cm) and a radius (unsided) from 4A (40–50 cm) were all so small and undeveloped that they could only be from neonates. A left distal humeral diaphysial fragment from 3E (30–40 cm), a right humeral shaft fragment with unfused articular end from 3B (70–75 cm), a damaged left dp4 with no occlusal wear (Grant Stage A) from 3 (10–20 cm), and an unerupted mandibular first molar from 1B (0–5 cm), represent at least three juvenile individuals based on spatial and chronological separation. Furthermore, tooth eruption and dental wear of the dp4s and permanent molars suggests individuals of a variety of ages, from perhaps a few months to 3 years old. But no pigs appear to have reached a substantial age before death (Table 10.7). The high proportion of juvenile or sub-adult pigs is consistent with a managed rather than a wild or feral pig population. However, the presence of neonatal and very young pigs of just a few months of age is not a pattern of kill-off seen in the bone assemblages of Layers 2 and 4 at Savidug Dune Site on Sabtang Island. Perhaps it indicates different methods of pig stalling and management on the two islands, and during different periods of occupation (see below).

Biometrical analyses of the Anaro pig molars indicates that they fall within the upper range of the Eurasian wild boar (*Sus scrofa*) recorded in Taiwan and China, suggesting that the morphotype represented in the Batanes was a large pig, unlikely to have been reduced much in size from its wild progenitor (Table 10.1). No example of LEH was recorded in any of the teeth.

A total of 68 caprine fragments were recorded from Anaro. Only the domestic goat, *Capra hircus*, was ever introduced to the Batanes Islands. All remains positively identified as caprines (including sheep as well as goats) are taken to be goat. Sheep were introduced to the Philippines, but only in the recent past. The fragments consisted primarily of loose teeth or tooth fragments (N=48), and a few cranial and post-cranial elements. Goat was identified in all trenches except Anaro 6. In Anaro 3, goat was primarily recovered from the upper 50 cm, with just four fragments in Trenches 3D (N=2) and 3G (N=2) at 60–70 cm.

Most of the molars demonstrate extensive wear indicating that the majority of animals were mature adults at the time of death (Table 10.8). Hillson (2005) noted that there is a considerable variation in the eruption timing of the teeth of different domestic goat breeds. But the presence of worn third molars suggests individuals older than 24 months (Moran and O'Connor 1994). A left mandibular dp4 from 1B (10–20 cm), a fragment of left mandible containing a dp2 from 3B (30–40 cm), and an unworn upper left first molar and unfused distal epiphysis from a metapodial from 3E (30–40 cm) suggest that some individuals also died before they reached maturity.

Table 10.8. Length and breadth measurements (mm) of the maxillary and mandibular dp4s to M3s, together with tooth wear stages, of goats recovered from Anaro. All measurements for molar length are the greatest length of each tooth. L = length, Ba = breadth of anterior cusps, Bm = breadth of middle cusps (dp4 and M3 only), Bp = breadth of posterior cusps, D = damaged.

Location	Max. Depth	Element	Side	Biometrics										Toothwear		
				M1L	M1Ba	M1Bp	M2L	M2Ba	M2Bp	M3L	M3Ba	M3Bm	M3Bp	M1	M2	M3
Maxilla																
1B	25-30	M1	R	12.4	9.22	D								E		
3	30-35	M1	L	13.68	D	D								G		
3G	30-35	M1	L	11.21	9.65	9.16								F		
3B	15-20	M2	L				15.72	D	D						F	
3A	15-20	M2	L				15.32	12.15	10.35						D	
9	Oct-20	M2	R				13.69	10.83	12.43					?		
3E	30-40	M3	L							19.64	11.95		10.37			D
3G	20-30	M3	R							20.06	12.43		10.23			J
Mandible																
3B	35-40	M1	L	11.36	6.92	6.77								D		
3A	35-40	M1	L	12.13	7.32	7.48								F		
3E	30-40	M1	L	12.24	6.58	6.73								unworn		
3	20-25	M2	R				14.77	D	D					?		
3A	15-20	M2	L				13.06	7.84	7.81						B	
1B	15-20	M3	L							D	8.21	7.82				G
3B	35-40	M3	R							22.3	7.92	7.94				C

Table 10.9. A comparison of the mandibular tooth row lengths (mm) from the cranial end of the canine alveolus to the caudal margins of the M2 of the viverrid archaeological specimen from Anaro 6 (80-90 cm) and a number of *Paguma larvata* (subsp.) and *Paradoxurus hermaphroditus* specimens held within the mammal section of Naturalis, Leiden, and the zooarchaeology laboratory, Archaeological Studies Program (ASP), University of the Philippines; all taxonomic nomenclature follows the original labels for museum specimens.

Species	Sex	Facility/ Accession No.	Tooth row length (mm)
Archaeological specimen	\	Anaro 6 (80-90 cm)	37.66
Paguma larvata taivana (Taiwan)	F	Mammal Sec. Naturalis 20861	39.24
Paguma larvata taivana (Taiwan)	F	Mammal Sec. Naturalis 20860	39.55
Paguma larvata taivana (Taiwan)	M	Mammal Sec. Naturalis 20911	34.87
Paguma larvata (Borneo)	F	Mammal Sec. Naturalis 34668	45.93
Paguma larvata leucomystax (Sumatra)	F	Mammal Sec. Naturalis 14672	50.57
Paguma larvata leucomystax (Sumatra)	F	Mammal Sec. Naturalis 15750	52.46
Paguma larvata leucomystax (Sumatra)	M	Mammal Sec. Naturalis 1370	50.61
Paguma larvata leucomystax (Sumatra)	F	Mammal Sec. Naturalis 20778	48.45
Paradoxurus hermaphroditus (Brunei)	\	Mammal Sec. Naturalis 20765	41.66
Paradoxurus hermaphroditus (Sumatra)	\	Mammal Sec. Naturalis 324	42.37
Paradoxurus hermaphroditus (Sumatra)	F	Mammal Sec. Naturalis 34681	41.96
Paradoxurus hermaphroditus (Sumatra)	M	Mammal Sec. Naturalis 20312	43.63
Paradoxurus philippinensis (Philippines)	M	Mammal Sec. Naturalis 34737	42.48
Paradoxurus hermaphroditus (Palawan)	\	Zooarchaeology Lab. ASP A0095	38.43
Paradoxurus hermaphroditus (Palawan)	\	Zooarchaeology Lab. ASP A0044	44.65

Body part representation is difficult to assess from the few fragments recorded at Anaro, but several meat-yielding elements such as the humerus and scapula are represented, as well as teeth and skulls (Fig. 10.5). Some small fragments of vertebrae and rib within the upper 50 cm of Anaro 3 that could only be identified as 'large mammal' might be parts of caprines, as well as pigs.

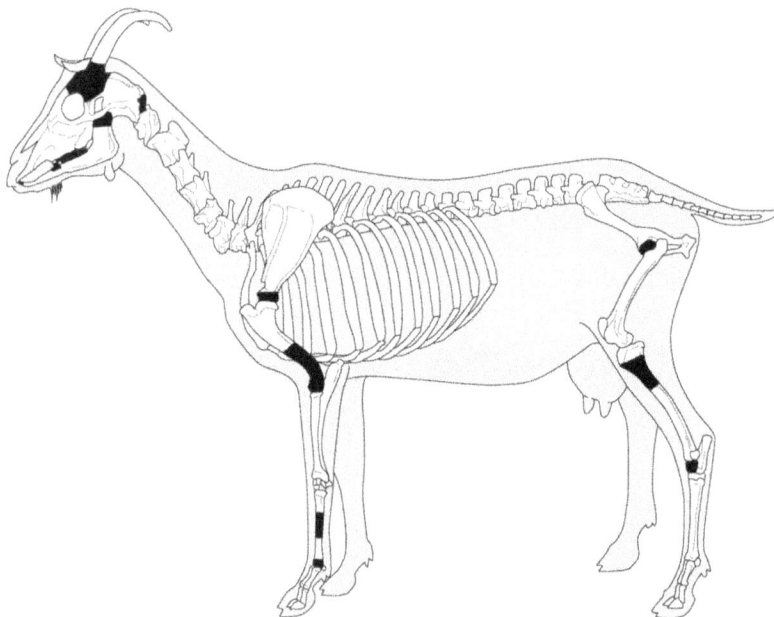

Figure 10.5. The goat body part representation (shaded) from Anaro.

Source: Philip Piper.

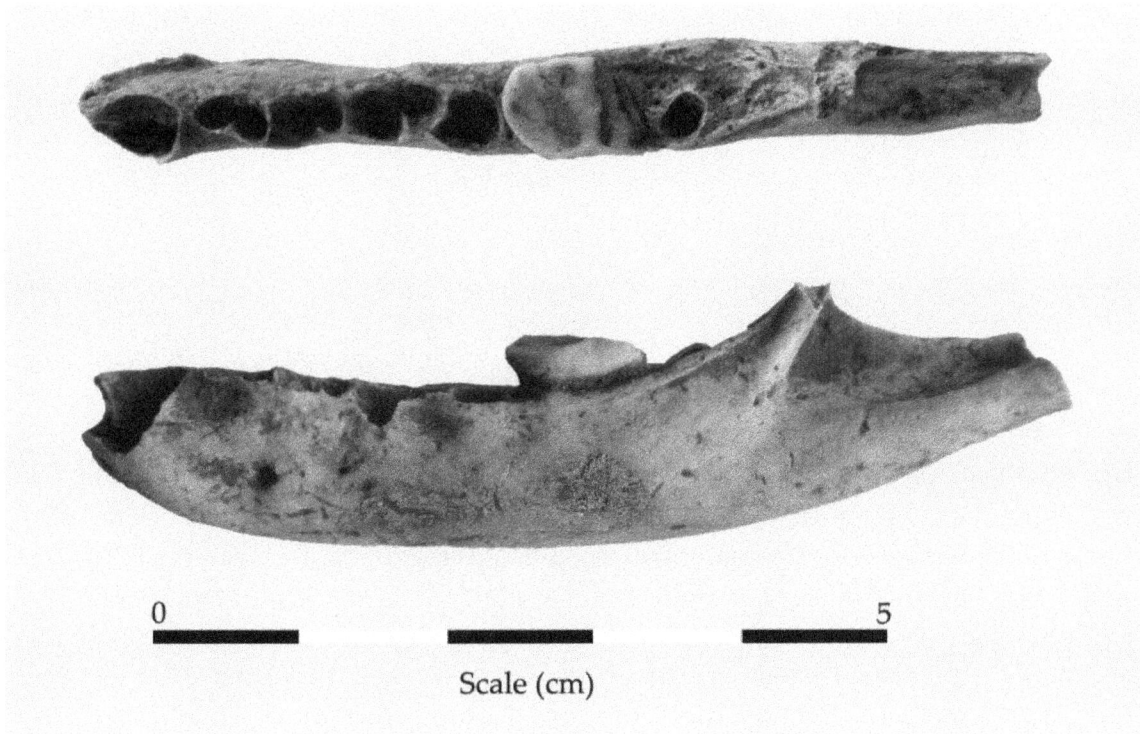

Figure 10.6. The occlusal (above) and labial (below) aspects of the viverrid left mandible from Anaro 6 (80–90 cm).

Source: Philip Piper.

The lengths and breadths of caprine molars overlap with those recorded from 14th – 17th century AD East Timor (Amano and Piper 2011). Indeed, measurements were not significantly different from those taken on modern domestic goats housed at the University of the Philippines, Archaeological Studies Program.

The bones of a viverrid also occur in small numbers (N=8) throughout the Anaro archaeological sequence, with the earliest occurrence possibly recorded in Anaro 6 at 110-120 cm. One mandible from Anaro 6 (80-90 cm) consisted of a complete mandibular body, from the cranial aspects of the canine alveolus to the ventral portions of the mandibular ramus. It still contained a first molar (Fig. 10.6), so heavily worn that it has completely lost its crown morphology and caudal portions. The specimen was taken to the Natural History Museum (Naturalis) in Leiden, Netherlands, for comparison with the two most likely species to be represented, the common palm civet (*Paradoxurus hermaphroditus*) and the masked palm civet (*Paguma larvata*). Attempts at differentiation using tooth morphology and the locations and alignments of the empty alveoli were inconclusive. Measurements of the mandibular length from the cranial end of the canine alveolus to the caudal margins of the second molar alveolus indicates that the specimen falls within the range of *Paguma larvata taivana*, the small Taiwanese subspecies of masked palm civet, but is also comparable in size to the small sample of modern comparative specimens of common palm civet held within the zooarchaeology collection, Archaeological Studies Program, University of the Philippines (Table 10.9). Taxonomic identification will need to await recovery of fragments with more diagnostic features (see below). A left humerus from Anaro 3A (45–50 cm) with an unfused distal articular end indicates the presence of sub-adults and suggests that Itbayat was home to a breeding population of civet cats. A small right calcaneus from the subsurface in Anaro 7 could indicate that civet populations, that are unknown on the island now, survived until relatively recently.

Seven bird bones were recorded from Anaro, none of similar size or morphology to the chicken skeleton. A fragment of proximal right tibiotarsus from Anaro 3F (40-50 cm) bears an oblique cut mark on its postero-lateral surface, close to the articular end, indicating that this specimen was butchered and consumed. Three indeterminate snake vertebrae were recovered from Anaro 1B (25–30 cm and 40–45 cm) and 2A (10–15 cm).

Bone artefacts from Anaro

Two complete and five fragments of bone and tooth artefact were recovered from Anaro, as well as a waste fragment from artefact production. A male pig lower canine from Anaro 3C (60–65 cm) was deliberately split longitudinally (length 39.21 mm, maximum width 7.06 mm), and its occlusal surface ground down to remove rough edges (see Fig. 8.11 K). A transverse notch was ground out on the same split side of the specimen for the secure attachment of a cord or line. This specimen was probably used as a fishing gorge.

Another fragment of bone from Anaro 3A (80–90 cm) has been roughly ground on all surfaces to form a circular profile and to taper into a point at either end. The specimen is 35.25 mm in length and has a maximum width of 2.69 mm. It was probably also a fishing gorge (Fig. 10.7).

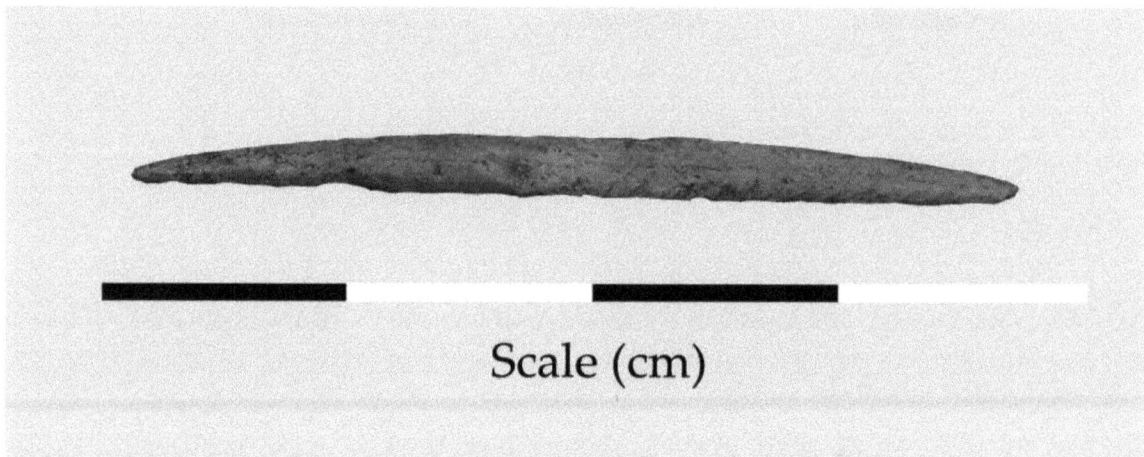

Figure 10.7. A probable fishing gorge from Anaro 3A (80–90 cm).

Source: Philip Piper.

Two fragments of bone from Anaro 3 (70–75 and 80–85 cm) have diameters of 3.37 mm and 1.9 mm respectively, suggesting they are from two different artefacts (fragment lengths = 39.39 mm and 17.49 mm respectively). Both are split transversely, but it is clear they have been ground on all surfaces to produce a circular profile and to taper to a point. There is no evidence of a notch on either specimen, but microscopic analysis of the tip indicates no rotational wear that would suggest use as awls. It is possible that both are broken fishing gorges or projectile points.

A fragment of male pig left lower canine, 56.57 mm in length and 11.27 mm in maximum width has a transverse fracture at the cranial end and longitudinal break towards the caudal end. The occlusal surface has regular transverse striations and grooves that appear to be too deep and regular and cover too much of the surface to reflect the natural wear caused by the pig upper and lower canines when they grind against each other. It is possible that this fragment of canine was used as some sort of scraping or planing tool for materials such as wood. Similar tools were recently recorded by Piper et al. (2010) from the Neolithic site of An Son in southern Vietnam. One of these examples had resin adhering to the labial and lingual surfaces close to the caudal end of the tooth, indicating it had almost certainly been hafted.

Torongan Cave: Taxonomy

Of the 121 bone fragments from Torongan, 96 (79.3%) were recovered from within the upper 30 cm of the excavation. The upper 5 cm consisted primarily of bone fairly recently introduced to the site, including one human hand phalanx and one toe phalanx. Three domestic animals are represented within the archaeological record, the pig (NISP = 4), goat (NISP = 8), and as a surface find a fragment of bovine metacarpal. The goat remains are all restricted to the upper 25 cm of deposit, whereas one of the four pig fragments was recovered from a depth of 55 cm. This would suggest that there is some stratigraphic and chronological integrity, with the upper 25 cm at Torongan post-dating the introduction of goats to Itbayat, and the lower deposits pre-dating it.

The assemblage also includes four Viverridae fragments, including a femur and humerus, all from the upper 25 cm. The distal end of the humerus has unfused epiphyses, which suggest that breeding populations of this taxon inhabited the surroundings of Torongan Cave. In addition, a rib and vertebra of a small snake species were recovered from 30 cm and 50 cm respectively.

Below 45 cm depth, and with the exception of two very small and severely eroded pig tusk fragments, the Torongan bone assemblage consisted entirely of rat and bat bones. The excellent condition of the small vertebrate remains suggests that, if anthropic derived midden bone had been deposited on the site, it would still be represented. Thus, the taphonomic heterogeneity of vertebrate remains suggests that at least the lower 25 cm of deposit represents nothing more than reworking and redeposition of waterborne deposits, intermixed with some cultural material, as suggested by the geomorphological and archaeological interpretations for the site (chapter 2).

Savidug Dune Site: Taxonomy

In total, 291 specimens (24%) of the terrestrial animal bone assemblage (including marine turtles) could be identified to class or higher taxonomic level. Of these, 279 could be securely placed within layers 2, 4 and 5. The most common taxon was the pig, accounting for 234 (80.4%) of the identified bones. It is probably safe to conclude that the majority, if not all, of the unidentified 'large mammal' bone fragments are from pigs (Table 10.10).

Just 11 bone fragments in layer 5 could be identified to taxon, including a fragment of pig lumbar vertebra, a complete right 2nd metatarsal, and a fragment of left 3rd metacarpal. Another eight were severely weathered and abraded pieces of marine turtle carapace and/or plastron and ribs.

Savidug Dune Site layer 4

Seventy-five pig bones could be securely provenanced to layer 4, with at least four individuals represented, based on left maxillary fragments. The small number of pig mandibles and maxillae (NISP = 6) with teeth are all from adult individuals, with at least three of the specimens exceeding three years of age at the time of death (Bull and Payne 1982). These include the fused right distal tibia in R7-9 (110-120 cm) from an individual greater than 18 months of age, and two axial metapodials with fused distal ends from a pig in excess of two years old (Bull and Payne 1982). A fused distal articular end of a left humerus in C10 (100-110 cm) belonged to an animal in excess of one year old, but this is likely to belong to cultural layer 2.

There is little that can be said from the few mandibular and maxillary teeth recovered from this phase, except that the teeth are relatively large and fall within the expected size range for the comparative examples of *Sus scrofa* from Taiwan and China (Table 10.11).

Many of the high meat-yielding bones from pigs, such as the scapula, humerus and pelvis were recorded, as well as loose teeth and extremities. This suggests that most elements in the skeleton are represented in the archaeological record (Fig. 10.8).

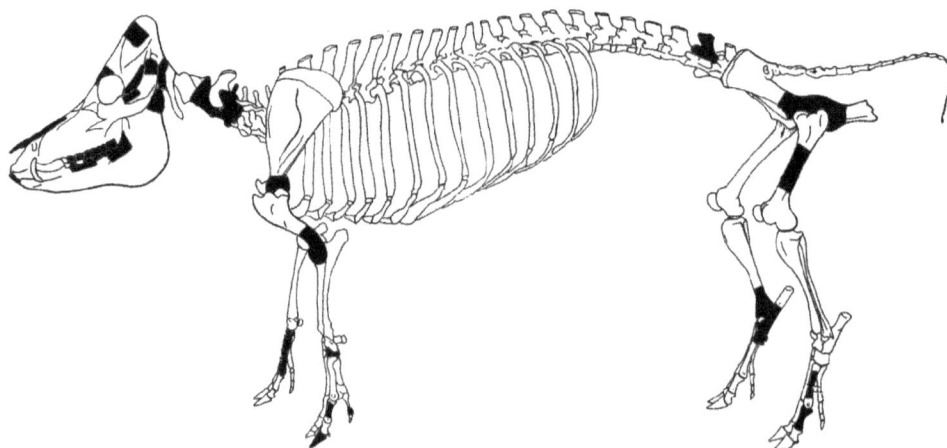

Figure 10.8. The pig body part representation (shaded) from Savidug Dune Site layer 4.

Source: Philip Piper.

Three fragments of dog were recorded in QR 7-9 layer 4, a basioccipital at 120-130 cm and the proximal end of a right scapula at 110-120 cm (Fig. 10.9). A fragment of right mandibular condyle from 110-120 cm, also from a dog, has eight transverse cut marks on the labial margins of the neck of the mandibular condyle, suggesting that this individual was possibly butchered for consumption, or perhaps the skull or mandible was removed as a trophy or for display (Fig. 10.10).

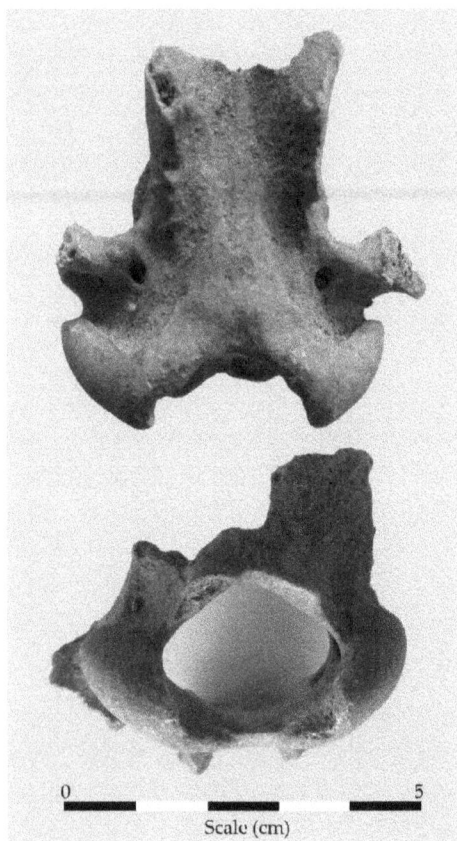

Figure 10.9. The ventral (above) and caudal (below) aspects of a dog basioccipital from Savidug Dune Site QR 7-9, 120–130 cm.

Source: Philip Piper.

Figure 10.10. A dog right mandibular condyle from Savidug Dune Site QR 7-9, 110–120 cm, with eight transverse cut marks on the neck (in approximate anatomical position).

Source: Philip Piper.

Table 10.10. The number of identified specimens (NISP) from layers 2, 4 and 5 in Savidug Dune Site.

Class	Taxon	Layer 2	Layer 4	Layer 5	Total NISP
Reptilia	Testudine	1	16	8	25
Aves	Bird indet.	3	5	0	8
Mammalia	Rat-sized murid	6	0	0	6
	Rattus sp.	1	0	0	1
	Canis familiaris	0	3	0	3
	Sus scrofa (domestic)	129	102	3	134
	Cervid indet.	2	0	0	2
	TOTAL	**142**	**126**	**11**	**179**

Table 10.11. The length and breadth measurements (mm) of the maxillary and mandibular dp4s to M3s of the pigs recovered from Savidug layer 4. All measurements for molar length are the greatest length of each tooth. L = length, Ba = breadth of anterior cusps, Bm = breadth of middle cusps (dp4 and M3 only), Bp = breadth of posterior cusps.

Grid	Depth	Side	P4L	P4W	M1L	M1Wa	M1Wp	M2L	M2Wa	M2Wp	M3L	M3Wa	M3Wm	M3Wp	M1	M2	M3
Maxilla																	
R7-9	120-130	R	12.14	12	14.34	13.81	13.69	20.62	16.47	16.97					F	A	
R7-9	112	L	11.55	12.18	15.5	14.73	14.86	21.24	18.63	18.65	35.2	21.03	19.14	13.93	J	F	A
R7-9	120-130	L					14.56	22.74	17.85						H	G	
R7-9	130	R						20.82	15.52	14.98						D	D
Mandible																	
R7-9	113	R			16.09	11.95	12.7	20.95	16.28	16.37	40.04	17.93	17.62	12.1	K	G	D
R7-9	130	R									43.32	17.55	17.34	15.66			A

Table 10.12. The length and breadth measurements (mm) of the maxillary and mandibular dp4s to M3s of the pigs recovered from Savidug layer 2. All measurements for molar length are the greatest length of each tooth. L = length, Ba = breadth of anterior cusps, Bm = breadth of middle cusps (dp4 and M3 only), Bp = breadth of posterior cusps, D = damaged.

Grid	Depth	Side	dp4L	dp4	M1L	M1Wa	M1Wp	M2L	M2Wa	M2Wp	M3L	M3Wa	M3Wm	M3Wp	dp4	M1	M2	M3
Maxilla																		
B11	50-60	L	13.67												F			
B11	50-60	L	12.7												B			
M28	50-60	R	14.25												F			
A9	60-70	R	11.49												D			
B10	50-60	L	12.52												B			
A9	90-100	L	12.67												D			
B10	40-50	L																
B10	60-70	L			13.66	13.91	14.07	17	18.14	17.9						G	D	
B10-11	100-120	L			14.73	14.75	14.55	18.32	17.84	16.92						F	D	

Table 10.12. Continued.

			Biometrics															Tooth Wear			
Grid	Depth	Side	dp4L	dp4	M1	M2	M3	M1L	M1Wa	M1Wp	M2L	M2Wa	M2Wp	M3L	M3Wa	M3Wm	M3Wp	dp4	M1	M2	M3
A9	90-100	L			K	F	C	14.98	13.87	14.09	20.06	17.72	16.98	38.46	20.36	17.72	11.7		K	F	C
C10	100-110	L			D	B		16.67	13.84	13.93	20.31	18.39	18						D	B	
B11	90-100	R			A			16.24	14.72										A		
C11	20-40	L			D			14.36	14	13.18									D		
L28	50-60	R			E			16.02	13.42	13.75									E		
A9	90-100	R				C					D	D	16.59							C	
Mandible																					
C9	40-50	R	16.32	6.64	8.6													B			
C9	40-50	L	16.23	6.23	7.89													E			
M28	50-60	?	15.98	6.30	8.95													G			
B10	50-60	L	15.76	5.98	7.68													B			
K29	30-40	?	D	D	7.58													D			
B10	50-60	L				11.36	10.88											D			
B11	90-100	L				12.18	8.24	15.97	10.66	10.89	20.29	14.34	14.12						D	B	
B10	40-50	R						14.5	10.73	11.68									A		
C11	40-50	R						15.55	9.69	11.2									B		
B11	90-100	R						15.18	10.59	11.19									C		
B11	40-50	R						15.56	10.72	11.82	17.6	14.64							F	B	
C9	40-50	?						15.1	\	\									A		
B10	40-50	R									17.53	13.95	13.78						UNE		
C10	60-70	R									19.52	12.63	13.82							UNE	
B10-11	100-120	R												39.04	16.76	15.69	12.12				
C11	50-60	R												33.92	19.35	17.82	13.14				A

The proximal end and shaft of a murid right femur from QR 7-9 (120-130 cm) is somewhat distinctive. The element is smaller than expected for a rat-sized murid, although the proximal diaphysis is unfused and could potentially have been a sub-adult. The dorsal margins of the greater trochanter and the whole of the lesser trochanter are missing. There is a noticeable medial-orientated curvature in the shaft below the neck. The 3rd trochanter is broad and merges with the ventral margins of the greater trochanter. The 3rd trochanter is also more developed and distinct than in commensal murids (including mice) and extends further down the femoral shaft. This is potentially a fragment of femur from a native (endemic) murid species, rather than an introduced one.

Five small fragments of bird long bone and a possible coracoid were recorded in QR 7-9 at depths between 120 and 150 cm. A single, small fragment of right tibiotarsus shaft with the dorsal portion of the extensor canal underneath the supratendinal bridge is remarkably similar in both size and morphology to three comparative specimens of chicken (*Gallus gallus*) held in the Archaeological Studies Program, Zooarchaeology Laboratory, University of the Philippines. This specimen was recorded in Q/R 7-9 at 110-120 cm and thus dates to *c.*500–300 BC (Fig. 10.11). Fifteen severely weathered and abraded fragments of turtle carapace and/or plastron were also recovered from layer 4.

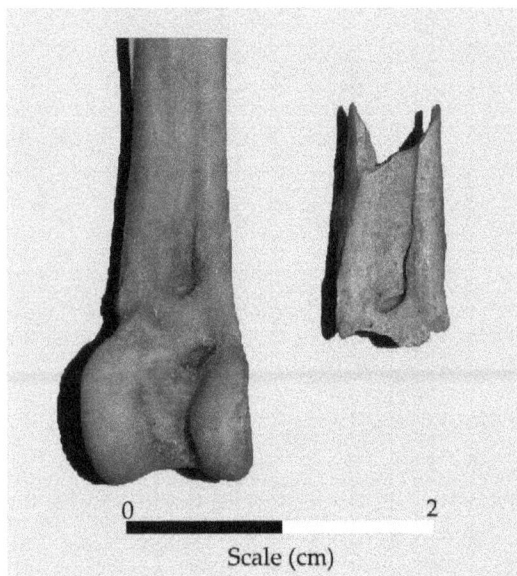

Figure 10.11. A fragment of right tibiotarsus shaft from Savidug Dune Site Q/R 7-9, 110-120 cm, with the dorsal portion of the extensor canal underneath the supratendinal bridge (right). This is remarkably similar in both size and morphology to three comparative specimens of chicken (Gallus gallus) held in the University of the Philippines Archaeological Studies Program, Zooarchaeology Laboratory (left).

Source: Philip Piper.

Savidug Dune Site layer 2

Layer 2 produced 156 identifiable fragments of pig. Based on upper left first molars, at least five individuals are represented (Table 10.12). There is a relatively high proportion of dp4s in the assemblage (N = 14) from at least four individuals. All retain their roots, indicating that they were not shed naturally but represent animals killed at or below 12-18 months of age. The maxillary and mandibular first and second molars demonstrate a range of ages at death from unerupted to moderately worn, but none shows the advanced Grant wear stages associated with considerable age. Only one of the three recovered M3s demonstrates any kind of occlusal wear (Grant Stage C) and comes from a slightly older individual than the majority of the assemblage. No LEH was recorded in any of the teeth.

The conclusion reached from the dental remains that pigs were killed at a young age is supported by the presence of right and left unfused innominates from juvenile individuals in B9 (60-70 cm), C9 (40-50 cm) and C10 (40-60 cm). A humeral shaft fragment with unfused distal end in C9 (30-40 cm) is from a pig less than one year old.

Body part representation is hard to ascertain from the small number of identifiable fragments, but both high meat-yielding bones such as the humerus, femur and pelvis are all represented as well as parts of the skull, loose teeth and extremities, suggesting all parts of the pig skeleton were entering the archaeological record (Fig. 10.12).

In addition to the pig bones, three bird bones including a humeral shaft fragment of a 'chicken-sized' bird (A10, 20-40 cm) and several rat-sized murid bones were also identified in layer 2. A rat left mandible from N27 (20-30 cm) has a first molar with the antero-lingual cusp much larger than the antero-labial, and when viewed from above is centrally placed in the anterolobus. The antero-labial cusp is offset and located slightly posteriorly of the antero-lingual cusp. As a result, the metaconid and entoconid have a steeper slope towards the posterior than the protoconid and hypoconid. The posterior cingulum is relatively large. A small cusplet on the anterolabial side of the protoconid is present. This distinctive tooth morphology places this specimen within the genus *Rattus*.

Intriguingly, a heavily worn deer right lower second molar was recovered from L27 (0-20 cm). The cranial end of the tooth is missing and it is worn almost to the pulp cavity, but is still distinctively that of a cervid (Fig. 10.13). The tip of a deer antler tine was also identified in C10 at 100-110 cm. There is no indication that this specimen was curated in any way that would suggest import from elsewhere and use either as a tool or a decorative piece. This raises the possibility that a deer species was once present on Savidug. A single fragment of marine turtle plastron was identified in M27 (40-50 cm).

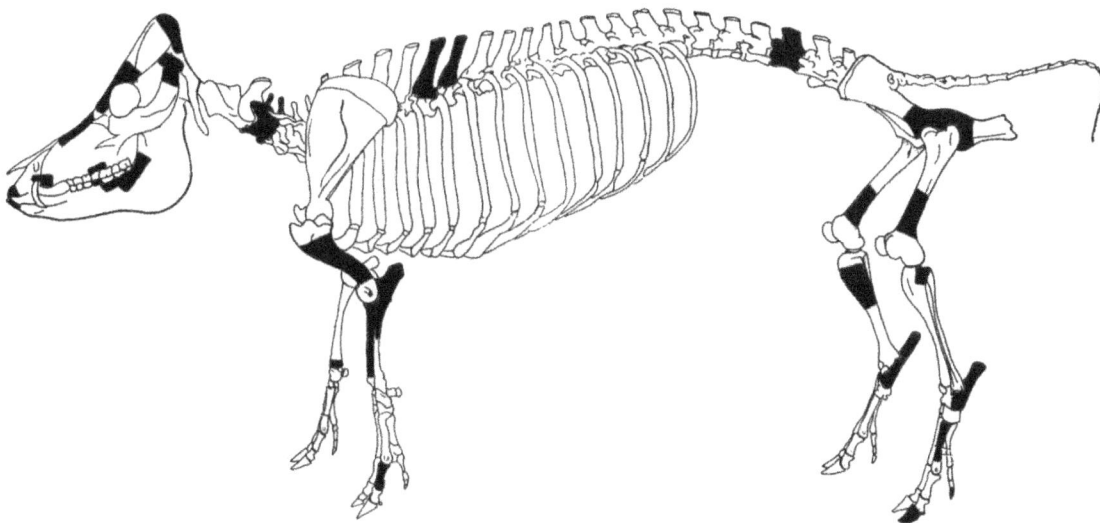

Figure 10.12. The pig body part representation (shaded) from Savidug Dune Site layer 2.

Source: Philip Piper.

terra australis 40

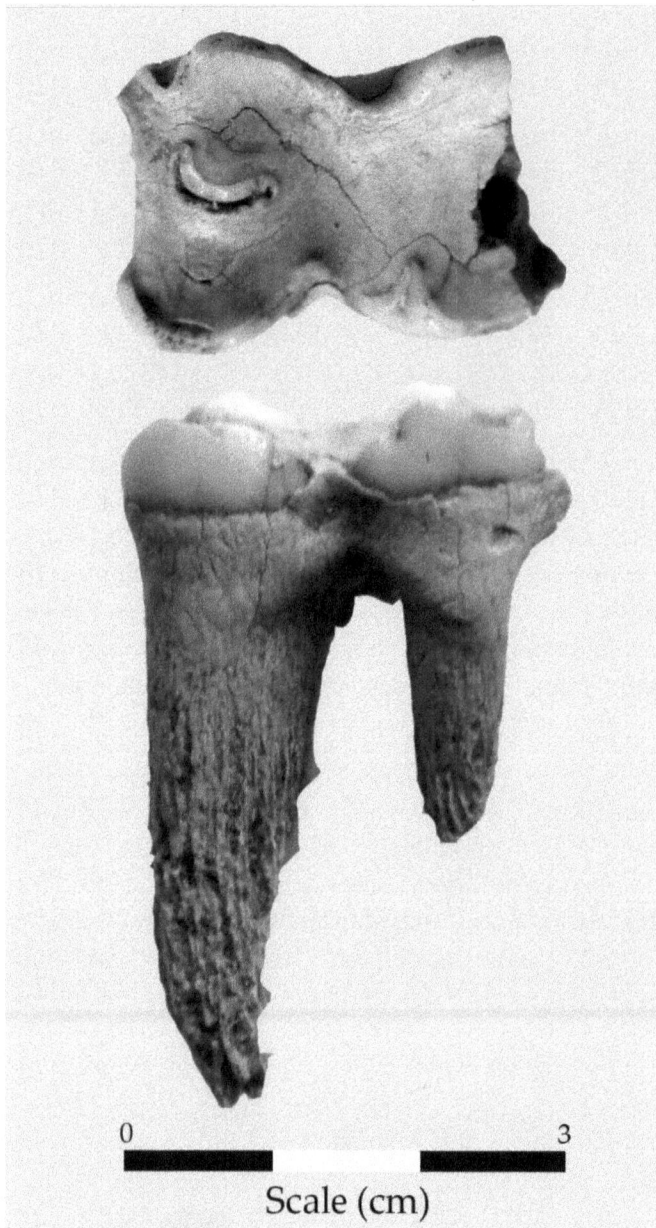

Figure 10.13. The labial (below) and occlusal (above) aspects of the heavily worn cervid right lower 2nd molar recovered from Savidug Dune Site L27 at 0-20 cm.

Source: Philip Piper.

Pamayan: Taxonomy

The most common mammal remains recorded in Pamayan are goat (N=50), with bones recovered throughout the sequence from near the base at 100 - 105 cm to the sub-surface. This indicates that the Pamayan shell midden developed after the introduction of the goat to the Batanes Islands.

Goats appear to have been killed at a variety of ages at Pamayan. Only a single dp4 was recovered, from 85–90 cm, and most of the molars are moderately to heavily worn suggesting they are from mature individuals. The assemblage contains an unworn maxillary second molar from 75–80 cm, an unfused right innominate from 100–105 cm, and an unfused lumbar vertebra centrum and neural arch from 95–100 cm.

The pig is represented by 33 fragments distributed throughout the archaeological sequence, from the base at 100-105 cm to within the upper 15 cm. It is difficult to build an age profile from the fragmentary remains but there are at least two juvenile pigs, based on the presence of two upper left dp2s. There is a left upper dp2 from 30-35 cm, an unerupted second molar at 40-45 cm still the process of development and with no root formation, a sub-adult calcaneus at 50-55 cm, and an unfused right ilium at 70-75 cm. At least one adult is also represented by a right 2nd metacarpal with fused distal epiphyses at 70-75 cm.

A single murid right femur, a small weathered piece of turtle plastron and 14 indeterminate bird bone fragments were also identified in the assemblage. None of the bird bones approximated the chicken in size.

Finally, a small fragment of turtle carapace or plastron 15.65 mm in length, with a maximum width of 8.36 mm and thickness 4.26 mm, retains part of a cut and shaped rounded end. On one side the cortical bone remains, on the other the cancellous bone has been ground flat to produce the desired thickness. The function of this small fragment of artefact is unknown.

Discussion and conclusions

In the earliest phases of site occupation (layer 5) in Savidug Dune Site the only identifiable non-fish vertebrate remains are those of the pig (*Sus scrofa*) and marine turtle. This suggests that pigs were present on Sabtang by at least 1200 BC. A pig bone from Torongan Cave was recovered from a similar depth (50–55 cm) as a fragment of *Turbo* shell dated to 1384–1095 cal. BC (WK 14641), and could indicate that suids were introduced to Itbayat even earlier. Analyses of the pig teeth from the Batanes Islands indicates that all specimens are similar in size and morphology to those of the Eurasian boar *Sus scrofa* from China and Taiwan and fall outside those expected for the Philippine warty pigs (*S. philippensis* and *S. cebifrons*). These species, endemic to the Philippine archipelago, have a distinctive tooth morphology and small size (reflected in the size of the teeth) that makes them easily distinguishable from introduced domestic pigs in the zooarchaeological record (see Amano et al. in press for discussion).

It is known that pigs were probably introduced to Lanyu Island, between the Batanes Islands and Taiwan, long enough ago to become a genetically distinctive island native population (Wu et al. 2007). These Lanyu pigs are closely related to East Asian *Sus scrofa*, from which they derive. However, there is no evidence of a human presence on the Batanes Islands prior to the Neolithic and it is likely that pigs were translocated to these islands during this period. There are too few pig remains to reach any solid conclusion about management strategies in the earliest Phase 4 assemblages. During the proto-historic period there appears to have been a preference towards slaughtering sub-adults and young adults within the first year or two of life.

At Anaro, the remains of several neonatal pigs were also recovered. In modern pig populations nearly 80% of pre-weaning mortality occurs within the first three days after birth (Svendsen 1982), and approaches 60% in free-ranging 'feral' pigs (Barber and Coblenz 1986). If pigs had been free-ranging around the Anaro site then neonates would have been deposited at farrowing sites, locations where the sows chose to give birth. It is highly unlikely that these casualties would have entered the archaeological record, as farrowing sites would be away from human disturbance, if sows had that choice. Thus, the presence of neonates in the archaeological record during this phase of occupation could be an indication that, whilst Anaro was occupied, pig populations were stalled in and around the human habitations. In this regard, Jirobei (in Yamada 2007: 326) recounts a late 17th century battle between two chiefdoms on Batan Island in which several hundred people were killed. Inter-community violence and theft during this late period of prehistory might have encouraged communities to corral pigs within settlements, rather than allowing them to range freely as they perhaps had done in the past. In more practical terms, there may have simply been a need a restrain pigs from causing damage by rooting through valuable food gardens.

At Anaro 3, goat bones occur within the upper 50 cm of most excavated trenches. The only exceptions are trenches 3D and 3G, where two fragments each were recovered from 60–70 cm. These might indicate disturbance or simply a greater depth in these squares to the upper, later horizons. On Sabtang Island, goats are present throughout the Pamayan sequence, but they are absent from the upper cultural layer in the Savidug Dune Site. If bones from Savidug Ijang site are really those of goat, as reported by Dizon (1998), then they were perhaps present there in the 12th century AD. Taking all the current evidence into consideration, it would appear that goats were introduced to the Batanes prior to seventeenth century European contact, and must have thus been acquired from a source other than European vessels.

It is difficult to ascertain the source of the Batanes goats, but it is significant that their introduction occurred in rough correlation with the appearance of Chinese porcelain. In the Philippines, patterns of long-distance exchange, which first emerged during the later centuries BC and early centuries AD, began to intensify towards the mid-late first millennium AD (Bacus 2004). This timeline appears to fit with the introduction of the goat to the Batanes Islands.

Zooarchaeological records of goat are scarce throughout Mainland and Island Southeast Asia. Medway (1963) reported the discovery of a fragment of goat in the upper few inches of deposit in the West Mouth of Niah Cave. These fragments remain undated, but are undoubtedly of fairly recent origin. Glover (1986: 205) reported that *Capra/Ovis* remains first appear in the archaeological sequence in the cave of Uai Bobo 2, East Timor, in Horizon VII (4000-3000 BC) and Horizon IX (2000-1500 BC). He also noted that goat bones were recovered in quantity only in Uai Bobo 1 Horizon V and Uai Bobo 2 Horizon X, dated to about AD 200-600 and 500-1 BC respectively. We regard all these dates as probably too early for the introduction of the goat to the region, especially considering that caprines only appear in the zooarchaeological record of China at 2000 BC, and then only in small numbers (Jing and Flad 2002).

An explanation for these seemingly early records of goat in Timor might be explained by the common contemporary use of caves as goat herding pens (Sue O'Connor pers. comm.). This practice is possibly of some antiquity and could have caused considerable disturbance and re-working of goat bones into old deposits. A study of the animal remains from the indigenous fortified settlements of Vasino and Macapainara has demonstrated that goats were present there during the early to middle 15th century AD, and probably prior to this date (Amano and Piper 2011; Piper and Amano 2011).

Bird bones are relatively rare in the zooarchaeological assemblages, but a single fragment of bird right tibiotarsus shaft with marked similarities in both size and morphology to the chicken was recorded in Savidug Dune Site layer 4. This corresponds with a date close to 500 BC. It is possible that chickens were introduced fairly early in the prehistory of the Batanes Islands. They were certainly present when Dampier visited in 1687, albeit in rather small numbers. He wrote

> Here are plenty of goats and abundance of hogs; but few fowls, either wild or tame. For this I have always observed in my travels, both in the East and West Indies, that in those places where there is plenty of grain, that is, of rice in one and maize in the other, there are also found great abundance of fowls; but on the contrary few fowls in those countries where the inhabitants feed on fruits and roots only. The few wild fowls that are here are parakeets and some other small birds. Their tame fowl are only a few cocks and hens. (Blair and Robertson 1903-9, Vol. 39, pp. 99).

This scarcity of chickens on the islands and the propensity of fragile bird bones to break up easily might explain their rarity in the archaeological record. Bird bones also present particular identification challenges, and this tentative identification of chicken rests on a single tibiotarsus shaft. Confirmation of the presence of chickens in Batanes in prehistory awaits further identifications of well-stratified, species-diagnostic specimens.

Three fragments of dog (*Canis lupus familiaris*) from Savidug Dune Site layer 4 also indicate that this domestic animal was already present in Batanes by 2500 years ago. The recent evidence for dogs at Nagsabaran in northern Luzon dates to a similar age, and demonstrates that the domestic dog was widespread in the northern Philippines by the middle of the first millennium BC (Piper et al. 2009; Amano et al. in press). The proximal end of a dog 3rd left metatarsal and the distal end of the same or different metapodial were recovered from Square 3, layer 4, during the 2004 Callao Cave excavation in the Peñablanca region of northern Luzon (Fig. 10.14). This layer is dated by an AMS C14 sample of charcoal to 1650–1470 cal. BC (Mijares 2006: 37). There is no evidence of wild canids ever inhabiting Luzon, and it is likely that this specimen is from a domestic dog. However, the association between the date and the bone fragments is tentative. It is not definitive evidence for a 2nd millennium BC presence of dog in the Philippines, but it suggests that earlier dog remains might yet be found in the archipelago.

Figure 10.14. Though coated in concretion, this specimen is still identifiable as the proximal end of a dog 3rd left metatarsal, recovered from Square 3, layer 4, during the 2004 excavations at Callao Cave, northern Luzon.

Source: Philip Piper.

Cut marks on a dog right mandibular condyle from Savidug QR7-9 (110-120 cm) would seem to indicate that dogs were eaten, at least occasionally. This interpretation is corroborated by the journal of Jirobei (in Yamada 2007: 325), who states that men ate dog meat during his three-year stay on Batan between 1668 and 1670. This would appear to have been a dietary habit that dated back at least 2500 years.

A fragment of deer antler tine in the Savidug Dune Site and a heavily worn deer mandibular second molar were also recovered from layer 2 suggesting the possibility that a deer population once existed on Sabtang. But this will require further verification through the recovery of more zooarchaeological remains.

Turtle remains are common in Savidug Dune Site layers 4 and 5, but are extremely scarce in layer 2. The diminishing numbers of marine turtle remains possibly reflects prehistoric over-hunting.

Jinsuke Uji (in Yamada 2007: 333) wrote of his late 17th century Batan observation that "there are many water buffaloes which look like large cows." This suggests that the water buffalo (*Bubalus bubalis*) was introduced before the mid-17th century. Jinsuke Uji also visited Sabtang and noted numerous water buffalo there too. The only fragment of bovine recorded in this project was a small fragment of the proximal end of a bovine metacarpal from the subsurface of Torongan Cave, and this piece looks relatively modern. There is also a small fragment of molar column from Savidug Dune Site, at 50–60 cm (cultural layer 2), that could potentially be from a bovine. This provides very tentative evidence that bovines might have been present on Sabtang about a thousand years ago. Dampier made no reference to the presence of buffalo *per se*, but did indicate that 'armour' was made of buffalo hide. It is possible that bovines were introduced and later extirpated to be re-introduced again in the 18th century. Recent analysis of a bone assemblage from the site of Nagsabaran in northern Luzon has produced evidence for a buffalo presence there as early as 500 BC (Amano et al. in press) indicating source populations of bovines were present in the Philippines. Further archaeological research and zooarchaeological analyses are necessary to resolve the outstanding issue of the prehistoric presence of bovines in the Batanes Islands.

An interesting feature of the Itbayat assemblage is the presence of a civet cat throughout the archaeological sequence, from at least 1000 BC to the fairly recent. There are no specimens that identify the archaeological remains with any certainty to species, but based on size and morphology it was most likely to be either the widely distributed common palm civet (*Paradoxurus hermaphroditus*) or the Taiwanese subspecies of masked palm civet (*Paguma larvata taivana*). The remoteness of the islands would suggest that the civet cat was deliberately introduced. However, independent colonization of Itbayat by civet cats without human intervention is not impossible. Esseltyn and Oliveros (2010) argue that the shrew *Crocidura tanake* invaded the islands of Batan and Sabtang from Taiwan in this way, and subsequently diversified.

The same civet cat is not yet recorded on Sabtang, suggesting a limited distribution across the archipelago. More definite resolution and species identification would thus have important implications for understanding prehistoric contact between the Batanes and surrounding islands. The common palm civet is absent from Taiwan and would most likely have been introduced from the Philippines, whereas there are no records of the masked palm civet in the Philippines.

The common palm civet is also known to have been translocated from the Sunda biogeographic region to certain Wallacean islands, including Sulawesi, Nusa Tenggara and the Aru Islands (Heinsohn 2003; van den Bergh et al. 2009). However, no geometric morphometric or genetic analyses have been attempted to try and find the sources of these ethnophoretic populations. The masked palm civet and common palm civet could have provided additional sources of protein and fur on islands with impoverished faunas, and both are considered excellent predators of commensal rodents (Heinsohn 2003).

The presence of rat-sized cranial and post-cranial elements indicates that rodents were active on the island from the earliest periods of human activity. A single *Rattus* sp. mandible from Savidug Dune Site indicates that an introduced commensal species inhabited the islands during prehistory. In addition, the zooarchaeological study has produced records of unidentified native birds, from passerine to chicken-sized, on Itbayat and Sabtang that are likely to have been part of the native avifauna. There was also a small snake on the former island. However, there is currently no evidence in the archaeological record for a large (4.5–4.8 m long) snake, of a size that Jinsuke Uji (in Yamada 2007: 333) claimed to be caught and eaten on Batan during the 17th century.

Acknowledgements

The preliminary research for chapter 10 was undertaken by Shawna Hsiu-Ying Yang under the supervision of Terry O'Connor, as part of a visiting fellowship to the Department of Archaeology, University of York, UK, funded by a European Community Marie Curie MEST-CT-2005-020601 PALAEO grant. Philip Piper and Noel Amano undertook a further detailed analysis of the remains within the zooarchaeology laboratory of the Archaeological Studies Program, University of the Philippines, funded by a special grant from the Chancellor's Office to Drs Piper and Mijares as part of the Bioarchaeology Initiative. The authors of chapter 10 would like to thank the National Museum of the Philippines for permitting the zooarchaeological assemblages from the Philippines to be sent to the Department of Archaeology, University of the Philippines, for initial study.

11

Ichthyoarchaeological Investigation of Neolithic to Recent Fishing Practices in the Batanes Islands

Fredeliza Campos

The recovery of fish bone assemblages of Neolithic to recent date (1200 BC to AD 1500) in Batanes has generated significant new information on the early fishing practices of the region. As part of a wide-ranging project to understand the palaeoenvironmental history and human prehistory of the islands, the analysis of the fish remains suggests utilization of inshore and offshore marine species dating back as far as 1200 BC. In particular, the results show consumption of the common dolphinfish *Coryphaena hippurus* L., a pelagic bony fish hunted and much revered by the present-day inhabitants of the islands. The presence of the dolphinfish in the archaeological record demonstrates the antiquity of an open ocean fishing tradition, implying an ability to construct sophisticated fishing vessels. The study also examines butchery techniques and fish processing in the prehistory of the region.

The analysis of fish remains is essential to understanding past maritime subsistence strategies, particularly in island communities such as the Philippines. The country has a large aquatic resource base that forms part of the most diverse marine community in the world (Carpenter and Springer 2005; Ekman 1953). The seas off the Philippine Islands with their long coastlines support an abundance of fish, with a recent count of over 3000 marine species (Froese and Pauly 2012), providing an easily accessible food resource. Fish constitute a big portion of the Filipino diet and by far the largest source of protein in that diet (Florentino 1996; Florentino et al. 1985).

However, the overall role of fish in Philippine prehistory has not been clearly established. Substantial analysis and interpretation of fish remains recovered from archaeological sites has been scarce, both within the country and in Southeast Asia generally. Mudar (1997) included fish remains in her assessment of past animal consumption in four archaeological sites: Plaza Independencia (14th century AD) and Santo Niño (AD 1350 - 1900) in Cebu City, Tanjay (AD 1000 - 1600) on Negros, and Sohoton I Cave (after 8500 BC) on Samar. Sohoton 1 is of particular interest because it indicates catching of inshore reef fishes before the Neolithic, and transport from the coast to the cave. Elsewhere in Southeast Asia, Neolithic (1400 - 500 BC) fishing strategies of the inhabitants of Bukit Tengkorak on the east coast of northern Borneo have been explored (Ono 2004), as well as in southern Taiwan (Li 1989, 2000). Interestingly, these studies underscore reliance on reef fish and only minimal exploitation of pelagic fish.

For freshwater species, several studies have focused on fishing strategies within the Mekong River system. For instance, riverine fish remains have been identified from several archaeological sites in Cambodia (Voeun 2003). Thosarat (2010) has examined fishing strategies at the Neolithic site of Ban Non Wat (starting *c.*1700 BC) in northeast Thailand. Piper et al. (2012) discuss fishing in the early agricultural settlement site of An Son (starting *c.*2000 BC) in southern Vietnam. The presence of freshwater fish in the huge shell middens of the Cagayan Valley (1000 BC to AD 500) has been reported since 1987 (Garong and Toizumi 2000), but earlier excavations such as those conducted by Cabanilla (1972) and Thiel (1989) did not report substantial fish bone assemblages. All of these studies have strengthened the burgeoning field of ichthyoarchaeology in the region, and should now expand into the study of fish butchery, a topic virtually untouched in the archaeology of Southeast Asia.

In the Batanes Islands, the fish bones recovered by the initial Philippine-Australian excavations on Batan in 2002 were analysed by Szabó et al. (2003). Their relatively small numbers, due to an initial concentration on rock shelter occupations, implied that fishing was only an occasional subsistence pursuit. This contradicted both early and modern-day accounts that described fishing, along with livestock, as principal livelihoods among the local inhabitants (see chapter 2). However, the succeeding open site excavations on Itbayat and Sabtang Islands produced denser fish bone fragments, which underpin the research reported here. These remains form one of the largest fish bone assemblages so far encountered in Philippine archaeology.

Three sites in Batanes were covered for this study: Anaro on Itbayat, with Savidug Dune Site (Nadapis) and Pamayan on Sabtang. These sites contain important chronological sequences from an early phase of habitation (though not the earliest) around 1200 BC to the period just before European contact. The study reveals that some of the contemporary fishing traditions and methods of preparation observed among Batanes inhabitants have a deep antiquity, particularly exploitation of the common dolphinfish, *Coryphaena hippurus* Linneaus, 1758 (Perciformes: Coryphaenidae).

The fish bone assemblage

In total, the assemblage consists of 2396 fish bone fragments from the above-mentioned excavation sites. Due to logistical problems with sieving, the bones from Anaro were hand-collected, and this has inevitably biased the assemblage towards large, easily identifiable fragments. The larger assemblages from Savidug Dune Site and Pamayan were dry sieved and all fragments were collected.

The fish bones were primarily identified through direct morphological comparison using the modern comparative collection of tropical fish established by the author for the Archaeological Studies Program at the University of the Philippines (UP-ASP 2010). Initial segregation and preliminary identification procedures followed Leach (1986, 1997). Other prominent neurocranial, appendicular and axial elements, particularly vertebrae, were also analysed. Selected bone fragments and all anthropogenic modifications, such as cut and scrape marks, were identified according to osteoarchaeological conventions (Potts and Shipman 1981), acknowledging that materials other than stone could potentially have been used in the butchery process (see Campos 2009 for full analytical data).

Due to the high diversity of fishes in tropical seas, it is difficult in most cases to identify fish bones to anything higher than family level. An exception is the common dolphinfish, for which the distinctive porosity and morphology of its skeletal elements make identification possible to species level. On the other hand, family-level identifications for the subclass Elasmobranchii could not be made due to the lack of a sufficient comparative collection. The overall size of the assemblage did not permit meaningful comparisons in potential variability in fishing strategy between sites and time periods. But the presence and absence of certain fish taxa provide evidence for the fishing strategies employed on both Itbayat and Sabtang islands.

The species identification of Coryphaenidae permitted an approximation of body lengths, based on modern comparative specimens. The method employed is modified from Casteel (1976) using equation $L_1/Q_1 = L_2/Q_2$; where L_1 is the unknown snout-to-tail length or total length (TL) of the excavated fish; L_2 is the known TL of the comparative fish specimen. Q represents measurements of the vertebra: Q_1 is either the antero-posterior length, dorso-ventral depth, or medio-lateral width (cranial and caudal end) measured from the excavated vertebral fragment; and Q_2 is the corresponding measurement from the comparative vertebra. The weights of the archaeological specimens were estimated based on modern weights of Coryphaenidae recorded by Uchiyama and Boggs (2006). However, distribution of body fat varies tremendously between individuals, so these estimated weights should only be considered as an approximate supplement to the calculated TL.

Taxonomic representation

The smallest fish bone assemblage was recovered from Anaro and consists of 210 fragments, of which 65 could be identified to taxon. Nonetheless, the assemblage is relatively diverse considering its size. It contains Elasmobranchii (sharks and/or rays), Serranidae (groupers), Lutjanidae (snappers), Haemulidae (sweetlips), Sparidae (sea breams), Lethrinidae (emperors), Carangidae (jacks and trevallies), Coyphaenidae (dolphinfish), Labridae (wrasses), Scaridae (parrotfish), Siganidae (rabbitfishes), Sphyraenidae (barracudas), Scombridae (tunas and mackerels), Balistidae (triggerfish), Tetraodontidae (pufferfish), and Diodontidae (porcupine fish). The results suggest that a variety of reef fishes were caught along with the pelagic dolphinfish during the occupation of the Anaro site.

Of the 885 fragments analysed from Savidug Dune Site, 544 could be confidently assigned to the layer 2 upper cultural horizon, and a further 341 fragments to the lower cultural horizon in layers 4 and 5, all from Trench Q/R 7-9 below 1.2 m depth. The raw NISP calculations show a predominance of Diodontidae (43.4%) (Table 11.1), but this merely reflects the quantity and toughness of the dermal spines. These sharp, specialized fish scales cover certain species for protection against predators and considerably outnumber recognized skeletal elements in other teleosts. Their robustness, high resistance to decay and abundance in a single individual means that they substantially elevate the NISP for the taxon beyond their overall importance within the assemblage. Of note is the high number of Coryphaenidae fragments (n=91) identified in layer 2, which even exceeded Diodontidae (n=73).

All three layers in Savidug Dune Site contain a variety of inshore and offshore fishes, similar in Anaro, but with the addition of Acanthuridae (surgeonfish) and the absence of Tetraodontidae (Table 11.1). It appears that a variety of techniques were used in inshore reef fishing. There was, however, a notable difference in the numbers of Coryphaenidae remains recovered between layers. In layer 2, 36% of the identified fish remains are Coryphaenidae, represented primarily by vertebrae (n=74). In archaeology, fish identification using vertebrae can be unreliable, but in the case of the common dolphinfish this particular element is characteristic of the species. Other elements, namely premaxilla, maxilla, articular, preopercle, subopercle, and dentary also represent Coryphaenidae, and support its definite occurrence, if not prominence, in this layer. Several pharyngeal teeth and cranial elements from other fish taxa are also recorded, suggesting that most anatomical elements were introduced into the site. The abrupt decrease of Coryphaenidae in layer 4 (n=4) would seem to suggest a marked increase in the importance of dolphinfish from the prehistoric to protohistoric periods, but this is contradicted by their rarity at Pamayan, discussed below. The basal deposits of Savidug Dune Site contained only 26 identifiable fish bone fragments, which were of Serranidae, Lethrinidae, Carangidae, Coryphaenidae, Scaridae, Acanthuridae, Balistidae and Diodontidae.

The Pamayan shell midden at the back of Savidug village is roughly contemporary with layer 2 at Savidug, with Song dynasty and later Chinese import ceramics and a basal date of AD 1420-1630 (see chapter 5). It yielded a total of 1328 fish bones, of which 355 (26.73%) were identified to taxon (Table 11.1). Fifteen fish taxa were identified in the assemblage, with Diodontidae and Acanthuridae the most abundant based on their numerous spines and pterygiophores. Other bones were identified as Serranidae, Carangidae, Coryphaenidae, Lutjanidae, Lethrinidae, Labridae, Scaridae, Siganidae, Scombridae, Balistidae, and Tetraodontidae. Additionally, two taxa not recorded at Anaro or Savidug but present in the Pamayan assemblage included Belonidae (needlefish) and Nemipteridae (threadfin bream). However, in contrast to layer 2 at Savidug, the Pamayan assemblage contained only three (0.8%) Coryphaenidae vertebrae. Planar (antero-posterior) lengths of complete vertebrae fragments were taken which reflect relative sizes of individuals, and these measurements show that the Pamayan fish bones were markedly smaller (2-20 mm) than those from Savidug (4-40 mm).

The occurrence of *Coryphaena hippurus* in all three sites presents an opportunity to estimate the sizes of this fish caught in prehistory. With approximately ±100 mm variation from the estimated lengths, the archaeological specimens were caught as adults but most likely had not yet reached maximum sizes. The majority were estimated to have been between 1 m and 1.4 m in length (snout-to-tail length or TL; Tables 11.2 and 11.3). Although more than one vertebra could potentially have come from the same individual in layer 2, the distribution of calculated TLs in the assemblage suggests that several individuals of different length are represented. Modern fisheries data for this species in the northern Pacific, regularly caught in Hawaiian waters, suggest body weights of as much as 29 kg for 1.5 m long females (Uchiyama and Boggs 2006). From Savidug Dune Site, the largest estimated individual was around 2 m in length, similar to the maximum size reported for modern common dolphfinfish (Allen 2000; Broad 2003). A dolphinfish of this size can weigh up to 40 kg (Burton and Burton 2002; Massutí 1997).

Butchery and fish processing

Though cut marks are generally rare on archaeological fish bones (Colley 1990: 216-217; Lyman 1994: 439), at least 34 Batanes fragments bear distinct cut, chop, and scrape marks (Table 11.4). The modified bones include vertebrae, vertebral spines, dorsal and fin spines, dermal spines, pharyngeal plates and, notably, a Coryphaenidae right dentary. These cut marks further verify the human consumption of reef fishes from families such as the Carangidae, Balistidae and Diodontidae, as well as the pelagic Coryphaenidae. The locations of the cut marks on the lateral surfaces of vertebrae suggest filleting and the division of the carcass into pieces, and scraping off meat closely attached to the axial skeleton. The marks concentrated along the opercular areas and posterior cephalic vertebra strongly suggest common fish preparation processes such as the removal of gill rakers and other internal organs. The excision of spinous structures, such as the sharp first dorsal spine of the Balistidae (Fig. 11.1) and the dermal spines of Diodontidae (Fig. 11.2) are techniques used by contemporary fishermen of the Batanes Islands, wherein the latter were often deliberately burned or buried on site (Paz et al. 1998).

Table 11.1. NISP of fish bones recovered from the islands of Itbayat (Anaro) and Sabtang (Savidug Dune Site and Pamayan). Information on habitat and size range are taken from Allen (2000), Broad (2003), and Helfman et al. (2009).

Taxon	Anaro	Pamayan	Savidug Dune Site			HABITAT	SIZE RANGE (Total Length)
			Layer 2	Layer 4	Layer 5		
Elasmobranchii	12	0	1	3	0	offshore, insular shelves and slopes	generally large (> 1 m)
Belonidae	0	1	0	0	0	inshore, pelagic surface	large (100 cm)
Serranidae	4	4	14	7	2	inshore, offshore (depth to 200 m)	small to very large (8-270 cm), most species <50 cm
Lutjanidae	4	3	7	6	0	inshore (depth to 100 m), brackish	medium to large (25-100 cm)
Haemulidae	1	0	1	0	0	inshore	medium to large (30-100 cm)
Sparidae	1	0	0	0	0	inshore, offshore, brackish	medium to large (35-65 cm)
Lethrinidae	5	6	9	11	1	inshore (depth to 30 m), coral reef edges	medium to large (25-90 cm)
Nemipteridae	0	1	0	0	0	offshore, coral reef edges	medium (15-35 cm)
Carangidae	3	3	7	1	1	offshore, outer coral reef walls	medium to very large (20-100 cm)
Coryphaenidae	10	3	91	4	2	offshore, pelagic surface	very large (up to or over 200 cm)
Labridae	11	5	9	6	0	inshore (depth to 100 m)	7-60 cm (some larger), most species 15-40 cm
Scaridae	2	5	16	3	2	inshore	small to medium (20-130 cm)
Siganidae	1	3	2	0	0	inshore	medium (30-55 cm)
Acanthuridae	0	23	4	9	1	inshore	medium to large (21-90 cm), most species 25-40 cm
Sphyraenidae	1	0	2	0	0	inshore, outer coral reef edges	medium to very large (155-180 cm)
Scombridae	1	1	1	0	0	offshore, pelagic surface	medium to very large (35-240 cm), most species 100-200 cm
Balistidae	5	7	16	0	1	inshore	medium (20-60 cm)
Tetraodontidae	2	2	0	0	0	inshore	small to large (7-90 cm)
Diodontidae	2	288	73	95	16	inshore	medium to large (30-70 cm)
TOTAL	65	355	253	145	26		

Table 11.2. Estimated TLs (cm) of Coryphaenidae calculated from the abdominal vertebrae found in Layer 2 of the Savidug Dune Site. The resultant values are considered to be no more than general estimates of head to fork length. Ant1 = Anterior medio-lateral width; Ant2 = Anterior dorso-ventral width; Post1 = Posterior medio-lateral width; Post2 = Posterior dorso-ventral width.

Specimen No.	Square No.	Depth (cm)	Length	Ant1	Ant2	Post1	Post2	Average (Approx.) length (cm)
SB489	C-11	50-60	-	199.9	206.7	-	-	203.3
SB130	B-10	70-100	148.4	-	-	-	154.5	148.5
SB131	B-11	80-90	-	141.2	145	-	-	143.1
SB195	C-10	60-70	134.5	124	129.4	121.9	134.3	128.8
SB100	B-10	70-100	131.5	135.8	129.3	117.1	127.5	128.2
SB66	B-10	50-60	136.2	122.6	126.2	121.1	128.6	126.9
SB3	A-9	60-70	129.9	119.9	127.3	123.1	130.1	126.1
SB148	B-11	90-100	-	122.3	121.8	-	-	122.1
SB190	C-10	40-60	-	122.2	127.1	118.6	120.2	122
SB50	B-10	20-40	102	121	124.9	131	120	119.8
SB1	A-9	50-60	115.7	110.7	129.9	-	105.6	115.5
SB51	B-10	50-60	-	984.2	-	-	-	98.4

Table 11.3. Estimated TLs (cm) of Coryphaenidae based on the caudal vertebrae found in Savidug Dune Site, Layer 2. The resultant values are considered to be no more than general estimates of head to fork length (TL).

Specimen	Square	Depth (cm)	Vertebra length	Anterior medio-lateral width	Anterior dorso-ventral width	Posterior medio-lateral width	Posterior dorso-ventral width	Average (approx.) length (cm)
SB18	A-9	90-100	148.5	-	-	-	-	148.5
SB102	B-10	70-100	158.1	-	138.5	-	140.8	145.8
SB171	C-10	40-50	-	136.2	137.7	-	-	136.9
SB319	C-10	70-80	134.4	127	-	-	144.2	135.2
SB146	B-11	90-100	138.1	132.9	127.5	138.1	131.2	133.5
SB68	B-10	50-60	143.3	121.1	126.8	-	-	130.4
SB30	B-9	50-60	126.2	126.6	139.4	108.9	124	125
SB69	B-10	50-60	-	-	-	121.6	127.9	124.7
SB35	B-9	70-80	141.5	-	118.2	114.6	122.3	124.2
SB155	B-11	60-70	-	123.7	123.9	-	-	123.8
SB65	B-10	50-60	-	120.4	127	-	-	123.7
SB167	C-9	40-50	-	119.9	124.9	-	-	122.4
SB147	B-11	90-100	128.4	118.5	127.2	110.8	-	121.2
SB67	B-10	50-60	124.4	112.7	119.9	110.8	120.2	117.6
SB197	C-10	60-70	107	-	124	121	117.3	117.3
SB48	B-9	80-90	111	-	-	111.7	118	113.6
SB31	B-9	50-60	112.9	110.9	115.5	109.8	105.6	110.9
SB192	C-10	50-60	-	109.2	111.3	-	-	110
SB149	B-11	90-100	118.7	103.1	109.2	107	111.2	109.9
SB101	B-10	70-100	116.9	-	-	101.7	109.1	109.2
SB48	A-9	60-70	105.8	-	101.9	96.2	101	101.2
SB150	B-11	90-100	98.6	-	-	-	-	98.6
SB64	B-10	50-60	69.2	80.9	-	80	76.9	76.7

Source: Primary data assembled by the author.

Table 11.4. The fish bone fragments from Anaro, Savidug Dune Site and Pamayan that carry signatures of human processing. Abd. = abdominal.

Site	Square	Depth	Element	Taxon	Description
Anaro	3B	70-75	Vertebra	Unidentified	Oblique chop mark completely cutting off the specimen from the dorso-anterior facet towards the ventro-posterior end
Savidug	B11	40-50	Atlas	Coryphaenidae	Scrape marks on the antero-dorsal aspect of the centrum and chop mark coming from the dorsal aspect that completely cut off the posterior end of the bone fragment
Savidug	C10	40-50	1st dorsal spine	Balistidae	10.81 mm severe cut mark near the proximal end of the right lateral aspect; 2.22 mm cut mark on right postero-lateral facet; distinct cut mark, note relatively large size of the fish prob. on its maximum size
Savidug	C10	40-50	Fin spine	Unidentified	Oblique 3.66 mm cut mark on the distal end
Savidug	C10	40-60	Abd. vertebra	Coryphaenidae	5.53 mm and 2.95 mm cut marks on the ventral aspect near the anterior end
Savidug	C10	40-60	Abd. vertebra	Coryphaenidae	Oblique chop mark that completely cut off the posterior end of the specimen; 13.79 mm cut mark on the left mid-lateral facet and minor cuts on the anterior end
Savidug	G10	Sp4	Abd. vertebra	Coryphaenidae	3.39 mm cut mark on the ventral left lateral aspect of the specimen
Savidug	C11	50-60	Abd. vertebra	Coryphaenidae	14.58 mm scrape mark on the mid-anterior end of the left lateral facet; 9.58 mm scrape mark on the left mid-lateral aspect; mid-left side of the vertebra's body; combination of chopping-scraping motions
Savidug	C11	50-60	1st dorsal spine	Balistidae	3.84 mm and 3.25 mm cut marks on the right postero-lateral facet; marks indicates attempts to cut off the hard spine
Savidug	B9	50-60	Caudal vertebra	Coryphaenidae	16.63 mm and 8.65 mm cut marks near the anterior end of the left lateral aspect; modern marks on the left mid-lateral aspect
Savidug	B10	50-60	Fin spine	Unidentified	2.95 mm and 2.1 mm cut marks on the lateral aspect near the proximal end
Savidug	B10	50-60	Neural spine	Coryphaenidae	Bone tool; non-modified spine
Savidug	C10	50-60	1st dorsal spine	Balistidae	Cut to remove the tip/dorsal end of the spine from left side; a few cut marks beside the cut end
Savidug	B11	50-60	Right dentary	Coryphaenidae	7.25 mm severe cut mark with numerous small cut marks on the antero-medial aspect
Savidug	B11	70-80	Vertebra	Unidentified	Oblique chop mark coming from the left lateral aspect completely cutting off the posterior end of the vertebra
Savidug	L28	70-80	Fin spine	Unidentified	Bone point implement; missing tip, transverse shaft fracture, appears to be ground obliquely, no evidence of polish
Savidug	B10	70-100	Abd. vertebra	Coryphaenidae	Deep 7.36 mm oblique cut on the left mid-lateral aspect; 6.21 mm cut on the left posterior lateral aspect; 5.97 mm cut on the left dorso-lateral aspect proximal end of the neural spine; scrape marks on the right posterior lateral aspect possibly as a result of chopping off the posterior end of the vertebra to cut the fish through its dorso-ventral axis; posterior end of the vertebra was completely cut off; cutting and chopping action coming from the left lateral side of the fish done to cut the specimen into pieces; chopping off completely the posterior end of the vertebra
Savidug	B10	70-100	Caudal vertebra	Coryphaenidae	15.13 mm scrape marks with minor cut marks on the anterior end of the right lateral aspect possibly to debone the fish

Table 11.4. Continued.

Site	Square	Depth	Element	Taxon	Description
Savidug	B11	90-100	Caudal vertebra	Coryphaenidae	12.44 mm scrape marks on the inferior right lateral aspect; 8.51 mm scrape marks on the left antero-dorsal aspect near the anterior proximal base of the neural spine
Savidug	A9	90-100	Caudal vertebra	Coryphaenidae	7.93 mm and 3.26 mm cut marks on the left mid-lateral aspect combined with severe scrape marks
Savidug	A9	90-100	1st dorsal spine	Balistidae	6.45 mm cut mark on the anterior aspect near the proximal end; looks like a cord was tied around it and pulled out
Pamayan	A	15-30	Abd. vertebra	Coryphaenidae	Chop mark that completely cut off the posterior end of the vertebra
Pamayan	A	25-30	Dermal spine	Diodontidae	2.61 mm four small cut marks near the central shaft
Pamayan	A	50-55	Vertebra	Unidentified	5.77 mm oblique cut mark on the posterior end of the left lateral aspect
Pamayan	A	65-70	Left quadrate	Carangidae	5.65 mm deep cut mark with small, numerous ones near the antero-mid lateral aspect
Pamayan	A	65-70	Haemal spine	Unidentified	4.71 mm and 6.09 mm cut marks on the lateral aspect
Pamayan	A	95-100	Haemal spine	Unidentified	Small transverse cuts

Figure 11.1. Deep oblique cut mark on the right lateral aspect near the base of a Balistidae 1st dorsal spine from Savidug Dune Site.

Source: Fredeliza Campos.

The most striking butchery evidence recorded is on Coryphaenidae vertebrae, which suggests methods of carcass preparation. Cut and chop marks on the ends and through vertebrae can possibly be explained by misplaced attempts to divide the carcass by cutting between adjoining vertebrae. For example, a Coryphaenidae cephalic vertebra has been sliced through from the dorsal aspect, with a right hand rotation through the lateral left side to the ventral margins, and an atlas has been cut in half at an approximate 55° angle, with only the caudal portion remaining. The angle suggests a cut made from the left side from the dorso-caudal aspect towards the ventro-cranial aspect. Both these examples resulted in the decapitation of the fish. Interestingly, cut and scrape marks associated with filleting were generally located on the left lateral aspect of vertebrae (n=8), compared with just one on the right side. Synthesizing the location and orientation of butchery signatures, it can be suggested that filleting of fish was often undertaken by a right-handed person. The cut mark shown in Fig. 11.3 and the scrape marks in Fig. 11.4 are all located on the left lateral side, and the orientation and morphology of the modifications show directionality from caudal end (tail) towards the cranial end (head). It could be surmised that the fish was laid on a surface with its head being held in the weaker left hand, the stronger right hand held the cutting implement, and the filleting motions were from the caudal towards the cranial end of the fish. Cutting in this direction permits the butcher to pass the knife between the overlapping scales, making de-scaling and de-skinning easier.

Figure 11.2. Prominent anthropogenic marks on Diodontidae dermal spines from Pamayan.

Source: Fredeliza Campos.

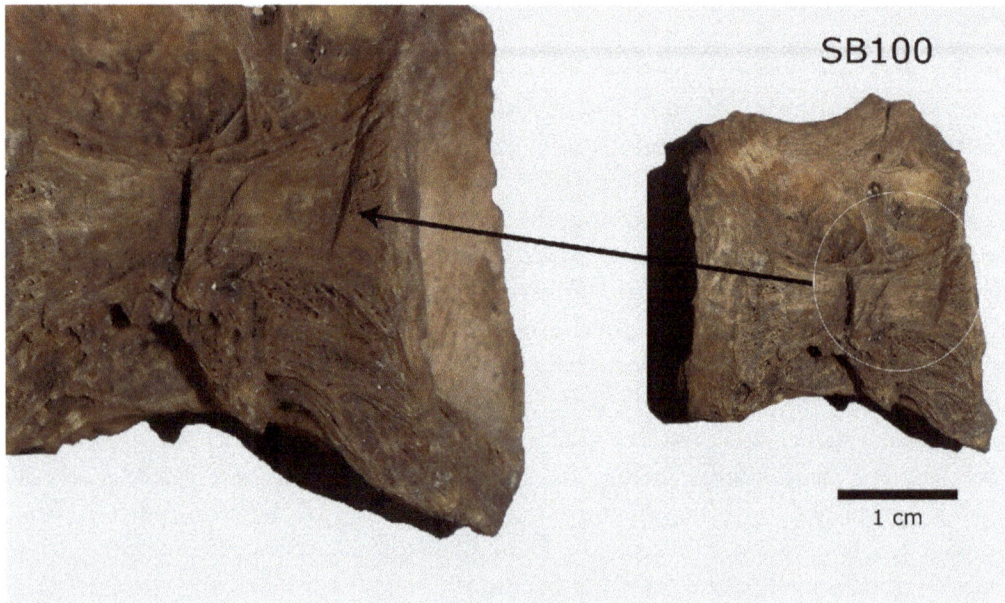

Figure 11.3. Two large dorso-ventral orientated cut marks on the left lateral aspect of a Coryphaenidae abdominal vertebra from Savidug Dune Site.

Source: Fredeliza Campos.

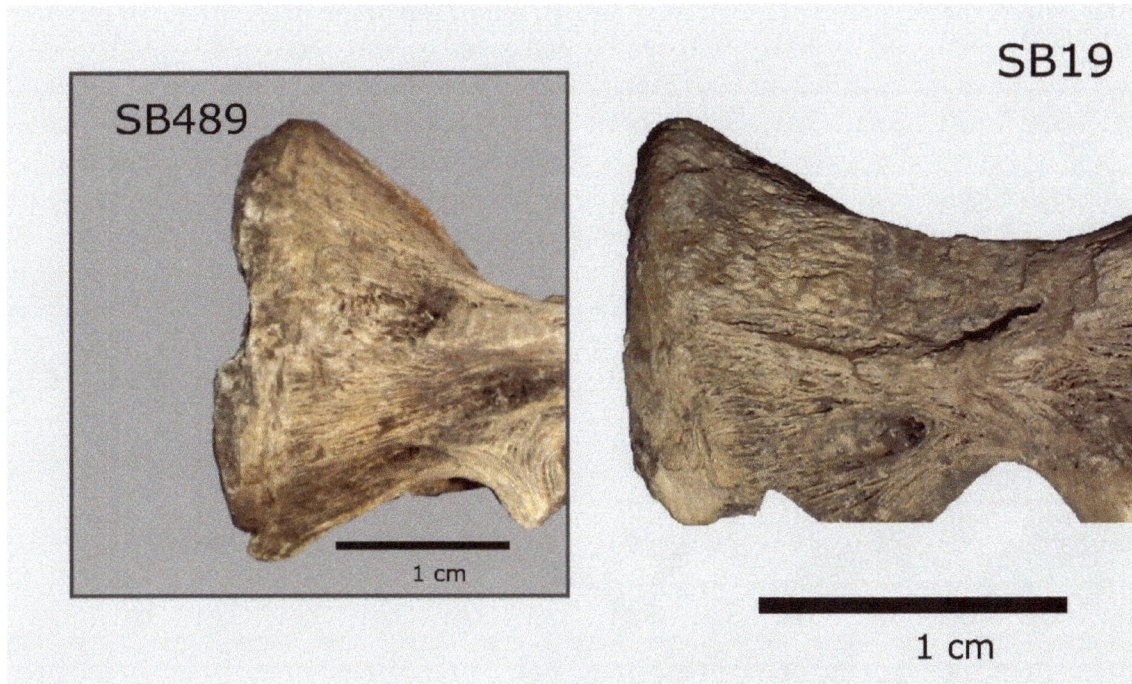

Figure 11.4. Scrape marks on the dorsal surfaces of the left lateral aspect of two Coryphaenidae vertebrae from Savidug Dune Site.

Source: Fredeliza Campos.

In the markets of Manila, contemporary fishmongers employ similar methods of filleting fish. The difference is that they remove the fillets from both sides of the vertebral column, a tradition not observed in the Batanes fish bones, where cut and scrape marks were found mostly on one side of the vertebrae. This butchery pattern can be explained by the modern Ivatan tradition of removing just one large fillet from a single side of the carcass along the vertebral column, sometimes decapitating the fish, and then hanging both fillets out to dry on a large wooden rack (Fig. 11.5). The earliest examples of this type of butchery on a Coryphaenidae vertebra was from Savidug Dune Site QR 7-9 at 100-110 cm (lower cultural layer), with other examples within the younger layer 2 and Pamayan assemblages. This would suggest that the practice of dolphinfish filleting and hanging on drying racks could potentially extend back at least 2500 years, and appears to have continued until the present time. Archaeological evidence from Anaro for methods of dolphinfish processing is currently still lacking.

Discussion

The ichthyoarchaeological materials from Batanes present opportunities for a critical assessment of the role of fish in the diet of the early inhabitants of the islands. There are at least 1 subclass, 17 families and 1 species in the combined faunal assemblages. It appears a variety of common inshore reef fishes, including groupers, snappers, parrotfishes, emperors, jacks/trevallies and triggerfishes were being caught around the coasts. Table 11.1 lists the diverse habitats of these fishes and implies that varying strategies must have been employed in relation to what could be caught throughout the year. Vertebrae length measurements show that the largest fish caught were the inshore emperor fish (Lethrinidae) and the pelagic dolphinfish (Coryphaenidae).

Yang (2006) has recorded notched stone fishing sinkers in the archaeological record from Batan Island dating to as early as 1200 BC (chapter 8), and more examples were recovered from Savidug.

Stone sinkers can be used either for nets or tied to fishing lines as weights. Some cut pieces of shell, also from Anaro 3, look very similar to the shell hook preforms illustrated by Li (2002: 63) from Eluanbi in southern Taiwan (see chapters 8 and 12 for discussion of the Anaro examples). Perforated *Turbo* long units from the upper cultural layer at Savidug are also discussed in chapter 8, and the tentative suggestion is made there that they might have been trolling lure shanks, used with thorn or bone points. Indeed, fishing gorges produced from a male pig lower canine and bone have been identified in the archaeological record from the Cagayan valley (Piper et al. 2009), and these would have been effective for capturing carnivorous fish with relatively large mouth sizes, such as the Serranidae. During the 2005 excavation at Anaro, at least three similar fishing gorges were found (Fig. 11.6). Their sizes indicate that medium to big individuals (over 50 cm long) and species more resistant to being caught in nets, such as parrotfish and triggerfish, were being targeted.

Figure 11.5. Contemporary filleting and drying of dolphinfish in the Batanes Islands.

Source: Roel Manipon.

Considering the location of the Batanes Islands and the periodically rough seas, resources would have been most accessible throughout the year near the shore. However, the rapid falling away of the seabed immediately offshore from the islands would have meant that a combination of baited angling hooks, baited and unbaited trolling lures, traps, nets and suitable ocean-going canoes could have been employed to ensure perennial supplies of fish.

Figure 11.6. Fishing gorges from Anaro.

Source: Fredeliza Campos.

The Ivatan maintain a special reverence for dolphinfish that is still central to rituals that mark the beginning of the fishing season (Hornedo 2000; Mangahas 1994, 1996; Severino 2003). Fishing for dolphinfish coincides with the summer (March – May), when their migration occurs. A similar situation exists in Lanyu Island, located off the southeast coast of Taiwan, which also has ethnographic evidence of dolphinfish exploitation by the Yami population, who speak a Batanic language (de Beauclair 1986; Hsü 1982). The five vertebrae recovered from the sealed context of layer 4 in trench Q/R 7-9 suggest that the practice of offshore fishing for this species can be traced back in Batanes for at least 2500 years. However, it is difficult to ascertain the relative importance of dolphinfish in the early fishing economies of Batanes from a limited number of bones recovered from small trenches.

The modern Ivatan use lines baited with flying fish and motorised outrigger canoes to travel offshore for dolphinfish. A similar strategy has been observed among the local inhabitants of southern Taiwan, who use nylon trolling lines with either flying fish or plastic lures trailing behind the boat (Li 1994, 2002). The propensity for pelagic fishing evidenced in the rough seas off the Batanes islands and Taiwan would suggest a more sophisticated vessel than would be required just to fish in shallow inshore reefs, perhaps with sail technology for trolling, as suggested by Li (2002). Hung et al. (2011) argue that these pelagic fish hunting traditions in the Marianas, southern Taiwan, Lanyu and Batanes might be an indication of cultural connections between these localities during the period of initial Austronesian migration beyond Taiwan. Possibly, the ichthyoarchaeological records of southern Taiwan and the Philippines are hinting at the existence of a maritime technology that permitted people to make the 2300 km open-ocean crossing between the Philippines and the Marianas around 3500 years ago (Carson et al. 2013).

However, although the common dolphinfish is present in the zooarchaeological record from Batanes, it does not yet parallel the evidence for vigorous offshore fishing identified in nearby southern Taiwan (Campos and Piper 2009). Here, archaeological records from Eluanbi on the southernmost tip of Taiwan have shown that people specialized in open-ocean fishing, primarily for Coryphaenidae, and also for the much larger and more powerful Istiophoridae/Xiphiidae (marlins, sailfish and swordfish), from at least 1500 BC onwards (Li 2000, 2002). Size estimation is not possible for other taxa apart from the common dolphinfish, but it would be interesting to see if bigger individuals of taxa such as Serranidae, Scombridae, and Carangidae, as well as Elasmobranchii, were caught offshore. Aggregation among pelagic fishes is also common, particularly between Scombridae and Coryphaenidae (Castro et al. 2002; Hall 1992).

Finally, although Coryphaenidae appear regularly in tropical waters, their presence is otherwise rare in the archaeology of the Indo-Pacific region (Amesbury and Hunter-Anderson 2008; Foss Leach pers. comm. 2009). The database held at the Museum of New Zealand Te Papa Tongarewa contains information on more than 75 tropical Pacific island sites and more than 125 sites in New Zealand. But none outside the Mariana Islands contain dolphinfish. The focus of prehistoric fishing throughout most of the Pacific appears to have been on inshore reef fishes (Leach and Davidson 2006; Leach et al. 1998).

Conclusion

The ichthyoarchaeological record from the Batanes indicates that the inhabitants have a long tradition of marine fishing. Nineteen different taxa were identified, comprising species commonly found over inshore reefs, such as triggerfish, porcupine fish, parrotfish and wrasses, and species from pelagic zones like the common dolphinfish. Similar reef fishes and the pelagic dolphinfish were recovered from both Itbayat and Sabtang, and from all periods of occupation, perhaps indicating that communities on both islands were participating in both inshore and offshore fishing. From Savidug Dune Site and Pamayan there appears to have been continuity in fishing tradition from the late Neolithic through the protohistoric period and up to recent times.

The archaeological record shows that fishing for Coryphaenidae has a long tradition in Batanes, stretching back at least 2500 years. Size estimations suggest that the ancient dolphinfish were of a similar size to those presently available in commercial markets. The lengths of the prehistoric specimens from Batanes ranged from 1 m to 1.4 m, with the largest individuals reaching over 2 m and weighing perhaps as much as 40 kg. The hunt for this particular fish certainly entailed sophisticated skills and technological acuity that would have encouraged the use of a sail together with trolling lures.

Finally, evidence for carcass processing suggests that the common practice today, in which the fish is divided longitudinally and the fillets hung to dry in the sun, is also an ancient technique.

12

Shell Midden from the Batanes Excavations

Katherine Szabó, Shawna Hsiu-Ying Yang, Timothy Vitales and Brent Koppel

Midden shell was present at a number of the sites excavated in the Batanes during the course of this project. While sample sizes and states of preservation are highly variable, the variety in terms of site type, geographic location, and chronology allows for a summary overview of shellfish exploitation throughout the prehistoric sequence of the Batanes Islands. Drawing upon these variables, we will situate each assemblage within its spatio-temporal context and compare and contrast midden shell deriving from different islands, different geographic situations (e.g. sea caves, inland shelters, open sites) and different time periods.

The Batanes shell samples and analytical approaches

Due largely to taphonomic factors, molluscan remains were not recovered from all sites excavated in the Batanes. Some sites, such as Sunget, had very small samples of only a handful of shells or shell fragments, and such samples are not dwelt upon in discussions here. Sites that produced enough shell to warrant detailed analysis and discussion are presented in Table 12.1. For sites that produced shell, there is variability in how much of the excavated sample was studied. For excavations where time and expertise was available for on-site analysis, the entirety of the excavated shell sample was studied. Where there were logistical or other constraints, shell midden deposits were sub-sampled using a variety of strategies.

Table 12.1. The analysed samples of Batanes shell midden.

Island	Site	Total sample MNI	Total sample NISP
Batan	Sunget	13	21
	Mavuyok a Ahchip	304	951
	Dios Dipun	362	642
Itbayat	Anaro (Area 3)	1328	1591
	Torongan	842	1113
Sabtang	Savidug Dune Site 2006		
	Layer 2	103	211
	Layer 4	126	292
	Savidug Dune Site 2007	467	not recorded
	Pamayan	not recorded	2752

Analysis was undertaken by the three first-named authors; individually or in combination depending on the season and attendant logistics. As a rule, Szabó undertook the analysis of material excavated from Batan and Itbayat, while Yang carried out the analysis of midden material from Sabtang Island transported to Australia, and Vitales the equivalent material that remained in the Philippines. Material from Batan Island was studied during the course of the excavation season and not retained, while shell midden from Itbayat and Sabtang was transported to and studied at The Australian National University (ANU) or National Museum of the Philippines.

Shells and shell fragments were identified to the lowest possible taxonomic level – generally species or genus. Quantification was numerical rather than weight-based, with both MNI (minimum number of individuals) and NISP (number of identified specimens present) fragment counts being recorded. Details of breakage and the presence of any taphonomic modifications were recorded by all analysts. They include burning, beach-rolling, utilisation of the shell by hermit crabs, carnivorous gastropod borings and deliberate human modification related to either meat extraction or artefact production. The finer points of recognition of all of these alterations of shell surfaces were the subject of extended discussions amongst the three analysts, with second opinions through joint analysis or exchange of photographs generally reinforcing interpretations. Given this, we are confident that all three analysts were recognising and recording the same range of shell modifications.

Worked shell was recovered from some of the excavated sites, but the only sizeable samples derived from Anaro and Savidug Dune Site. Some of these artefacts were transported back to Australia for further analysis, while the rest of the worked shell remained in Manila for study at the National Museum of the Philippines. The worked shell taken to Australia was studied by Szabó and Koppel, and their analysis is presented separately at the end of this chapter.

Batan Island: Sunget, Mavuyok a Ahchip and Diosdipun

Limited amounts of shell were recovered from the Sunget, Mavuyok a Ahchip and Diosdipun sites on Batan Island in 2002. All excavated shell from these sites was studied on Batan by Szabó during the course of the field season and the results subsequently published (Szabó et al. 2003). These results will not be reiterated here, but results of the Batan Island midden analyses will be compared to the results from sites on Itbayat and Sabtang islands.

Itbayat Island: Torongan and Anaro

The Torongan cave site was excavated over two seasons, with samples from the 2005 excavation being brought back to Australia for study. This included all excavated shell from squares C, D, X and Z. The Anaro shell samples mainly derive from the second season of excavations and were returned to Australia for analysis by Szabó. Included are full shell samples from Anaro 3 squares A, B and C. Smaller shell samples from areas 1(b), 5 and 6 were also analysed, but with only a handful of shells each, discussion of shellfish use at Anaro has relied upon the results from Anaro 3.

Sabtang Island: Savidug Dune Site and Pamayan

Shell samples from the 2006 excavations at Pamayan and the test excavations at the Savidug Dune site were retained and transported to Australia for comprehensive analysis. These samples were studied by Yang with assistance from Szabó. Most of the shell derives from either the upper (layer 2) or the lower (layer 4) cultural layer, with only a handful of shells retrieved from the uppermost reworked agricultural soil. A further sample of midden shell deriving from the lower cultural layer from the 2007 excavations in Savidug Dune Site (QR/7-9) was studied by Timothy Vitales at the National Museum of the Philippines.

Results

Identification and quantification of the various midden samples produced a set of results that showed distinct variation in composition. Here, the results of shell midden analysis for Torongan Cave, Anaro, Savidug Dune Site and Pamayan are presented, followed by a consideration of the differences between the samples in terms of local environment and topography, as well as chronological placement.

Torongan Cave

The excavated shell provides a snapshot of the complexities of the site formation processes at Torongan as a whole. Situated at the landward end of a sea cave, which itself sits atop the outlet of the Torongan River, sources for marine, freshwater and terrestrial molluscs are all in the immediate vicinity, and all contribute to the excavated shell samples. Of the non-marine shell, terrestrial snails account for 40% of the overall assemblage (n = 337 individuals), and the freshwater species *Melanoides tuberculata* makes up a further 2% (n = 14) (Fig. 12.1). Marine shells constitute 59% of the Torongan shell sample, but 51% of the total assemblage is comprised of only two species: the upper intertidal periwinkle *Tectarius tectumpersicum* and the limpet *Collisella striata* (n = 267 and 159 respectively). Other marine shell taxa collectively contribute only 8% (n = 65).

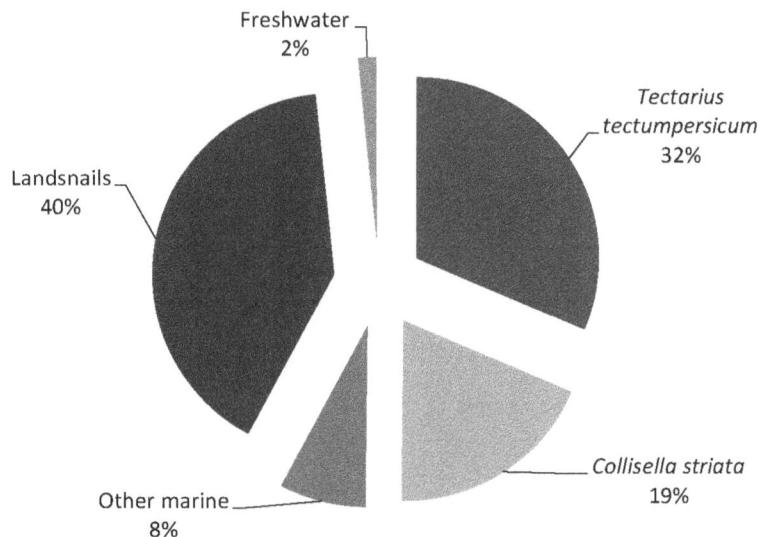

Figure 12.1. Graph to show the relative proportions of terrestrial, upper intertidal and 'other' marine shell excavated from Torongan in 2005. Values are derived from MNI counts.

Source: Katherine Szabó.

Species within the Littorinidae such as *Tectarius temtumpersicum* typically dwell high up the shore-line, at and above the high-tide mark, with limpets such as *Collisella striata* dwelling only slightly lower down (Morton and Raj n.d.: 10). Given the general layout of Torongan Cave, it is likely that both *Tectarius tectumpersicum* and *Collisella striata* could be gathered, live, from the area immediately around the seaward cave entrance. This would explain their dominance within the midden, and also reinforce the interpretation that Torongan was used largely for temporary or short-term shelter. Over 75% of the *T. tectumpersicum* shells are missing their spires, suggesting that these were deliberately removed to more easily extract the flesh.

The remaining marine molluscs present in the Torongan shell assemblage come from nineteen species, with no species represented by more than nine individuals. All species are characteristic of littoral hard-shore habitats, and include turbinids (*Turbo setosus, T. argyrostomus, T. chrystostomus*), neritids (*Nerita plicata, N. costata, N. undata*), chitons (*Acanthopleura* sp.) and carnivores in the Muricidae (*Thais armigera, Drupa clathrata, Purpura persica*). A number of the *Thais* spp. specimens show evidence of hermitting, indicating that original midden shells were removed from the midden by hermit crabs who deposited their old shells in exchange (see Szabo 2012).

The consistent presence of terrestrial hermit crab (*Coenobita* spp.) remains within the assemblage further confirms their presence at Torongan.

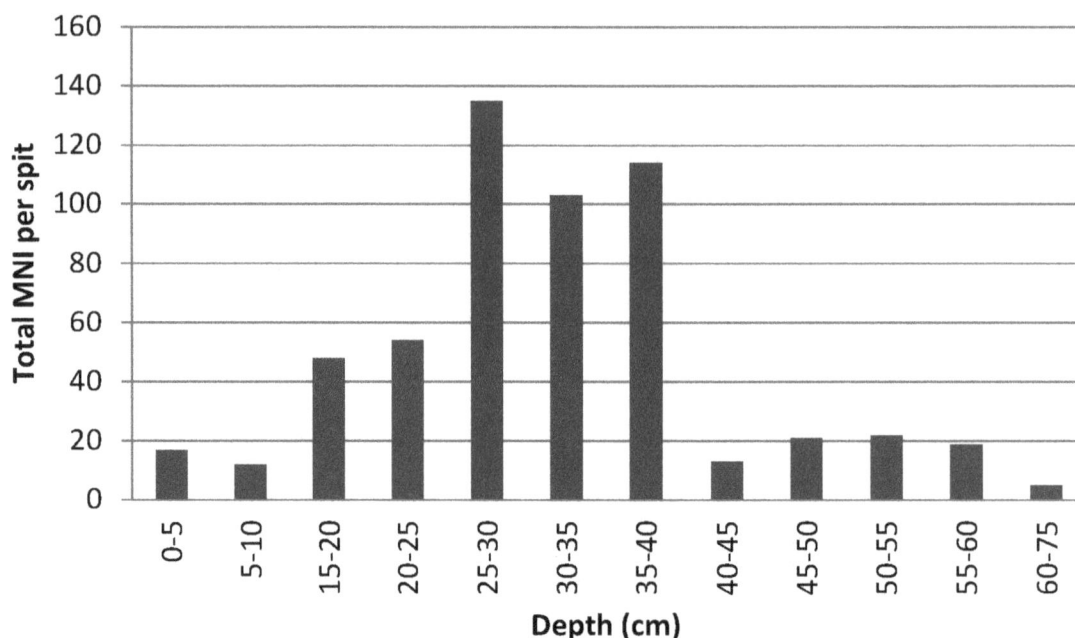

Figure 12.2. Graph to show the total number of shells (MNI) recovered from each spit of square C, Torongan Cave, Itbayat Island.

Source: Katherine Szabó.

Within the land snail component of the assemblage, the 2-3 cm long *Pythia scarabaeus* (Ellobiidae) dominates, making up 94% of the sample (n = 322). Although many members of the Ellobiidae are mangrove-swamp dwellers, *P. scarabaeus* is associated more with terrestrial coastal vegetation such as *Pandanus* screw-pines. Although a number of larger land snails native to the Batanes are still collected as a culinary item, and there is evidence that terrestrial snails were eaten in the past (Szabó et al. 2003), *P. scarabaeus* was not among those species listed as edible by locals, and it is likely that the accumulations in Torongan Cave represent a natural death assemblage. The remaining land snails are a mix of arboreal (e.g. *Helicostyla* spp., *Chloraea* sp.) and ground-dwelling (e.g. *Cyclophorus* sp., *Ryssota sagittifera batanica*) species, with each taxon only being represented by one to three individuals. While the strong preponderance of *P. scarabaeus* could be interpreted as reflecting deliberate human collection, it is just as likely that the structure of the terrestrial snail assemblage simply reflects the nature of local vegetation and topographic conditions.

Shell occurs at all depths of the Torongan deposits, but there is considerable variation in gross abundance through the sequence. The greatest densities of shell are found in a band between 25 cm and 40 cm depth, thus sitting above the in-washed topsoil layer (Fig. 12.2). This observation holds not only for the marine shell, but also the land snail component which indicates that the land snails were not washed in with the soil, but have accreted at the same pace as the rest of the assemblage. Interestingly, this depth-distribution pattern is not matched by that of the potsherds (Table 2.1) where numbers of sherds are higher in the in-washed soil layer. It is unclear whether subtle taphonomic actions are at play here or whether the use of shell intensified through time.

Anaro

Lying about two kilometres inland, the marine shell present within the Anaro deposits is clearly the result of deliberate human transport. Small shell samples were recovered from areas 1b (n = 10), 5 (n = 18) and 6 (n = 15), with the only sizeable sample coming from Area 3 (n = 1328 MNI). Given this, discussion here will be restricted to the results generated from the study of Anaro 3.

Shell is not distributed evenly either spatially or depth-wise within Anaro 3. The majority derive from the rockshelter square 3A (n = 934 MNI). Whether this is because the focus of deposition was within the rockshelter, or whether the 3A deposits have been protected from the elements by their position behind the drip line, is unclear. With regards to vertical patterning, molluscan remains are concentrated strongly towards the base of all squares (Fig. 12.3); a pattern possibly enhanced by the alkaline conditions of the limestone bedrock. However, this need not suggest a more ephemeral human presence at Anaro in from ~90cm upwards, since the pattern is not replicated by depth-distribution counts for potsherds (Tables 6.1 and 6.2). Sherd sample sizes are comparable for all levels between 20 cm and the base of the site at 110 cm.

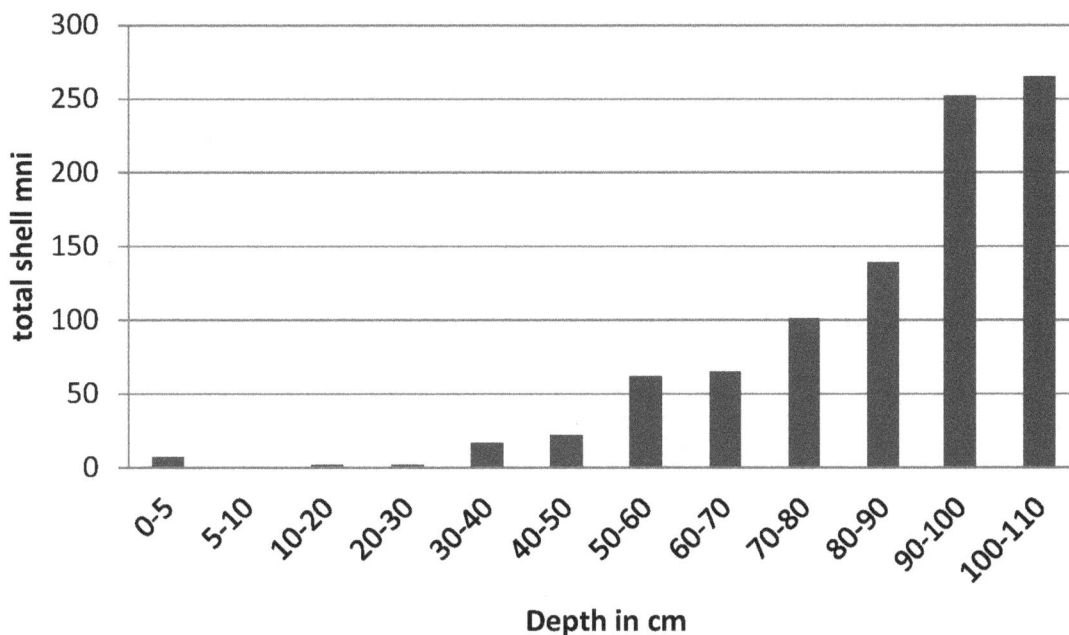

Figure 12.3. Graph to show the increasing density of shell by depth in Anaro 3A, Itbayat Island.

Source: Katherine Szabó.

In contrast to Torongan, and despite being much further inland, terrestrial snails make up only 4% of the Anaro Area 3 shell total (Fig. 12.4). Fourteen different species of land snail are present, including a mix of arboreal (e.g. *Helicostyla* spp.) and ground-dwelling (e.g. *Ryssota sagittifera batanica*) taxa. Although quite diverse for a small sample, only two species are represented by more than ten individuals: *Cyclophorus* sp. (n = 12) and *Pythia scarabaeus* (n = 14). *P. scarabaeus* is generally associated with coastal vegetation, as witnessed by the high totals of this species at Torongan, and it is likely that the Anaro 3 specimens were transported to the site with *Pandanus* leaves, which are used extensively in the Batanes for weaving.

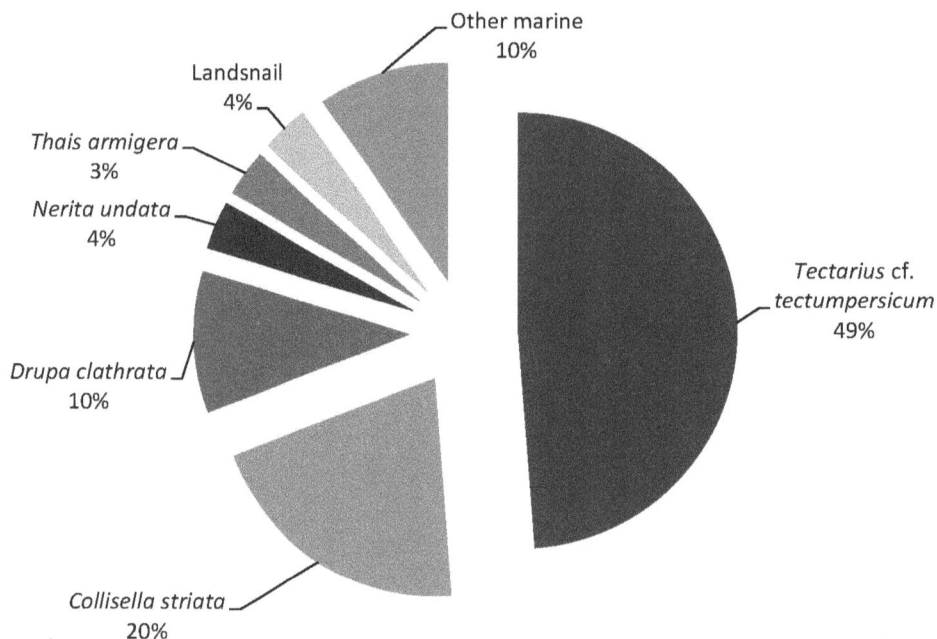

Figure 12.4. Graph to show the relative proportions of major species, land snails and 'other' marine shell excavated from Anaro Area 3. Values are derived from MNI counts.

Source: Katherine Szabó.

The two upper-shore species, *Tectarius tectumpersicum* and *Collisella striata*, which dominated at Torongan, also dominate at Anaro, collectively composing nearly 70% of the Anaro 3 shell assemblage. The remaining 27%, comprising 'other' marine taxa, is dominated by rocky shore gastropods, including relatively high numbers of carnivorous species (e.g. *Drupa clathrata* n = 139, *Thais armigera* n = 46). These species are usually associated with hard-shore colonial bivalves such as mussels and rock oysters, which are only represented at Anaro 3 by a single fragment of rock oyster (*Saccostrea* sp.). Indeed, the total bivalve sample for Anaro 3 is completed by only a further two fragments of *Asaphis violascens*. Given that rocky shore bivalve prey species often adhere to the substrate (e.g. oysters, mussels, and in the Crustacea, barnacles), it is possible that only the meat was collected by Anaro residents, whereas gastropods which required more time-consuming extraction techniques were transported back to the site.

Of the marine component of the Anaro 3 shell assemblage, a group of typically sub-littoral taxa stand out, including the large Green Snail (*Turbo marmoratus*), Giant Clams (*Tridacna* spp.) and *Nautilus pompilius*. During analysis, fragments of these taxa were associated with shell-working based on morphology and surface features, and will be discussed further in the section on shell-working below.

Savidug Dune Site

The 2006 excavation in the stratified Savidug Dune Site produced two distinctive molluscan assemblages. These came from the upper cultural layer 2 with 103 shells (MNI), and from the lower cultural layer 4 with 126 shells (MNI). Although small, these samples are comparable in size. They are not only internally diverse, but also contrast with each other. The 2007 excavation in trench QR/7-9 produced a further 471 shells (MNI), all associated with the lower cultural layer 4. A further 40 shells (MNI) were deemed not to be subsistence refuse due to evidence of hermit crab occupation or the action of littoral taphonomic processes, indicating post-mortem collection by Savidug Dune Site residents.

Thirty-seven different species were identified within the layer 2 sample. Given the sample size, this is very diverse, with the majority (twenty-four) of species being represented by a single fragment or individual. Indeed, only six species were represented by more than five individuals, three of which were species of cowrie (*Cypraea annulus, C. moneta, C. caputserpentis*), one was the small gastropod *Nerita albicilla*, and the remaining two were terrestrial snail species (*Bradybaena mighelsiana, Helicostyla* sp.) (Fig. 12.5). Of these six taxa, it is probable that the land snails were self-introduced into the deposits, and five out of six *Nerita albicilla* specimens show clear traces of *Coenobita* sp. hermit crab use. Evidence of hermit crab use is also seen on most or all specimens of tritons (Ranellidae), rock shells (Thaidinae, Muricidae (Fig. 12.6), tulip shells (Fasciolariidae) and dog whelks (Nassariidae).

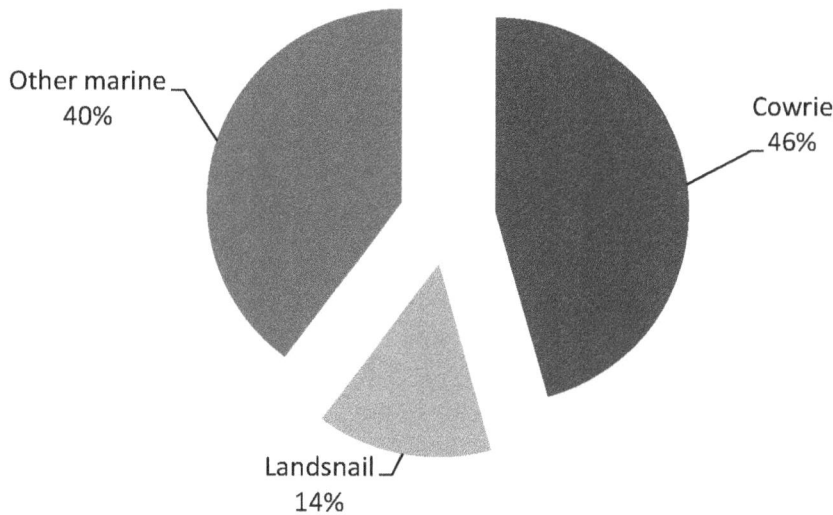

Figure 12.5. Graph to show the relative proportions of major species, land snails and 'other' marine shell excavated from layer 2 of the Savidug Dune Site. Values are derived from MNI counts.

Source: Katherine Szabó.

As noted by the excavators (chapter 4, and especially Table 4.1), small cowrie shells were particularly common within deposits at Pamayan and the Savidug Dune Site. In Savidug layer 2, the remains of *Cypraea annulus, C. moneta* and *C. caputserpentis* comprise 46% of the total sample of shells (MNI). Levels of fragmentation are high, with fragment (NISP) counts being over double the individual (MNI) counts for these three species (Fig. 12.7). Given the narrow-apertured morphology of cowrie shells, such high levels of fragmentation are probably the product of deliberate breakage by Savidug Dune Site residents to extract the flesh for consumption.

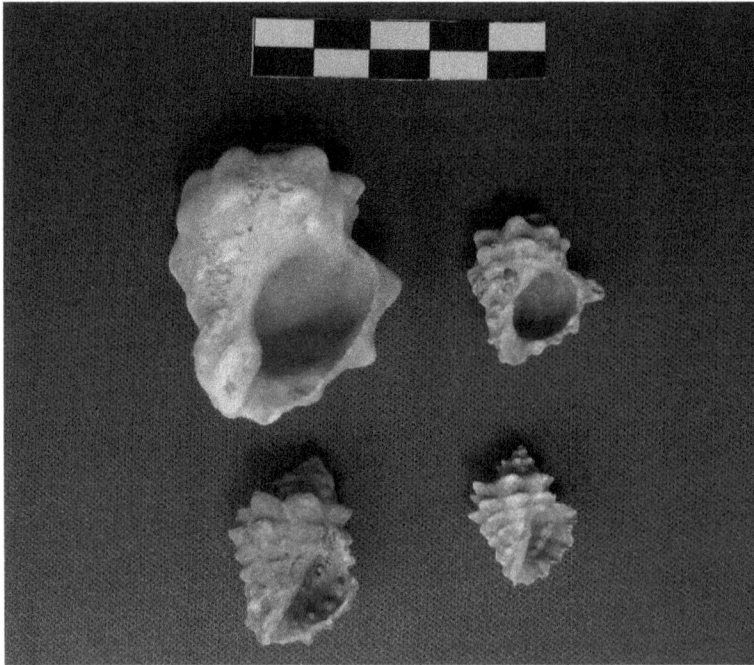

Figure 12.6. Four *Thais tuberosa* specimens from Savidug Dune Site. The upper two show evidence of *Coenobita* sp. hermit crab occupation while the lower two specimens do not. Note the denticles/teeth within the apertures as well as the D-shaped aperture shape of the lower examples in contrast with the worn interiors and circular aperture shape of the upper examples.

Source: Shawna Hsiu-Ying Yang.

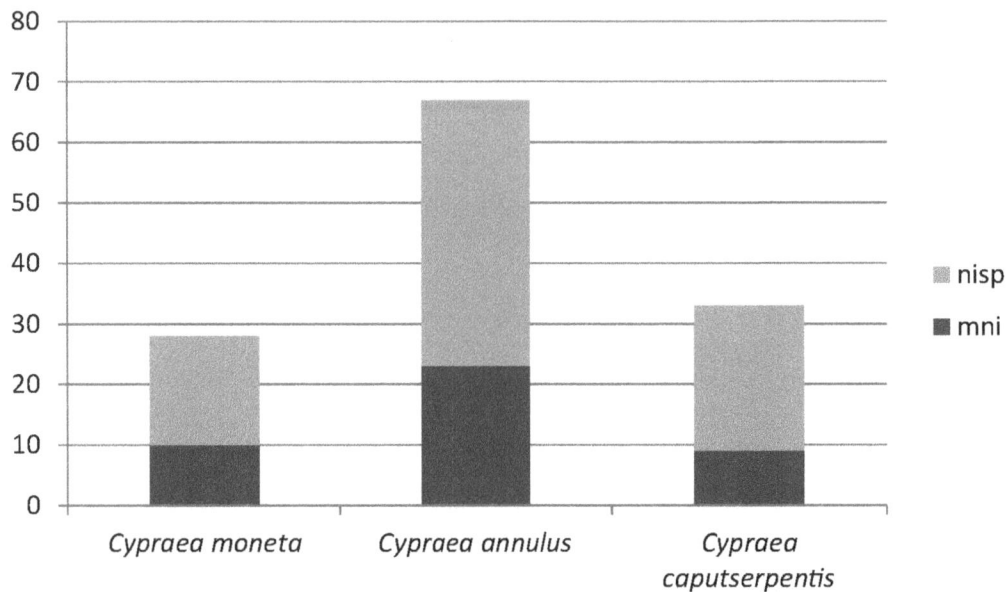

Figure 12.7. Dominant species of cowrie represented in layer 2 of the Savidug Dune Site showing levels of fragmentation by comparing fragment (NISP) with estimated minimum number of individual shell (MNI) counts.

Source: Katherine Szabó.

Whilst cowrie shells were clearly dominant within the layer 2 shell assemblage, the same was not true of layer 4. The 2006 layer 4 shell sample is only slightly larger than that of layer 2 (n = 126 MNI). It is also very diverse, with forty-one different species being identified. Although twenty of these species are represented by a single fragment or individual, taxa represented by five or more individuals are more numerous and are spread more evenly than seen in layer 2. Despite the layer 4 shell assemblage being larger, cowries make up only 23% (n = 28) (Fig. 12.8). The contribution of land snails is comparable in both relative (15%) and absolute (n = 19) terms to that recorded for layer 2.

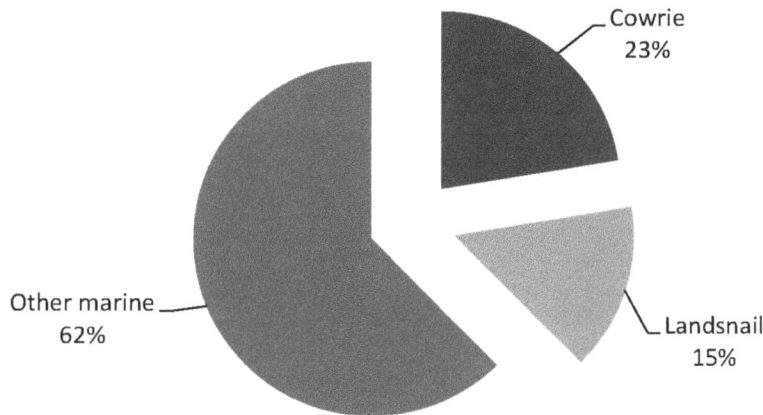

Figure 12.8. Graph to show the relative proportions of cowries, land snails and 'other' marine shell excavated from layer 4 of the Savidug Dune Site in 2006. Values are derived from MNI counts.

Source: Katherine Szabó.

'Other' species of marine shell make up 62% of the layer 4 sample; considerably more than in layer 2. For comparative purposes, all identified shell species/taxa from layers 2 and 4, together with their associated MNI counts, are listed in Table 12.2. Although numbers are consistently low, it is notable that larger species such as the turbinids (*Turbo chrysostomus, Turbo argyrostomus*) are only present in layer 4, as are the larger limpet species (*Cellana testudinaria*), tulip shell (*Filifusus filamentosa*), giant clam (*Tridacna maxima*) and various medium-sized species in the Trochidae (*Trochus maculatus, Trochus histrio*). In short, the layer 4 assemblage has a greater number of larger-bodied taxa.

The 2007 sample from layer 4 in QR/7-9 presents a slightly different picture. A total of fifty-nine species was identified in the sample of 467 shells (MNI) excluding those specimens/species that were deemed not to represent subsistence remains. Cowries make up a slightly larger percentage (30%) than in the 2006 layer 4 sample (Fig. 12.9), but this is still considerably less than in the younger layer 2 assemblage. As with the 2006 layer 4 sample, a range of larger gastropods and bivalves were present, including *Turbo argyrostomus* and *Tridacna maxima*. Limpets were again present, making up 13% of the sample, contrasting with their complete absence in layer 2. The land snail component is overwhelming dominated by the arboreal *Helicostyla leai* (n = 86, 97% of the land snail component of the assemblage), which suggests a presence of tree cover in the vicinity of the site at this time. It is also notable that of the 138 cowrie specimens, 90 are *Cypraea caputserpentis* while the smaller species *Cypraea annulus* and *C. moneta*, which are dominant in layer 2, are only represented by six individuals each. The remaining 36 cowries are a mixture of large (e.g. *Cypraea arabica, C. mauritania*) and medium-sized (e.g. *Cypraea talpa*) species.

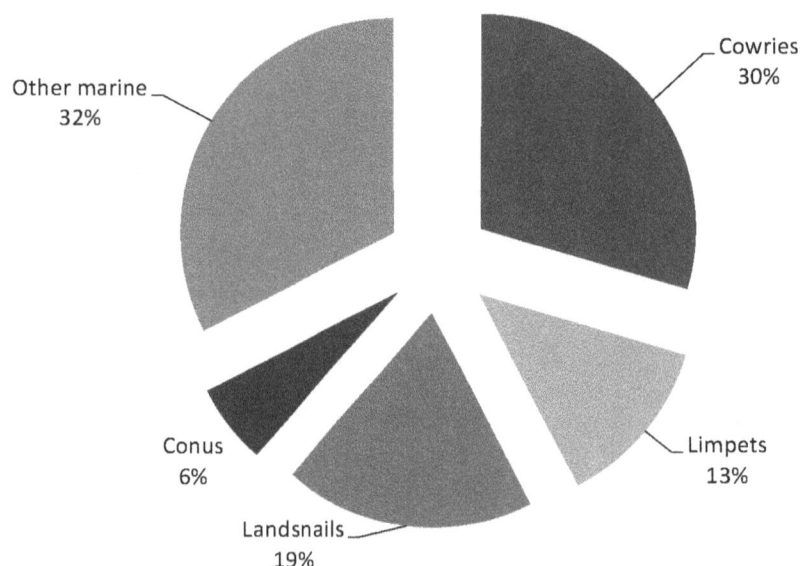

Figure 12.9. Graph to show the relative proportions of cowries, land snails and 'other' marine shell excavated from layer 4 of the Savidug Dune Site in 2007. Values are derived from MNI counts.

Source: Katherine Szabó.

It is possible that the much stronger representation of cowries, and more generally small gastropod species, in layer 2 is a reflection of heavy human predation on local molluscan resources through time. However, it is equally possible that the inshore habitats themselves were dynamic in composition. For example, an increase in terrestrial sediment input into the littoral zone might have impacted upon taxa which dislike silty conditions, such as trochids and turbinids. Sustained human gardening and associated landscape modification could provide such an increase in terrestrial sediments in the littoral zone, with humans indirectly affecting the structure and composition of intertidal molluscan populations. Much larger samples would be required to begin to differentiate between direct and indirect human-induced causes of change in local molluscan populations, as well as the potential impact of non-human environmental variables.

Pamayan

The Pamayan molluscan assemblage is contemporaneous with layer 2 of the Savidug Dune Site, and indeed a number of commonalities are apparent. The Pamayan shell sample derives only from section A (chapter 4). Fifty per cent of the shell, composed of the largest and most identifiable fragments, were retained from excavations and transported to Australia for further analysis. It is this sample that is discussed here.

The Pamayan sample was recorded using NISP fragment counts, without accompanying MNI calculations. The section A shell assemblage was overwhelming dominated by small cowrie fragments (*Cypraea* spp.) which comprised 79.5% (n = 2188 NISP) of the total sample (n = 2752). As can be seen in Fig. 12.10, the representation of *Cypraea* is consistently high at all levels, demonstrating a clear focus upon the gathering of small cowrie shells through time at Pamayan. The remaining 20.5% of the shell assemblage is composed of a mix of land snails (n = 226 NISP) and a variety of marine species (n = 338) (Fig. 12.11).

Table 12.2. Savidug Dune Site 2006: Identified shell species/taxa from layers 2 and 4, together with their associated MNI counts.

Species	Layer 2	Layer 4
Bradybaena mighelsiana	8	13
Thais armigera	1	11
Cypraea annulus	23	9
Cypraea caputserpentis	9	9
Cypraea spp.	3	7
Asaphis violascens	2	6
Nerita polita	2	5
Thais tuberosa		5
Vasum turbinellum	2	5
Conus spp.	4	5
Cellana radiata	1	4
Nerita albicilla	6	4
Tridacna maxima		4
Trochus maculatus	2	3
Turbo argyrostomus		3
Turbo chrysostomus		2
Cerithium sp.	1	2
Morula uva		2
Helicostyla sp.	6	2
Helicostyla effusa		2
Chloraea sp.	1	2
Cellana testudinaria		1
Trochus histrio	1	1
Trochus sp.		1
Clanculus sp.		1
Turbo marmoratus	1	1
Tectarius sp.		1
Strombus mutabilis		1
Cypraea moneta	10	1
Cypraea arabica	1	1
Cypraea mauritania		1
Drupa rubusidaeus		1
Drupa morum		1
Drupa sp.		1
Gyrineum natator		1
Bursa bufonia	1	1
Filifusus filamentosa		1
Modiolus sp.	1	1
Chama cf. lazarus		1
Tellina scobinata	1	1
Tellina palatum		1
Nerita plicata	1	
Cerithium echinatum	1	
Rhinoclavis sinensis	1	
Clypeomorus sp.	1	
Cypraea tigris	1	
Semiricinula turbinoides	1	
Cymatium sp.	1	
Cynatium muricinum	1	
Nassarius cf. luridus	1	
Cantharus undosus	1	
Mitra cf. mitra	1	
Siphonaria atra	1	
Trachycardium sp.	1	
Atactodea striata	1	
Periglypta puerpera	2	

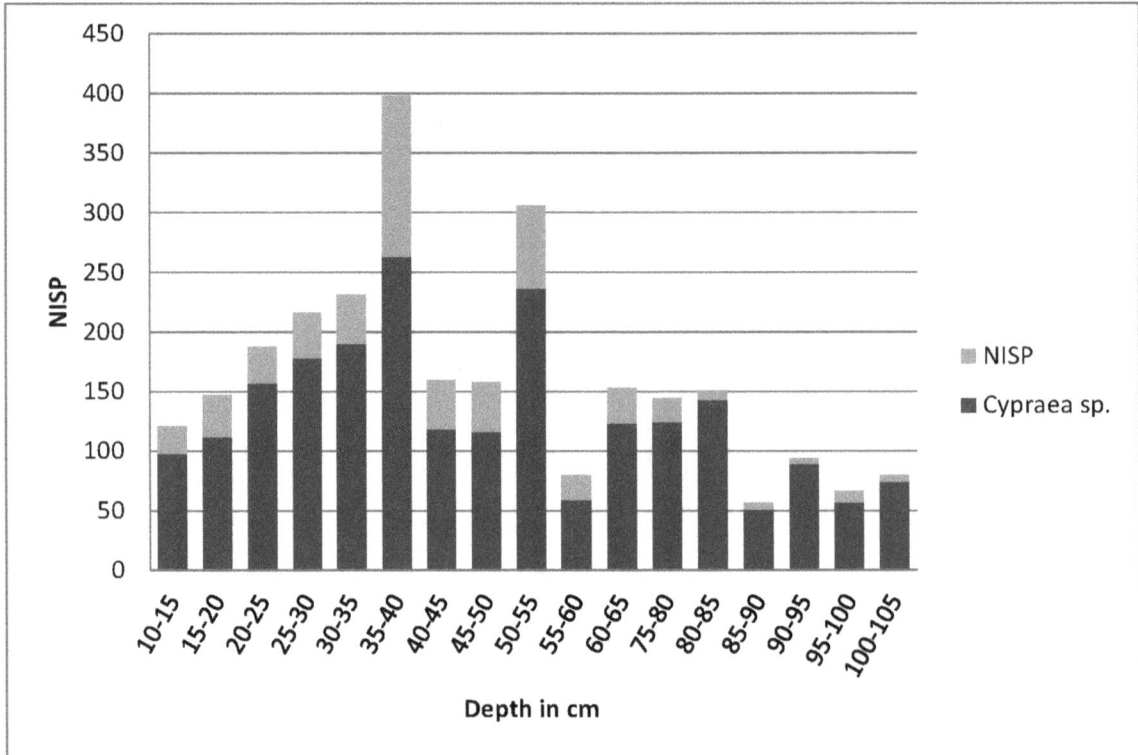

Figure 12.10. Graph to show the relative proportion of cowrie shells (*Cypraea* spp.) within the total shell sample at all levels from Pamayan section A.

Source: Katherine Szabó.

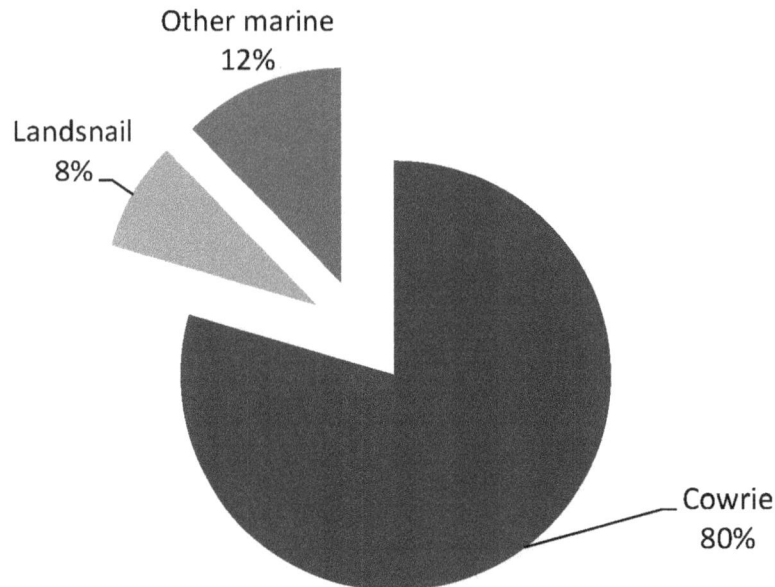

Figure 12.11. Graph to show the relative proportions of cowrie shells, land snails and other marine species at Pamayan. Values are derived from MNI counts.

Source: Katherine Szabó.

Within the land snail sample two species were identified, with the common, cosmopolitan, *Bradybaena mighelsiana* composing 81% and *Pythia scarabaeus* a further 8%. The remainder of land snail fragments (n = 24) were not able to be identified. The high incidence of *B. mighelsiana* suggests an open, disturbed landscape in the immediate vicinity of the site during the time of midden formation.

Marine species other than *Cypraea* spp. were represented by between six to sixty fragments per taxon and were made up of a variety of hard shore (e.g. *Nerita plicata*, *Turbo* spp., *Cellana* sp., *Trochus maculatus*) and soft shore (e.g. *Strombus* spp., *Periglypta puerpera*, *Asaphis violascens*) species. No particular patterning of hard shore/soft shore taxa by depth was apparent.

Discussion

The composition of the shell midden samples from Batan, Sabtang and Itbayat islands reflect the relatively exposed and hard-shore-dominated coastlines of the Batanes Islands as a whole, while also showing some degree of temporal and spatial variation. The most notable contrast is between the shell middens of the earliest-known period of Batanes prehistory (Torongan and Anaro) and the most recent (Pamayan and Savidug Dune Site layer 2). Despite the fact that Torongan is situated right by the sea and Anaro inland, both middens are dominated strongly by two upper-intertidal rocky shore gastropods, *Tectarius tectumpersicum* and *Collisella striata*. Living high on exposed littoral rocks, these species are easily accessible and, in the right habitat, plentiful. Certainly at Torongan there seems to have been little impetus to venture further down the intertidal zone – perhaps due to the proximity of high intertidal and 'splash zone' habitats at the mouth of the cave. The Anaro assemblage presents a more balanced picture of intertidal rocky shore species, with the strong showing of carnivorous species hinting that beds of rocky shore bivalves such as oysters or mussels may also have been targeted.

A very different picture of shellfish gathering is seen within Savidug Dune Site layer 2 and the Pamayan midden. In these late prehistoric deposits small cowries including *Cypraea annulus*, *C. moneta* and *C. caputserpentis* dominate. These are the three most common species of cowrie and can be found in a range of littoral habitats, including reef flats, amongst the shelter of rocks or within turtle-grass (*Thalassia*) beds (Demond 1957:303, Abbot 1982:152). Certainly, intertidal reef flats and seagrass beds host many species of mollusc, many much larger than these three cowrie species. A number of larger intertidal reef-flat and seagrass species are present in the layer 4 sample from Savidug Dune Site, demonstrating that species of conches (*Strombus* spp.), turban shells (*Turbo* spp.) and topshells (*Trochus* spp.) were locally available in earlier times. Nevertheless, even in the layer 4 Savidug Dune Site assemblage, small cowries make up nearly one-quarter of the total sample. The passage of time recorded at Savidug Dune Site, supplemented by the Pamayan data, shows the decline in numbers of medium to large mollusc species. Population pressure stemming directly from human predation may well have been a factor, as suggested in chapter 4, but the fact that many of the species which disappeared from the record are coral reef-flat dwellers, which generally eschew turbid conditions (e.g. *Trochus* spp., *Turbo* spp.), hints that terrestrial erosion – perhaps accelerated by human activity – likely impacted littoral habitats and communities.

Sites from Batan Island have little information about shellfishing to add to the early part of the Batanes sequence, with faunal preservation at the early Sunget site being poor (Szabó et al. 2003). However, at the other end of the sequence, the later prehistoric Mavuyok a Ahchip coastal site yielded a sample large enough to allow some conclusions about shellfish use to be drawn (n = 304 MNI). As with Torongan, the Mavuyok a Ahchip site is located at the landward entrance of a sea cave and is most easily accessed from the sea. However, unlike Torongan, upper intertidal gastropods do not dominate at Mavuyok a Ahchip, and a more diverse collection of larger intertidal species (such as various species in the Turbinidae and Trochidae) contribute to the overall total. Indeed, at Mavuyok a Ahchip, only a single *Tectarius tectumpersicum* and six *Cypraea annulus* shells are present. This suggests that the late prehistoric focus on small cowrie collection seen in the late-sequence Sabtang sites was a local rather than universal phenomenon.

As a cramped space that is not easily accessible, Mavuyok a Ahchip does not show any evidence of having been used for any considerable length of time. Indeed, as with Torongan, it is possible that this was a sheltering spot for fishers, reef-gleaners or those in boats. Thus, while there is no evidence of heavy or sustained predation upon local shellfish at the site, there is evidence for the consumption of land snails. The most common mollusc species within the Mavuyok a Ahchip sample was the large (~ 8 cm diameter) terrestrial snail *Ryssota sagittifera batanica* (n = 34), only occasional fragments of which were found at other sites. A number of these shells were also recovered near-complete from within hearths. Land snails are still collected and consumed on occasion in the Batanes, and Parkinson et al. (1987:47) note that species of *Ryssota* are actively collected for food and bait in various places throughout the Philippines. The combination of easily-accessible upper intertidal marine species and large land snails suggests that shellfish gathering at Mavuyok a Ahchip was focused on proximity and accessibility of molluscs, rather than the systematic gathering seen at other Batanes sites.

While Mavuyok a Ahchip offers evidence of the collection and consumption of large land snails, substantial land snail totals at other sites, especially Torongan, do not necessarily imply human gathering and consumption. Within the Anaro and Torongan shell samples there is no observable bias towards large land snails species or contextual evidence to suggest their use as a food resource. Indeed, the land snail assemblages of both sites reasonably reflect the habitats of the surrounding environments. The differences in land snail numbers between Torongan and Anaro are most likely explained by site topography and geographic location. At Torongan, the landward mouth of the cave faces a slope and material from above has accumulated around the cave entrance. These sorts of locations are often a natural catchment for empty snail shells that enter the deposits from the surrounding thickets of coastal vegetation, such as *Pandanus* trees. Anaro, on the other hand, is set on and around the crest of a hill and thus lacks the natural catchments of Torongan. Here, land snails are more likely to have entered the site from surrounding, sparser vegetation, or on plant material introduced into the site by its human residents.

Conclusions from midden analysis

There are no conspicuous shell middens or dense midden accumulations in the Batanes that would point to heavy human predation of local shellfish populations. Nevertheless, it is clear that molluscs were being consistently collected and consumed throughout the known sequence. The changing species representations evidenced at the Sabtang sites, with an increasing focus on the collection of small cowries through time, implies fairly slim littoral pickings by the late prehistoric period. However, at no point in the Batanes sequence are middens dominated by medium to large intertidal species, such as the various *Turbo* and *Trochus/Tectus* species. Habitats supporting such species were certainly present, and their ephemeral occurrence in earlier deposits attests to their presence in the Batanes in the past. Their virtual absence thus raises the question of whether Torongan and Anaro record the initial settlement of the Batanes, or whether there are earlier sites which contain the sort of shell midden that would be expected from the targeting of unexploited shellfish populations.

Observations on shell-working at Anaro

A collection of 49 pieces of worked shell, blanks and preforms from Anaro was transported to Australia for further study at The Australian National University and the University of

Wollongong. There were no finished, formal artefacts, but a number of recognisable preforms were present. The sample studied in Australia provides a number of insights into raw material selection, the types of artefacts being produced in shell and the manner of their production.

Molluscan raw materials at Anaro

Worked shell at Anaro derived only from two species of shell: the Giant Clam *Tridacna maxima* and the large Green Snail *Turbo marmoratus*. Both of these are large species, from between 20–30 cm in length for *T. maxima* to a maximum diameter of around 25–30 cm for *T. marmoratus*, which contrasts sharply with the small average size of shell species recorded within the midden. Both *T. maxima* and *T. marmoratus* generally occupy shallow subtidal habitats and thus would be beyond the reach of casual subsistence gleaning within the intertidal zone. This demonstrates that larger species than those represented in the midden were available beyond the low-water mark, and that an effort was made to access the subtidal zone for the purposes of shell-working. Anecdotal evidence from a number of older residents on Batan Island confirmed that shallow diving for *Turbo marmoratus* shells, of value in the mother-of-pearl industry, took place locally until relatively recently.

The worked *T. maxima* pieces (n = 4) are not especially well preserved, with acid dissolution in response to matrix conditions affecting most surfaces. Normally, modifications such as worm or sponge boreholes, pitting of surfaces by microalgae, or adhesions such as barnacles or worm tubes would indicate post-mortem collection by humans. But, given the partial dissolution of the surface layers, it is difficult to state with confidence that the shells were collected live as opposed to being collected empty within the intertidal zone.

The *Turbo marmoratus* pieces (n = 45) are in somewhat better condition. The surfaces are generally well preserved, although many pieces have split longitudinally as the organic layers cementing the sheets of nacre/mother-of-pearl have degraded. None of the modifications indicating post-mortem collection were noted amongst the *T. marmoratus* fragments, suggesting that the shells had been collected live. The presence of two worked *T. marmoratus* opercula also offers support for this interpretation. The majority of fragments, as well as the two recorded opercula, show clear evidence of modification, demonstrating that the presence of *T. marmoratus* fragments was associated with artefact production rather than subsistence gathering.

Formal shell artefact types at Anaro

Most of the worked shell fragments recovered at Anaro and examined in Australia cannot be linked to the production of particular formal artefact types; they are simply fragments with cut or chipped edges with the intent of working unclear. Despite this, the presence of some preforms in both *T. maxima* and *T. marmoratus* indicate at least a subset of the artefacts produced from these materials.

The worked *T. maxima* sample consists of four unfinished adzes/gouges (Fig. 12.12; and see also Fig. 8.14 E). All examples have been roughly hewn from a complete valve and have no to little evidence of grinding. One example utilises a rather squat and convex valve which results in a very curved cutting edge. Given this, it has been tentatively assigned as a gouge rather than an adze.

Within the collection of *Turbo marmoratus* worked shell pieces there were four broken preforms which clearly indicated rotating fishhook production. Three of these are shown in Fig. 12.13 (and see also 8.14 E). The outlines and inner shank surfaces of the preforms had been chipped into shape with a sharp point utilising largely flat shell from the body whorl of a *T. marmoratus*. None of the preforms showed evidence for the use of cutting or sawing techniques to achieve the basic form.

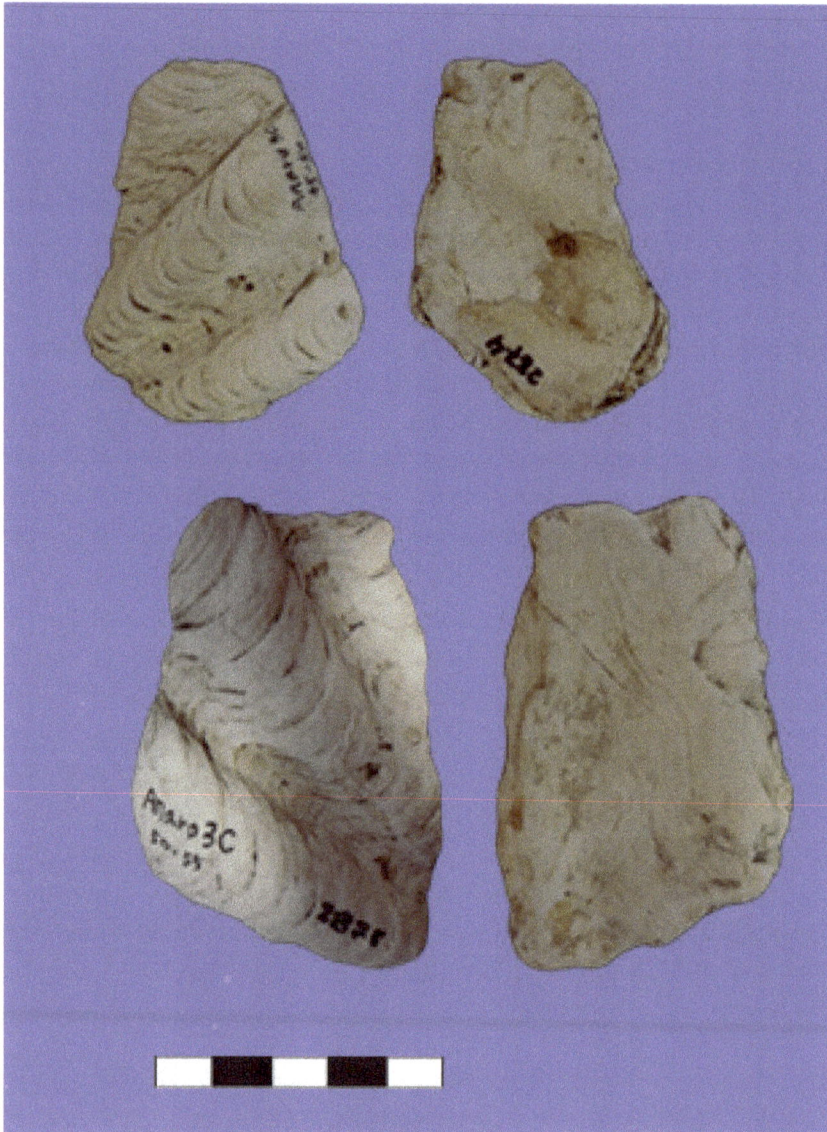

Figure 12.12. Two broken *Tridacna maxima* adze preforms, both from Anaro 3C (National Museum of the Philippines accession numbers II-2004-1-2874 and II-2004-1-2875). The upper example (II-2004-1-2874) was recovered from a depth of 45-50 cm and the lower one (II-2004-1-2875) from 50-55 cm.

Source: Katherine Szabó.

These rotating fishhook preforms are closely paralleled by examples recovered from the O-luan-pi site of southern Taiwan (Li 1983). Here too, pieces of *T. marmoratus* body whorl have been reduced through a process of chipping rather than cutting or sawing. Both an outer circular form and inner circular surface have been fashioned through these techniques. Again, no finished examples are present. At O-luan-pi, worked *T. marmoratus* shell was recovered from within all cultural layers, but only pieces recovered from Cultural Phase 3, dated to *c.*3000 uncal. BP, have these distinctive shapes.

Other evidence of shell-working

The majority of the Anaro worked shell assemblage consists of fragments of *Turbo marmoratus* showing signs of working, although the intentions behind the working are unclear. Included in this category are both opercula and body fragments of *T. marmoratus*.

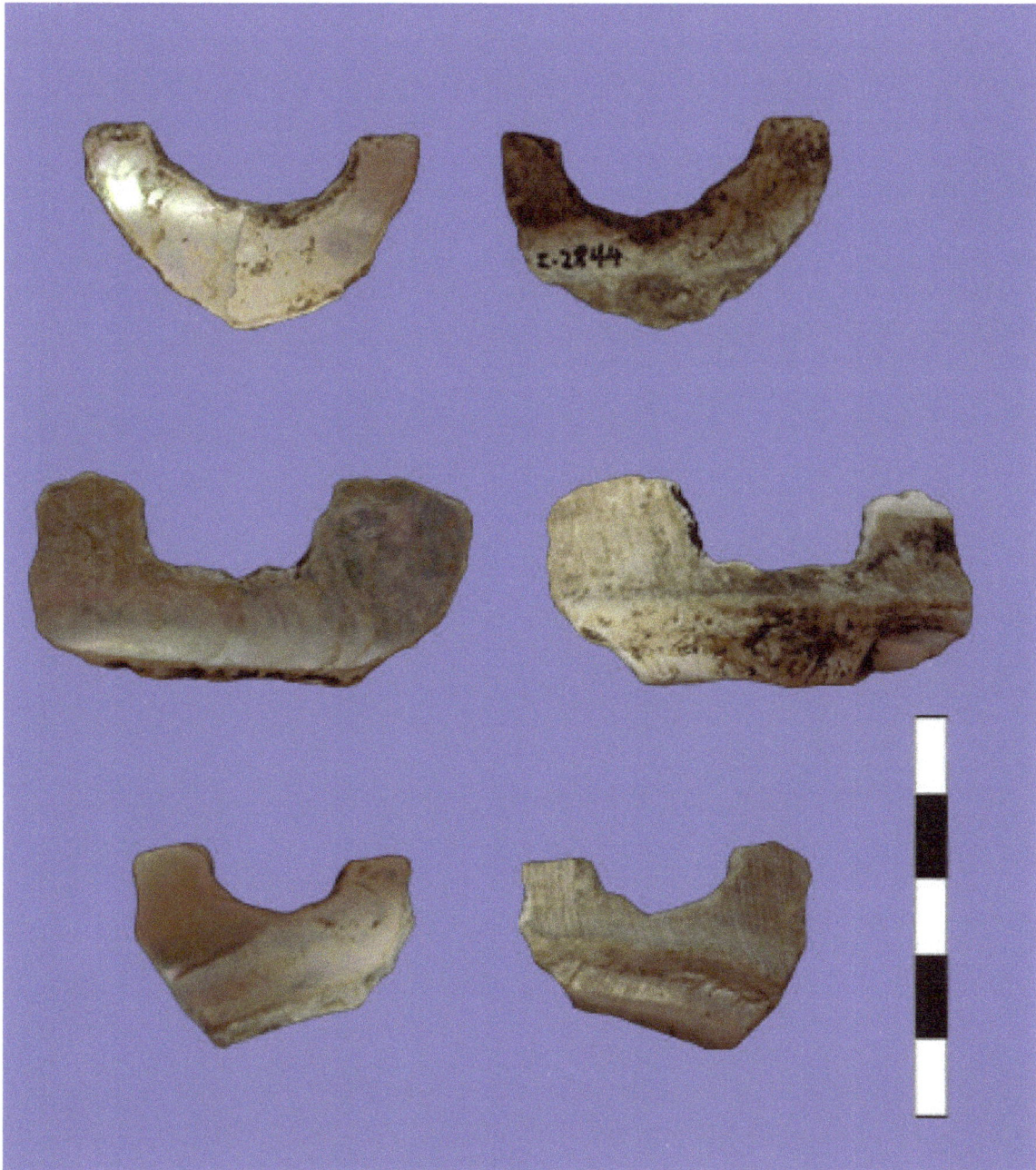

Figure 12.13. Three *Turbo marmoratus* rotating fishhook preforms from Anaro. The upper is from Anaro 3B recovered at a depth of 100-110 cm (National Museum accession number II-2004-1-2844). The middle and lower are from Anaro 3A 40-50 and 70-80 cm respectively (II-2004-1-2842 and II-2004-1-2843).

Source: Katherine Szabó.

There are two reduced opercula within the sample. One is in good condition, with evidence of either deliberate or incidental shell removal along one half of the circumference (Fig. 12.14, top; see also Fig. 8.14). The other has been more extensively reduced to form a near bilaterally-symmetrical disc, but it is in poor condition with clear traces of working obscured (Fig. 12.14, bottom). In both cases, the focus appears to have been on generating a sharp edge by removing sections of the periphery and ventral face of the operculum. Similar artefacts were also recorded in some numbers at O-luan-pi (Li 1983), within deposits associated with all four cultural phases

(5200-4800, 4000, 3000 and 2500 uncal. BP respectively). However, the O-luan-pi specimens show a lesser degree of working than that seen in the Anaro 6 example (Fig. 12.14, bottom). In Li's 1983 O-luan-pi report they are termed 'scrapers', which is also a possibility at Anaro.

The best-represented category of shell artefacts at Anaro are worked fragments of *Turbo marmoratus*. Most have at least one cut edge, some also with evidence of chipping (Fig. 12.15). Where the knobbled keel section around the perimeter of the body whorl is present it most often shows evidence of grinding (Fig. 12.15, top and middle). The grinding would imply that the raised keel was destined to form some part of an artefact under construction, although the eventual form and purpose of this artefact is unknown. Other body whorl portions that do not incorporate the keel variously show signs of cutting and chipping (Fig 12.15, bottom), but as a collective follow little discernible patterning.

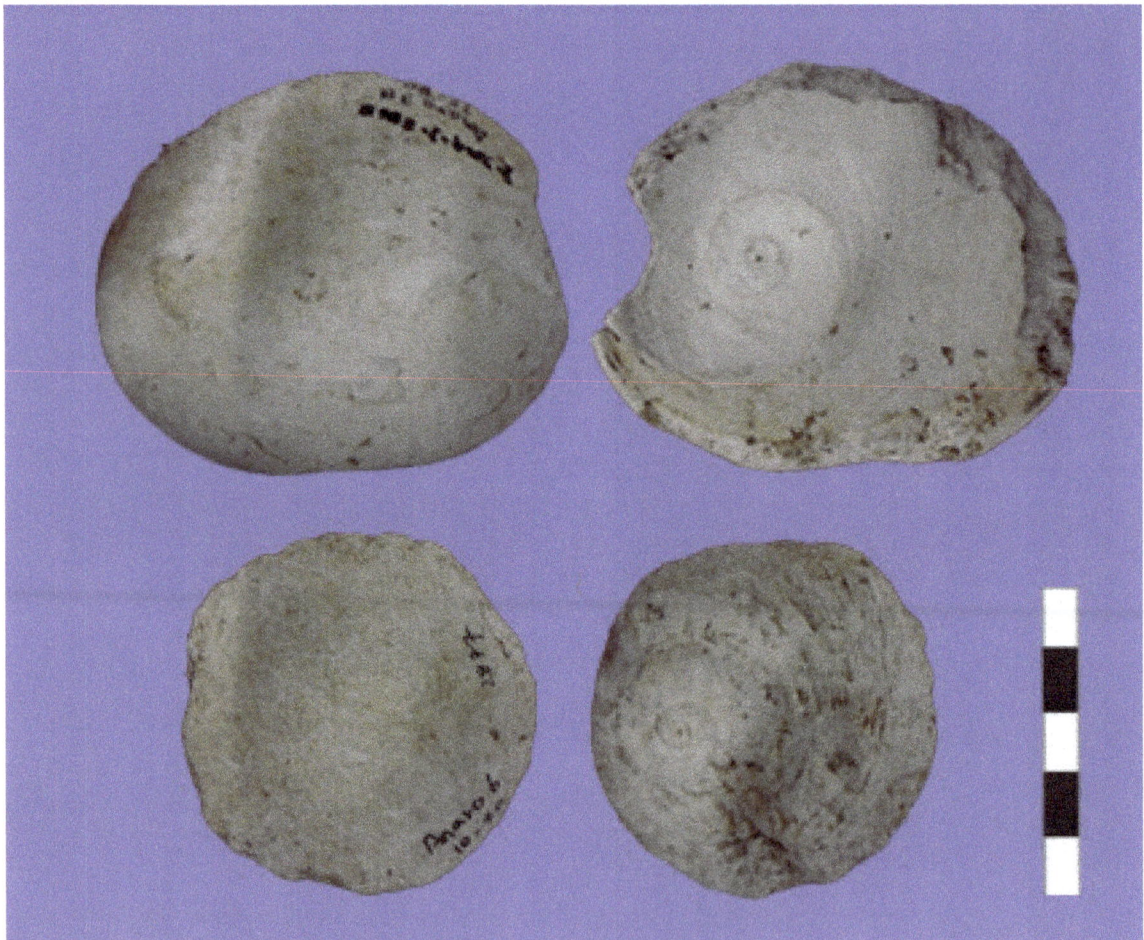

Figure 12.14. Two reduced *Turbo marmoratus* opercula. The upper is from Anaro 3B 70-80 cm (II-2004-1-2868), the lower from Anaro 6 10-20 cm (II-2004-1-2877).

Source: Katherine Szabó.

Discussion

The worked shell assemblage from Anaro is restricted both in size and variety. Only two raw materials were selected for working: *Tridacna* spp. and *Turbo marmoratus*. However, the fact that these two species occur in littoral habitats that do not coincide with the littoral zones represented in the midden demonstrates that particular effort was made to source these species for artefact production.

Figure 12.15. Three worked *Turbo marmoratus* body fragments. The upper and middle are central sections of body whorl containing part of the knobbly keel that runs around the perimeter of the shell. In both cases, the keel surface has been ground smooth. Both fragments also have a long cut edge (A: no accession number, Anaro 3A 40-50 cm; B: II-2004-1-2870, Anaro 3B 90-95 cm). The lowest has three cut edges along with a chipped notch (C: II-2004-1-2824 Anaro 3A 70-80 cm).

Source: Katherine Szabó.

Tridacna and *T. marmoratus* are widely used raw materials for artefact production in the tropical island Asia-Pacific region (Ronquillo 1998; Szabó 2005; Szabó *et al.* 2007), but most frequently occur with shell artefacts made from other materials, such as *Conus* spp., *Trochus niloticus*, *Nautilus pompilius* and/or a selection of other less frequently used taxa [ed.: see chapter 8 for a discussion of artefacts made from such materials in Savidug Dune Site on Sabtang]. Thus, while raw material choice at Anaro falls within the regional pattern of selection, it is notable for being so narrow.

The restricted nature of raw material selection may be linked to the observation that there was a clear focus on tool, rather than ornament, production at Anaro. In other locales, tools were produced in raw materials such as *Conus* spp. and *Trochus niloticus*, but the majority of artefacts associated with these raw materials are generally ornamental.

Despite a concerted focus on only two shell taxa for artefact production, the range of working techniques applied to these materials indicates considerable expertise in handling and working shell. This is particularly visible with the worked *Turbo marmoratus*, where evidence of direct percussion, secondary percussion or pressure flaking, sawing with the blade parallel to the shell surface, cutting with the blade perpendicular to the shell surface and grinding are all present.

Such expertise in terms of techniques applied, as well as clear preferences regarding raw materials, suggests that the shell-working present at Anaro was part of an established tradition. There are clear similarities with worked shell excavated from the southern Taiwanese site of O-luan-pi. Temporally, Anaro corresponds to the mid-sequence of O-luan-pi, and the worked *Turbo marmoratus* in particular suggests technological and cultural ties. O-luan-pi contains a wider range of raw materials, but not more than one would expect given the larger sample.

Further south such parallels are harder to see, with *Turbo marmoratus* not really becoming an important raw material in the Philippines or Indonesia until the Metal Age ~2000 years ago (Szabó 2005). *Turbo marmoratus* shell was used within early Lapita sites of southwestern Oceania for the fashioning of rotating fishhooks at a slightly earlier date (Szabó 2005), but if and how the Lapita and Batanes/southern Taiwan traditions of fishhook manufacture in *T. marmoratus* are related remains to be established. Nevertheless, the small sample of worked shell from Anaro strongly suggests the expansion of southern tip Taiwanese Neolithic culture beyond its borders to influence, directly or indirectly, patterns of culture at Anaro.

13

The Batanes Islands and the Prehistory of Island Southeast Asia

Peter Bellwood and Eusebio Dizon

The Batanes research has covered 4000 years of prehistory, with evidence gleaned from many archaeological sites located on four different islands. The chronological sequence of changes in artefacts and their stylistic attributes, especially in pottery, Taiwan nephrite and other lithic artefacts (Fig. 14.1), will form a keystone in the broader understanding of northern Philippine prehistory and relations with adjacent regions. Archaeological data can often be frustrating in their ambiguity, scarcity and level of preservation, but within the whole corpus of data from Batanes there are many observations that can be made with a high degree of confidence.

Some of these observations are based on negative data. For instance, absolutely no archaeological evidence was found to indicate that the Batanes Islands were discovered or settled prior to the Neolithic. Admittedly, lack of recovered evidence need not always reflect a total absence, but in the case of the Batanes it is hard to avoid the assumption, from the red-slipped and cord-marked pottery in Torongan and Reranum Caves, that the first humans to settle these islands permanently came from Neolithic Taiwan in the centuries around 2000 BC. By soon after 1500 BC, at Sunget, Savidug and Anaro, the evidence of Taiwan nephrite and slate, domestic pigs and dogs, red-slipped and stamped pottery, pottery spindle whorls, side-notched stone net sinkers, and grooved and stepped stone adzes reinforces the existence of very strong links with Taiwan. All of these items have a much greater likelihood of origin in Taiwan and southern China than they do from the Wallacean region that lies directly to the south of Batanes, in the main Philippines and central/eastern Indonesia.

Nevertheless, there might be a very significant difference here between early ephemeral visits by hunter-gatherers from Taiwan or Luzon, and actual settlement of the Batanes by a population that remained permanently in place and grew in numbers thereafter. The archaeological record might be showing us the latter, in the form of the Batanes Neolithic, and masking any faint traces of the former. The Batanes Islands are very small and depauperate in native resources, being neither part of Sundaland nor indeed ever linked by dry land to any other region. This makes it possible that any hunter-gatherer settlements in Batanes during the Pleistocene or early Holocene might not have survived for long, just as many of the more remote offshore islands adjacent to Australia (Kangaroo Island, Bass Strait Islands) were abandoned as they became cut off by postglacial sea level rise. Similar points have been made about small islands in eastern Indonesia, for instance by

Ono et al. (2008), although it must be remembered that these small Indonesian islands at least have an archaeological record of a fleeting Palaeolithic presence in caves. The Batanes Islands do not, despite also having quite numerous caves.

Nevertheless, two other observations render a slim possibility of occasional pre-Neolithic non-sedentary settlement in Batanes at least worthy of consideration. Firstly, using parallels from the many remote Oceanic islands settled by Austronesian-speaking populations, particularly in Polynesia, we might expect that the Batanes Islands hosted many species of bird and reptile at the time of first human arrival, and that these would have been rapidly extirpated by human hunters (Steadman 2006). Alas, however, the bone records from Torongan and Reranum were too poor to reveal clear evidence on this issue, so the issue remains open. Likewise, reflecting on the relative scarcity of shell midden in Batanes, the authors of chapter 12 ask if sites such as Torongan and Anaro record the initial settlement of the Batanes, or whether there might be earlier sites which contain the sort of shell midden that would be expected from the targeting of unexploited shellfish populations. So far, there are no such sites. Is this because the records are too poor, or is it possible that pre-Neolithic hunters had already extirpated many resources before Neolithic settlers arrived? At present, we do not know.

Two other rather more disappointing negatives from the Batanes research also merit comment here, before focusing on the more positive results of the research. Firstly, we were not lucky in finding human remains, except for a single skeleton of very late prehistoric date with no grave goods from Dios Dipun shelter on Batan, and some small fragments of human bone from the Savidug jar burials. We know nothing about the biological affinities, health, or stable isotope dietary signatures of the first Batanes islanders. Added to this, we have virtually no archaeobotanical record for Batanes. Reasons for this are discussed in an appendix to this chapter.

Moving now towards positive evidence, derived from what we did rather than did not find, we have a strong sequence of artefact variation covering the past 4000 years in Batanes, both in basic presence-absence terms and in details of stylistic attributes. Some sites have also produced good records of animal exploitation, both marine and terrestrial, as discussed in chapters 10 to 12. One general conclusion is evident, and this is that the Batanes Islands were not just settled once from Taiwan and thereafter isolated until Jirobei and Dampier arrived in the late seventeenth century. There are indications that arrivals from Taiwan, and probably movements in the other direction as well, happened on many occasions.

For instance, it is unlikely that all the Taiwan nephrite and slate artefacts found in Batanes were brought in by just one founder canoe. It must be remembered that Taiwan nephrite was taken to many regions of Southeast Asia in the period from 500 BC to AD 500 (Hung et al. 2007; Hung and Bellwood 2010), rendering it obvious that contacts with Taiwan at this time happened much more than once. They also happened long before this time, given the evidence from Sunget (c.1000 BC), and the two Taiwan nephrite bracelet fragments found at the base of Nagsabaran in the Cagayan Valley (c.2000-1500 BC; see chapter 9). The Batanes Islands must also have received frequent contacts from Luzon moving in the other direction, given the extent of island intervisibility (chapter 2). In the same direction, a Batanic language (Yami) was carried in late prehistory from Itbayat to Lanyu Island, just southeast of Taiwan. Exactly when this occurred is not clear, but it is generally assumed that the ancestral Yami language arrived from Batanes in Lanyu after initial settlement of that island from Taiwan, the latter presumably during the earlier phases of the Neolithic.

In terms of general Taiwan-Batanes contact via the mediation of Lanyu Island, the dramatic discoveries made between 1978 and 1982 at the site of Rusarsol on Lanyu (Hsu 2008) are of very great relevance. This site has yielded Anaro circle-stamped type 1 pottery, pelta-shaped nephrite debitage identical to the pieces from Anaro shown in Fig. 9.7, slate knives, a biconical spindle whorl, possible clay earrings, and other sherds of red-slipped pottery and pottery appendages similar to Batanes examples. At Anaro, such materials date to the later part of cultural phase 2 in the Batanes sequence, *c.*500 BC to AD 1, as discussed in chapters 5 and 6. There is also a corrugated rim from Rusarsol with stamped half-circle decoration almost identical to one from Mitangeb on Siayan Island (Fig. 6.10, top). The Rusarsol assemblage is not in itself directly dated, and appears to be mixed with much younger imported Chinese ceramics, suggesting that the site might have several chronological components. It is also not known if any of the Rusarsol pottery artefacts actually came from Batanes, or were produced in Lanyu. But whatever the answer, it is clear that Itbayat and Lanyu were in very definite contact between at least 500 BC and the early centuries AD.

Another conclusion must be that Batanes prehistory, at least as known through the past 4000 years, shows no sign of any hiatus in occupation or dramatic cultural replacement, except for the possibility of a period of fairly localised abandonment of central Batan following the Iraya eruption around AD 500. This raises the probability that the initial Neolithic inhabitants of Batanes were the relatively direct ancestors of the people who lived there at the end of prehistory, and likewise of the modern Ivatans and Itbayaten (Ross 2005). This ancestry may extend to the modern Yami of Lanyu as well, given that Yami is a Batanic and not a Formosan language.

It is interesting that the Batanic languages as a whole (Ivatan, Itbayaten and Yami) have a very low internal diversity, despite the fact that they subgroup uniquely with no other Philippine languages. This presumably reflects the ease and frequency of interisland communication for people with a competent technology of boat construction. The Batanic languages are therefore deeply rooted within the major Malayo-Polynesian subgroup of the Austronesian language family, even if they remain internally rather undifferentiated. This suggests that the Batanes Islands populations have behaved linguistically as inhabitants of a single interlinked archipelago throughout their prehistory, rather than as residents of completely separate islands whose populations never came into contact.

Exactly how much contact occurred between Batanes and Lanyu is not so clear, and a recent Y chromosome and mitochondrial genetic survey has found rather few traces of gene flow between Ivatans and Yami (Loo et al. 2011). However, the very clear archaeological evidence of contact between Itbayat and Lanyu around 2000 years ago, discussed above, cannot be ignored. In this case the contact obviously involved some population movement since it was across sea, by boat.

Turning now to some specific aspects of the Batanes archaeological record, the artefact and economic sequences recovered have been described fully in chapters 6 to 12, and some of the main observations are shown in Fig. 13.1, also printed earlier as Fig. 5.3. The four major phases recognised within Batanes prehistory are based on visible changes in artefact decoration and style, and are not intended to be rigid and non-overlapping. Phase 1, with its red-slipped plain pottery from Torongan and Reranum, and limited amounts of cord-marked pottery from Reranum, is still rather fugitive and known only from caves. Phase 2 (outer limits 1300 BC to AD 1) is perhaps the most prominent in all of Batanes prehistory, being represented by large assemblages from the major open sites of Sunget, Anaro, and Savidug Dune. The range of artefacts with Taiwan parallels in Phase 2 is quite remarkable, as mentioned so many times during the course of this monograph. After 500 BC, this was also the phase of major importation of Taiwan nephrite and slate into Batanes and Lanyu, the former worked from blanks at Anaro and Rusarsol into circular ear ornaments similar to the *lingling-o* ornaments of early Metal Age date found across so many regions of Southeast Asia. Indeed, as discussed in chapter 6, the pottery sequence from Anaro allows us to divide Phase 2 into two subphases, as defined by variations in the stylistic composition of stamped circle motifs on pottery.

However, the strong Phase 2 emphasis on pottery decoration using motifs created *purely* from rows of stamped circles was always rather unique to Batanes, with direct parallels existing only in

Taiwan and in offshore Taiwanese sites such as Youzihu on Ludao Island and Rusarsol on Lanyu Island. This rather obsessive focus on stamped circles was a little different from the varieties of circle stamping combined with zones of punctate or dentate stamping that characterised sites in the Cagayan Valley of Luzon (e.g. Magapit, Nagsabaran, Irigayen) and elsewhere in the Philippines (e.g. Batungan Caves on Masbate Island), in the early culture of the Mariana Islands (House of Taga and Achugao), and in Lapita sites in Oceania (Carson et al. 2013). This might relate to a relative self-containment of the Batanes stylistic scene, suggesting that these islands in themselves were not sources of major colonising voyages to the south or east.

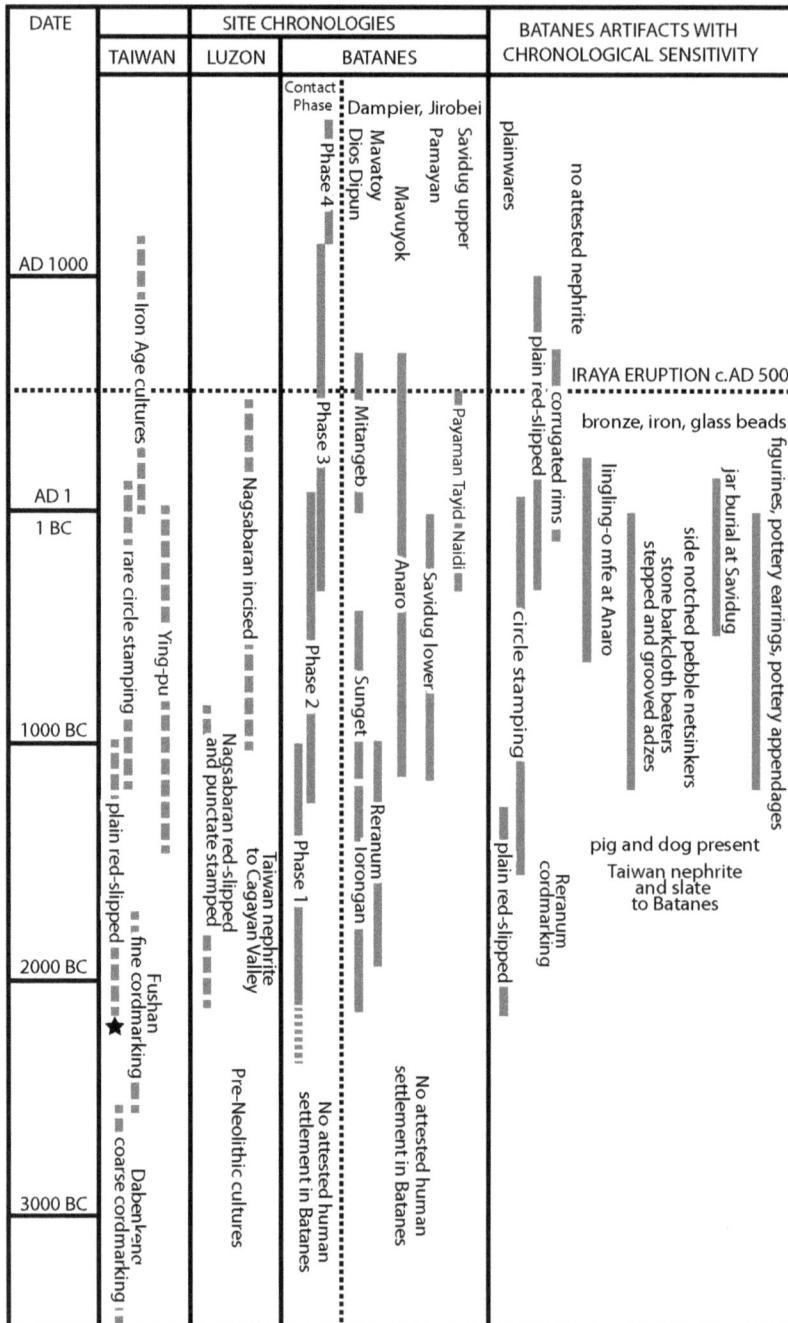

| DATE | SITE CHRONOLOGIES | | | BATANES ARTIFACTS WITH CHRONOLOGICAL SENSITIVITY |
	TAIWAN	LUZON	BATANES	

Figure 13.1. The four proposed phases for Batanes prehistory, together with radiocarbon chronologies for the excavated Batanes sites, and contemporary cultural manifestations in Taiwan and Luzon.

★ Chaolaiqiao

Source: Peter Bellwood.

This final point, of course, brings up the role of the Batanes Islands in the whole saga of Austronesian origins and migrations across Island Southeast Asia, into Oceania, and even to Vietnam and Madagascar. This monograph is not the place to repeat the many observations made over many years on this issue by the senior editor, who has published recent summaries elsewhere of the out-of-Taiwan hypothesis for Austronesian origins, involving human migration rather than language shift or "cultural diffusion" alone (Bellwood 2011a, 2011b; Bellwood et al. 2011). This *Terra Australis* monograph on Batanes archaeology has been published as a source of data, rather than as an argument for or against a specific historical position in the field of Austronesian origins. Its purpose is to allow readers to examine and assess some very significant data for themselves, relating to human movements between Taiwan and the northern Phipippines during the past 4000 years, in order to have an opinion, should they wish one, on this much-debated issue.

Appendix: Archaeobotanical and Palaeoenvironmental Observations

Janelle Stevenson and Peter Bellwood

Flotation was tried on several Batanes sites, but was rarely successful owing to a general lack of charcoal in the seasonally wet and dry soil conditions. For instance, it was carried out at Sunget and Mavuyok a Ahchip during the first season of fieldwork on Batan in 2002. Abundant charred plant material was recovered from the latter site, a protected cave with deposits of very recent date, but Sunget by comparison had only a small amount. Unfortunately, expertise to identify the recovered botanical samples was not available and this line of research eventually lapsed.

Sediments for phytolith analysis were also collected in 2002 from Sunget, Mavuyok a Ahchip and Dios Dipun, with excellent recovery from the last two caves. However, both assemblages were overwhelmed by non-diagnostic grass phytoliths. The Sunget phytolith samples came from the ancient subsoil, beneath the Iraya ash, which had lost its original topsoil layer at some point in the past. As a consequence, the sediments were phytolith poor.

Palaeoenvironmental investigations

Depositional sites outside the archaeological context, such as natural lakes and swamps, can contain important information on how landscapes have changed over time as a result of climate change, large-scale natural events (e.g. volcanic eruptions) and human disturbance. These sites contain fossil pollen, spores and charcoal laid down stratigraphically over time. The pollen and spores are derived from plants in the surrounding landscape and are indicators of how the vegetation has changed. Charcoal tells us how important fire has been in shaping these past landscapes (Bennett and Willis 2001). However, coherent records from swamps and lakes can only be constructed if the sediments that have accumulated, sometimes over tens of thousands of years, remain largely undisturbed by human activities and other natural forces.

A programme of environmental research in the Batanes was planned in 2002 to investigate (1) how perturbations of climate during the last ten to twenty thousand years might have affected the environment of the islands; (2) how quickly and to what degree Neolithic people changed the Batanes environment; and (3) how the eruption of Mount Iraya at AD 500 affected the landscape, and the story of its subsequent recovery.

In 2002 we carried out reconnaissance for suitable sites in Batan, Sabtang and Ivuhos. It soon became apparent that the steep topography and the lack of any permanent, natural and undisturbed bodies of water in Batanes were going to present problems. We identified a natural body of water behind the coastal dunes near Savidug on Sabtang Island, but unfortunately this shallow sedimentary deposit had been disturbed recently by cattle and people. In 2007, it was completely dry and full of buffalo wallows.

As the lake sediments from Savidug proved to be unsuitable for analysis, the decision was made to investigate the potential of less traditional sites for palaeoenvironmental research. We therefore collected material using a simple soil auger from several valley fills on Batan Island, and from a low-lying point behind a sand dune in the north of Ivuhos Island. These sites were not considered ideal for fossil pollen analysis, as pollen is best preserved in either waterlogged sediments or sediments that are permanently dry. Under conditions of repeated wetting and drying the pollen decomposes (Bennett and Willis 2001). On returning to Australia these samples for pollen analysis were processed, but, as suspected, pollen was not preserved.

Further attempts were made in 2004 (Itbayat) and 2007 (Sabtang) to locate suitable sites for palynological coring. However, in each case the 'potential' sites returned modern basal dates. The conclusion was drawn from this latter work that accelerated land clearance, dam construction and the introduction of water buffalo in recent times had led to increased sedimentation, rendering it extremely difficult to locate suitable research locations. Since 2007, the palaeoenvironmental research of Janelle Stevenson in the northern Philippines has shifted to northern Luzon and the Central Cordillera. The results of this have been and will continue to be published elsewhere (e.g. Stevenson et al. 2010).

References

Abbot, R. 1982. *Kingdom of the Seashell*. Bonanza Books, New York.

Allen, G. 2000. *Marine Fishes of Southeast Asia*. Periplus, Singapore.

Amano, N. and P. Piper 2011. A report on the animal remains from the 2009 archaeological excavations at Vasino in East Timor. An unpublished report produced for S. O'Connor and J. Fenner of The Australian National University, Canberra, Australia.

Amano, N., P. Piper, H. Hung and P. Bellwood in press. Introduced domestic animals in the Neolithic and Metal Age of the Philippines, and evidence of human subsistence strategies and behavior at Nagsabaran, northern Luzon. *Journal of Island and Coastal Archaeology*.

Amesbury, J. and R. Hunter-Anderson 2008. An analysis of archaeological and historical data on fisheries for pelagic fishes in Guam and northern Mariana Islands. A report prepared for the Pelagic Fisheries Research Program, Joint Institute for Marine and Atmospheric Research, School of Ocean and Earth Science and Technology, University of Hawai'i at Mānoa. Micronesian Archaeological Research Services, Guam.

Anderson, A. 2005. Crossing the Luzon Strait: archaeological chronology in the Batanes Islands, Philippines and the regional sequence of Neolithic dispersal. *Journal of Austronesian Studies* 1(2): 25-46.

Anggraeni, T. Simanjuntak, P. Bellwood and P. Piper, in press. Neolithic foundations in the Karama valley, West Sulawesi, Indonesia. *Antiquity* (Durham, UK).

Aoyagi Y., M. Aguilera, H. Ogawa and K. Tanaka 1993. Excavations of the Hill Top site, Magapit shell midden in Lal-Lo Shell Middens, Northern Luzon, Philippines. *Man and Culture in Oceania* 9: 127-155.

Ardika, I. 1991. Archaeological Research in Northeastern Bali, Indonesia. Unpublished PhD thesis, Australian National University.

Ardika, I. and P. Bellwood 1991. Sembiran: the beginnings of Indian contact with Bali. *Antiquity* 247: 221-32.

Bacus, E. 2004. The archaeology of the Philippine archipelago. In I. Glover and P. Bellwood (eds) *Southeast Asia: From Prehistory to History*, pp. 257–281. RoutledgeCurzon, London.

Barber, D. and B. Coblenz 1986. Density, home range, habitat use and reproduction in feral pigs on Santa Catalina Island. *Journal of Mammalogy* 67(3): 512-525.

Barbosa, A. 1979. A preliminary archaeological report on the Lattu-Lattu Cave excavation. Manila: National Museum (unpublished manuscript).

Barretto, G., A. Mijares and R. Santiago 1998-2003. Preliminary exploration of the Vatang stone boat-shaped marker. *Ivatan Studies Journal* V-X: 39-48.

Behrensmeyer, A. 1978. Taphonomic and ecologic information from bone weathering. *Paleobiology* 4: 150-162.

Bellwood, P. 1988. *Archaeological Research in South-eastern Sabah*. Sabah Museum Monograph no.2, Kota Kinabalu.

_____. 2005. Coastal South China, Taiwan, and the prehistory of the Austronesians. In Chen Chung-yu and Pan Jian-guo eds, *The Archaeology of the Southeast Coastal Islands of China*, pp. 1-22. Taiwan: Executive Yuan, Council for Cultural Affairs. ISBN 986-00-2638-6.

_____. 2006. The dispersal of Neolithic cultures from China into Island Southeast Asia: standstills, slow moves, and fast spreads. In Institute of Archaeology, Chinese Academy of Social Sciences (ed.), *Prehistoric Archaeology of South China and Southeast Asia*, pp. 223-34. Beijing: Cultural Relics Publishing House.

_____. 2007a. Southeast China and the prehistory of the Austronesians. In Tianlong Jiao ed., *Lost Maritime Cultures: China and the Pacific*. Bishop Museum Press, Honolulu.

_____. 2007b. *Prehistory of the Indo-Malaysian Archipelago*. 2nd edition. ANU E Press, Canberra.

_____. 2011a. Holocene population history in the Pacific region as a model for world-wide food producer dispersals. *Current Anthropology* 52, No. S4: 363-78.

_____. 2011b. The checkered prehistory of rice movement southwards as a domesticated cereal – from the Yangzi to the Equator. *Rice* 4: 93-103.

_____. 2013. Southeast Asian islands: archaeology. In I. Ness and P. Bellwood (eds) *Encyclopedia of Global Human Migration*. 5 volumes (Volume 1, Prehistory), pp. 284-92. Wiley-Blackwell, Chichester, Oxford and Malden.

_____. in press. The Neolithic in Vietnam. In Andreas Reinecke, ed., *Treasures of Vietnamese Archaeology*. Museums of Herne, Chemnitz and Mannheim and the German Archaeological Institute. To be published in German and Vietnamese.

Bellwood, P. and E. Dizon 2005. The Batanes Archaeological Project and the "Out Of Taiwan" hypothesis for Austronesian dispersal. *Journal of Austronesian Studies* (Taitung, Taiwan) 1: 1-33.

_____. 2008. Austronesian cultural origins: out of Taiwan, via the Batanes Islands, and onwards to western Polynesia. In A. Sanchez-Mazas, R. Blench, M. Ross, I. Peiros and M. Lin (eds) *Past Human Migrations in East Asia: Matching Archaeology, Linguistics and Genetics*, pp. 23-39. Routledge, London.

Bellwood, P., G. Chambers, R. Ross and H. Hung 2011. Are "cultures" inherited? Multidisciplinary perspectives on the origins and migrations of Austronesian-speaking peoples prior to 1000 BC. In B. Roberts and M. Van der Linden (eds) *Investigating Archaeological Cultures: Material Culture, Variability and Transmission*, pp. 321-54. Springer: Dordrecht.

Bellwood, P., H. Hung and Y. Iizuka 2011. Taiwan jade in the Philippines: 3000 years of trade and long-distance interaction. In P. Benitez-Johannot (ed.) *Paths of Origins: Austronesia in the Collections of the National Museum of the Philippines, the Museum Nasional Indonesia, and the Netherlands Rijksmuseum voor Volkenkunde*, pp. 30-41. ArtPostAsia, Manila.

Bellwood, P., G. Nitihaminoto, G. Irwin, Gunadi, A. Waluyo and D. Tanudirjo. 1998. 35,000 years of prehistory in the northern Moluccas. In G.-J. Bartstra (ed.) *Bird's Head Approaches*, pp. 233-75. *Modern Quaternary Research in Southeast Asia* 15. Balkema, Rotterdam.

Bellwood, P., J. Stevenson, A. Anderson and E. Dizon 2003. Archaeological and palaeoenvironmental research in Batanes and Ilocos Norte Provinces, northern Philippines. *Bulletin of the Indo-Pacific Prehistory Association* 23: 141-61.

Bellwood, P., J. Stevenson, E. Dizon, A. Mijares, G. Lacsina and E. Robles 2008. Where are the Neolithic landscapes of Ilocos Norte? *Hukay* 13: 25-38. Manila.

Bennett, K. and K. Willis 2001. Pollen. In J. Smol, H. Birks and W. Last (eds) *Tracking Environmental Change Using Lake Sediments. Volume 3: Terrestrial, Algal and Siliceous Indicators*, pp. 5-32. Kluwer Academic Publishers, Dordrecht.

Beyer, H. 1947. Outline review of Philippine archaeology by islands and provinces. *Philippine Journal of Science* 77:205-374.

_____. 1948. *Philippine and East Asian Archaeology*. National Research Council of the Philippines Bulletin 29. Quezon City.

Blair, P. and Robertson, E. 1903-1909. *The Philippine Islands 1493-1898*. Cleveland, 55 vols.

Blust, R. 2013. Southeast Asian islands and Oceania: Austronesian linguistic history. In I. Ness and P. Bellwood (eds) *Encyclopedia of Global Human Migration*. 5 volumes (Volume 1, Prehistory), pp. 276-83. Wiley-Blackwell, Chichester, Oxford and Malden.

Broad, G. 2003. *Fishes of the Philippines: A Guide to the Identification of Families*. Anvil Publishing Inc, Pasig City, Philippines.

Bull, G. and S. Payne 1982. Tooth eruption and epiphysial fusion in pigs and wild boar. In B. Wilson, C. Grigson and S. Payne (eds) *Ageing and Sexing Animal Bones from Archaeological* Sites, pp. 55-71. BAR British Series 109, Oxford.

Bullock, P., N. Fedoroff, A. Jongerius, G. Stoops and T. Tursina 1985. *Handbook for Soil Thin Section Description*. Waine Research Publication, Albrighton, UK.

Burton, M. and R. Burton 2002. Dolphinfish. In *International Wildlife Encyclopedia* (3rd ed., p. 693). Marshall Cavendish, New York.

Cabanilla, I. 1972. Neolithic Shellmound of Cagayan: The Lal-lo Excavation. Unpublished Field Report No. 1, Archaeology Division, The National Museum of the Philippines, Manila.

Cameron, J. 2001. Textile technology and Austronesian dispersals. In G.R. Clark, A.J. Anderson and T. Vunidilo(eds) *The Archaeology of Lapita Dispersal in Oceania*, pp. 177-183. Pandanus Books, Canberra.

_____. 2002. Textile Technology in the Prehistory of Southeast Asia. Unpublished PhD thesis, Australian National University.

_____. 2006. The origins of bark cloth production in Southeast Asia. In M.Howard (ed) Bark Cloth in Southeast Asia, pp. 65-74. White Lotus Press, Bangkok.

_____. 2007. Report on the spindle whorl from the Linaminan Site, Palawan. *Hukay* 11: 28-9.

_____. 2008. Prehistoric interaction in the Asian Mediterranean. In Gu Xiao Song and Tana Li (eds) *Two Corridors and One Rim*, pp. 99-110. Academy of Social Sciences, Nanning.

Cameron, J. and M. Mijares 2006. Report on an analysis of spindle whorls from Callao Cave, Penablanca, Northeast Luzon, Philippines. *Hukay* 9: 5-13.

Campos, F. 2009. The Ichthyoarchaeology of Batanes Islands, Northern Philippines. Unpublished Master of Science thesis, Archaeological Studies Program, University of the Philippines.

Campos, F. and P. Piper 2009. A preliminary analysis of the animal bones recovered from OLPII Site 2006, southern Taiwan. In C-W. Cheng, Cultural Change and Regional Relationships of Prehistoric Taiwan: a Case Study of Oluanpi II Site: Appendix B. Unpublished PhD thesis, National Taiwan University.

Carpenter, K., and V. Springer 2005. The center of the center of marine shore fish biodiversity: the Philippine islands. *Environmental Biology of Fishes* 72: 467-480.

Carson, M., H. Hung, G. Summerhayes and P. Bellwood 2013. The pottery trail from Southeast Asia to Remote Oceania. *Journal of Island and Coastal Archaeology* 8: 17-36.

Casteel, R. 1976. *Fish Remains in Archaeology and Paleo-Environmental Studies*. Academic Press, New York.

Castro, J., J. Santiago and A. Santana-Ortega 2002. A general theory on fish aggregation to floating objects: an alternative to the meeting point hypothesis. *Reviews in Fish Biology and Fisheries* 11: 255-277.

Chang, K. 1969. *Fengpitou, Tapenkeng and the Prehistory of Taiwan.* Yale University Publications in Anthropology 73, New Haven.

Chia, S. 2003. *The Prehistory of Bukit Tengkorak.* Sabah Museum Monograph 8, Kota Kinabalu.

Chu, C. 1990. *Investigation on the Neolithic Sites in the Estuary of Mawuku River, Taidong).* Unpublished Masters thesis, National Taiwan University, Taipei. (in Chinese)

Colley, S. 1990. The analysis and interpretation of archaeological fish remains. In M. B. Schiffer (ed) *Archaeological Method and Theory* (Vol. 2, pp. 207-253). The University of Arizona Press, Tucson.

Cooper-Cole, F. C. 1915. *Traditions of the Tinguian: a Study in Philippine Folklore.* Field Museum of Natural History, Chicago.

Cox, M. 2013. Southeast Asian islands and Oceania: human genetics. In I. Ness and P. Bellwood (eds) *Encyclopedia of Global Human Migration.* 5 volumes (Volume 1, Prehistory), pp. 293-301. Wiley-Blackwell, Chichester, Oxford and Malden.

Cummins, J. (ed) 1962. *The Travels and Controversies of Friar Domingo Navarette, 1618-1686.* Cambridge University Press, Cambridge.

Dang, V., Q. Vu, T. Nguyen, T. Ngo, K. Nguyen and L. Nguyen 1998. *Prehistory and Protohistoric Archaeology of Ho Chi Minh City.* Yonth Press, Ho Chi Minh City. (in Vietnamese)

De Beauclair, I. 1972. Jar-burial on Botel Tobago Island. *Asian Perspectives* 15: 167-176.

_____. 1986. *Ethnographic Studies: The Collected Papers of Inez de Beauclair.* Southern Materials Center, Taipei.

De la Torre, A. 2000. Preliminary report of the Lal-lo, Cagayan Archaeological Project: Clemente Irigayen Property. In H. Ogawa (ed.) *Excavation of the Lal-lo Shell Middens*, pp. 93-128. Tokyo University of Foreign Studies (unpublished report).

_____. 2003. Ulilang Bundok: secondary jar burials at Calatagan. In C. O. Valdes (ed.) *Pang-alay: Ritual Pottery in Ancient Philippines.* The Ayala Foundation, Manila.

De Leon, A. 2008. Pottery and Cultural Interaction from 3000 to 600 BP Batanes, Northern Philippines. Unpublished Masters thesis, University of the Philippines, Diliman.

Demond, J. 1957. Micronesian reef-associated gastropods. *Pacific Science* 11(3): 275-341.

Dewar, R. 2003. Rainfall variability and subsistence systems in Southeast Asia and the western Pacific. *Current Anthropology* 44: 269-88.

Dickinson, W. 2006. First petrographic appraisal of sand tempers in prehistoric potsherds from Luzon, Batan-Itbayat, and Taiwan. Unpublished Appendix 4 in Swete Kelly 2008, pp. 747-63.

Dizon, E. 1998. Stones of the sea. In G.S. Casal, E.Z. Dizon, W.P. Ronquillo and C.G. Salcedo (eds) *Kasaysayan the Story of the Filipino People Vol. 2, The Earliest Filipinos*, pp. 127-133. Asia Publishing Company Limited, New York.

_____. 1998-2003. Batanes Archaeological Project: 1996-1997 status report. *Ivatan Studies Journal* V-X: 9-18.

_____. 2000. Archaeology of Batanes Province, Northern Philippines: the 1996-1997 status report. *Bulletin of the Indo-Pacific Prehistory Association* 19: 115-24.

Dizon, E. and J. Cayron 1998-2003. Archaeological excavation of a stone boat-shaped burial at Locality No. 1, Nakamaya, San Antonio, Batanes. *Ivatan Studies Journal* V-X: 19-28.

Dizon, E. and R. Santiago 1994. Preliminary report on the archaeological investigation in Batan, Sabtang and Ivuhos Islands. *Ivatan Studies Journal* 1: 7-49.

Dizon, E., R. Santiago and M. Bolunia 1995-97. Report on the archaeological acitivties in Ivuhos and Sabtang Islands from February to March 1996. *Ivatan Studies Journal* 2-4: 30-63.

Dobney, K. and A. Ervynck 1998. A protocol for recording enamel hypoplasia on archaeological pig teeth. *International Journal of Osteoarchaeology* 8(4): 263-274.

Dobney, K., A. Ervynck, U. Albarella and P. Rowley-Conwy 2007. The transition from wild boar to domestic pig in Eurasia, illustrated by a tooth developmental defect and biometrical data. In U. Alberetta, K. Dobney, A. Ervynck and P. Rowley-Conwy (eds) *Pigs and Humans: 10,000 Years of Interaction*, pp. 30-41. Oxford University Press, Oxford.

Duff, R. 1970. *The Stone Adzes of Southeast Asia.* Canterbury Museum, Christchurch.

Ekman, S. 1953. *Zoogeography of the Sea.* Sidgwick and Jackson, London.

Ervynck, A. and K. Dobney 1999. Lining up on the M1: a tooth defect as a bio-indicator for environment and husbandry in ancient pigs. *Environmental Archaeology* 4: 1-8.

Esseltyn, J. and C. Oliveros 2010. Colonization of the Philippines from Taiwan: a multi-locus test of the biogeographic and phylogenetic relationships of isolated populations of shrews. *Journal of Biogeography* 37: 1504-1514.

Faylona, P. 2003. The Dipnay Supuan jar burials in Batanes. *Philippine Quarterly of Culture and Society* 31: 119-29.

Florentino, R. 1996. Contribution of major food items on caloric and protein intake of Filipinos. Micro Impacts of Macroeconomic Adjustment Policies (MIMAP) Research Paper No. 23, MIMAP-Philippines Project Management Office, Manila.

Florentino, R., G. Villavieja, T. Valerio, A. Domdom and E. Red 1985. Fish consumption patterns in the Philippines. *ASEAN Food Journal* 1(2): 63-69.

Fox, R. 1970. *The Tabon Caves.* National Museum Monograph, Manila.

French, C. 2003. *Geoarchaeology in Action: Studies in Soil Micromorphology And Landscape Evolution.* Routledge, London.

Froese, R. and D. Pauly (eds) 2012. *FishBase.* World Wide Web electronic publication, www.fishbase. org.

Fuller, D., L. Qin, Y. Zheng, Z. Zhao, X. Chen, L. Hosoya and G. Sun 2009. The domestication process and domestication rate in rice. *Science* 323: 1607-10.

Garong, A., F. Mihara et al. 2010. Carbon and nitrogen isotope anaysis using human bones and hair from Philippine burial sites. *Bull. Graduate School of Social and Cultural Studies, Kyushu University* 16: 25-43.

Garong, A. and T. Toizumi (eds) 2000. *The Archaeological Excavation of the Shell Midden Sites in Lal-Lo, Cagayan.* Dept. of Philippines Studies, Tokyo University of Foreign Studies, Tokyo.

Gaza, T. and Y. Yamada 1999. *Atlas of Itbayat Place-names.* Himeji Dokkyo University, Himeji.

Glover, I. 1986. *Archaeology in Eastern Timor.* Terra Australis Vol. 11. ANU E-Press, Canberra.

Gonzalez, P. 1966. *The Batanes Islands.* University of Santo Tomas Press, Manila.

Grant, A. 1982. The use of toothwear as a guide to the age of domestic ungulates. In B. Wilson, C. Grigson and S. Payne (eds) *Ageing and Sexing Animal Bones from Archaeological Sites*, pp. 91-99. BAR British Series 109, Oxford.

Gunadi, N., H. Simanjuntak, Suwarno, T. Hartono and Budijanto 1978. *Laporan Ekskavasi Gunung Piring (Lombok Selatan)*. Berita Penelitian Arkeologi 17, Jakarta.

Hall, M. 1992. The association of tuna with floating objects and dolphins in the Eastern Pacific Ocean. VII. Some hypotheses on the mechanisms governing the associations of tunas with floating objects and dolphins. Paper presented at the International workshop on fishing for tunas associated with floating objects, 11-14 February 1992, La Jolla, California.

Harlow, G. and S. Sorensen 2005. Jade (nephrite and jadeitite) and serpentinite: metasomatic connections. *International Geology Review* 47: 113–146.

Heaney, L. 1985. Zoogeographic evidence for middle and late Pleistocene land bridges to the Philippine Islands. *Modern Quaternary Research in SE Asia* 9: 127-44.

Heinsohn, T. 2003. Animal translocation: long-term human influences on the vertebrate zoogeography of Australasia (natural dispersal versus ethnophoresy). *Australian Zoologist* 32(3): 350-376.

Helfman, G., B. Collette and D. Facey 2009. *The Diversity of Fishes*. Wiley-Blackwell, Oxford.

Hidalgo, C. 1996. *The Making of the Ivatans*. Cognita TRC, Pasig, Philippines.

Higham, C. and L. Lu 1998 The origins and dispersal of rice cultivation. *Antiquity* 72: 867-77.

Johnson, E. 1985. Current developments in bone technology. In M. B. Schiffer (ed.) *Advances in Archaeological Method and Theory*, pp. 157-235. Academic Press, New York.

Hillson, S. 2005. *Teeth*. Cambridge University Press, Cambridge.

Hornedo, F. 2000. *Taming the Wind: Ethno-Cultural History on the Ivatan of the Batanes Isles*. UST Publications, Manila.

Hsu, S. 2003. Report on the Lanyu High School site, Yu You Village, Lanyu. Paper presented at a Workshop on Lanyu Studies. Taipei: Academia Sinica. (in Chinese)

_____. 2008. Research report on Rusarsol site of Yayo village in Lanyu. *Journal of Austronesian Studies* 2(1): 55-84. (in Chinese)

Hsü, Y. 1982. *Yami Fishing Practices: Migratory Fish*. Southern Materials Center, Taipei.

Hung, H. 2004. A sourcing study of Taiwan stone adzes. *Bulletin of the Indo-Pacific Prehistory Association* 24: 7-70.

_____. 2005. Neolithic interaction between Taiwan and northern Luzon: the pottery and jade evidences from the Cagayan Valley. *Journal of Austronesian Studies* 1, no. 1: 109-34.

_____. 2006. Distribution of Taiwan nephrite and its implications for Southeast Asian archaeology. In Institute of Archaeology, Chinese Academy of Social Science (ed.) *Southern China and Southeast Asia Archaeology*, pp. 324-340. Cultural Relics Press, Beijing. (in Chinese)

_____. 2008. Migration and Cultural Interaction in Southern Coastal China, Taiwan and the Northern Philippines, 3000 BC to AD 1: The Early History of the Austronesian-speaking Populations. Unpublished PhD Thesis, Australian National University, Canberra.

Hung, H. and P. Bellwood, 2010. Movement of raw materials and manufactured goods across the South China Sea after 500 BCE: from Taiwan to Thailand, and back. In *50 Years of Archaeology in Southeast Asia: Essays in Honour of Ian Glover*, eds B. Bellina, L. Bacus, O. Pryce and J. Wisseman Christie, pp. 234-43. Bangkok: River Books.

Hung, H., M. Carson, P. Bellwood, F. Campos, P. Piper, E. Dizon, M. Bolunia, M. Oxenham and C. Zhang 2011. The first settlement of Remote Oceania: the Philippines to the Marianas. *Antiquity* 85: 909-26.

Hung, H., Y. Iizuka and R. Santiago 2004. Lost treasure from beyond the sea: a prehistoric jade bell-shaped bead excavated in the Philippines. *The National Palace Museum Research Quarterly* 21: 43-56. (in Chinese with English abstract: pp. 213)

Hung, H., Y. Iizuka, T. Yui and R. Santiago 2005. A missing jade mine: studies on the white jade adzes from the Philippines. *Field Archaeology of Taiwan* 10(1): 79-104. (in Chinese)

Hung, H., Y. Iizuka and P. Bellwood 2006. Taiwan jade in the context of Southeast Asian archaeology. In E. Bacus, I. Glover and V. Pigott (ed.) *Uncovering Southeast Asia's Past*, pp. 203-15. National University of Singapore Press.

Hung, H., Y. Iizuka and 8 other authors 2007. Ancient jades map 3000 years of prehistoric exchange in Southeast Asia. *Proceedings of the National Academy of Sciences, USA* 104: 19745-50.

Hung, H., K. Nguyen, P. Bellwood and M. Carson in press. Coastal connectivity: long-term trading networks across the South China Sea. *Journal of Island and Coastal Archaeology.*

Iizuka, Y, P. Bellwood, H. Hung and E. Dizon 2005. A non-destructive mineralogical study of nephritic artefacts from Itbayat Island, Batanes, northern Philippines. *Journal of Austronesian Studies* 1, no. 1: 83-108.

Iizuka, Y., P. Bellwood, I. Datan and H. Hung 2006. Mineralogical studies of the Niah West Mouth jade *Lingling-o.Sarawak Museum Journal* LXI (82): 19-29.

Iizuka, Y. and H. Hung 2005. Archaeomineralogy of Taiwan nephrite: a sourcing study of nephritic artefacts from the Philippines. *Journal of Austronesian Studies* 1: 33-79.

Iizuka, Y., H. Hung and P. Bellwood 2007. A non-invasive mineralogical study of nephritic artefacts from the Philippines and surroundings: the distribution of Taiwan nephrite and implications for Island Southeast Asian archaeology. In Janet Douglas, Paul Jett and John Winter (eds) *Scientific Research on the Sculptural Arts of Asia*, pp. 12-19. Freer Gallery of Art/Arthur M. Sackler Gallery and Smithsonian Institution, Washington DC.

Isorena, E. 2004. The Visayan raiders of the China coast. *Philippine Quarterly of Culture and Society* 32: 73-95.

Jenks, A. 1905. *The Bontoc Igorot.* Bureau of Public Funding, Manila.

Jiao, T. 2007. *The Neolithic of Southeast China.* Cambria, Youngstown, N.Y.

Jing, Y. and R. Flad 2002. Pig domestication in ancient China. *Antiquity* 76: 724-732.

Johnson, E. 1985. Current developments in bone technology. In M.B. Schiffer (ed.) *Advances in Archaeological Method and Theory* vol.8, pp.157-235. Academic Press, New York.

Kano, Tadao 1942. Prehistorical perspective on Ludao off the east coast of Taiwan. *Jinruigaku Zasshi (Journal of the Anthropological Society of Nippon)* 57: 110-34. (in Japanese)

_____. 1946. *Studies in the Ethnology and Prehistory of Southeast Asia*, Vol. I. Yajima Shobo Press, Tokyo. (in Japanese)

_____. 1952. *Studies in the Ethnology and Prehistory of Southeast Asia)*, Vol. II. Yajima Shobo Press, Tokyo. (in Japanese)

Kirch. P. and D. Yen 1982. *Tikopia.* Bishop Museum Press, Honolulu.

Koomoto, M. 1983. General survey in Batan Island. In University of Kumamoto (ed.) *Batan Island and Northern Luzon*. pp. 17-68. University of Kumamoto, Faculty of Letters, Japan.

Krieger, H. 1942. *People of the Philippines*. Smithsonian Institution, Washington.

Kuhn, D. 1988. *Science and Civilization in China. Volume 5: Chemistry and Chemical Technology. Part IX: Textile Technology: Spinning and Reeling*. Cambridge University Press, Cambridge:.

Larson, G., T. Cucchi and 30 others 2007. Phylogeny and ancient DNA of *Sus* provides insights into Neolithic expansion in Island Southeast Asia and Oceania. *Proceedings of the National Academy of Sciences, USA* 104: 4834-9.

Leach, B. 1986. A method for the analysis of Pacific island fishbone assemblages and an associated database management system. *Journal of Archaeological Science* 13: 147-159.

_____. 1997. *A Guide to the Identification of Fish Remains from New Zealand Archaeological Sites*. New Zealand Journal of Archaeology Special Publication, Wellington.

Leach, B. and J. Davidson 2006. *Analysis of Faunal Material from an Archaeological Site at Ylig, Guam*. Museum of New Zealand Te Papa Tongarewa, Wellington.

_____. 2008. *The Archaeology of Taumako*. New Zealand Journal of Archaeology Special Publication, Wellington.

Leach, B., M. Fleming, J. Davidaon, G. Ward and J. Craib 1988. Prehistoric fishing at Mochong, Rota, Mariana Islands. *Man and Culture in Oceania* 4: 31-62.

Leake, B.E. with 21 co-authors 1997. Nomenclature of amphiboles. *American Mineralogist* 82: 1019-37.

Li, K-C. 1983. *Report of Archaeological Investigations in the O-Luan-Pi Park at the Southern Tip of Taiwan*. Department of Anthropology, National Taiwan University, Taipei. (in Chinese)

Li, K-S. 2010. Three pointed lingling-o ear pendants unearthed from Jiuxianglan site and the related questions. In C.F. Tong and H.M. Lin (eds) *Essays from 2009 International Conference on Austronesian Studies*, pp. 141-164. National Museum of Prehistory, Taidong. (in Chinese)

Li, K-T. 1989. *Prehistoric Fishing Activities in the Oluanpi Park Area*. Research Project Report No. 66, Administrative Bureau of the Kenting National Park, Pingtung.

_____. 1994. *Coastal Adaptation in Southern Taiwan: a Case Study of Kuei-shan Site*. The Planning Bureau of National Marine Biology Museum, Kaohsiung.

_____. 2000. Change and stability in the dietary system of prehistoric O-luan-pi inhabitants in southern Taiwan. *Bulletin of the Indo-Pacific Prehistory Association* 20: 159-164.

_____. 2002. Prehistoric marine fishing adaptation in southern Taiwan. *Journal of East Asian Archaeology* 3(1/2): 47-74.

Lien C. 2002. The jade industry of Neolithic Taiwan. *Bulletin of the Indo-Pacific Prehistory Association* 22: 55-62.

Lien C. and W. Sung 1989. *Archaeological Investigation of the Peinan Site: The Park Area Study*. Occasional Paper 15, Dept. Anthropology, National Taiwan University, Taipei (in Chinese)

Liu, Y., M. Qiu and W. Fu 1995.*A study of Prehistoric Culture on Ludao Island*. Academia Sinica, Taipei. (in Chinese)

Llorente, A. 1983. *A Blending of Cultures: The Batanes 1686-1898*. Historical Conservation Society, Manila.

Loo, J., J. Trejaut, J. Yen, Z. Chen, C. Lee and M. Lin 2011. Gentic affinities between the Yami people of Orchid Island and the Philippine islanders of the Batanes Archipelago. *BMC Genetics* 2011: 12:21. http://www.biomedcentral.com/1471-2156/12/21.

Loofs-Wissowa, H. 1980-1. Prehistoric and protohistoric links between the Indochinese peninsula and the Philippines. *Journal of the Hong Kong Archaeological Society* IX: 57-76.

Lyman, R. 1994. *Vertebrate Taphonomy*. Cambridge University Press, Cambridge.

Mangahas, M. 1994. Mataw, Amung Nu Rayon, Anitu/Man, the 'Fish of Summer', and the Spirits. an Ethnography of Mataw Fishing in Batanes. Unpublished M.A. thesis, University of the Philippines, Diliman, Quezon City.

_____. 1996. Mataw fishing in Batanes. *Aghamtao* 8: 1-12.

Marshall, L. 1989. Bone modification and 'the laws of burial'. In R. Bonnichsen and M.H. Sorg (eds) *Bone Modification*, pp. 7-24. University of Maine Center for the Study of the First Americans, Orono.

Massutí, E. 1997. Biology of *Coryphaena hippurus* Linnaeus, 1758 (Pisces: Coryphaenidae) in the Western Mediterranean. Unpublished Ph.D. thesis, Universitat de les Illes Balears, Spain.

Matthews, P. 1996. Ethnobotany, and the origins of *Broussonetia papyrifera* in Polynesia. In R. Green (ed.) *Oceanic Culture History*, pp. 117-32. New Zealand Journal of Archaeology Special Publication, Dunedin.

Medway, Lord. 1963. Niah Cave animal bone V1. New records. *Sarawak Museum Journal* 11 (NS 21-22): 188-191.

Meijaard, E. 2001. Successful sea-crossings by land mammals: a matter of luck, and a big body. *Geological Research and Development Centre, Special Publication* 27: 87-92. Bandung.

Mijares, A. 1996. Report on the preliminary archaeological reconnaissance of Abra de Ilog, Occidental Mindoro, Philippines. *National Museum Manila Papers* 6 (2): 27-39.

_____. 2006. Unravelling Prehistory: The Archaeology of Northeastern Luzon. Unpublished PhD thesis, Australian National University.

Mijares, A. and C. Jago-on 2001. Archaeological survey of Itbayat Island, Batanes Province, northern Philippines. *Philippine Quarterly of Culture and Society* 29: 296-308.

Mijares, A., C. Jago-on, and P. Faylona 2003. In search of prehistoric Itbayaten settlements. *Philippine Quarterly of Culture and Society* 31: 26-45.

Mijares, A., R. Santiago and A. Dado 1998-2003. The 1997 archaeological exploration and test excavation of Rakwaydi site, Mahatao, Batanes. *Ivatan Studies Journal* V-X: 29-38.

Milgram, B. 2007. Re-crafting tradition and livelihood: women and bast fibre textiles in the upland Philippines. In R. Hamilton and B. Milgram (eds) *Material Choices: Refashioning Bast and Leaf Fibres in Asia and the Pacific*, pp. 119-132. UCLA, Fowler Museum of Cultural History, Los Angeles.

Moran, N. and T. O'Connor 1994. Age attribution in domestic sheep by skeletal and dental maturation: a pilot study of available sources. *International Journal of Osteoarchaeology* 4: 267–28.

Morton, J. and U. Raj n.d. *The Shore Ecology of Suva and South Viti Levu. Introduction to Zoning and Reef Structures – Soft Shores, Book One*. University of the South Pacific.

Mudar, K. 1997. Patterns of animal utilization in the holocene of the Philippines: a comparison of faunal samples from four archaeological sites. *Asian Perspectives* 36: 67-105.

Nguyen, K. 2007. Stone Age archaeology in Vietnam. *Vietnam Archaeology*, no. 2 for 2007: 53-64.

Ogawa, H. 2000. *Excavation of the Lal-lo Shell Middens*. Tokyo University of Foreign Studies (unpublished report).

_____. *Archaeological Research on the Lower Cagayan River.* Tokyo University of Foreign Studies (unpublished report).

Olsen, S. and P. Shipman 1988. Surface modification on bone: trampling versus butchery. *Journal of Archaeological Science* 15: 535-553.

Ono, R. 2004. Prehistoric fishing at Bukit Tengkorak, East Coast of Borneo Island. *New Zealand Journal of Archaeology* 24: 77-106.

Ono, R., S. Soegondho and M. Yoneda 2009. Changing marine exploitation during late Pleistocene in northern Wallacea. *Asian Pespectives* 48: 318-41.

Parkinson, B., J. Hemmen, and K. Groh 1987. *Tropical Landshells of the World.* Verlag Christa Hemmen, Wiesbaden.

Paz, V. 2002. Island Southeast Asia: spread or friction zone? In P. Bellwood and C. Renfrew (eds) *Examining the Language/Farming Dispersal Hypothesis*, pp. 275-86. McDonald Institute for Archaeological Research, Cambridge.

Paz, V., A. Mijares et al. 1998. Batanes Expedition Report (unpublished). Archaeological Studies Program, University of the Philippines, Quezon City.

Piper, P. 2003. Rodents, Reptiles and Amphibians: A Palaeoecological and Taphonomic Study of the Micro-Faunal Remains Recovered from Archaeological Settlement Sites. Unpublished Ph.D thesis, University of York.

Piper, P. and N. Amano 2011. A report on the animal remains from the 2009 archaeological excavations at Macapainara in East Timor. Unpublished report produced for S. O'Connor and J. Fenner of The Australian National University, Canberra, Australia.

Piper, P., F. Campos and H. Hung 2009. A study of the animal bones recovered from pits 9 and 10 at the site of Nagsabaran in northern Luzon. *Hukay* 14: 47-90.

Piper, P., F. Campos, N. Dang, N. Amano, M. Oxenham, C. Bui, P. Bellwood and A. Willis 2012. Early evidence for pig and dog husbandry from the Neolithic site of An Son, Southern Vietnam, *International Journal of Osteoarchaeology.* DOI: 10.1002/oa.2226 (published online 6 February 2012).

Potts, R. and P. Shipman 1981. Cutmarks made by stone tools on bones from Olduvai Gorge, Tanzania. *Nature* 291: 577-580.

Quizon, C. and J. Cameron 2009. The Banton Cloth. Paper presented at the 19th Indo-Pacific Prehistory Association Congress, Vietnam Academy of Social Sciences, November 29th – December 5th 2009.

Richard, M., R. Maury, H. Bellon, J. Stephan, J. Boirat and A. Calderon 1986. Geology of Mt Iraya and Batan Island, northern Philippines. *Philippine Journal of Volcanology* 3, part 1: 1-27.

Ronquillo, W. 1998. Tools from the sea. In G. S. Casal, E. Z. Dizon et al. (eds) *The Earliest Filipinos*, pp. 63-75. Asia Publishing Company, Manila.

Ross, M. 2005. The Batanic languages in relation to the early history of the Malayo-Polynesian subgroup of Austronesian. *Journal of Austronesian Studies* 1, no. 2: 1-24. Taitung, Taiwan.

Sathiamurthy, E. and H. Voris 2006. Maps of Holocene sea level transgression and submerged lakes on the Sunda Shelf. *Natural History Journal of Chulalongkorn University, Supplement* 2: 1-43.

Scheans, D. and J. Laetsch 1981. An analysis of the ceramic materials from three habitation sites, Batan Island, Batanes Province. *Philippine Quarterly of Culture and Society* 9: 33-55.

Severino, H. (director) 2003. *"Ginto ng Dagat":* the chase for *dorado* [video documentary], *iWitness: the GMA documentaries.* Philippines: GMA 7.

Snow, B., R. Shutler, D. Nelson, J. Vogel and J. Southon 1986. Evidence of early rice cultivation in the Philippines. *Philippine Quarterly of Culture and Society* 14: 3-11.

Snow, B. and R. Shutler 1985. *The Archaeology of Fuga Moro Island*. San Carlos Publications, Cebu City.

Solheim, W. 1960. Jar burial in the Babuyan and Batanes Islands. *Philippine Journal of Science* 89(1): 115-48.

_____. 1984-5. The Nusantao hypothesis. *Asian Perspectives* 26: 77-88.

Steadman, D. 2006. *Extinction and Biogeography of Tropical Pacific Birds*. University of Chicago Press, Chicago.

Stevenson, J., F. Siringan, J. Finn, D. Madulid and H. Heijnis 2010. Paoay Lake, northern Luzon, the Philippines: a record of Holocene environmental change. *Global Change Biology* 216: 1672-88.

Stoops, G. 1998. Key to the ISSS Handbook for thin section description. *Natuurwetenschappen Tijdschrift* 78: 193-203.

Sung W-H., C. Yin, S. Huang, C. Lien, C, Tsang, C, Chen and Y. Liu 1992. *Preliminary Evaluation of the Major Prehistoric Sites of Taiwan*. Ethnological Society of China, Special Project Series 1, Taipei.

Svendsen, J. 1992. Perinatal mortality in pigs. *Animal Reproduction Science* 28: 59-67.

Swete Kelly, M. 2008. Prehistoric Social Interaction and the Evidence of Pottery in the Northern Philippines. Unpublished PhD thesis, Australian National University.

Szabó, K. 2005. Technique and practice: Shell-working in Island Southeast Asia and the Western Pacific. Unpublished Ph.D. thesis, Australian National University.

Szabó, K. 2012. Terrestrial hermit crabs (Anomura: Coenobitidae) as taphonomic agents in circum-tropical coastal sites. *Journal of Archaeological Science* 39:931-941.

Szabó, K., Brumm, A. and Bellwood, P. 2007. Shell artefact production at 32,000 BP in Island Southeast Asia: thinking across media? *Current Anthropology* 48: 701–723.

Szabó, K., Ramirez, H., A. Anderson and P. Bellwood 2003. Prehistoric subsistence strategies on the Batanes Islands, northern Philippines. *Bulletin of the Indo-Pacific Prehistory Association* 23: 163-171.

Thiel, B. 1986-87a. Excavations at Arku Cave, northeastern Luzon, Philippines. *Asian Perspectives* 27:229-264.

_____. 1986-87b. Excavations at the Lal-lo shellmiddens. *Asian Perspectives* 27:71-94.

_____. 1989. Excavation at Musang Cave, northeastern Luzon, Philippines. *Asian Perspectives* 28: 61-81.

Thosarat, R. 2010. Fish and shellfish. In C. Higham and A. Kijngam (eds) *The Excavation of Ban Non Wat, Part Two: The Neolithic Occupation*, pp. 169-188. Fine Arts Department of Thailand, Bangkok.

Tsang, C. 2000. *The Archaeology of Taiwan*. Council for Cultural Affairs, Executive Yuan, Taipei.

_____. 2005. On the origin of the Yami people of Lanyu as viewed from archaeological data. *Journal of Austronesian Studies* 1(1): 135-151. (in Chinese)

Tsang, C., K. Li and C. Chu 2006. *Footprints of Ancestors: Archaeological Discoveries in Tainan Science-Based Industrial Park*. Tainan County Government, Tainan. (in Chinese).

Uchiyama, J. and C. Boggs 2006. Length-weight relationships of dolphinfish, *Coryphaena hippurus*, and wahoo, *Acanthocybium solandri*: seasonal effects of spawning and possible migration in the Central North Pacific. *Marine Fisheries Review* 1-4: 19-29.

Valerio, M. 1995-7. Botanical explorations in Ivuhos and Adequey Islands, Batanes. *Ivatan Studies Journal* 2-4: 139-76.

Van den Bergh, G., H. Meijer and 8 others 2009. The Liang Bua faunal remains: a 95 k.y.r. sequence from Flores, East Indonesia. *Journal of Human Evolution* 57(5): 527-537.

Voeun, V. 2003. Fishbones from archaeological remains from Angor Borei. In A. Karlstrom and A. Kallen (eds) *Fishbone and Glittering Emblems: Southeast Asian Archaeology 2002, Museum of Far Eastern Antiquities*. Stockholm: Ostasiatiska Musee.

Von den Driesch, A. 1976. *A Guide to the Measurement of Animal Bones from Archaeological Sites*. Peabody Museum of Archaeology and Ethnology, Bulletin No. 1, Cambridge, Mass.

Wheeler, R., A. Ghosh and K. Deva 1946. Arikamedu: an Indo-Roman trading-station on the east coast of India. *Ancient India* 2: 17-124.

Wu, C., Y. Jiang, H. Chu, S. Li, Y. Wang, Y. Li, Y. Chang and Y. Ju 2007. The type I Lanyu pig has a maternal genetic lineage distinct from Asian and European pigs. *Animal Genetics* 38: 499-505.

Yamada, Y. 2007. *An Itbayat Chronicle*. Himeji Dokkyo University, Himeji.

Yang, S. 2006. Fishing Sinkers in the Batanes Islands (Philippines) and Taiwan, and Further Relationships with East Asia. Unpublished Archaeology MA Thesis, Australian National University.

Yang, T. T. Lee, C. Chen, S. Cheng, U. Knittel, R. Punongbayan and A. Rasdas 1996. A double island arc between Taiwan and Luzon: consequence of ridge subduction. *Tectonophysics* 258: 85-101.

Ye, M. 2001. *Research on the Huagangshan Culture*. National Museum of Prehistory, Taidong. (in Chinese)

Zheng Y., G. Sun, L. Qin, C. Li, X. Wu and X. Chen 2009. Rice fields and modes of rice cultivation between 5000 and 2500 BC in east China. *Journal of Archaeological Science* 36: 2609-2616.